# Creolizing Contradance in the Caribbean

In the series **Studies in Latin American and Caribbean Music,**
edited by Peter Manuel

Also in this series:

Cathy Ragland, *Música Norteña: Mexican Migrants Creating a Nation between Nations*

Alejandro L. Madrid, *Sounds of the Modern Nation: Music, Culture, and Ideas in Post-Revolutionary Mexico*

Christopher Washburne, *Sounding Salsa: Performing Popular Latin Dance Music in New York City*

David F. Garcia, *Arsenio Rodríguez and the Transnational Flows of Latin Popular Music*

Sergio Navarrete Pellicer, *Maya Achi Marimba Music in Guatemala*

Peter Manuel, *East Indian Music in the West Indies: Tân-Singing, Chutney, and the Making of Indo-Caribbean Culture*

María Teresa Vélez, *Drumming for the Gods: The Life and Times of Felipe García Villamil, santero, palero, and abakuá*

Edited by Peter Manuel

# Creolizing Contradance in the Caribbean

TEMPLE UNIVERSITY PRESS
Philadelphia

Temple University Press
Philadelphia PA 19122
*www.temple.edu/tempress*


Published 2009
Printed in the United States of America

Library of Congress Cataloging-in-Publication Data

Creolizing contradance in the Caribbean / edited by Peter Manuel.
p. cm. — (Studies in Latin American and Caribbean music)
Includes bibliographical references and index.
ISBN 978-1-59213-734-3 (cloth : alk. paper)
1. Dance—Caribbean Area. 2. Dance music—Caribbean Area. 3. Music—Caribbean Area.
4. Country-dances—Caribbean Area. 5. Quadrille (Dance)—Caribbean Area.
I. Manuel, Peter, 1952–
GV1631.C74 2009
793.3′19729—dc22

2008043730

ISBN 13: 978-1-59213-735-0

011012-P

# Contents

PETER MANUEL

# 1 / Introduction

## *Contradance and Quadrille Culture in the Caribbean*

A region as linguistically, ethnically, and culturally diverse as the Caribbean has never lent itself to being epitomized by a single music or dance genre, be it rumba or reggae. Nevertheless, in the nineteenth century a set of contradance and quadrille variants flourished so extensively throughout the Caribbean Basin that they enjoyed a kind of predominance, as a common cultural medium through which melodies, rhythms, dance figures, and performers all circulated, both between islands and between social groups within a given island. Hence, if the latter twentieth century in the region came to be the age of Afro-Caribbean popular music and dance, the nineteenth century can in many respects be characterized as the era of the contradance and quadrille. Further, the quadrille retains much vigor in the Caribbean, and many aspects of modern Latin popular dance and music can be traced ultimately to the Cuban contradanza and Puerto Rican danza.

Caribbean scholars, recognizing the importance of the contradance and quadrille complex, have produced several erudite studies of some of these genres, especially as flourishing in the Spanish Caribbean. However, these have tended to be narrowly focused in scope, and, even taken collectively, they fail to provide the panregional perspective that is so clearly needed even to comprehend a single genre in its broader context. Further, most of these publications are scattered in diverse obscure and ephemeral journals or consist of limited-edition books that are scarcely available in their country of origin, not to mention elsewhere.[1] Some of the most outstanding studies of individual genres or regions display what might seem to be a surprising lack of familiarity with relevant publications produced elsewhere, due not to any incuriosity on the part of authors but to the poor dissemination of works within (as well as outside) the Caribbean. Meanwhile, current generations of scholars, for better or worse, have tended to devote their attention primarily to the more distinctively Afro-Caribbean side of the music and dance spectrum, and especially to contemporary commercial popular genres like salsa and reggae.

This volume addresses this scholarly lacuna by presenting a set of area studies covering all the major contradance and quadrille traditions that have flourished in the Spanish-, French-, and English-speaking Caribbean. Rather than being a motley collection of diverse articles reflecting the authors' idiosyncratic interests, the volume aims to treat each area in a relatively consistent manner, covering historical development, musical and choreographic aspects, and a set of relevant sociocultural themes and approaches. Each area article synthesizes extant published scholarship with the authors' own original research. The Introduction seeks to further unify the presentation by offering general background material as well as suggesting some of the panregional perspectives that are so essential to a holistic appreciation of the contradance and quadrille complex. (The Introduction and subsequent chapters, however, are works of the individual authors and represent their own interpretations and perspectives, rather than any particular perspective of the editor.)

The contradance and quadrille, far from flourishing solely in the insular Caribbean, have taken root in various forms and at various times throughout the Americas, from Peru to Vermont. Particularly relevant has been their presence in the mainland Caribbean Basin countries. Thus, the exclusion of these areas from consideration in this volume is in some ways artificial and reifying. A holistic study of the Cuban and Puerto Rican contradanza should properly encompass its closely linked Venezuelan and Mexican counterparts, just as this volume's panorama of the Caribbean quadrille is inherently flawed for slighting Belize and Panama—not to mention New Orleans and the southern United States. However, proper incorporation of these areas might then oblige further consideration of the North American as well as South American hinterlands, with their closely related contradance and quadrille traditions, at which point the problem of sprawl would become acute and the entire topic too unwieldy. Hence the decision has been made, with reservations, to limit the focus of this study to the island traditions, to direct interested readers to other literature,[2] and to hope that other scholars may ultimately generate the more broadly inclusive panoramas that the subject requires. As it is, the authors regret that even certain Caribbean island traditions have been covered inadequately in this book. Further, even the pan-Caribbean focus of this volume has presented vexing challenges to coherent presentation; these, indeed, can be seen to commence with the book's very title, which, as a sort of unsatisfactory compromise, uses what cognoscenti will notice as an unidiomatic variant "contradance" rather than the more conventional but language-specific terms "contra dance," "country dance," "contredanse," or "contradanza." Throughout this volume, the reader may note that we continue to use the term "contradance" in contexts where a generic, panregional sense is intended, while using the other terms to denote specific regional genres.

The contributors to this volume are aware that different readers may use it in different ways; many, we assume, will attend only to one or two individual area chapters, perhaps in conjunction with the Introduction, while a few zealots may actually read the book from cover to cover. In the interests of enabling the individual chapters to be read more or less on their own, we have covered certain sorts of material in more than one chapter (and especially in the Introduction and individual chapters), affording a degree of repetition that will hopefully be regarded with indulgence by those who notice it. At the same time, in order to keep this to a reasonable minimum, readers of individual chapters are on occasion referred to other chapters or to the Introduction for further coverage of a given point.

## Contradance and Quadrille in Europe

The contradance and quadrille reigned for over a century as the favored social dances of Western Europe, especially England, France, and the Netherlands. As social phenomena they were particularly important as vehicles for collective recreation and self-definition on the part of the rising middle classes, in contrast to the courtly and hidebound minuet. As musical idioms, their orbit ranged from the untutored fiddler, to the petty-bourgeois dilettante composer, and on to the great Mozart himself. Yet in many respects their greater importance lay in the choreographic realm and their place in the broader history of European social dance, which merits some consideration here.

The social dances of seventeenth- and early-eighteenth-century Western Europe reflected the class divisions of the era. The most characteristic dances of the lower classes were group (or "choral") dances based around ring formations or single- or double-line formats. Some of the latter were to be performed only by men, such as the morisca/moresque and the related English Morris dance. Others could involve mixed couples; in the branle, couples arrayed in an open file or closed circle performed a series of chain-type figures. Other couple dances were "open," in that the partners did not touch; in this category was the Spanish *zarabanda* (sarabande), evidently of Afro-Latin derivation, which featured men and women in double lines advancing, retreating, and posturing in a manner that was sensual enough to be intermittently banned. In the elite ballrooms, the most characteristic dances were technically difficult and complex open couple dances, especially the minuet, which epitomized courtly refinement, particularly in France, prevailing in roughly the years 1650–1750. Every aspect of the minuet, from the strictly hierarchic order of the dancers' entry to the measured bowing and dipping of the dancers themselves, was formalized and stylized in order to reflect a sense of aristocratic restraint, propriety, and elegance. The development of dance notation in 1700 led to the publication of dance manuals, enabling nobles throughout Western Europe to imitate and emulate the Versailles court dances.

By the latter 1700s, the spread of bourgeois capitalism was undermining traditional social hierarchies and inspiring new democratic ideals, which swept through Europe and had deep and diverse effects on the arts. The growing middle classes developed a fondness for group dances, especially the contradance, which in fact had arisen more than a century earlier. While some have argued for a French origin of the dance, the prevailing scholarly consensus traces its origin to sixteenth-century England, whence it crossed the Channel to become enthusiastically adopted and domesticated in France and Holland. In France, the word "country" was phonetically adapted, rather than translated, to "contre," which also aptly characterized the format of "counterposed" male and female lines;[3] hence its easy, though still curious, reincorporation to English as "contra dance" (which today is most typically applied to the more Americanized derivative).

One of the most important features of the contradance (to commence use of this generic term for the entire complex) was the way that its popularity cut across social classes. While originating in the latter 1500s as a rustic folk dance, it was soon being danced at the court of Queen Elizabeth I (r. 1558–1603), by masters and servants together (Sachs 1937: 420). Although subsequently a staple of elite ballrooms, it also became a popular dance idiom of the rising bourgeoisie, especially insofar as this new class borrowed aristocratic forms while its own ideals were still taking shape (see, e.g., Sachs 1937: 428). With the advent of commercial publishing for middle-class readers, the dance's spread was both reflected and intensified by the publication of instruction manuals, especially John Playford's *The English Dancing Master,* which appeared in eighteen editions between 1651 and 1728.[4] From the latter 1600s, the dance was taken up in France, enjoying particular popularity in the court of Louis XIV (r. 1643–1715), who was himself an enthusiastic dancer; by the time of the French Revolution of 1789, the contredanse had come to replace the minuet as the opening dance at formal balls held by the queen. In subsequent years, French aristocrats freely adapted new figures from staged versions of operatic contredanses. As it gained in popularity, the contradance, although of English origin, came to be thought of in many circles as an essentially French entity, especially as French elite culture became the model for much of Europe. From 1700 the rule of the Italo-French Bourbon family in Spain further promoted the spread of the French-style contradance to that country, as did Napoleon's occupation of the peninsula in 1808.

The seventeenth- and eighteenth-century English/French country dance could be danced in a circle, a square of two or four couples, or, most typically, the "longways" format, whose initial and subsequently recurring basic format arrayed the men and women in two lines facing each other. This configuration itself was not new; Curt Sachs, in his magisterial *World History of the Dance,* observes, "The circle and single file are the basic forms of all choral dancing, and the majority of the figures go back to the Stone Age. . . . Even the way the men and women are placed in a double row, facing each other and divided in pairs, has already been pointed out in numerous African tribes, among the bailas of Rhodesia, the bergdamas and bolokis of the Congo. The fundamental primitive theme is once again, the battle of the sexes with the ensuing attack and flight, union and separation" (1937: 415). What distinguished the longways country dance was the sequential entrance of the couples, the particular figures employed, the flexibility with which it accommodated new figures (and melodies), the original and stylistically contemporary music, and the new social significance of the dance. As with revivalist American country and contra dancing today, the traditional country dance offered the pleasure of social dancing to those who were not necessarily skilled or trained as dancers. While participants in elite contradances might feel inclined or obliged to master a variety of intricate steps, in many formats, all that was needed was a basic familiarity with the conventional figures (such as do-si-do, star, chain, balance, and allemande), whose sequence could be directed by convention or a caller. In a typical format, after lining up in longways style, dancers would perform a specific sequence of figures, each lasting eight bars of music and about a half minute, with subsequent partners, proceeding down the lines and back again, eventually returning to their original partners. Alternately, the caller might organize the two lines into "minor sets" of four dancers each, who perform figures with each other and then split up to execute the same figures with the adjacent sets, thus proceeding down the lines.

By the 1800s the longways style had spread to Spain, Saint-Domingue (later Haiti), and the Spanish Caribbean. Although its prevailing mood could be either genteel or rowdy, in its spirit of collective fun it contrasted dramatically with the ceremonious and dainty minuet, which it increasingly came to replace. Sachs (1937: 398) quotes Franco-Martinican chronicler Médéric Louis Elie Moreau de Saint-Méry (henceforth Saint-Méry) as saying that people "had come to feel that a party is not a course in etiquette," such that after allowing the periwigged grandparents a brief obligatory minuet, the spirited contradancing would commence in earnest. As Cuban musicologist and novelist Alejo Carpentier notes, the contradance "was an honest figure dance, with a certain good-natured gallantry, and did not require an enormous choreographic ability from the dancers" ([1946] 2001: 145).

As a musical genre the European contradance was in some respects unremarkable and standardized, with its typically plain, major-key, diatonic melodies and simple harmonies structured in two eight-bar phrases, each of which would typically be repeated, with the entire AABB structure (briefer than a minute) being reiterated as long as was necessary or desired. However, these very features identified the genre as contemporary or even modern by eighteenth-century standards, in contrast, for example, to the long-winded Baroque "spinning out" phrases, with their elaborate sequences and contrapuntal intricacies. Moreover, the simplicity of the music was deemed suitable to its function as dance accompaniment; as Jean-Jacques Rousseau wrote, since the tunes "are often re-performed, they would be disgusting if of a heavy composition."[5] The eight-bar phrases also corresponded to the length of the individual dance figures, whose sequences would then be repeated with different partners. While the contradance was thus not a vehicle for lofty innovation or elaboration, Mozart, Beethoven, Rameau, Gluck, and other classical composers—along with innumerable lesser dilettantes—penned their own contradances, some of which were adapted in ballrooms.

Most of the over nine hundred country dances in the Playford editions were in 6/4 time, although duple meter became increasingly popular. In Playford's presentation, as in the numerous dance manuals of the eighteenth century, each dance was presented as a specific melody with a prescribed set of figures, though in practice a dance could be performed to any appropriately metered piece (as is the case in country and contra dancing today). Composers and dance ensembles further enriched the music by liberal borrowing of current operatic airs and other urban songs. Figure 1.1 shows a modern notation of the first eight bars of a typical country dance, "The Elector of Hanover's March," whose original is presented in the 1710 edition of Playford's compendium. In that edition, the staff notation, designated "longways for as many as will," accompanies, like the other dances, prose instructions for the figures (e.g., "The firft Man go under the fecund Couple's hands, the firft Woman do the same, change Places, Foot it, and caft up"). The melody exhibits a striking feature of several of the Playford country dances—the presence of what would later be called the "habanera" rhythm, a trademark of the nineteenth-century Cuban contradanza.[6] In fact, in this tune the habanera rhythm is not merely present but serves as a basic recurring pattern.

**Figure 1.1** "The Elector of Hanover's March," from Playford, *The Dancing Master*, 1710.

In the mid-1700s the format of dancing in square formation had become especially popular in France and typically came to be designated as the "French" style (*contredanse française*), as opposed to the original "English" longways style. This French contradance variant also evolved into the quadrille, which derived from a variety of sources. One precedent was the earlier French dance called *le cotillon*, which, taking its name from a popular tune, was incorporated into contredanse format as a variant for two couples and exported to England in the 1760s as the "cotillion." Refitted by dance masters with new choreographies for four couples, it dispensed with the need for couples to wait their turn in the lines and soon developed its own characteristic figures and lively music. In France around the same time, the quadrille emerged from the *cotillon*, taking its own name, according to various accounts, from a contemporary card game or from the Spanish *cuadrillo* (a diminutive for "four," and cf. *cuadrado*, "square"). According to some sources, aside from the cotillion and contradance, another inspiration for the new dance was the seventeenth-century form of equestrian quadrille consisting of show formations executed by four mounted horsemen, as are still performed in horse shows today.

The quadrille adopted the French tradition of structuring contredanse sessions as "pot-pourris" of two or three contredanses strung together. Standardizing this sort of structure, in the early 1800s the French quadrille assumed the form of a conventional suite of five units (called "figures"), whose music originally consisted of contredanse tunes in alternating triple and duple meters. In the 1820s the quadrille per se became formalized as musicians composed new music for the sections, and the genre assumed the form of a suite of five movements, separated by brief pauses, with fixed figures, named "*Le pantalon*" (trousers), "*L'été*" (summer), "*La poule*" (hen), "*La pastourelle*" (shepherd girl), and "*Finale*." Each of the five items had a conventional, although flexible, series of dance figures, each set to four or eight bars of music; hence, for example, the figures in *Le pantalon* might consist of English chain, balancé, turn partners, ladies' chain, half promenade, and half English chain. Although certainly a social dance, the quadrille could retain something of the character of a "spectacle" dance insofar as individual couples danced inside the squares while others rested and watched.

In 1815 the French quadrille, typically performed with violins, flutes, and piano, was introduced to London and subsequently became a standard Victorian court dance. In tandem with its Continental counterpart, its popularity extended to the middle and lower classes, and its performers freely borrowed tunes from diverse sources. By the 1840s it had become widely popular in Berlin and elsewhere on the Continent, danced by bourgeois and working-class men and women and also cultivated as a simple piano piece. It had also spread to Spain in the 1830s. Quadrille music, like contradances, often consisted of adaptations of opera melodies. An offshoot of the quadrille was the Lancers, which, after being invented in Ireland in 1817, went on to become popular in Europe in the 1850s. Although the quadrille's appeal declined in the latter 1800s, by this time it and the Lancers had taken root in the Caribbean, both from French and English sources.

Sachs characterizes the contradance as introducing the bourgeois epoch (1937: 428) in the genre's rejection of the minuet's stale formality and its appeal to the emergent middle classes. The contradance can also be seen as a transitional genre in the metanarrative of the evolution and, in the decades around 1800, the definitive triumph of independent couple dancing, with partners loosely embracing in ballroom style. In Europe, the primary vehicles for this development were the waltz and later the polka. The waltz differed from its predecessor the minuet in its ballroom-style embrace, its absence of prescribed figures, and, above all, its spirit of passion, expression, and "naturalness" that replaced the minuet's stiffness and artificiality and the stately ceremoniousness of the rigodón. The contradance itself had also spurned that courtly prissiness, but its emphasis on collectively performed figures, often dictated by a caller, eventually came to be seen as artless calisthenics. Sachs quotes a commentator from around 1800: "Our figure dances without character and expression [are] the most artificial and ridiculous foot play. . . . The empty changing of the sets, the alternation of these dead geometrical figures is nothing but sheer mechanism. . . . [The true dance] must have soul, express passion, imitate nature" (1937: 429). Hence the revolutionary (and accordingly controversial) waltz, which in a Viennese ballroom could be genteel and refined in its way or in a petty-bourgeois dance party could be vigorous and sensual.

The independent couple dance, in the European form of the waltz, reflected triumphant bourgeois ideology not only in its cult of "naturalness" and expression but also in its unprecedented and exclusive celebration of the individual and his or her consort, rather than the broader community. The fundamentally asocial character of the dance could be easily appreciated if one were to imagine an eighteenth-century contradance, or a modern square dance, at which one couple, in blatant disregard of the others, were to dance intimately by themselves in a corner. Goethe wrote of how joyous it was to "hold the most adorable creature in one's arms and fly around with her like the wind, so that everything around us fades away" (in Sachs 1937: 430). Of course, primary among the things that faded away was the community—in this case, in the form of the other dancers. In the contemporary terms of Karl Marx and Fredric Engels, community—in its traditional cohesive sense—was one of the things that melted into thin air with the full emancipation of the bourgeois worldview. Impersonal mass marketing of commodities replaced local village craftsmen and undermined traditional occupations with their networks of guilds and feudal bonds; the establishment of the individual as the basic socioeconomic unit vitiated the traditional social fabric; and the advent of capital undid an entire social order of feudal hierarchies and reciprocal obligations: "All fixed, fast-frozen relations, with their train of ancient and venerable prejudices and opinions, are swept away. . . . All that is solid melts into air, all that is holy is profaned" ([1847] 1959: 10). The spirit of the independent couple dance reflected the same individualism that came to permeate the arts, including the introspective poetry of Wordsworth, the self-conscious subjectivity of impressionist painting, the nuanced character portrayals of contemporary novels, and even the closed, narrative form of the classical sonata, with its thematic melodies that, like fictional protagonists, wander afar and then dramatically return home. Inseparable from these phenomena was Romanticism, with its emphasis on "naturalness," the purported nobility of the peasantry, and sentimental love. All these developments were grounded not in some set of superstructural aesthetic coincidences but in the triumph—at once destructive and liberating—

of a capitalist economic order that would exert similar effects on culture in the Caribbean.

## Contradance and Quadrille as Caribbean Dances

Any serious inquiry into the history of creole dances in the Caribbean is inevitably confounded by a set of obstacles. Foremost is the shortage of contemporary documentation, including an essentially complete absence of viewpoints expressed by subalterns in the colonial period. Another obstacle is the confoundingly inconsistent use of terminology, both within the Caribbean itself and as compared with European usages of the same terms. Such words as "contradanza," "danza," and "quadrille" might in different contexts refer either to musical or choreographic features; the same term (like "merengue" or "tango") might denote very different genres, while different terms (like "habanera," "danza," or, again, "tango") might be used to denote the same genre. In the Spanish Caribbean, "danza" might designate either a specific genre or be a general term for "dance"; similarly, the Spanish term *cuadrilla* (quadrille) could denote either the specific dance by that name, any formation of four dancers, or a suite dance of four successive figures (e.g., minuet, rigodón, *lancero*, and contradanza). In Cuba, as seen in Chapter 2, the words "contradanza" and "danza" were used with prodigious inconsistency, albeit with a tendency toward using the latter to denote the couple dance that prevailed from the 1850s. In Puerto Rico, discussed in Chapter 3, "contradanza" generally connoted the old-style Spanish group dance, with the couple dance introduced in the 1840s being initially known as "merengue" and, subsequently, "danza." In the Dominican Republic, the new style evidently came in the form of the Puerto Rican "merengue," but that term later came to denote the familiar popular music and dance genre, with the exception of the salon "merengues" of the 1920s, which might be regarded as hybrids with danzas in Puerto Rican style. If such confusion were not sufficient, in the context of the 1850s Puerto Rican danza/merengue and the modern Dominican merengue, the term "merengue" also denoted the extended melodic sections following the introductory *paseo*.

At the risk of repeating data, the following pages survey the Caribbean contradance and quadrille as dance formats, then as musical idioms, as historically evolving entities, as exemplars of creolization, and, lastly, as sites of sociocultural contention and negotiation. Most patently visible in retrospect are the general trends. One of these has been the aforementioned grand transition, paralleling European developments, from collective figure dancing to independent couple dancing. In the Spanish Caribbean the vehicle for this transformation was not the waltz, which was never more than a subsidiary genre. Perhaps because of its distinctive triple meter, the waltz, despite being of interest to composers in Cuba and elsewhere in the form of the *vals tropical*, did not lend itself to the process of musical creolization, which foregrounded duple-metered genres and marginalized the rest. Rather, it was the rhythmically more varied and flexible contradance itself whose choreography changed dramatically in the course of the century and whose role in the transformation to couple dancing was fundamental rather than incidental. Further, as a musical idiom, in the Spanish and French Caribbean the contradance played a seminal role in the development of the commercial popular dance styles, from that of the Cuban danzón to the Haitian méringue (mereng), that would flower in the early twentieth century. Meanwhile, in the French and English Caribbean, the quadrille variants remained group dances but tended to acquire a neotraditional, even folkloric status; hence the transition to couple dancing involved not their transformation but rather their gradual marginalization, with popular, predominantly couple-style dances, such as *konpa*, reggae, soca, and zouk, replacing them as mainstream dance formats.

## Caribbean Dance Forms

The colonial-era Caribbean to which the contradance and quadrille were imported was not a choreographic and musical wasteland. Rather, by the late 1700s a number of European and African dance and music genres had taken root in the region, with varying degrees and sorts of modifications, and creolized new ones had been emerging since the late 1500s, when the Afro-Mexican *zarabanda* (sarabande) was exported to Spain. Thus the trajectories of the contradance and quadrille were conditioned from the start by their interaction with other genres, including neo-African ones that had no counterparts in Europe.

The contradance and quadrille must further be appreciated in both their choreographic and musical dimensions, which did not always exhibit identically parallel sorts of creolizations and modifications. In many ways the more dramatic changes involved dance rather than music per se, in interaction with other forms of Caribbean dancing. In general, the gamut of colonial-era Caribbean dances (like that of dances elsewhere) can be seen as corresponding to a set of contrasting categories.

One group of distinctions involves the contrasts between collective group ("choral") dances, couple dances, and solo dances. The category of collective dances would include neo-African religious dances, such as those still performed in Cuban Santería and Haitian Vodou ceremonies, in which all dancers perform more or less synchronized movements in accordance with the spirit being praised and, in some cases, the section of the song. It would also comprise various traditional ring dances described in colonial-era accounts, such as the calenda (calinda, kalenda), which I discuss below.

Solo dances themselves, as well as many forms of couple dancing, may also fall into the category of "spectacle" genres (to use Sachs's term) performed to an audience of sorts. Aside from various dances described in eighteenth-century chronicles,[7] quintessential examples of such formats would be traditional

Afro-Cuban rumba and Afro–Puerto Rican *bomba*, in which single couples or solo dancers take turns dancing in the center of a ring of others watching and singing (a format especially common in Africa). Colonial chroniclers described a variety of such dances, including those in which, as in *bomba*, a solo dancer interacts with a lead drummer.[8] Forms of the Spanish-derived dances such as the archaic bolero and *cachucha* could also be performed by couples or by a solo dancer amid a circle of viewers. Spectacle dancing of this sort would contrast with what could be categorized as social dancing, without any formal or informal audience.

For their part, couple dances could be "open" forms, in which partners do not touch, or "closed" forms, most characteristically with the partners loosely embracing in ballroom style. The closed ballroom posture was uncommon in Europe before the spread of the waltz around 1800, and it was not only absent in Africa but also long regarded by many Afro-Caribbeans as indecent (however lewd their own dances seemed to Europeans). Hence open couple dances tended to predominate on both the European and Afro-Caribbean sides of the spectrum in the colonial era. Some such dances, such as the *zarabanda* and fandango, were genres of "*ida y vuelta*" or "coming and going"—that is, creolized products evolving jointly on both sides of the Atlantic.[9] Also in the open couple dance category were such genres as the *seis* of Puerto Rican peasants and the fandango, which flourished in diverse forms on both sides of the Atlantic. Although couple dances of any sort were uncharacteristic of traditional African dancing, in their open form they were documented from early on in the Caribbean, reflecting the early commencement of creolization. A European visitor described one such dance in 1707, evidently in Jamaica, in which slaves in their finest European-style attire danced to the accompaniment of drums: "The negroes dance always in couples, the men figuring and footing, while the women turn round like a top, their petticoats expanding like an umbrella; and this they call *waey-cotto*" (in Abrahams and Szwed 1983: 285).

Prior to the advent of the contradance and quadrille, the predominant European salon dances were either independent open couple dances, such as the minuet, or collective dances, such as the rigodón, in which couples, when formed in figures, were interdependent and generally not touching, performing the same figures at the same time, perhaps as guided by a caller. This collective open format was also the basis of the contradance and quadrille. Group couple dances could also be to varying degrees unstructured and free, with each couple more or less on its own—the format that was revolutionary in the waltz, and, in its wake, the later forms of Caribbean contradance. Finally, of course, dances could vary in their overall spirit and character, from the ceremonious and dainty minuet to the informal and festive rumba.

Significant precursors of the contradance were Afro-Caribbean dances in which the men and women were arranged in two lines, facing each other. In 1724 French priest R. P. Labat published his *Nouveaux Voyages* containing a revealing account of the calenda (which, like "bamboulá," became a generic colonial term for neo-African dances) that he saw danced by slaves in 1698 during his travels in Santo Domingo and elsewhere:

> That which delights them most and is their favorite diversion is the calenda, which comes from the Guinea coast and judging by its antecedents, from the kingdom of Ardá [Allada]. The Spanish learned it from the blacks and dance it throughout the Americas, in the same manner as the negros. Given the nature of the gestures and movements of this dance, the masters who live morally have prohibited it, and try to maintain the prohibition, which is far from easy, since the dance is so popular that even the children, when barely able to stand, try to imitate their parents in dancing, and would pass entire days in this fashion. The dancers array themselves in two lines, facing each other, the men on one side and the women on the other. The spectators form a circle around the dancers and drummers. The most gifted sings a tune, improvising lyrics on some contemporary theme, and the refrain is repeated by all the dancers and onlookers, accompanied by clapping. The dancers raise their arms, as if they were playing castanets, they leap, spin, approach to within a few steps of each other and then withdraw, following the music, until the drum signals them to approach and bump their thighs together, that is, the men against the women. Upon seeing them, it looks like they are bumping their bellies, though it is clear that only their thighs sustain the encounter. Withdrawing immediately with pirouettes, they repeat the exercise with these supremely lascivious movements as often as is guided by the drum, which signals them again and again. On occasion they join arms and take a few turns, shaking their hips and kissing.
>
> One can well appreciate, then, how immodest this dance may be, in spite of which it is so pleasing to the Spaniards and creoles of America, and so in use among them, that it constitutes the better part of their entertainments and even enters their religious devotions.
>
> They dance the calenda in their churches and Catholic processions, and the nuns even dance it on Christmas Eve in a stage erected in the choir loft, in front of the railings, which are left open so that the public can have the aid of these good souls dedicated to the birth of our Savior. . . . And I would like to think that they dance it with noble intent, but how many spectators would judge them as charitably as do I?[10]

Several decades later, Saint-Méry offered a similar description of a calenda in Saint-Domingue, with its two lines of men and women alternately approaching and withdrawing to the accompaniment of drumming and responsorial singing (1797–98: 44–45).[11] This Afro-Caribbean dance formation was scarcely limited to the Caribbean, as Dom Peretty documented yet another instance of it, akin to the calenda, in Montevideo (Uruguay) in 1763, stating (like Labat) that it derived from "Ardra" in West Africa (in Galán 1983: 73). In Africa itself, the double-file dance format has been documented from the nineteenth century, as among the Bakongo seen in 1882 by J. H. Weeks, who wrote:

> Two lines are formed—one of men and the other of an equal number of women. The drum is placed at one end of the line, and all begin to clap, chant, shuffle, and wriggle together. A man then advances, dancing, and a women from the opposite line advances a few paces and they dance thus a few moments, usually a yard or so apart, but sometimes they approach nearer and strike their abdomens together, then they retire, and others take their places, and so on right down the lines; and thus they proceed over and over again. (Weeks 1914: 128)

Given the popularity in Africa of the double-file choral dance form, to which the calenda belonged, its cultivation by African-born slaves in eighteenth-century Saint-Domingue should not be surprising. What is significant here are the dance's affinities to the longways style of contradance. The popularity of the calenda and similar dances—among both blacks and creole whites and mulattos—clearly contributed to the subsequent adoption of the longways-style contradance, in various creolized forms. Indeed, the only substantial musical or choreographic difference between the calendas witnessed by Labat and a modern Haitian-derived Cuban *tumba francesa* dance or Martinican calinda might lie in the latter's use of specific contradance-derived figures. Saint-Méry also indicated how the calenda included sections in which men and women would dance as couples, reflecting an early form of hybridization with dances like the contradance (see Courlander 1960: 128). As Dominique Cyrille has observed, even the custom of structuring contradances and quadrilles as suites cohered with extant West African practices (see Nketia 1965: 5, 23). These structural affinities, she notes, provided grounds for the easy blending of African and European traditions and enabled neo-African ritual practices to be rearticulated in the guise of colonial dances.

## Caribbean Contradancing

In the Spanish Caribbean, the group contradanza, both in Spanish- and French-style forms, appears to have existed since the latter 1700s, thriving until the mid-1800s. In its heyday of over a half century, it employed many of the figures that are still used in traditional and modern country dancing in Europe and the United States. (See Chapter 2 for a comparison and contrast of the Cuban contradanza and modern North American country/contra dancing.) Most of these figures (such as those discussed in Chapter 2) would have derived from European contradance figures, although, given the fondness for novelty in some contexts, new steps and movements were also introduced.

Some figures would correspond to counterparts in other contemporary dances. For example, the contradance's opening *paseo* section had analogous passages in the Spanish bolero dating from the late 1700s and in the early-twentieth-century Argentine tango; the *paseo* also constituted a counterpart to the promenade of the contemporary mazurka, quadrille, schottische, reel, and Lancers. In the contradanza—especially the Puerto Rican danza and Dominican salon merengue—the *paseo* could serve as an introductory section that allowed dancers to array themselves properly on the ballroom floor. In the case of a controversial dance, such as the 1850s merengue, it could even serve to lure to the floor unsuspecting dancers who might otherwise be reluctant to indulge in the more libertine (*sandungo*) couple dance that followed; sometimes musicians might repeat the *paseo* until the floor was full. In a repeated Cuban contradanza and the later danzón (as in the archaic Spanish bolero), the *paseo* could recur throughout the dance, allowing some welcome respite in the sultry Caribbean climate.

Gradually, throughout the Spanish Caribbean and unevenly in the French Caribbean, the practice of collectively performing figures—whether fixed by convention or directed by a caller—came to be seen as old-fashioned and inhibitingly structured. To some extent inspired by the waltz, with which the contradance was often paired in performance, the new format allowed couples to dance independently, embracing loosely—or perhaps intimately—in ballroom posture. The break with the older style was not complete, as certain contradanza figures could be retained, in disarticulated form, by the couples, and the accompanying music seems to have undergone a gradual process of creolization rather than a dramatic rupture. To some extent, in Cuba the transition constituted a focus on the final *cedazo* figure of the contradanza, which traditionally consisted of independent couple dancing, like the last figure of some quadrille styles. Nevertheless, the change was radical enough to occasion spirited, if unsuccessful, opposition by traditionalists who felt that the new dance style was asocial and indecent, as it allowed intimate embracing and sensual hip-swaying. Much of the scanty documentation of the mid-nineteenth-century contradanza variants consists of bilious condemnations by moralists offended by the new style in which partners could whisper and embrace amorously—perhaps separating by a few inches only if some officious martinet shouted "*¡Que haya luz!*" ("Let there be light [showing between the two of you]!"). In Haiti, the change came in the form of the méringue, a couple dance that, according to Jean Fouchard ([1973] 1988: 96–97), replaced the collective *carabinier*, a derivative of the contredanse.

Throughout the Spanish Caribbean, collective longways-style dancing effectively disappeared, except in the *tumba francesa*, where contradance figures are still performed to neo-African-style drumming. In the Dominican Republic, contradanza choreography, as practiced in the context of the local *tumba*, declined after the 1860s, henceforth persisting primarily in a *tumba* variant documented as performed by a few octogenarians in the 1970s. In Haiti the contredanse itself survives as a collective rural folk dance, which is also standard in the repertoires of folkloric troupes. Its dance steps also contributed to the formation of such group dances as the *carabinier* and, more significantly, the once-pervasive méringue. It is perhaps elsewhere in the French Caribbean—Martinique, Guadeloupe, Dominica, and St. Lucia—that contradance-related choreography has survived most vigorously, in the form of the quadrilles and calindas that are still performed in various contexts. Thus, longways-style contradance formation has persisted in genres like the Jamaican "camp" format of quadrille and the Martinican calinda. In some cases, the modern tendency to dance in intimate embrace has to be explicitly prohibited, just as might have occurred 150 years ago; in 1988 Michael Largey (as he relates in Chapter 6) witnessed a contredanse in rural Haiti where the caller was obliged to chastise two partners for dancing too closely, shouting "*Nou pap danse konpá isit!*" ("We don't dance *konpá* here!")—*konpá* or *compas* being the late-twentieth-century commercial popular dance and music genre.

A curious feature of the transition to intimate couple dancing is that, to some extent, as in Europe itself, socially it appears to have originated both from above and below. The immediate model and precursor for independent couple dancing was the waltz, imported to the Caribbean from the bourgeois salons of Paris, Vienna, and elsewhere. Caribbean conservatives opposed to the new dance style found themselves in the awkward position of criticizing a social practice derived from the fashionable metropolitan elite. At the same time, some contemporary critics of the new format denounced it as exhibiting the uninhibited lewdness associated with Afro-Caribbeans. Ironically, African slaves and many of their descendants—including Haitians known by Melville Herskovits as late as 1937 (264)—tended to regard as vulgar and immoral the European practice of embracing while dancing.

For its part, the quadrille, after being introduced to the French Caribbean and the British West Indies in the decades around 1800, did not undergo the same transition to couple dancing, instead persisting as a collective suite dance, while public tastes inexorably gravitated toward modern dance styles associated with commercial popular music. As Cyrille notes, most French Caribbean quadrilles were choreographed in the standard square formation formed by four couples, while some—especially that called *lakadri* of southern Martinique—have followed the eighteenth-century French longways-style contredanse formation. French Caribbean quadrilles span a continuum stretching from distinctively Afro-Caribbean dance styles to other formats closer to European models. In the former category is rural Martinican *bèlè linò*, whose music consists solely of percussion and call-and-response singing and whose dance style is clearly more African and lively than that of other quadrille variants. Though categorized locally as a quadrille, the quadrille aspects of the *bèlè linò* consist only of the format of a suite of movements in different rhythms, certain

European-derived choreographic features, and the configuration of a "square" of four couples. More recognizably European in format are certain Martinican "indoor" quadrille variants, such as the Lancers, the *pastourelle*, and the *haute-taille*, with its caller-like *commandeur*; the Guadeloupean quadrille of Grand-Terre, with its staid, slow, and restrained movements, also contrasts markedly with dances like the vigorous and upbeat Martinican calinda. Most Caribbean quadrille dance styles require a fair amount of learning and rehearsal, even in comparison to other European-derived genres, and hence they traditionally enjoy a sort of prestige vestigially associated with the plantocracy.

A distinguishing feature of the quadrille (aside from its four-couple formations) is the format of a suite of movements—most typically, five—which may differ according to locale. In many cases, the final movement is a distinctively local dance form. A typical format in Guadeloupe and Dominica is for the first figure to be an introductory march (like a promenade or Spanish Caribbean *paseo*) leading to a waltz; the subsequent figures, as guided by the *commandeur*, retain the traditional French designation of *pantalon*, *été*, *poule*, and *pastorelle*, with the final figure being a biguine in couple dance style. In Martinique, the *haute-taille* consists of three contredanses, two biguines, and, lastly, a *mazouk* or creole mazurka, and the *pastourelle* starts with three waltzes and then segues to a *mazouk* and a polka. Jamaican quadrilles might include such European-derived dances as waltz, polka, schottische, and jig, as well as a local mento; dancers might comport themselves either in ballroom couple format or in longways style. In Haiti, the quadrille (*kadri*) is poorly documented, except as an independent couple dance with distinctive music.

Perhaps because the quadrille (Spanish: *cuadrilla*) came relatively late to Spain, it did not enjoy extensive or long-lasting popularity in the Spanish Caribbean. In the mid-1800s its presence, along with that of the waltz and polka, was noted in Cuba and Santo Domingo, but it later disappeared in Cuba and barely survived in the Dominican Republic in the twentieth century. Dominican folklorist Fradique Lizardo (1974: 65–72, 190) encountered a form of quadrille in three-movement suite form in the early 1970s, but the dance has not been documented there since.

## Contradance and Quadrille as Caribbean Music

### *Caribbean Contradances*

If the terms contradance and quadrille derive from and primarily denote choreographic configurations, both entities have also flourished as distinctive sets of music genres, which played crucial roles in the region's music history. In the Caribbean, as in Europe, contradance and quadrille flourished in a variety of musical forms, from the simple, repeated ditty played by a Trinidadian fiddler to the elegant, Chopinesque Puerto Rican piano danza of Manuel Tavárez.

In certain contexts, the musical and choreographic aspects of the contradance and quadrille styles have seemingly operated independently of each other. In the 1840s–50s, spirited campaigns were waged in Puerto Rico and the Dominican Republic against the merengue as a dance form, but its evidently distinctive music was not seen as objectionable. Meanwhile, such genres as *tumba francesa* and certain styles of West Indian quadrille combine patently European-style choreographies with syncopated, drum-dominated music of overwhelmingly Afro-Caribbean flavor. In other contexts, forms of the contradance—especially Cuban and Puerto Rican light-classical piano danzas—took on their own lives independent of dance, as salon or concert pieces, in which capacity they can be enjoyed today as performed from notations. On the whole, however, the contradance and quadrille as musical entities tended to develop in tandem with their existence as dance genres, exhibiting the same general processes of creolization and indigenization, and the same sorts of orientations, depending on context, toward class, race, and local or panregional characters.

During their heydays—especially the nineteenth century—local contradance and quadrille styles were often pre-eminent music genres, constituting the focuses of musical interest for many Caribbean composers, performers, and listeners. At the same time, as dance-music genres they also coexisted with a variety of other dance-music styles, whose presence is sometimes obscured in studies devoted to the contradance or quadrille. At one end of the Caribbean music spectrum flourished the varied Afro-Caribbean or neo-African dance-music genres, including those associated with Haitian Vodou, Jamaican Kumina, or Cuban Santería, or the diverse secular entertainment dance musics, such as Cuban rumba, Puerto Rican *bomba*, Dominican *palo*, or the "big drum" music of Carriacou. As music forms, such genres exhibited a strongly Afro-Caribbean flavor in their emphasis on syncopated rhythm, their formal structures based on repetition of ostinatos and call-and-response patterns, and their ensembles consisting solely of percussion instruments—most typically, three drums. At the other end of the sociomusical gamut lay music of purely classical European style or origin, from the motets of eighteenth-century Cuban composer Esteban Salas to the Italian operas performed in various port towns by local or visiting troupes. On the whole, contradance and, to a lesser extent, quadrille flourished in an intermediate stratum of social dance music in which European and African, black and white, and elite and plebian participants mingled and inspired each other in a grand process of creolization.

The realm of colonial-era social dance music included various genres that were quite distinct from the contradance in origin and style. One example would be the Cuban *zapateo*, with its Spanish-derived string-based instrumentation, modal-tinged melodies, and fast, hemiola-laden rhythms in 6/8 meter. In the French and Spanish Caribbean, strictly European-style genres, such as waltz (*vals*), rigodón, paso doble, polka, schottische, *lanceros*, mazurka, and minuet, were all performed alongside contradance variants, often with no particular prominence given to the latter; in the early decades of the twentieth century, these could be supplemented by the American-derived fox-trot or two-step.[12] It may be assumed that most of these pieces were of foreign composition, although many would have been written by obscure local composers. Many such pieces became thoroughly indigenized in the sense of being incorporated into local folk performance formats, as with the odd mazurka being played by a Puerto Rican *jíbaro* (peasant) music ensemble. Nevertheless, it may be said that they were never celebrated as national creole musics per se, as was the case, for example with the early-twentieth-century *vals criollo* ("creole waltz") and "*fox trot inkaico*" ("Inca fox-trot") in Lima, Peru (see Lloréns Amico 1983). Similarly, Caribbean-composed waltzes never achieved more than local or ephemeral popularity, nor did they play seminal roles in the evolution of subsequent commercial popular genres.

Understanding Caribbean contradance and quadrille variants as musical entities involves attention to their melodic aspects, their rhythms, their ensemble formats, and their manner of execution—which may all, in fact, differ significantly in style. For example, looking at the score of a quadrille violin melody from Dominica, one might infer that the piece is wholly in conventional, nondescript European style, but only through actually hearing the piece performed, with its syncopated rhythms played on frame drum, scraper, and shaker, would one appreciate the extent to which it has become creolized and effectively Afro-Caribbeanized. Accordingly, several nineteenth-century chroniclers testified to the distinctively creole manner of playing contradances on piano and to the inability of European pianists to play them properly (Alonso [1849] 2002: 15; Dueño Colón [1913] 1977: 22; Ramírez 1891: 69). Similarly, in looking at the piano score of a Cuban contradanza of the 1850s we are unable to get much sense of how it would have sounded when performed by a contemporary dance band, not to mention precisely how and in what spirit it was danced.[13] As Cuban musicologist Natalio Galán artfully observed, the task of the historian in confronting such scores is akin to trying to discern the scent of a violet found between the pages of a grandmother's book, while not confusing its faint odor with that of the paper or the ink (1983: 42).

On the whole, in terms of their melodic and harmonic aspects, the Caribbean contradances and quadrilles are predominantly mainstream European in style. Hence, for instance, in Cuban contradanzas one would seldom hear the Andalusian harmonies (e.g., the A minor–G–F–E cadence) that characterize such genres as flamenco or the Cuban *punto carvalho*, nor does one encounter the distinctively ambiguous tonicity, with its cadences "on the dominant," that pervades so many Latin American genres, from the Venezuelan *joropo* to the Mexican *jarabe* (see Manuel 2002). Also absent in Caribbean contradances and quadrilles are the sorts of African modal melodies that distinguish such genres as the Cuban *rumba columbia* (see Manuel and Fiol 2007). Rather, both contradance and quadrille melodies throughout the Caribbean tend to have straightforward diatonic melodies in regular four- or eight-bar phrases, accompanied by relatively simple common-practice harmonies, all in a style that became established in vernacular and classical Western music of the eighteenth century.

In the Caribbean crucible, with its distinctive Afro-Caribbean presence, musical creolization—to some extent synonymous with Afro-Caribbeanization—took place primarily in the dimension of rhythm (Galán 1983: 66). One manifestation of this process would be a general tendency toward syncopation. Another related Afro-Caribbean rhythmic trait is the use of rhythmic ostinatos, to an extent and in a manner uncharacteristic of any kind of traditional European music of the time.[14]

A third distinctive creole rhythmic element in the Caribbean contradance consists of the specific ostinatos themselves, comprising in particular a set of four or five interrelated rhythmic cells, most commonly used as accompanimental rather than melodic figures. Although scholars have argued about the origins of these specific patterns, their use as ostinatos is presumed to be of African or at least Afro-Caribbean derivation. Cuban ethnologist Fernando Ortiz cautioned against hasty conclusions about origins:

> The extraordinary abundance of rhythms in the musical tradition of the Negro can sometimes provoke the hasty and erroneous assumption that this or that musical work is of African origin. What rhythms could possibly exist that have not been drummed somewhere by Negro musicians? . . . [A] rhythmic formula, like a simple geometric figure (a triangle, a zigzag, a circle, a spiral, etc.), can be found at the same time in diverse cultures, a relationship between them being neither necessary nor probable.[15]

While questions of origins are best discussed in reference to the particular rhythms themselves, what is perhaps most important is that their use as ostinatos became trademarks of creole Caribbean music, whose adoption clearly derives from the input of Afro-Caribbean and mixed-race performers.

Such issues are particularly manifest in relation to the pattern variously called the "habanera rhythm" or, by Cuban musicologists, the tango or congo rhythm, which was a hallmark of the Cuban contradanza. Cuban and Puerto Rican musicians might also informally refer to it by the culinary mnemonics "ma-*ní* tos-*tao*" (roasted peanuts) or "ca-*fé* con *pan*" (coffee with bread), respectively. Shown in Figure 1.2, this pattern can also be counted as "ONE-and-two-AND-THREE-and-FOUR-and," repeated without pause (or, if one prefers, 3-1-2-2). The rhythm is hardly unique to Afro-Caribbean music, as it recurs in music forms as diverse as the North African *mahuri* meter, a thirteenth-century Cantiga de Santa María from Spain (Galán 1983: 226), several of the coun-

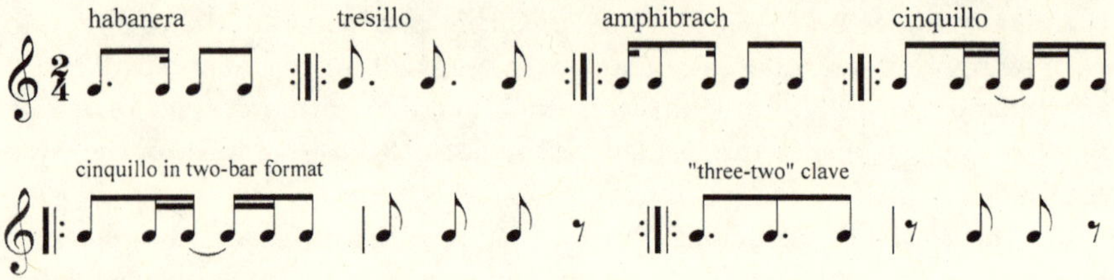


**Figure 1.2** Creole ostinatos: habanera rhythm, *tresillo*, "amphibrach," *cinquillo/quintolet*, *cinquillo* in two-bar format, three-two *clave*.

try dance melodies notated in Playford's seminal seventeenth-century compendium, German peasant folk songs of the nineteenth century (see, e.g., Marothy 1974: 238), and processional drumming of Ibiza, Spain.

Nevertheless, the habanera rhythm, especially as an ostinato, became especially pronounced and stylistically significant in the Caribbean, where its prominence was clearly due to Afro-Caribbean input. Hence it features conspicuously as a composite ostinato in Afro-Cuban *Iyesá* drumming and in Santería *batá* music (in the first section of the *aguere* for Ochosi), both traditions being of West African Yoruba derivation. It is also common in Afro-Dominican *palo* drumming (see Davis 1976: 269). As discussed in Chapter 2, the rhythm came to figure prominently in *guarachas* of the late 1700s and became a recurrent and characteristic ostinato in the Cuban contradanzas that flourished from then until the 1880s, when the danzón came into vogue. Its prominence in the slaves' drumming that resounded in New Orleans's Congo Square until 1851 is strongly suggested by its pervasive recurrence in Louis Gottschalk's 1848 piano piece "Bamboulá" inspired by such music (see Sublette 2008: 123–125).

As notated in nineteenth-century Cuban contradanza piano scores, the habanera pattern typically constituted a left-hand ostinato (especially but not only in the second [B] section of the bipartite piece), and occasionally surfaced in right-hand melodies and accompaniments as well. In the mid-century decades, vocal songs based on this form performed by *tonadilla* theatrical troupes in Cuba and Spain were often called "tango," a term often used in Cuban parlance for this pattern (which also occurs in the early Argentine tango itself, in the years around 1900). From the 1850s, such songs—including that later immortalized in Bizet's *Carmen*—might also be called "habaneras," especially outside Cuba itself, leading to the common designation of the ostinato as the "habanera rhythm" in the English-speaking world. The habanera rhythm has long outlasted the contradanza itself, constituting a standard bass pattern in the bolero, the chachachá, and, in a modified form, the percussion ostinato in Trinidadian soca and Spanish Caribbean reggaetón.

Another common creole contradance rhythm is that which Cuban musicologists call the *tresillo*, which could be represented as 3-3-2 or "ONE-two-three-ONE-two-three-ONE-two" (or, less fluidly, "ONE-and-two-AND-three-and-FOUR-and").

While the term "*tresillo*" (which should not be translated as "triplet") can be used for convenience, the rhythm is far too basic and abundant in world music to be attributed to Cuban provenance. However, it is uncharacteristic of traditional European and Anglo-American music and has clearly entered Latin and American vernacular music through Afro-Latin influence.[16] The *tresillo* occurs in the melodies and bass patterns of several Cuban contradanzas (such as "Tu madre es conga" ["Your Mother Is Congolese"] of 1856) and Puerto Rican danzas, as well as in Cuban *guarachas* of the late 1700s. It is perhaps more prominent in other genres, such as the processional conga, the *son*, and the Charleston.

Closely related to the habanera rhythm is the pattern that, again following Cuban musicological practice, may be called the "amphibrach" and may be rendered as "ONE-AND-TWO-AND-THREE-and-FOUR-and" or 1-2-1-2-2. It differs from the habanera pattern only in adding an accent on the second eighth note. As with the habanera rhythm, scholars might advance various theories about its origin and discover its appearance in this and that music culture. However, in the case of Caribbean music, its origin must certainly be attributed to West Africa, where the pattern is a fairly common bell ostinato.[17] It was presumably established as a characteristic feature of Caribbean creole songs as early as 1762, the publication date of a volume of English country dances containing the syncopated song, "A Trip to Guadeloupe" (see Galán 1983: 80–85). The pattern is at least as common as the habanera rhythm, figuring prominently in the Cuban and Puerto Rican danza (especially when the habanera rhythm occurs in the bass), the Haitian-Cuban *tumba francesa*, the Brazilian creole *lundú* and *maxixe*, and, indeed, innumerable other Hispanic and French Caribbean genres, not to mention ragtime. In effect, it constitutes a hallmark of creole Caribbean Basin music, primarily as a melodic pattern but also, as in *tumba francesa*, occasionally as an accompanimental ostinato.

An equally fundamental creole rhythm in the contradance complex is what Cubans call the *cinquillo*, which can be rendered as "ONE-and-TWO-AND-three-AND-FOUR-and" (or 2-1-2-1-2—like a *tresillo* with added anacruses before the second and third beats). The *cinquillo* is presumably of West African origin. It figures prominently in several Afro-Caribbean traditional music contexts, including Santería *batá* rhythms (*toques*) played for the *orishas* (spirits) Obatalá, Ochún, and Olokun, certain Haitian Vodou rhythms (such as *banda*), Martinican bèlè, and in the *sicá* and *cuembé* styles of Afro–Puerto Rican *bomba*. Possibly deriving from Franco-Haitian influence, it went on to play a prominent role in creole Caribbean music, especially contradance variants. In Haiti and Martinique, where some musicians call it the *quintolet*, it pervades creole music, including the biguine and the traditional méringue (including such songs as "Chouconne," whose melody is better known elsewhere as that of "Yellow Bird"). During the Haitian Revolution in the years around 1800, it accompanied refugees to eastern Cuba, where it soon became commonplace in creole songs. Surfacing in Havana and Santiago contradanzas of the 1850s, it went on to become the basic rhythm of the danzón and the second section of the Puerto Rican and Dominican danzas, all as emerging in the 1870s. In these genres it was typically presented in the creolized form of an ostinato in which it is followed by a measure of two or three quarter notes, typically in the pattern "ONE-and-TWO-AND-three-AND-FOUR-and-ONE-and-TWO-and-THREE-and-four-and."[18] In the resulting form of a syncopated measure followed by an unsyncopated one, it coheres with the Cuban *clave* pattern (in its "three-two" form), a structural ostinato in Cuban rumba, *son*, and modern salsa. The *cinquillo* also figures prominently as a melodic pattern in Trinidadian calypso and various other genres animated by the colonial-era "French connection."

Hearing two genres as different as thunderous Vodou *banda* drumming and an elegant piano danza of Tavárez, it might be difficult to imagine any formal affinity between them. Yet both are undergirded by the *cinquillo*—as a straightforward, insistent ostinato in the *banda*, and in the piano danza as a gently lilting left-hand syncopation, typically rendered with such leisurely rubato that it is almost unrecognizable. Puerto Rican historian Ángel Quintero-Rivera refers to its presence in the latter context as a "camouflaged drum" (1994), in the sense that the rhythm derives from Afro-Caribbean genres like *bomba*; in some contexts the camouflage was scarcely present at all, leading conservative commentators, such as essayist Braulio Dueño Colón in 1913, to denounce the presence of the "grotesque and anti-aesthetic *bomba* rhythm" in the danza ([1913] 1977: 17). In other contexts one might alternately choose to regard the *cinquillo* as a generalized creole rhythm that came to pervade a gamut of Caribbean musics, to very different effects. Indeed, if in Vodou drumming it is intended to precipitate spirit possession, in a danza of Tavárez it is perhaps more subliminally redolent of a creole sensuality, like the drowsy swaying of palm trees on a hot afternoon.

In terms of style, context, and general character, the rowdy Afro-Caribbean *tumba francesa* and the genteel Tavárez piano danza could be regarded as representing extreme ends of a broad contradance-family continuum. The remainder of this gamut could be seen as comprising more "mainstream" varieties of contradances, in the form of dance and music subgenres with various shared choreographic and musical features, flourishing especially in the nineteenth and perhaps early twentieth centuries in Cuba, Haiti, Puerto Rico, and the Dominican Republic. These contradances might take place in various settings, with diverse sorts of accompanying ensembles. In an elite ballroom, the ensemble might typically include one or two clarinets, violins, trumpets, a contrabass, and percussion—all typically played by mulatto or black professional musicians who would likely be reading from handwritten scores. In more humble circumstances, the music might be provided by a single melody instrument, such as a fiddle or flute, accompanied by a guitar (or guitar variant) or even a harp, in which case the musicians might be performing familiar tunes from memory. Another ensemble format was the military brass band, typically playing in a town plaza, which, in the preamplification days, played at a volume that was thrilling and otherwise unparalleled in the music world.

A distinctive feature of the contradance complex was the way it constituted a continuum between art music and vernacular music. The same danza written as a parlor piano piece by Tavárez could be performed by a humble *jíbaro* (peasant) group at a rural Puerto Rican fiesta. Similarly, the 1839 Cuban novel *Cecilia Valdés* mentions an actual contemporary contradanza, "Caramelo vendo," which "became popular among all social classes." Meanwhile, evidence suggests that many musicians themselves traversed this continuum, playing in an aristocratic ballroom one night and in a boisterous plebian fiesta (in Cuba, perhaps called *bachata* or *changüí*) the next.

The formal structure of contradance subgenres also varied. Perhaps the simplest would be the *tumba francesa*, which consists essentially of drummed ostinatos with a sung vocal litany. More typical was the Cuban form of contradance that retained the English-derived bipartite AABB form, with the first section (the *prima*) often segueing to a second section (*segunda*) that was more enlivened by the creole rhythms (typically the *cinquillo* or habanera patterns). Since such a rendering still lasts less than a minute, in the dance context the piece would be repeated many times and might segue to another composition. The form of the Puerto Rican danza was similar, except that the piece was typically extended not by repetition but by composing a longer B section, adding a third (C) section, and/or introducing a lengthy passage in which the bombardino (saxhorn) would perform arpeggio-laden solos.

The first section of a piece was often referred to as the *paseo* (promenade), in accordance with the stylized strolling that it could accompany. In many Cuban contradanzas and most danzones, the *paseo* section does not differ dramatically in style or intensity from the other section (or sections, in the case of the danzón). However, in other cases, the *paseo* would be distinct in style; in many Cuban contradanzas and in the standard Puerto Rican danza, it would lack the syncopated creole rhythms (habanera or *cinquillo*) that would pervade the subsequent section(s). In Dominican danzas and salon merengues (as in many early-twentieth-century standard merengues), the *paseo* would have a march-like character, often in straight eighth or sixteenth notes.

## *Caribbean Quadrilles*

The creole Caribbean quadrille has flourished in a variety of musical forms. Perhaps the primary feature distinguishing it as a genre is its formal structure, typically comprising a suite of five or six separate sections, each with distinctive music and choreographic figures. The suite format thus can accommodate a variety of otherwise distinct musical genres, including creole forms of jig, reel, schottische, mazurka, waltz, biguine, and contradance. Like most forms of contradance, the quadrille is predominantly an instrumental idiom, although sung lyrics can occasionally be added (as with Puerto Rican and Dominican danzas and the Cuban habanera); in the *haute-taille* style of Martinique, the *commandeur* voices an ongoing monotone chant, calling steps, exhorting the dancers, and making other miscellaneous comments.

Today as before, quadrilles are played by a variety of characteristic ensembles in the Caribbean, many of them assembling in an ad hoc, informal manner where precise instrumentation depends on availability of performers. On the most Afro-Caribbean end of the spectrum is the *bèlè linò* of Martinique, whose quadrille-format dancing is accompanied by the bèlè drum, *tibwa* (*ti-bois*, a small stick-beaten log), and call-and-response singing, without any melodic instrument. A more typical format, like that of the "indoor" Lancers, *haute-tailles*, and *pastourelles* of Martinique and Guadeloupe, involves a melodic instrument—most often a violin or accordion—accompanied by percussion instruments. The latter typically include some sort of drum (whether a cylindrical drum, a frame drum, or a tambourine) and perhaps a scraper, a shaker, and/or a triangle; the drummer often plays in a lively, assertive manner rather than merely unobtrusively keeping time. Quadrille ensembles in Dominica (the latter called "jing-ping" bands) are similar, with the accordion accompanied by tambourine, bamboo scraper (*syak, gwaj*), maracas (*cha-chas*), triangle, and perhaps a "boom-boom" bamboo tube blown more or less as a percussion instrument. The traditional Bahamanian "rake 'n' scrape" ensemble features an accordion, a goombay drum, and a saw, with other instruments, such as guitar, banjo, or shak-shak (shakers), added if available. Jamaican quadrille groups might include fiddle, clarinet, flute, concertina, and various percussion instruments, such as tambourine, triangle, and scraped jawbone of a horse. All these ensembles, depending on the occasion, might in modern times be augmented by guitars, wind instruments, a drum set, and perhaps electric bass. Nevertheless, the most common format of a single melody instrument accompanied by rhythm instruments affords a prevailingly percussive texture and, in some ways, a pronounced Afro-Caribbean flavor. However, the violin-tambourine-triangle ensemble has also been typical of quadrille groups in Brittany, France; in that sense, it is only the syncopated rhythms and ostinato-based tunes rather than the instrumentation and texture that might distinguish a Caribbean quadrille as creole.

Quadrille melodies, like those of Caribbean contradances, are predominantly European in character, although they may be enlivened by conventional improvised embellishments and syncopations, as when St. Lucian fiddlers alternate phrases (and often renditions of a given tune fragment) in binary and ternary meter. The structure of individual movements in a suite is often informal; Jocelyne Guilbault (1985: 55) notes how a fiddler may construct a section by freely repeating or alternating two or three short tunes. In some cases, the fiddler may seem to be playing melodic fragments rather than full-blown, eight-bar melodies. Quadrille tunes in Guadeloupe and Martinique often consist of arpeggiated ostinatos rather than song-like melodies or sectional passages.

Musical forms vary from place to place, although the "*La poule*" movement is invariably in 6/8 meter; in such places as Côte Sous-le-Vent in Guadeloupe, the other movements are mostly creole polkas. In many locales, tunes might be fixed by convention, although elsewhere, as in Guadeloupe, musicians freely add new compositions or borrowed melodies to the repertoire. In general, Caribbean quadrille styles, given their informality and variety, exhibit fewer of the conspicuous, recurrent, and distinctive creole rhythms, such as the *cinquillo* and amphibrach, that pervade so many contradance variants. However, in Guadeloupe and elsewhere, one may hear the triangle and *tibwa* sticks playing syncopated ostinatos, such as a 3-3-3-3-4 pattern; the semichanted, ongoing *commandements* of the *rigaudonnier* (caller) may also reflect a *cinquillo*-like pattern.

On the whole, the quadrille has flourished in the Caribbean as an orally transmitted folk music and dance, typically played by amateur, albeit often skilled, performers who have not had formal training in music. Thus, the customary fiddle-and-percussion quadrille group would contrast markedly with a nineteenth-century Cuban or Puerto Rican danza *típico* ensemble led by musically literate wind players who play their pieces from written scores. Accordingly, the innumerable Spanish Caribbean danzas formally composed for the elite salon or ballroom have no particular counterparts in the more informal and lower-class quadrille realm. European composers, such as the younger Johann Strauss, wrote numerous quadrilles, but no such light-classical tradition seems to have existed for the Caribbean quadrille. These contrasts, however, do not derive from any intrinsic differences between the contradance and quadrille per se but rather have to do the cultural milieus of the islands where they flourished. As will be discussed below, the contradanza was cultivated primarily in the "settler colonies" of the Spanish Caribbean, with their vibrant nineteenth-century creole cultures, while the quadrille flowered more in the "plantation colonies" of the British West Indies and the French Lesser Antilles, where a sense of bourgeois musical nationalism did not develop in the nineteenth century. However, quadrilles were familiar in nineteenth-century Cuba, and their suite format constituted one precedent and likely source for the danzón emerging in the 1870s, with its multisection rondo form.

## Historical Trajectories of the Caribbean Contradance and Quadrille

Reconstructing the routes by which the contradance and quadrille variants spread through the Caribbean, and their evolutionary trajectories in individual islands, is a challenging undertaking. It is not only undermined by a general paucity of documentation but can also involve traversing a minefield of nationalistic sensitivities, which at times are only exacerbated by modern notions of political correctness. In many cases, musical and choreographic elements traveled independently in several directions at once, with the Caribbean serving as a fertile petri dish of creole entities that circulated, intersected, and cross-pollinated. Despite the analytical difficulties posed by such complexities, the need for a pan-Caribbean perspective, both diachronic and synchronic, is obvious and is in some ways only heightened by the existence of so many potentially useful scholarly studies of individual local traditions. Most aspects of the dissemination and evolution of the contradance and quadrille throughout the region are discussed in the individual chapters in this volume; the following paragraphs attempt a very cursory overview of the peregrinations of the contradance and quadrille in the region.

Uncertainty regarding the spread of the contradance commences from the very first stages of its introduction to the Caribbean in the early or mid-1700s. By that time the contradance, in longways style and other forms, was well established not only in its cradle of England and its strongholds of Holland and France but also in Spain. It seems likely that by the mid–eighteenth century the contradance had taken root in Havana, as introduced primarily by Spaniards, but also possibly by the English, who occupied the city in 1762–63, and even by visiting French vessels, with their sailors, merchants, and nobles. By the 1760s, the French contredanse was being danced in Saint-Domingue (Haiti) and Martinique. French Caribbean planters and wealthy merchants brought dance masters from Paris in order to keep up with metropolitan styles and maintain the social status associated with fine dancing. At the same time, however, domestic slaves and free mulattos were also learning to dance contredanses and other genres, in order to mimic white aristocrats, to distinguish themselves from field slaves, and, it may be said, simply to have fun. As Cyrille notes, earlier in the 1600s, planters and missionaries had already attempted to teach European dances, such as the *passé-pied* and *courante*, to slaves in order to wean them from their supposedly barbaric African dances. Plantation owners would be especially pleased to own a few slaves who could provide dance music on fiddle, flute, and other instruments, and it is clear that many slaves eagerly took advantage of opportunities to learn these instruments. By the time of the Haitian Revolution, former slaves and mulattos of varied social standings were avidly cultivating the contredanse and quadrille for their own enjoyment and social elevation. As Saint-Méry wrote in the late 1700s, "Freedmen are wild about dancing and choose exactly the same dances as their former masters. What formerly was forbidden fruit becomes thereby the tastier" (in Stevenson 1981: 52–53). Mulattos and other people of color were also animated by the ideals of freedom and equality associated with the French Revolution, and learning quadrilles and contradances—even from the same dance masters as whites—represented one form of achieving this equality.

As African ways of moving and playing inexorably reasserted themselves, the process of musical creolization became overt in various parts of the Caribbean, primarily in the form of Afro-Caribbean syncopations in both melody and accompaniment. Hence a syncopated habanera rhythm pervades the bass part of the 1803 "San Pascual Bailón," the first documented Cuban contradanza, and other Haitian songs from subsequent decades are enlivened by *cinquillos* and amphibrachs. During this period the Spanish-style contradanza, a figure dance of open couples, would also have established some presence in Puerto Rico, as brought both from the metropole and by Venezuelan and Colombian upper-class refugees fleeing Simón Bolívar's anticolonial insurrection. Meanwhile, from the early 1800s French and British colonists and travelers introduced or reinforced the quadrille in their colonies, including such islands as St. Lucia, Dominique, and Guadeloupe that changed hands at various times.

In the years around 1800, Saint-Domingue/Haiti came to exert a powerful musical influence, both through the vitality of its creole culture as well as through the impact of refugees of diverse races and classes fleeing the Revolution. The Franco-Haitian impact was particularly strong in the nearby asylum of Oriente (eastern Cuba), where the creolized contradance soon took root. Franco-Haitian influence was also pervasive in the eastern, Spanish-speaking part of Hispaniola (Santo Domingo, subsequently the Dominican Republic), which was ruled by the French in 1801–5 and occupied by independent Haiti in 1822–44. Despite the lack of documentation—and the corresponding abundance of competing origin theories—it seems clear that by the 1840s a Haitian-derived style of longways contradance called *tumba* (or *tumba dominicana*) was flourishing in Santo Domingo. Musical and choreographic influences, however, were typically mutual and multidirectional; thus, for example, while French refugees from Saint-Domingue flooded Santiago de Cuba around 1800, the next generations saw prominent Santiago composers and bandleaders, such as Lino Boza, performing extensively in Haiti, whose own economy and urban culture had declined dramatically.

The ongoing military campaigns in the Spanish and French Caribbean in some ways disrupted civic and cultural life, but in other ways they helped spread music and dance forms. Military bands played important roles in this process by performing vernacular dance genres for public entertainment as well as pompous marches for parades. Regiments brought from one island to another exchanged musical materials with the populations of the areas they were posted in. Oral traditions also attribute several genres to specific military occasions, including the Haitian and Dominican *carabinier/carabiné* (supposedly first danced by carbine-wielding Haitian soldiers invading Santo Domingo in 1805), or the merengue (allegedly first created as a song mocking a cowardly Dominican general after an 1844 battle against the Haitians). Military bands also provided much of the instruments, the musical training, and the orchestration models for smaller dance bands in the nineteenth century.

During the 1840s, in Havana the collective figure contradanza was being definitively eclipsed by a new style—inconsistently called danza—emphasizing independent couple dancing, occasionally with controversial hip movements and a more syncopated rhythmic accompaniment. With the ongoing maritime traffic between Cuba and Puerto Rico, this new style—under the name "merengue"—evidently reached Puerto Rico, perhaps with the entourage of the count of Mirasol, General Rafael Arístegui, who visited the island from Cuba in 1844. The new genre soon became the rage in Puerto Rico, leading to its official prohibition in 1849 by the colonial governor Juan de la Pezuela in San Juan. In Puerto Rico, the primary and perhaps sole lasting effect of this decree appears to have been the gradual renaming of the merengue with the more dignified term "danza." Meanwhile, this merengue—evidently a contradance variant quite distinct from the modern Dominican genre of the same name—was evidently exported to Santo Domingo, where it provoked another conservative backlash. While the immediate impact of this journalistic campaign is not clear, by the latter 1800s the Puerto Rican–style danza, especially modeled on the pieces of Juan Morel Campos, had become a standard salon dance. Probably it coexisted not only with a new, rustic style of merengue in the Cibao valley but also with a salon version of the old *merengue contradanzeado*, which may have become increasingly indistinguishable from and absorbed into the danza.

The 1850s–70s constituted in some respects the heyday of the Cuban contradanza (or danza), which flourished both as a dance and as a light-classical piano genre. But if Cuba appears to have led the region in the early establishment of the contradance, it was also in Cuba that the genre first expired, as it was effectively eclipsed in the 1880s by the more lively and syncopated danzón, with its rondo structure and pervasive *cinquillos*. In Puerto Rico, however, the danza flourished with continued vigor, absorbing influences (especially the *cinquillo*) from and coexisting with the Cuban-style danzón. As in Cuba, the danza thrived both as a popular dance and as a salon piano idiom, with the elegant piano compositions of Tavárez reaching unprecedented heights of sophistication. The Puerto Rican danza remained vital until the 1930s, when it gave way, depending on contexts, to the Cuban-derived *son* and bolero or to the American-style fox-trot and other imports. Meanwhile, the three-part Puerto Rican danza seems to have provided the primary model for a derivative danza style in Curaçao, as cultivated by composer Jan Gerard Palm (1831–1906) and his successors.[19] During these same early decades of the twentieth century, the danza and a revived form of parlor *merengue contradanzeado* were cultivated in the Dominican Republic, as was a salon méringue in urban Haiti. In the 1930s, however, all these neoclassicist creolisms came to be seen as quaint and gave way to more modern popular styles.

Despite such inexorable decline, vestigial contradance variants managed to survive, in various forms and in varying degrees of vitality, until the latter twentieth century and even to the present. As mentioned, rural forms of Dominican *tumba* and quadrille were documented in the 1970s and adopted by some folkloric groups; in Haiti, contredanse is still encountered in rural areas and in the stage shows of folkloric groups. Meanwhile, conservatory pianists in Puerto Rico and Cuba still learn the evergreen compositions of Saumell, Cervantes, and Tavárez. It is perhaps in Puerto Rico that the contradance has proved most durable. Traditional familiar danzas are still performed at various occasions, including weddings, especially as the first dance, in which the bride dances with her father. Danzas survive in the repertoires of *jíbaro* musicians, and through the 1960s one could purchase LPs of accordionists, crooners, and other ad hoc ensembles performing their simplified arrangements of such evergreens as "Laura y Georgina." Even the occasional modern commercial popular song, such as El Topo's well-known "Verde Luz," may adhere essentially to the format of a danza.

If the history of the Caribbean contradance is inadequately documented, even less is known about the early history of the quadrille in the region, especially since it has flourished primarily as a lower-class practice of little interest to literate elites. The quadrille was introduced by British and French colonists in their respective domains in the late eighteenth and early nineteenth centuries, just as it was taking European ballrooms by storm. In islands that changed hands, such as St. Lucia, quadrille seems to have been brought by both colonial powers. In accordance with its popularity in the courts and aristocratic ballrooms of Europe, in the Caribbean the quadrille was initially reserved for the plantocracy elite; although subsequently adopted by lower classes, quadrille dancing requires some practice and in some contexts retains an association with social elevation and propriety.

Insofar as they flourished as folk genres, the West Indian quadrille styles did not achieve the level of professional cultivation that elevated the Cuban and Puerto Rican danza to the status of a light-classical art. At the same time, however, while the danza declined definitively after the 1930s, in some Caribbean locales the quadrille, in its persistent humble form, has endured. There is no doubt that its popularity has eclipsed with the advent of the mass media, modernity, and the panoply of new alternative forms of music and dance, from soca to reggae. Hence, for example, Rebecca Miller describes the late-1990s quadrille scene in Carriacou as consisting of a single performing group, with a sole, octogenarian fiddler (2005); there, as to some extent elsewhere, quadrille suffers from being seen as a derivative colonial-era dance, unlike "big drum" dance and music, which is celebrated nowadays as an oppositional Afro-Caribbean entity. Similarly, while quadrille persists in Guadeloupe and Martinique, it is in some contexts bypassed in the revived Afrocentricity that currently celebrates more neo-African forms, such as *gwoka* and bèlè.

Nevertheless, the quadrille (*kwadril*) remained a lively tradition in the 1980s in St. Lucia, as documented by Guilbault (1985), and is still performed by groups in Martinique and Guadeloupe, who alternate hosting balls incorporating enthusiasts of different generations and social backgrounds. In Dominica, quadrille has come to be celebrated as a national dance, being foregrounded with particular prominence at the Heritage Festival held every October. Guilbault notes that the relatively old age of quadrille participants in St. Lucia does not necessarily indicate stagnation but rather reflects that many people take an interest in the genre only as they age. Quadrille-type dances, whether by that name or not, seem to have survived most dynamically in Martinique and Guadeloupe, where they have been focal genres in ballroom dances until recently. At present, although still danced as part of mutual-aid projects and yuletide "*bal quadrille*" celebrations, they are more typically performed on stage at festivals and competitions, and for tourists, by groups who must rehearse the complicated choreography. Most significantly, since the 1980s quadrille variants in the French Caribbean (including Dominica and St. Lucia) have been promoted in inter-island festivals as emblems of a shared Creole Antillean culture—like the Creole language itself—that distinguish islanders from metropolitan French culture.

## Unity and Diversity

The Caribbean contradance and quadrille family comprises a vast and unruly set of genres that in many ways resists a unifying pan-regional perspective. Even broad generalizations about contradance and quadrille families, or between English, French, and Spanish realms are blurred by overlapping choreographic or musical features, internal disjunctions, and, of course, the prevailing insufficiency of data about the present as well as the past. Much might be gleaned, for example, from a study of quadrille melodies in the French and English Caribbean, exploring tune families, shared songs, and transformations and perpetuations of European models; however, neither have island-specific compendia of tunes been compiled, nor have researchers performed the sort of panregional studies that could enable such a project.

The most broad and obvious categorizations would distinguish a Spanish Caribbean contradance family, with some presence in the French Caribbean, from a set of English and French Caribbean quadrille traditions. The contradance and quadrille, both in European and Caribbean incarnations, are of course related in origin and structure, although more specific affinities in the Caribbean are in some ways limited. We know that in Cuba in the nineteenth century, quadrilles and contradanzas might be danced at the same function, as performed by the same ensemble in presumably the same style. Today, as mentioned above, choreographies might also overlap, as in the Martinican *haute-taille* quadrille, whose first three figures might be in contredanse format. Still, while a quadrille tradition was documented in the rural Dominican Republic in the 1970s, on the whole, the quadrille, with its distinctive suite structure, has never flourished extensively in the Spanish Caribbean. Conversely, and perhaps more curiously, the contradance, despite its English origin, does not seem to have flourished in the British West Indies, although longways format may appear in some quadrille variants, such as Jamaican "camp" styles.

Musically, the contradance and quadrille families reflect certain affinities. While the salon contradanza may not have counterparts in the more orally transmitted West Indian quadrille traditions, the small and unpretentious ensembles that typically play quadrilles would certainly find counterparts in the lower category of ambulatory or informal groups that played contradanzas in Cuba in the nineteenth century, or even in the varied ad hoc trios and quartets, especially in *jíbaro* music, that played danzas throughout the twentieth century. Like some West Indian quadrilles passed down in oral tradition, many if not most of these danzas would have originally been written by trained composers, such as Juan Morel Campos. Both quadrilles and contradanzas tend to be structured in eight-bar sections, with simple (often only tonic and dominant) harmonies and diatonic melodies. Quadrilles documented in Carriacou by Miller (2005) tend, like Cuban contradanzas, to be in bipartite form. Repetition and extension patterns, not surprisingly, may vary, as in the loose and variable schemes found in St. Lucia quadrilles (see Guilbault 1985: 55). Forms of rhythmic creolization tend to differ; the rhythmic icons of Spanish Caribbean and Haitian contradance variants—the *cinquillo*, amphibrach, and habanera rhythms—are not typical of French or English Caribbean quadrilles. These latter, rather, tend to have their own characteristic syncopations, which may even suggest three-against-two polyrhythms in the case of quadrilles in 6/8 meter (Miller 2005: 415). Haitian folk contredanses, with their simple melodic ostinatos punctuated by regular calls by a *commandeur*, closely resemble quadrilles in Guadeloupe.

Further research would undoubtedly unearth affinities and probably even shared melodies in the quadrille repertoires of the French and English Caribbean. Choreographic commonalities, for their part, are readily apparent, especially to participants in the interisland festivals bringing together quadrille groups from St. Lucia, Martinique, Dominica, and Guadeloupe. Cyrille finds clear awareness of a core vocabulary of quadrille dancing in these islands, whose practitioners often speak of their dance tradition as a shared legacy comparable to the Creole they speak. Similarly, Chapter 7 discusses the shared figures and terms that are found in quadrilles throughout much of the English-speaking Caribbean, as well as several correspondences to the contemporary French Caribbean and the Continental French quadrille that generated both traditions. These commonalities extend to Central America, as brought by migrant West Indian laborers in the decades around 1900. Most of these laborers came from Jamaica and elsewhere in the English-speaking West Indies, but Haitian workers are the likely source for the Garifuna contradance style called "*kujai*," presumably from the Haitian *coup d'jaill* (Kreyòl: *koudjay*) discussed in Chapter 6.

Connections between the contradanza (especially "danza") efflorescences in Cuba, Puerto Rico, and the Dominican Republic are especially overt and are scarcely surprising given the shared European origins of these traditions and the historical links between the three sites themselves. The documented Puerto Rican danzas of the 1860s closely resemble their Cuban models. In the next decades, the Puerto Rican danza—as well as the derivative Dominican danza and salon merengue and the Haitian salon méringue—developed its own distinctive features, particularly in terms of its extended formal structure; at the same time, however, in the *cinquillo* that pervaded its ensemble renditions, all these traditions bore an obvious similarity to the Cuban danzón of the same period. Meanwhile, the repertoires of Puerto Rican and Dominican dance bands in the decades around 1900 overlapped considerably, incorporating danzas, danzones, and the usual waltzes, two-steps, and the like.

The emergence of Dominican and Haitian salon merengue/méringue styles in the early decades of the twentieth century, although in some respects marginal phenomena, constituted another parallel with Cuban and Puerto Rican music scenes. Structural affinities, as well as such features as the *cinquillo/quintolet*, united all these variants. Moreover, as U.S. occupations intensified nationalistic sentiment in Haiti and the Dominican Republic (not to mention Puerto Rico) in the second and third decades of the century, even the attempts of local composers to differentiate their music from that of other islands tended to resemble each other. Hence, Dominican salon composers Juan Francisco García (1892–1974) and Haitian counterparts, such as Justin Elie (1883–1931), turned to vernacular local musics for inspiration and tried to fashion local piano merengues/méringues that would retain the spirit of the more extensively cultivated Cuban and Puerto Rican danzas while emerging from their shadow. Even the idiosyncratically different ways of notating the *cinquillo/quintolet* reflected a similar self-conscious concern with correct rubato-laden execution of the distinctively creole rhythms.[20]

## Creolization

The Caribbean contradance and quadrille are quintessential products of the creolization process that has animated most of what is distinctive about the region's culture. As deriving from linguistics, the term "creolization" originally denotes the process by which speakers of two or more distinct tongues, who meet on neutral territory that is the homeland of neither, create a pidgin lingua franca, which then becomes a first language for subsequent generations. This process is more than, say, the mixing of blue and yellow to make green, since people are active, creative agents, not inert chemicals, and the new human product, whether a language or a musical style, takes on a life of its own.

As applied to culture, the term "creolization," like its approximate synonym "syncretism," has been occasionally criticized for its tendency to imply that the two or more entities—whether musical styles, religions, or languages—that meet and blend are somehow pure and unalloyed (like primary colors), as opposed to the hybrid product of their encounter. The syncretic process that generated the Caribbean contradance and quadrille illustrates the importance of remembering that the formative elements in creolization may themselves be creolized rather than primordially pure entities. From a broad perspective, the Caribbean contradance and quadrille were products of the encounter of two dramatically distinct cultural heritages—the African and the European—though these contributions were themselves diverse and often internally syncretic. The European contradance and quadrille flourished in distinct regional and class-based variants in England, Holland, France, and Spain, which to some extent nourished each other, with the exchanges between England and France being the most extensive. The versions exported to the Caribbean were thus already creolized in their own way; a further sort of "neo-European" creolization occurred when the regional variants established in the Caribbean not only coexisted with but also cross-fertilized each other, in some cases independently of any particular sort of Afro-Caribbean influence.

Similarly, the African cultural entities that took root in the Caribbean were themselves products of ongoing interactions in Africa. In the Caribbean crucible, "African" music and dance, far from constituting a monolith, comprised a set of diverse traditions associated with people of varied ethnic origins who were obliged to interact in the new setting. Hence, for example, while one might like to pinpoint a specific African place of origin for such things as the *cinquillo* or amphibrach ostinatos, the prominence these rhythms assumed in Haiti and elsewhere must be attributed to a process of interethnic musical syncretism that then extended to "whiter" musical realms.

We can easily imagine instances of this sort of initial level of neo-European and neo-African syncretism in the Caribbean. Perhaps, for example, at an informal soirée in 1790 in Port-au-Prince one might encounter some local whites dancing a French-style contredanse to English jigs and reels provided by a fiddler and flautist serving on a visiting British merchant vessel; a local Franco-Haitian fiddler then joins the musicians and later teaches the tunes to his own friends. Outside the city, on a plantation in the nearby countryside, three musically inclined slaves from Dahomey, Yorubaland, and the Congo are playing together on some drums the local Dahomeyans have built; while their own traditional rhythms are all somewhat distinct from each other, they soon settle on one based around a pattern—the *cinquillo*—that is at least implicitly extant in the traditions of all three. Meanwhile, the trio, with their master's encouragement, has also learned to approximate a few contredanses on the two fiddles and a tambourine available in the "big house." The next and more overt level of creolization—between African and European traditions—occurs when they perform these at a dance party of their master and enliven the music with the *cinquillo* that has become a familiar rhythm to all of them. Meanwhile, the cultivation of such European-derived genres as the contradance and quadrille—like the adoption of European languages—also served to facilitate sociocultural interaction between ethnically diverse segments of the slave population.

Musical creolization in the Caribbean was a complex process that did not "just happen" but instead was inextricably conditioned by the power dynamics of the social groups involved. In the Caribbean, creolization invariably required a degree of openness and adaptation, both on the parts of whites as well as people of color. Just as black people might learn European quadrilles, so did many whites avidly take up Afro-Caribbean dances. Thus, as we have mentioned, in the eighteenth-century French Caribbean, Labat testified to the fondness of whites for dancing the calenda, while Saint-Méry related how plantation owners and other upper-class white people were performing Africanized dances, such as the *chica* and "minuet congo," alongside contredanses and minuets. (Meanwhile, other Caribbean commentators lamented how white women adopted their domestic slaves' "drawling, dissonant gibberish"—i.e., the local Creole language [see, e.g., Dayan 1995: 175].)

The plantation owner's house, with its socially intermediate stratum of domestic slaves and perhaps a few mulatto offspring of the white menfolk, would constitute one site for the sort of cultural interaction conducive to musical creolization. Another would be the military band, in which musicians of diverse races and social backgrounds would learn to play clarinet, cornet, and other instruments in order to perform marches, contradances, and other genres at both military functions and—perhaps while moonlighting—at civilian dances. Port towns would be particularly fertile sites of cross-fertilization, in which both plebian and elite locals would take avid interest in new songs and dances from abroad, and musicians and dancers of diverse backgrounds might on various occasions interact. Local theaters, as in Cap Français (Cap Haitien) in the late 1700s, presented pot-pourris including stylized versions of "negro dances" for the entertainment of white audiences (e.g., see Dayan 1995: 184). Another more specific meeting ground would be various institutions, such as Cuban *bailes de cuna*, in which young upper-class white men would fraternize with darker-skinned women, both on the dance floor and in the bedroom; in the former case, their dancing would typically be accompanied by an ensemble of mixed-race musicians whose syncopated renderings of contradanzas would be free from the admonitions of negrophobic moralists.

The ease and alacrity with which Afro-Caribbeans learned to play and dance contradances was attested to by many contemporary observers. Saint-Méry remarked in 1797, "Blacks, imitating whites, dance minuets and contradanzas. Their sense of attunement confers on them the first quality needed by a musician; for this reason many are good violinists, since this is the instrument they prefer. Quickly, they know, for example, that the B note is found over the third string, and the first finger should be placed on that string; by just hearing a tune, or remembering it, they learn it with utmost ease" (in Carpentier [1946] 2001: 145).

In 1808, a few years later, a visitor to the thoroughly Caribbean city of New Orleans similarly described a festivity in which black merrymakers divided into two groups—one to dance the bamboulá, and the other, the contradance (in Sublette 2008: 189).

The neo-African drumming heard on the Haitian plantation might have little in common with the elegant Bach invention played on the clavichord by the master's wife. Nevertheless, African and European traditions could easily intersect and cross-fertilize in the contradance and quadrille complex, with its varied and flexible sorts of ensemble formats and accompanimental rhythms and its dance formations that had close precedents in both Africa and Europe. Contradance and quadrille culture thus provided a fluid medium through which diverse music and dance elements as well as actual musicians and dancers could move and interact.

Particularly important in this process were people of color. In a nineteenth-century Caribbean milieu where whites did not regard the job of professional musician as prestigious, ensembles, whether playing for whites or blacks, tended to be staffed mostly by blacks and mulattos, leading one dismayed Cuban to lament with alarm in 1832, "The arts are in the hands of people of color." And while one mulatto clarinetist might take pride in socially distancing himself from the neo-African ways of the *bozal* (the fresh-off-the-boat slave), another might move easily and often between the two milieus. For their part, mulatto dancers—including the more or less public women at the *bailes de cuna*—might well dance in and help popularize a sensual style distinguished by the pendular hip movements so typical of much African dancing.

Creolization may in some contexts occur from the more or less natural collaboration of two communities that interact on neutral territory while remaining familiar with their own ancestral cultures. Most Caribbean white people, for example, presumably enjoyed a degree of at least potential access to European music and dance traditions, whether in the form of classical arts, jigs and reels, or neo-Hispanic *zapateos*. Colonial-era blacks, however, were more severely cut off from their ancestral traditions, especially as neo-African music, dance, and religion came to be energetically suppressed in the British West Indies and elsewhere.

In such a situation, creolization could be precipitated and intensified by a process of deculturation, in which one or more of the communities in question loses touch with its traditional culture. From the 1930s, E. Franklin Frazier (1932a, 1932b, 1939, 1957) argued that such was the case with Afro-Americans, who had been thoroughly stripped of their ancestral cultural traditions by the traumatic experience of slavery. Hence, Frazier argued, Afro-American culture, for all its vitality, had developed primarily as a derivative imitation of Euro-American culture—indeed, one could add, just as the emergence of Haitian Creole was accompanied by the forgetting of ancestral African languages. In the Caribbean, where most African musical traditions dwindled over the generations or were discouraged or actively repressed by white masters, the cultivation of creolized forms, such as the contradance and quadrille, may have constituted an obvious option for many black people. A Haitian Vodou chant pithily portrayed the dilemma of the slave alienated from African ancestry: "*Se Kreyol no ye, pa genyen Ginen anko*" ("We are creoles, who no longer have Africa"). What replaced inherited African tradition among Afro-Caribbeans was a shared experience of alienation and oppression.

In 1941 Herskovits's *The Myth of the Negro Past* challenged Frazier's portrayal of Afro-American deculturation, positing significant continuities between New World and African cultures and initiating a scholarly debate that continues, in various forms, to the present. In Herskovits's wake, many academics have exerted themselves in finding or hypothesizing African roots of

Afro-American and Afro-Caribbean practices. In the realm of the creolized contradance, obvious examples would include the prominent use of rhythmic ostinatos, specific patterns like the amphibrach and *cinquillo*, and the swaying hip movements enlivening couple dance styles from the mid-1800s, if not earlier. Africanisms are particularly overt in such genres as Haitian-Cuban *tumba francesa*, in which contradance choreography is accompanied by neo-African drumming. The use of quadrilles to induce spirit possession in Tobago, Montserrat, and elsewhere also represents an especially clear sort of Africanization of a European music tradition. Other practices may be seen as creolized adaptations of African traditions; Cyrille suggests, for example, that the ongoing stylized commentary declaimed by the *commandeur* in Martinique and Guadeloupe quadrilles may represent a perpetuation of a West African talking drum tradition. Leaving aside intangible concepts of supposedly African-derived "base patterns of performance" (Abrahams 1983: 33), origins of other practices may be less clear; for example, if an octogenarian quadrille fiddler in Carriacou consistently strays from standard Western intonation, is his playing an atavistic resurfacing of a hoary African modal tuning (as suggested by Miller 2005: 415), or is he simply playing out of tune—that is, as Frazier might argue, imperfectly imitating white culture? (And how could one tell the difference?)

One perspective that to some extent mitigates the Herskovits-Frazier opposition is to accept the reality of cultural loss on the part of many Afro-Caribbeans but to stress its positive aspect in the sense that it became a point of departure for dynamic creativity in the form of creolized expressive arts. Hence, for example, St. Lucian poet Derek Walcott has written eloquently both of the tragedy of such cultural loss and of the brilliant creativity that it engendered: "In time the slave surrendered to amnesia. That amnesia is the true history of the New World." Or, as a Trinidadian musician remarked to me, "I'm *glad* that the British banned our traditional drumming, because it inspired us to invent the steel drum." Thus many Afro-Caribbean performers of contradance and quadrille, from the slave fiddler on the eighteenth-century Haitian plantation to a trumpeter in an 1890s Puerto Rican danza ensemble, might have lost touch with ancestral Afro-Caribbean musics, but that alienation precipitated not stagnation or obsequious imitation but creation, in an inherently creole form. Liberated perforce from the inherited, unquestioned traditions of the past, and often animated by a self-conscious hybridity, Caribbean creole cultures were able to develop as intrinsically modern entities rather than as incompetent imitations of European forms. Creolization played an important part in Caribbean people's consciousness of being at once part of and separate from the Euro-American mainstream, and their ability to combine premodern African and New World features has accounted for much of the extraordinary power of Caribbean arts, especially music.

Further, to some extent, Afro-Caribbeans cultivated creole genres like the contradance and quadrille less because traditional neo-African forms were unavailable to them than because they actively preferred the new creole styles. Indeed, as mentioned, creolization in the Caribbean depended on a spirit of openness on the part of all communities involved. Many conservative whites vehemently denounced the creolization represented by the new contradance variants, which they perceived as lewd, unruly, and too tainted by black influence. For their part, we can assume that many black people preferred their traditional calendas and bamboulás to the dainty contradances and quadrilles that may have struck them as strange, dull, or even vulgar. Nevertheless, aside from the intrinsic pleasures offered by the contradance and quadrille, many Afro-Caribbeans, both during the slavery period and later, clearly felt that by performing these genres they could accrue some of the social status of the white masters and elevate themselves above their backward and perhaps more recently arrived African cousins who still danced the calenda. In the centuries before the negritude movement had stirred pride in African heritage, several accounts attested to the disdain with which creolized slaves and free blacks regarded *bozal* Africans and their rude music. Representative is James Kelly's 1831 description of Christmas celebrations on a West Indian plantation, where the creolized, Caribbean-born slaves danced to their fife and drum music (possibly quadrilles) in the center of the hall, while the Africans with their goombay dancing were crowded into the less desirable corners (in Burton 1997: 67, 34): "The one class [the *bozals*], forced into slavery, humbled and degraded, had lost everything and found no solace but the miserable one of retrospection. The other, born in slavery, never had the freedom to lose, yet did the Creole proudly assume a superiority over the African."

An 1823 visitor to Jamaica provided another telling description of the contrasting practices of the *bozal* and the Caribbean-born slave, and of the musical creolization process that was well evident in the country dancing of the latter:

> [The music of the *bozals*] is very rude; it consists of the goombay or drum, several rattles, and the voices of the female slaves. . . . In a few years it is probable that the rude music here described will be altogether exploded among the creole negroes, who show a decided preference of European music. Its instruments, its tune, its dances, are now pretty generally adopted by the young creoles, who indeed sedulously copy their masters and mistresses in every thing. A sort of subscription balls are set on foot, and parties of both sexes assemble and dance country dances to the music of a violin, tamborine, etc. But this improvement of taste is in a great measure confined to those who are, or have been, domestics about the houses of the white, and have in consequence imbibed a fondness for their amusements, and some skill in the performance. They affect, too, the language, manners, and conversation of the white; those who have it in their power have at times their convivial parties, when they will endeavour to mimic their mas-

> ters in their drinking, their songs, and their toasts; and it is laughable to see with what awkward minuteness they aim at such imitations. (In Abrahams and Szwed 1983: 301)

A modern, more charitable view might regard the slaves' attempts to imitate their masters' manners and music less as laughable than as an attempt to achieve power and status in an otherwise disadvantaged situation. Dancing the quadrille could be seen as a kind of opposition, expressed not in futile rebellion but in a carnivalesque and festive reclamation of the body and a playful appropriation of the recreational modes of the dominant culture (see Burton 1997). (However, there is no particular evidence to support the occasionally encountered view that, in dancing quadrilles and contradances, slaves were subversively mocking their masters.)

And yet, even a postcolonial perspective might disparage the Afro-Caribbean cultivation of genres like the quadrille as obsequious imitation and capitulation. In 1962, V. S. Naipaul wrote of a quadrille-type West Indian dance with his customary mixture of condescension and insight:

> By listening beyond the drums to the accordion, one could perceive the stringed instruments of two centuries ago, and see the dances which even now were only slightly negrofied, the atmosphere became thick and repellant with slavery, making one think of long hot days on the plantation, music at night from the bright windows of the estate house. . . . The music and motions of privilege, forgotten elsewhere, still lived here in a ghostly, beggared elegance: to this mincing mimicry the violence and improvisation and awesome skill of African dancing had been reduced. (1962: 231)

Politically incorrect as such a disparaging view of creole culture may seem, many West Indians might at least implicitly share Naipaul's sentiment, insofar as they have largely lost interest in such colonial-era dances. Except for some elders, most of today's West Indians are thoroughly tuned in to the cosmopolitan sounds of Bob Marley and Beenie Man. Fiddle-and-drum quadrille, while celebrated in some nationalistic circles as folklore, is seen by many as a relic of the days before Afrocentric negritude and Rastafari and before creolized black people had developed their own more modern, unique, and self-consciously Afro-Caribbean genres like reggae and salsa. Even in the realm of traditional folk musics, contradance and quadrille styles like the Martinican *haute-taille* came to be disparaged by some activists as lacking the "authenticity" of the more Afro-Caribbean bèlè. At the same time, as mentioned above, French Caribbean quadrille styles have also come to be upheld as icons of a shared creole culture—together with the Creole language itself—that links Guadeloupe, Martinique, St. Lucia, and Dominica.

## Patterns of Caribbean Creolization: Regional Distinctions

Creolization was the generative process that animated the evolution of all the Caribbean contradance and quadrille styles and made them distinctive and unique. At the same time, in different parts of the region creolization operated to different extents, in different manners, and with different historical timings. These differences account for some of the dramatically divergent forms that contradances and quadrilles assumed in the Caribbean.

While a region so diverse as the Caribbean does not lend itself to generalization, one can, with some equivocation, discern certain broadly divergent patterns of musical creolization, especially as pertain to contrasts between the British Caribbean and the Hispanic Caribbean—particularly Cuba. On the whole, in Cuba, creolization—as embodied in the contradanza—commenced relatively early, being well underway by the start of the nineteenth century. As we have seen, by the mid-century decades, in the Dominican Republic and Puerto Rico as well as in Cuba, local contradanza styles had emerged that were evidently danced and played by whites and people of color, often together. In Cuba and Puerto Rico the contradanza (or danza) came to flourish not only as a simple dance piece but also as a salon music genre cultivated by urban, formally trained amateur and professional composers of diverse races. By the 1840s in Cuba, and a few decades later in Puerto Rico, the local contradanzas had come to be recognized and celebrated as distinctively national, creole entities and in some contexts became explicitly associated with bourgeois nationalism and independence movements.

The contrasts with the British West Indies are striking. We do know from travelers' accounts that black slaves played and danced quadrilles and similar genres from the early 1800s (if not earlier), and slaves who learned to play fiddle and other instruments might provide dance music for the festivities of plantation owners. Nevertheless, there appears to have been no counterpart to the fluid cultural milieu existing in, for example, Havana, Santiago de Cuba, or Ponce, in which free whites and people of color not only composed but also collectively danced and performed contradanzas. While the quadrille may have been popular among both whites and blacks in the Anglophone Caribbean, it was neither cultivated as a vehicle for studied composition nor celebrated as a symbol of cultural nationalism. Instead, it survived primarily as a folk dance, and no West Indian equivalents to such Spanish Caribbean composers as Saumell and Tavárez exist. The quintessential West Indian quadrille ensemble was not a wind- and string-based *orquesta típica* of musically literate urban professionals reading from a score, but rather an unpretentious, ad hoc, fiddle-and-percussion trio recycling familiar, orally transmitted tunes. In general, creole culture came much later in the Anglophone Caribbean, and the quadrille played a less prominent role in it.

For its part, the French Caribbean lends itself less readily to generalization, especially since the cultural and historical trajectory of Haiti—independent from 1804—became so distinct from that of Martinique, Guadeloupe, and the lesser French Antilles. Evidence suggests that Martinique and especially Saint-Domingue were particularly dynamic and influential centers for musical creolization in the latter 1700s, with contredanses and quadrilles being actively performed by the growing numbers of free blacks and mulattos. In Haiti in the early 1900s a local urban cultivated form of méringue emerged that reflected both stylistic and ideological affinities with counterparts in the Spanish Caribbean. In terms of creolized quadrille and contredanse styles, the rest of the French Caribbean bears greater resemblance to the British West Indies, where these genres flourished more as folk idioms.

A variety of factors may explain the different patterns of musical creolization in the different colonial zones of the Caribbean. One argument would attribute the early and more intensive creolization in the Spanish and perhaps French Caribbean to a more open cultural attitude on the part of the colonists. The early Iberian colonists, unlike the bourgeois, more economically advanced English, were in some ways premodern, precapitalist people who, however racist in their own way, seem to have recognized Africans as human beings with their own culture. Unlike the more racially homogeneous English, the southern Europeans, according to this thesis, had a certain Mediterranean cosmopolitan nature bred from centuries of contact (whether amicable or not) with diverse Arabs, Jews, Gypsies, and Africans—hence, it could be argued, the evident ease with which so many Spanish-Caribbeans interacted on the dance floor or in the *orquesta típica* with people of color, and the openness to Afro-Caribbeans' musical and choreographic contributions, fostering the early and extensive emergence of local contradanza styles.

If such a culturally oriented hypothesis may seem essentializing or speculative, other more tangible factors may better explain the divergent trajectories of creole music in the nineteenth century. Perhaps the most important distinctions derived from the differences between plantation colonies like Jamaica, whose populations consisted primarily of slaves with a small white planter and administrative sector, and settler colonies like Cuba, which had a more diverse balance of whites, mulattos, slaves, and free blacks (over 20 percent in 1774). The large free black population—which had no counterpart in the British Caribbean (or, for that matter, the United States) before Emancipation—derived from more lenient Spanish manumission practices and the historically mixed economies based on family farms and cattle breeding in which people of diverse racial backgrounds intermarried over generations and worked, lived, danced, and made music together. In the early 1800s, the sugar plantation cultures that arose in Cuba and Puerto Rico had to adapt themselves to the already well-formed, racially fluid, and more lenient creole cultures, in which a genre like the contradanza could thrive. By contrast, in Jamaica, slaves, who constituted about 90 percent of the population in 1800, were subject to rigid cultural repression and could exert little cultural influence on local whites. Closer distinctions could also be made within individual islands themselves, contrasting plantation-dominated areas (e.g., western Cuba and northeastern Martinique) from hilly regions of family farms and greater racial fluidity (e.g., eastern Cuba and southern Martinique).

The Spanish Caribbean settler colonies, as suggested by that term, also differed from the West Indian plantation economies in attracting hundreds of thousands of European immigrants, who, over the generations, played crucial roles in fostering distinctive creole cultures in their new homelands. As mentioned above, by the 1840s many Cubans were already developing a sense of cultural nationalism, in which music genres like the contradanza were celebrated as distinctive idioms. As white Cubans and Puerto Ricans increasingly came to resent oppressive and exploitative Spanish rule, such a sentimental pride in local culture often came to overlap with a fierce political nationalism.

A comparable sense of creole cultural nationalism simply did not exist in the British Caribbean of the nineteenth century and would scarcely emerge until the mid–twentieth century. In general, the British colonies attracted relatively few settlers. As in eighteenth-century Saint-Domingue, many of those who did come were derelicts and mountebanks out to make a quick killing in the tropics. For their part, members of the British and French plantocracies often came for limited periods, remaining attached to Europe, where they invested their earnings and sent their children to be educated. The contrasts between the two sorts of colonies could be seen in their cities: Colonial Havana was an opulent and beautiful metropolis with fine cathedrals, mansions, and promenades, whereas the British Caribbean ports consisted of dreary warehouses surrounded by shantytowns, with a few bleak barns passing as the "great houses" of the rich. Accordingly, the British colonial elites made little attempt to develop their own art forms, developed no particular sense of local cultural or political nationalism, and took little interest in cultivating a genre like quadrille as a symbol of local creole culture.

## Contradance and Quadrille as Contested Sites

The contradance and quadrille might seem to be innocuous recreational genres, free from social or ideological dimensions and conflicts. In their most typical Caribbean forms, they constituted forms of "family entertainment" whose appeal transcended boundaries of class, race, and generation. Generally lacking lyrics, they were largely apolitical, secular, and innocent of the tendency toward controversial ribaldry that characterized other vernacular song forms. Their prevailing spirit, then as today, has been one of fun rather than transgression or protest. Nevertheless, both genres—like all forms of expression—have been inherently imbricated in the sociopolitical dynamics of their historical contexts. Whether explicitly or implicitly, they became associated with notions of comportment, social distinction, national identity, and even, in some cases, political agendas. Once established, they became so identified with social propriety that innovations or departures could provoke vigorous debate or even outright prohibitions; hence, for example, much of the early documentation of the Puerto Rican and Dominican merengue/danza comes in the form of journalistic polemics and the ban issued by the governor of Puerto Rico in 1849.

In Europe, as we have seen, the contradance and quadrille had their own set of diverse affective associations. On one level, in the eighteenth and early nineteenth centuries, they flourished as elite dances, whose correct and graceful execution was explicitly seen as a sign of aristocratic breeding and good taste. Under the guidance of professional dance masters, people of means learned to perform the figures with effortless elegance, avoiding any *faux pas*—literally, false step—that would betray poor taste and training. At the same time, as we have seen, the contradance and quadrille had certain democratic and populist aspects that distinguished them from stiff ceremonial dances, such as the minuet. Not only had the country dance first emerged as a folk dance, but it and the quadrille also became adopted, in diverse forms, by the rising bourgeoisie who enjoyed dance forms that were at once respectable but less formal and pompous than the minuet.

In the Caribbean, the contradance and quadrille acquired their own changing sorts of social significance in accordance with the social dynamics of the new setting. As Cyrille has documented, plantation owners in Martinique imported Parisian dance masters not only to keep up with the latest metropolitan fashions but also to maintain a sense of cultural superiority over their black slaves, whose dances they described as grotesque, crude, and vulgar, and that were all the more objectionable for being performed barefoot in the open air by scantily clad dancers. Yet by the latter 1700s, as we have mentioned, domestic slaves, handfuls of newly freed blacks, and the growing numbers of free mulattos were avidly imitating the contradance and quadrille as danced by the slave owners. Cyrille notes that French missionaries had earlier attempted to teach slaves the *passé-pied* and *courante* "so they [could] jump and entertain themselves at will with no indecent gestures" (Labat 1724: 2, 54), and they had encouraged musically inclined domestic slaves to learn to play fiddle and other instruments to accompany their dances. Subsequently, several commentators noted, often with bemusement, the enthusiasm with which mulattos, free blacks, and domestic slaves performed contredanses and quadrilles at dances where they would dress in their finest gowns and suits.

For many people of color during this period, it is clear that performing contradance and quadrille while dressed elegantly was not merely fun but served as a means of demonstrating superiority to others lower on the social hierarchy. As Cyrille notes in Chapter 5, newly freed blacks, for their part, might dance with domestic slaves at a party only with a sense of condescension, while petty-bourgeois mulattos cultivated social dances to demonstrate their superiority not only to blacks but also to lower-class whites. As I have suggested, scholars might differ as to whether such a strategy of social positioning should be regarded as a form of creative resistance to hegemony or, alternately, obsequious acquiescence to and even complicity with an unjust social hierarchy.

Two centuries later, with "massa day done" and new social hierarchies having long since replaced those of the slavery period, quadrille still retains some of its traditional prestige in such places as St. Lucia and Dominica. Quadrille is appreciated by some as a dance that requires training and rehearsal and accordingly accrues a certain sort of social status to its participants; in Guadeloupe, its dancers, as in earlier days, may also view it as more refined, European, and "respectable" than more African dances like the bèlè. Hence it is perhaps paradoxical that quadrilles, even with mundane lyrics, came to be associated with invocations of African ancestors in Trinidad or even with spirit possession in Tobago and Montserrat. With political independence, throughout the French and English Caribbean quadrille can also be celebrated as part of local traditional culture, performed by folkloric groups on various occasions and receiving some promotion via state-run competitions. As discussed in Chapter 7, quadrille has even come to be regarded as an icon of traditional culture among Carib Indians in St. Vincent and among Maroons in Jamaica. However, as I have suggested, its status is at the same time ambiguous, as many may see it as a relic of the colonial era, when people of color lacked a modern sense of black pride and had yet to develop assertive, self-consciously Afro-Caribbean genres like reggae and zouk.

As of the mid-1800s, contradance and quadrille could certainly still serve as recreation forms by which people of various races and levels of social status could distance themselves from rural plantation workers or even white country bumpkins and urban riffraff. However, especially in cities and towns in the Spanish Caribbean, the popularity of these social dances cut across many social boundaries, encompassing whites, blacks, and mulattos of diverse socioeconomic backgrounds. On one level, contradance culture was distinguished by fluidity and openness, performed by diverse people in diverse settings, and encompassed everything from the hyper-refined salon music of Tavárez to more syncopated and jaunty pieces with names like "Tu madre es conga" ("Your Mother Is Congolese") and "El mulato en el cabildo" ("The Mulatto in the *Cabildo* [Afro-Cuban club]"). At the same time, this very openness—as opposed, for example, to the rigidity of the minuet—meant that the boundaries of acceptability in the contradance and quadrille were often sites of contestation where representations of class, race, gender, and generation continually had to be negotiated. Hence negrophobic contradanza lovers objected to the incorporation of the *güiro* scraper, the excessive prominence given to Afro-Caribbean rhythms, and the titles too redolent of plebian or black culture (see Dueño Colón 1977). Particularly controversial, as we have discussed, was the advent of independent, intimate couple dancing, which negated the asexual, collective "family fun" orientation of the contradance and quadrille. It was evidently this waltz-inspired development (which negrophobes could not blame on black culture) that provoked the 1849 Puerto Rican ban on the merengue and the vitriolic denunciations by Dominican essayists a few years later.

While the incorporation of creole elements proved controversial, it enabled the contradanza in the Spanish Caribbean to become a celebrated emblem of local creole culture. The self-consciously creole character was particularly obvious in the colorful titles composers gave their contradanzas. Just as English country dances bore whimsical names, such as "Beggar Boy" and "Cuckolds All a Row," so did Cuban and Puerto Rican composers give their works titles invoking vernacular local speech and culture, such as "Ay, yo quiero comer mondongo" ("Oh, I Want to Eat *Mondongo* [a local stew]"), "Mandinga no va" ("Don't Go, Mandingo Lady"), and "Yo soy isleño y vendo maní" ("I'm an Islander and I Sell Peanuts"). By the early 1840s, Cuban contradanzas were being explicitly promoted as expressing the charm of creole culture. Such pride in local culture was not synonymous with political nationalism, just as a modern Puerto Rican lover of local music might well support continuation of the island's colonial status. Meanwhile, titles of some nineteenth-century Cuban contradanzas were explicitly loyalist or even celebrated annexation by the United States. However, creole cultural nationalism served, at the least, as a precursor to and precondition of political nationalism, and the two sentiments certainly overlapped. Hence, despite the fear of ferocious Spanish persecution, by the 1890s the Cuban danza had become implicitly or explicitly allied with the independence movement (Galán 1983: 172). Similarly, as Ángel Quintero-Rivera (2002) has described, in the latter 1800s the Puerto Rican danza became at least indirectly associated with proindependence sentiment, especially in the southern city of Ponce, with its nationalistic hacienda-owning protobourgeoisie that cultivated the support of working classes and petty-bourgeois merchants and artisans. While the music scene in the capital, San Juan, remained dominated by the military and the Church, a more varied and lively creole cultural ambience pervaded Ponce, a center for the agricultural export that was perpetually frustrated by imperial regulations. A vocal danza, "La borinqueña," became the island's anthem, whether with the official bucolic lyrics by Don Manuel Fernández Juncos or the militant ones penned by poet Lola Rodríguez de Tió in 1868. Even choreography came to acquire political overtones, as the collective Spanish-style contradanza, with its dictatorial bastonero, came to be associated by some people with despised Spanish rule, especially after Governor Pezuela attempted to ban its rival, the danza/merengue. The contentions surrounding dance styles were reminiscent of those in early-nineteenth-century Cuba, where the French-style contredanse was either despised or embraced, depending in part on one's attitudes toward Spanish rule.

In nineteenth-century Cuba and Puerto Rico, nationalist sentiment was naturally directed against Spain, with its backward culture and economy and its despotic, corrupt, and exploitative governance. In the Dominican Republic during the same period, the antagonist was Haiti, which remained a military threat and whose culture was demonized as barbaric. Musical borrowings between the three Spanish entities were not likely to be opposed on nationalistic grounds, especially insofar as they seemed to promote a shared creole Hispanic Caribbean culture. Hence, the danza/merengue introduced to Puerto Rico from Cuba in the 1840s did inspire criticism and even legal prohibition, but only because it was seen as indecent, not because it came from Havana. Likewise, when a few years later this merengue invaded Dominican salons from Puerto Rico, it provoked indignant journalistic opposition, but again on the grounds of indecency rather than its "foreign" origin (as discussed in Chapter 4).

By the early twentieth century, with Cuba independent and Puerto Rico a colony of the United States, the relations between nationalism, inter-island sentiments, and musical interactions became more problematic and complex. Thus, while the model for Dominican salon composers since the 1880s had been the danzas of Puerto Rican Juan Morel Campos, the second decade of the twentieth century saw a movement on the part of Dominican composers to transcend the benign Puerto Rican tutelage and develop a more distinctively national style of salon music. Hence Julio Arzeño urged his compatriot Dominican composers to seek inspiration in local music, and Julio Alberto Hernández, Juan Espínola, and Juan Francisco García composed pieces that, in spite of their close resemblance to Puerto Rican danzas, were nevertheless labeled "merengues"—a term that was by that point distinctly Dominican in resonance.

In Puerto Rico itself the danza's significance as a national icon was changing, both in terms of the genre's increasing decline in popularity and the change of colonial rulers. For the hacienda-owning class that was being bankrupted by American agribusiness, the danza—previously celebrated for its non-Spanish qualities—now became a symbol of refined Hispanic island culture, as opposed to commercial American culture. Hispanophilic essayist Antonio Pedreira put up a spirited defense of the danza in his classic 1934 study of the Puerto Rican cultural dilemma, *Insularismo*, in which he argued that the danza embodied the best aspects of Puerto Rican character—gentility, mildness, and aestheticism—the very qualities threatened by vulgar, crass, and materialistic Americanization. While the Cuban origins of the danza were not seen as an embarrassment, in 1935 Puerto Rican essayist Tomás Blanco urged local *plena* musicians to avoid "falling into plagiarizations of alien Cubanisms."

The ways in which the Puerto Rican danza has been a contested site have been particularly pronounced, partly due to the relative abundance of interpretive literature on the genre. Between the 1880s and the 1930s, writings by Salvador Brau, Braulio Dueño Colón, Antonio Pedreira, Tomás Blanco, and others at once provided astute insights into its role in island culture, reflected its changing meanings over the decades, and exposed some of the problematic biases that conditioned upper-class aesthetics. One of these biases, discussed by Aparicio, concerns the fondness of such literati as Pedreira for eulogizing the danza—allegedly like Puerto Rican character in general—as essentially feminine, in the sense of being gentle, docile, and languid. As Pedreira wrote, "The danza, like our landscape, is of a feminine condition, soft and romantic." Such an essentializing conceit, Aparicio notes, does justice neither to women nor to the danza, as illustrated by the fiery revolutionary lyrics written by Lola Rodríguez de Tió for "La borinqueña." Nor would it accommodate a 1981 danza, "Lolita," written by Vitín Calderón in honor of proindependence militant Lolita Lebrón, jailed for attempting to assassinate President Harry Truman. Meanwhile, although the heyday of the danza is long past, a bucolic vocal danza of Antonio "El Topo" Cabán Cale, "Verde luz," became an unofficial anthem of the island's progressive left (Aparicio 1998: chap. 1).

The conflicting and sometimes changing conceptions of local identity are manifest in their own way in attitudes toward the quadrille variants in the French Caribbean. As we have seen, many French Antillean quadrille dancers, like contredanse enthusiasts of the late 1700s, may take some pride today in the image of decency and propriety expressed in their dance, in contrast, for example, to more rowdy Afro-Caribbean dances like bèlè. However, this same European character of the dance stigmatizes it in the view of those whose sensibilities have been informed by the Afrocentric *negritude* movement and who see dances like *haute-taille* and *pastourelle* as reflecting capitulation to colonial European aesthetics.

Just as the affective significations of the contradance and quadrille have varied over time and place, so have its constitutive elements tended to submerge and resurface throughout the Caribbean over the generations. Thus a syncopated form of the habanera rhythm re-emerged in the 1970s as the heartbeat of Trinidadian soca and again in 1992 as the "riddim" of the Jamaica dancehall song "Dem Bow," which went on to form the rhythmic template of reggaetón. Similarly, the stentorian chanting of the Martinican quadrille *commandeur* reappears in the syncopated declamation of dancehall deejays, and (as the next chapter discusses) the rhythms, forms, and melodies of 1850s Cuban contradanzas resurface in twentieth-century *son* and *salsa*. In these correspondences the contradance and quadrille have served either as seminal original sources or as media for the transmission of elements from one genre or locale to another. Remote in time as the contradance and quadrille heyday grows, its legacy continues to animate Caribbean music, often in the most unanticipated ways.

## Notes

1. A short and preliminary but significant pan-Caribbean study is John Szwed and Morton Marks's "The Afro-American Transformation of European Set Dances and Dance Suites" (1988).
2. Regarding contradanza and quadrille traditions elsewhere in Latin America, see entries in *Diccionario de la Música Española e Hispanoamericana* (Casares 1999–

2002). For contradance and quadrille in the United States, see Ralph Giordano's *Social Dancing in America* (2006).

3. A similar French adaptation occurred in the same era with the dance name "allemande" ("German"), altered in the Gallic to "alamande" from "a la mande," meaning "[to take one's partner] by the hand."
4. Properly, *The English Dancing Master of Plaine and Easie Rules for the Dancing of Country Dances, with the Tune to Each Dance* (see Playford 1651). The entire book can be viewed on a few Web sites, including http://www.izaak.unh.edu/nhltmd/indexes.dancingmaster, whence Figure 1.2 is adapted.
5. In Rousseau's 1768 *A Complete Dictionary of Music*, quoted in Mikowsky 1973: 32.
6. For example, "London's Glory," "Marlborough House," "Ruben," "Kiddington Green," "The Pursuit," "Tipling John on the Riot Night," "The Slip," and "The Elector of Hanover's March."
7. See, e.g., Abrahams and Szwed 1983: 300.
8. See, e.g., Cynric Williams's 1826 account *Tour through the Island of Jamaica*, quoted in Burton 1997: 72.
9. The *zarabanda*, as a vernacular dance, was popular primarily in the early 1600s; the Andalusian-style fandango, as a dance form, flourished mostly in the eighteenth and nineteenth centuries.
10. Elsewhere the "charitable" good father Labat writes calmly of his administering some three hundred lashes to a slave caught with a wooden idol and then applying pepper sauce to the wounds (in Dayan 1995: 206).
11. Saint-Méry was governor of Saint-Domingue (Haiti) at the outbreak of the revolution and subsequently served as governor of Martinique, his birthplace. His voluminous writings and compilations of documents pertaining to the contemporary French Caribbean are a rich source of historical data. Dominique Cyrille is the source for quotations of Peretty and Weeks.
12. Edgardo Díaz Díaz (1990) provides much revealing data on the typical repertoire of Puerto Rican salon dances in the years 1877–1930.
13. Educated guesses can be made, as are represented, for example, by the ensemble recordings on *Cuba: Contradanzas & Danzones*, by the Rotterdam Conservatory Orquesta Típica, from which the track on this volume's compact disc derives (Nimbus NI 5502). Even these recreations may be controversial; for example, the recording's use of the *cinquillo* ostinato to accompany contradanzas of Saumell may not be representative of contemporary practice.
14. It should be recalled that ostinato-based high Baroque genres, such as the passacaglia, chaconne, and sarabande, appear to have derived in part from Afro-Latin music of the sixteenth and seventeenth centuries.
15. Ortiz 1965: 275–276, quoted in Mikowsky 1973: 77.
16. The *tresillo* can be seen from one perspective as a variant of the habanera rhythm. The latter can be regarded as a quarter note followed by two eighth notes, with the exception that the first eighth note is preceded by a decorative upbeat (the "AND") indicated above. However, if that "AND" is heard as a structural beat rather than an anacrusis, the subsequent "THREE" can be elided, affording the *tresillo*.
17. In Benin, Togo, and Ghana, the pattern is heard in the piece "Adzogbo." Ghanaian drummers refer to the pattern as *todzo* (David Locke, pers. comm.).

18. This is also a basic ostinato, called "al-wahda" in Arabic, used in Turkish and Arab urban popular music, typically as accompaniment to a *taqsim* or improvised instrumental solo. Depending on context, the rhythms in Figure 1.2 might be rendered in 4/4 rather than 2/4.

    Dominican folklorist Flérida de Nolasco (1948: 175) argued that the Caribbean contradanza and danza (along with the Dominican *mangulina* and *carabiné*) derive from the Cantigas of Santa María compiled by King Alfonso el Sabio of Spain in the thirteenth century. Reading from Julián Ribera's 1922 edition of the cantigas, she based her argument on the uses of the *cinquillo* in cantiga no. 318, which are indeed strikingly typical of a Puerto Rican danza or Cuban danzón. The fly in the ointment of her argument, however, lies in the fact that the creole-style rhythms occur not in the original melody but in the harmonized accompaniment added by Ribera. The intriguing question is what inspired Ribera to harmonize the cantigas in this most fanciful and anachronistic fashion. Perhaps he had recently come across some imported recordings of Los Negritos de Palatino or some such Cuban band, whose music was ringing in his ears when he sat down to harmonize the cantigas.
19. See danzas in Halman and Rojer 2008. I am grateful to Halman for sending me this volume. A popular danza by Palm, "Erani ta malu" ("Erani Is Sick"), is included on this volume's compact disc. It contains only two sections.
20. Such notational ambiguities were evident in the earlier contradanzas of Saumell, as can be seen in Figures 2.7–2.9. In Puerto Rico, composers preferred to write their *cinquillos* as sextuplets with tied third and fourth notes, as shown in Figure 3.2. Such Haitian salon composers as Justin Elie, following a tradition established in the 1880s, used alternating bars of 2/4 and 5/8, as shown in Figure 6.3. For his part, the Dominican García, in danzas like "Contigo," followed a more straightforward notation, such as would be followed by dance ensembles.

## References

Abrahams, Roger. 1983. *The man-of-words in the West Indies: Performance and the emergence of creole culture.* Baltimore: Johns Hopkins University Press.

Abrahams, Roger, and John Szwed. 1983. *After Africa: Extracts from British travel accounts and journals of the seventeenth, eighteenth, and nineteenth centuries concerning the slaves, the manners, and customs in the British West Indies.* New Haven, CT: Yale University Press.

Alonso, Manuel. [1849] 2002. "Bailes de Puerto Rico" (from *El Gíbaro*). In *Music in Puerto Rico: A reader's anthology.* Ed. and trans. Donald Thompson, 14–20. Lanham, MD: Scarecrow Press.

Aparicio, Frances. 1998. *Listening to salsa: Gender, Latin popular music, and Puerto Rican cultures.* Hanover, VT: Wesleyan University Press.

Blanco, Tomás. 1979. "Elogio de la plena." *Revista del Instituto de Cultura Puertorriqueña* 22:39–42 (from *Revista Ateneo Puertorriqueño* 1 [1935]).

Brau, Salvador. [1885] 1977. "La danza puertorriqueña." In *Ensayos sobre la danza puertorriqueña*, 1–13. San Juan: Institutos de Cultura Puertorriqueña.

Burton, Richard. 1997. *Afro-Creole: Power, opposition, and play in the Caribbean.* Ithaca: Cornell University Press.

Carpentier, Alejo. 2001. *Music in Cuba*. Ed. Timothy Brennan. Trans. Alan West-Durán. Minneapolis: University of Minnesota Press. Originally published as *La música en Cuba* (Mexico City: Fondo de la Cultura Económica, 1946).

Casares Rodicio, Emilio. 1999–2002. *Diccionario de la música española e hispanoamericana*. Madrid: Sociedad General de Autores y Editores.

Courlander, Harold. 1960. *The drum and the hoe: Life and lore of the Haitian people*. Berkeley: University of California Press.

Davis, Martha. 1976. "Afro-Dominican religious brotherhood: Structure, ritual, and music." Ph.D. diss., University of Illinois at Urbana-Champaign.

Dayan, Joan. 1995. *Haiti, history, and the gods*. Berkeley: University of California Press.

Díaz Díaz, Edgardo. 1990. "La música bailable de los carnets: forma y significado de su repertorio en Puerto Rico (1877–1930)." *Revista Musical Puertorriqueña* 5:2–21.

Dueño Colón, Braulio. [1913] 1977. "Estudio sobre la danza puertorriqueña." In *Ensayos sobre la danza puertorriqueña*, 14–21. San Juan: Institutos de Cultura Puertorriqueña.

Fouchard, Jean. [1973] 1988. *La méringue: Danse nationale d'Haïti*. Ottowa: Editions Lémeac. Reprint, Port-au-Prince, Haiti: Editions Henri Deschamps.

Frazier, E. Franklin. 1932a. *The free negro family*. Nashville: Fisk University Press.

———. 1932b. *The negro family in Chicago*. Chicago: University of Chicago Press.

———. 1939. *The negro family in the United States*. Chicago: University of Chicago Press.

———. 1957. *The negro in the United States*. Rev. ed. New York: Macmillan.

Galán, Natalio. 1983. *Cuba y sus sones*. Valencia: Pre-Textos.

Giordano, Ralph. 2006. *Social dancing in America: A history and reference*. Westport, CT: Greenwood Press.

Guilbault, Jocelyne. 1985. "A St. Lucian *Kwadril* evening." *Latin American Music Review* 6 (1): 31–57.

Halman, Johannes, compiler, and Robert Rojer, ed. 2008. *Jan Gerard Palm music scores: Waltzes, mazurkas, danzas, tumbas, polkas, marches, fantasies, serenades, a galop and music composed for services in the synagogue and the lodge*. Amsterdam: Broekmans and Van Poppel.

Herskovits, Melville. 1937. *Life in a Haitian valley*. New York: Alfred Knopf.

———. 1941. *The myth of the negro past*. New York: Harper and Brothers.

Labat, R. P. 1724. *Nouveaux voyages aux isles françaises de l'Amérique*. Paris: Delespine.

Largey, Michael. 2006. *Vodou nation: Haitian art music and cultural nationalism*. Chicago: University of Chicago Press.

Lizardo, Fradique. 1974. *Danzas y bailes folklóricos dominicanos*. Santo Domingo: Taller.

Lloréns Amico, José Antonio. 1983. *Música popular en Lima: Criollos y Andinos*. Lima: Instituto de Estudios Peruanos.

Manuel, Peter. 2002. "From Scarlatti to 'Guantanamera': Dual tonicity in Spanish and Latin American musics." *Journal of the American Musicological Society* 55 (2): 313–338.

Manuel, Peter, and Orlando Fiol. 2007. "Mode, melody, and harmony in traditional Afro-Cuban music: From Africa to Cuba." *Black Music Research Journal* 27 (1): 45–76.

Marothy, Janos. 1974. *Music and the bourgeois, music and the proletarian*. Budapest: Akademia Kiado.

Marx, Karl, and Fredric Engels. [1847] 1959. "The Communist manifesto." In *Marx and Engels: Basic writings on politics and philosophy*. Ed. Lewis Feuer, 1–41. New York: Doubleday.

Mikowsky, Solomon. 1973. "The nineteenth-century Cuban *danza* and its composers, with particular attention to Ignacio Cervantes (1847–1905)." Ph.D. diss., Teachers College, Columbia University. Published in Spanish as *Ignacio Cervantes y la danza en Cuba* (Havana: Editorial Letras Cubanas, 1988).

Miller, Rebecca. 2005. "Performing ambivalence: The case of quadrille music and dance in Carriacou, Grenada." *Ethnomusicology* 49 (3): 403–440.

Moreau de Saint-Méry, Médéric Louis Elie. 1797–98. *Description topographique, physique, civile, politique, et historique de la parte Française de L'Ile Saint-Domingue.* Vol. 1. Philadelphia.

Naipaul, V. S. 1962. *The middle passage.* London: Penguin.

Nketia, J. H. Kwabena. 1965. *Music, dance and drama: A review of the performing arts of Ghana.* Legon, Ghana: Institute of African Studies.

Nolasco, Flérida de. 1948. *Vibraciones en el tiempo.* Ciudad Trujillo (Santo Domingo): Editora Montalvo.

Ortiz, Fernando. 1965. *La africanía de la música folklórica de Cuba.* Havana: Editora Universitaria.

Pedreira, Antonio. [1934] 1973. *Insularismo.* Río Piedras: Editorial Edil.

Playford, John. 1651. *The English dancing master of plaine and easie rules for the dancing of country dances, with the tune to each dance.* London: Thomas Harper.

Quintero-Rivera, Ángel. [1986] 2002. "Ponce, la danza y lo nacional: Apuntes para una Sociología de la Música Puertorriqueña" [The danza: A sociopolitical view]. In *Music in Puerto Rico: A reader's anthology.* Ed. and trans. Donald Thompson, 71–84. Lanham, MD: Scarecrow Press.

———. 1994. "The camouflaged drum: Melodization of rhythms and Maroonage ethnicity in Caribbean peasant music." In *Music and black ethnicity: The Caribbean and South America.* Ed. Gerard Behague, 47–66. Miami: University of Miami.

Ramírez, Serafín. 1891. *La Habana artística.* Havana: Imprenta del E. M. de la Capitanía General.

———. 1928. "La Habana de otros tiempos." In *Evolución de la cultura cubana, Vol. 18,* 132–133. Havana: Imprenta Montalvo y Cardenas.

Ribera, Julián. 1922. *La música de las cantigas.* Madrid: Tipografía de la Revista de Archivos.

Sachs, Curt. 1937. *World history of the dance.* New York: Norton.

Stevenson, Robert. 1981. "Caribbean music history: A selective annotated bibliography with musical supplement." *Inter-American Music Review* 4 (1): 1–112.

Sublette, Ned. 2008. *The world that made New Orleans: From Spanish silver to Congo Square.* Chicago: Lawrence Hill Books.

Szwed, John, and Morton Marks. 1988. "The Afro-American transformation of European set dances and dance suites." *Dance Research Journal* 20 (1): 29–36.

Vega, Carlos. 1966. *El origen de las danzas folklóricas.* Buenos Aires: Ricordi Americana.

Walcott, Derek. 1974. "The muse of history." In *Is massa day dead? Black moods in the Caribbean.* Ed. Orde Coombs, 1–28. Garden City, NY: Anchor Books.

Weeks, John H. 1914. *Among the primitive Bakongo: A record of thirty years' close intercourse with the Bakongo and other tribes of equatorial Africa.* London: Seeley, Service.

PETER MANUEL

# 2 / Cuba

## *From Contradanza to Danzón*

If in the last century Cuban music has been known primarily for the mambo, the chachachá, and the *son* that generated salsa, in the nineteenth century by far the most predominant and distinctively *national* music was the contradanza, in the diverse forms it took over the course of its extended heyday. The contradanza (or "danza," as it was later called) was also the era's most seminal genre, parenting the habanera that graced European opera and music theater, the elegant figures of the *tumba francesa*'s *masón* dance, and, albeit ultimately, the mambo and chachachá themselves, which evolved from the danza's direct descendant, the danzón. Even some of the figures of modern salsa dancing derive from the contradanza, as do musical features of early-twentieth-century genres such as the *criolla*, *clave*, and theater *guajira*. Finally, while the roots of the Cuban *son* itself have customarily been ascribed to rural folk music of eastern Cuba, considerable evidence suggests that they are better sought in 1850s urban contradanzas of Havana and Santiago, thus calling for a revision of standard Cuban music historiography. Indeed, it is in some respects easier to enumerate those Cuban genres—such as Santería music or neo-Hispanic *punto*—which were *not* generated by or directly related to the contradanza.[1]

### Early History

Despite its centrality to Cuban cultural history, many aspects of the contradanza's career remain obscure and contentious. Just as some European scholars disagree as to whether the contradance originated in England, France, or elsewhere, so do some Cuban musicologists differ as to whether the contradanza in Cuba should be traced primarily to input from Spain, Saint-Domingue (Haiti), France, the English West Indies, or elsewhere.

The conventional scholarly and lay consensus, especially as established by novelist and musicologist Alejo Carpentier in his *La música en Cuba* ([1946] 2001), has been that the primary source of the Cuban contradanza was the French contredanse—whose form itself derived from the English longways country dance—as was introduced by refugees fleeing the Haitian Revolution (1791–1803). Carpentier's thesis deserves close examination, both for its merits and its fundamental problems.

The Haitian Revolution, which provoked prolonged chaos and destruction, precipitated the exodus of Saint-Domingue's white population, along with many of their slaves and large numbers of free blacks and mulattos. Many refugees emigrated to New Orleans and other French Caribbean colonies, but over fifteen thousand settled in nearby eastern Cuba (then called Oriente), especially in and around its main city of Santiago de Cuba (whose population prior to that influx was less than ten thousand). Many took up cultivation of coffee, sugar, and cotton, while others established themselves as urban merchants and businessmen.

In the decades preceding the Revolution, Saint-Domingue had hosted a lively cultural milieu, in contrast to provincial and sleepy Oriente and in keeping with its status as the economic dynamo of the Caribbean. The local French elite avidly cultivated the forms of dance and music—including the contredanse—that were popular among the Parisian bourgeoisie. Contemporary accounts indicate that many free blacks and even slaves adopted creolized forms of these arts, whether in the form of playing violin or flute or joining a contredanse, whose format of male and female lines replicated, with new figural variations, the Afro-Haitian calenda described in 1797 by Médéric Louis Elie Moreau de Saint-Méry (and cited in the previous chapter). As that keen observer noted, "Blacks, imitating whites, dance minuets and contradanzas. Their sense of attunement confers on them the first quality needed by a musician; for this reason many are good violinists, since this is the instrument they prefer" (in Carpentier 2001: 145 [1946: 125]). Once the diverse sorts of refugees had established themselves in eastern Cuba, they lost little time in fostering a more lively and cosmopolitan musical and artistic milieu than had existed previously on the island. Coffee plantation owners staged elegant soirées at their estates, with black musicians providing music on violin, flute, and other instruments. In Santiago de Cuba, as Carpentier (1946: 128–129) notes, their various activities included construction of a theater for staging dramas, comedies, and comic operas; the formation of a chamber orchestra and a black musical ensemble; the importation of pianos and other instruments; regular offerings of classical concerts, typically ending with a minuet; and, last but not least, the further popularization of the reigning bourgeois dance of the day, the contredanse.

The contradanza (as it was called in Cuba) subsequently flourished in Oriente, which, with its mixed economy based on trade and small-scale coffee cultivation, is generally regarded as fostering a more distinctively mixed, creole culture than did the more racially polarized, plantation-oriented central and western parts of the island. Accordingly, as Carpentier argues (1946: 128–129), the Franco-Haitian contredanse, as transplanted to Oriente, went on to constitute the basis for the more "mainstream" contradanza that flourished in subsequent decades in Havana. Some Oriente-style contradanzas, like other creole songs brought by the "*negros franceses*" (French blacks) to the region, displayed, at least as a passing figure, that most pervasive feature of Haitian music, what Cubans call the *cinquillo* (discussed below), which also figures prominently in arguments about the early history of the contradanza in Cuba.[2] Carpentier opines that the *cinquillo* pervaded the contradanzas of Oriente; in contrast, he argues, the rhythm was conspicuously absent in the Havana contradanza and did not surface in the music of that region until the advent of the danzón in the late 1870s. This distinction, he asserts, reflects how two schools of contradanza existed on the island, with the Santiago/Oriente contradanza flourishing to some extent independently of—and perhaps earlier than—the contradanza of Havana and Matanzas.

However, serious problems afflict Carpentier's historiography, starting with the contradiction between the supposed origin of the mainstream Havana contradanza in Santiago and the alleged contrast between the two regional styles. In fact, both these assertions appear to be incorrect or at least not documentable. An initial problem is what appears to be the complete absence of surviving Santiago contradanzas until around 1850—a good half century after the influx of French refugees had begun (and well after the publication of many contradanzas in Havana). This lacuna renders impossible any generalization about an alleged Santiago style of contradanza until the mid-1800s, by which time the few documented contradanzas suggest a style not dramatically different from their Havana counterparts.

Carpentier bases his argument about the contrasting styles on his assertion that the *cinquillo* pervaded the Santiago contradanzas and was completely absent in its Havana derivative. He cites only two Santiago contradanzas as examples of the use of the *cinquillo*: "La Santa Taé" and "La francesita" by Antonio Boza ([1946: 132] 2001: 150). "La francesita" (reproduced in Bacardí [1893] 1972: ii, 509) is a poor example, as it contains only a single *cinquillo*, used in passing (resembling, in this respect, two of the three other Santiago contradanzas I have encountered).[3] However, the B section of Boza's "La Santa Taé" (1852, reproduced in Pérez Sanjurjo 1986: 204) contains an interesting series of left-hand arpeggiated *cinquillos*, presented in the distinctively creole two-bar form (i.e., either followed or preceded by a bar in even eighth or quarter notes). The piece, discussed below, is a remarkable precursor of subsequent genres, especially the *son*, in the way its second section outlines what could be regarded as a twice-repeated four-bar chordal ostinato (//: i / iv / V / i ://), reiterating a rhythm cohering with the *clave* pattern pervading rumba and later Cuban popular dance music.

Striking as this piece may be, it presents a format that, rather than being unique to the Santiago contradanza, is found in at least a half dozen Havana counterparts, whose existence refutes Carpentier's claim for the absence of the *cinquillo* in the Havana contradanza. While the *cinquillo* surfaces only once in the entire oeuvre of famed contradanza composer Manuel Saumell (d. 1870); in its standard creole two-bar form it does figure prominently in these Havana 1850s contradanzas of lesser-known composers, including two by José Fernández de Coca, where it forms the basis for quasi-ostinato patterns, such as that of "La Santa Taé," as discussed below. It is also highlighted in Louis Moreau Gottschalk's music, such as his "Danza" of 1859. (Unfortunately, contradanza scores, written for piano, do not indicate rhythmic accompaniment patterns, which might have contained *cinquillos*.)

While evidence is thus insufficient to support an argument for a distinctive, *cinquillo*-based Santiago style, it is possible that the Franco-Haitian influx stimulated an early efflorescence of the contradanza in Cuba, coexisting with whatever tradition was germinating in Havana and Matanzas. By the 1830s, however, the Havana-area contradanza was flourishing to a far greater extent (and was accordingly better documented)[4] and as the century progressed could better claim the role of a "mainstream" tradition. As Havana's culture and economy boomed, the Santiago tradition presumably devolved to the status of a lesser provincial variant, perhaps more closely linked to vernacular song and lacking the light-classical dimension represented in Havana by Saumell and Ignacio Cervantes.

While the Franco-Haitian input may have invigorated the contradanza in Santiago from around 1800, it is quite likely that the genre, including in its longways form, had already been introduced to Havana from Spain, and perhaps from French and English visitors, several decades earlier. As Natalio Galán (1983) and Zoila Lapique Becali (1979) have independently argued, the creolization process that animated the Cuban contradanza thus predated the Franco-Haitian immigration. The French contredanse enjoyed considerable popularity in Spain from the early 1700s and would thus likely have been imported from that country to Cuba well before the Haitian Revolution. The advent of the French-descended Bourbon family to the Spanish throne in 1701 precipitated a new openness among the Spanish elite to Italian and French cultural influences, despite the protests of some xenophobes and ultranationalists. During the eighteenth century, although France was economically and politically backward, its elite culture, including the minuet and contredanse, came to be imitated throughout Western Europe, including Spain (see, e.g., Huertas 1989: 109; Esses 1992: 435). Hence the French-style contredanse (with its four-couple format) was not long in taking root in Spain; a 1714 reference attests to its popularity in Madrid (in Galán 1983: 70), and other references document its presence in dramatic interludes from the same decade (Esses 1992: 455). As the Spanish nobility avidly cultivated the art of dancing contradanza "a la francesa" (Huertas 1989: 111), manuals for performing the dance were published in Madrid in 1745 by Bartolomé Ferriol and, more expansively, by Pablo Minguet y Yrol in 1758 and in subsequent expanded editions.

Minguet's treatise, *Arte de danzar a la francesa*, describes the four different formats of contradanza—a pair of couples, a circle, a *cuadrada* or four couples, and the *largas*, or "*a lo largo* [roughly, 'lengthwise'], with all the gentlemen on one side and the ladies on the other, which is the form generally used by the English, the Scots, and so on."[5] Minguet specifically attests to the popularity of the French styles among the nobility (in Esses 1992: 446), and a 1796 publication asserted that in the course of the eighteenth century Spaniards all but forgot their local dances in favor of the contradanza (Juan Antonio de Zamácola, in Esses 1992: 458–459). Given the constant maritime traffic between Spain and Havana, it is inconceivable that the longways contradanza would not have taken root in Cuba by the 1760s, probably alongside the four-couple *cuadrada/quadrille* format that became increasingly popular among the French and identified with them.

Galán (1983: 60–64) offers further circumstantial evidence in favor of the presence of the French contredanse styles in Cuba throughout the 1700s. The extended visits to Havana of French ships, such as that of the Marquis of Coetlegon in 1701, with their squads of soldiers, sailors, and merchants must have familiarized *habaneros* (Havana-dwellers)—ever eager for contact with Europe—with contemporary Parisian fashions like the contredanse. Upper-class Cubans generally considered familiarity with French customs to be a concomitant of good breeding. Galán (1983: chap. 3–4) also cites a "country dance" published in London in 1762 entitled "A Trip to Guadeloupe," whose tune features a variant of the amphibrach[6] that came to pervade so many creole Latin American musics (as well as early ragtime—again, presumably, via Caribbean influence). Galán infers that this tune and its title indicate that a rhythmically creolized Caribbean contradance had already emerged by this time and, moreover, that if it reached as far as London, then it must certainly have reached Havana—especially in the course of the eleven-month occupation of that city by the British in 1762–63. In general, Galán points to the much-celebrated (or disparaged) fondness of contemporary *habaneros* for dancing, their avid interest in contemporary European fads, and the relative ease and rapidity with which Continental fashions and dances—from the waltz and minuet to the contradance—reached and circulated in the Caribbean. As he and Lapique Becali argue, the longways-style contradanza must have been well established, and the rhythmic creolization process well underway, in Cuba in the mid-1700s, such that the Franco-Haitian input would merely have reinforced, rather than initiated, the flourishing of the Cuban contradanza.

In his insightful 1973 doctoral dissertation on the Cuban contradanza, pianist Solomon Mikowsky, referring to earlier and less well-documented versions of such arguments, offers a well-reasoned argument in favor of Carpentier's thesis, asserting that the contradanza imported from Spain to Cuba was not the longways style adopted in Cuba but rather the Spanish contradanza, typically in 6/8 meter and danced primarily in square formation (*cuadrada*) or by two couples; hence it was not the form that generated the Cuban contradanza.

Mikowsky further points to contemporary Cuban sources associating the contradance with the French, not the Spanish, such as an 1809 Havana editorial denouncing the libertine and lewd influences of the blasphemous Gauls: "Now that we detest wholeheartedly the maxims of that degraded nation . . . why should we not banish from us the waltz (*balsa*) and the contradanza, inventions always indecent that diabolical France introduced to us?"[7] However, it should be noted that the loyalist Francophobia of the quoted correspondent was not shared by all Cubans, many of whom despised backward and imperial Spain and regarded France as a more liberal, fashionable, and cosmopolitan model. Galán also cites passages from around the 1830s attesting to a rivalry—and clear distinction—between the local and Spanish contradanzas (e.g., 1983: 128). Mikowsky (1973: 49–52) argues that the Spanish contradanza "failed without leaving a memory," while it was the Franco-Haitian style that took root, perhaps because its longways format cohered with Afro-Caribbean calenda-type dances, because it had already been creolized, and because so many Cubans (unlike the reactionary just quoted) took cosmopolitan Paris rather than reactionary and stuffy Madrid as a cultural lodestar. Mikowsky thus implicitly argues that the seminal role of the Franco-Haitian style predates the documented spread of the *cinquillo* in the 1870s.

However, a critic might point out that while the Francophobic editorialist of 1809 correctly attributed the prevailing contradanza style to diabolical France, that same contradanza might still have been introduced prior to and independently of the Franco-Haitian influx. That is, it is important to distinguish French inputs from Franco-Haitian ones per se. Thus, the French- and English-derived longways-style dance, the creole tango/habanera, and perhaps amphibrach rhythms may have been well established in Cuba by the late 1700s. Accordingly, Argeliers León cites a 1794 newsletter in Havana testifying to the existence of the contradanza in that city (1984: 275).

Moreover, while Mikowsky identifies the Spanish contradanza with *cuadrada* format, it is clear that the longways-style contradance also enjoyed considerable popularity in eighteenth-century Spain, even if it continued to be often referred to as the "English" style, in contrast to what had become the more characteristically French format of four couples (which evolved into the quadrille). Hence at a ball in New Orleans in 1802, an angry confrontation occurred between a group of Spaniards, who clamored for a longways "*contredanse anglaise*," and an equally vociferous faction of French creoles who demanded a "*contredanse francaise*" (in Sublette 2008: 240–241). As New Orleans and Havana were sister cities during this period, the longways-style contradance must have also been well established in the Cuban capital.

It may be ultimately impossible to definitively resolve the question of origins, as even Galán seems to suggest in labeling the genre "*anglofrancohispano-afrocubano*" (1983: 312). However, even that cumbersome categorization fails to distinguish between Continental French and Franco-Haitian forms of the genre. Further, it is clear that different dance and music styles coexisted even in Havana by 1832, when a local dance school offered instruction in English, Spanish, and Russian contradanza styles (Ramírez 1928: 132–133). While an account from Havana in 1793 claimed that French dance fashions prevailed there at that point (in Galán 1983: 110), various references from Havana and Camagüey a few decades later mention the popularity of the Spanish contradanza without mentioning other styles (see, e.g., those cited in Lapique Becali 1979: 67). At the same time, the arguments advanced on each side collectively serve well to document many aspects of the contradanza's early trajectory.

A relevant factor to keep in mind is not only that we know relatively little of musical life in eighteenth-century Cuba but also that it was not until the early 1800s that it truly began to flourish, especially in Havana, the nearby port of Matanzas, and Santiago. Only from that period can we document the appearance of music publications, local compositions in creole styles, classical and light-classical concerts, importations of musical instruments, and other features that heralded the dynamic music culture of nineteenth-century Cuba. Hence it is possible that even if a creolized form of the contradanza had existed in Cuba in the eighteenth century, it would not have been until the early 1800s—as heralded by the trumpets of "San Pascual Bailón" in 1803—that the Cuban contradanza, from its diverse Spanish, French, and English sources, came to truly flower and evolve into something distinctively creole.

## The Creole Contradanza in Its Sociomusical Milieu

Havana had hosted a lively entertainment scene from the sixteenth century throughout the colonial period. At any given time it would be serving as an entrepôt for hundreds of sailors—primarily but not only Spanish—allied to the dozens of ships docked in the harbor, refitting for their next trip. Given the hazards of pirates and tempests that attended their upcoming sea voyages, many off-duty sailors routinely indulged in wine, women, and song as if it were their last opportunity. In the early 1800s the city's cultural scene came to life dramatically. The main catalyst was the Haitian Revolution, which ended that colony's pre-eminence as a sugar exporter, opening the way for Cuba to step into that role and emerge as the economic powerhouse of the region and one of the richer countries in the world. The subsequent sugar boom generated unprecedented wealth, a new level of class stratification, and leisure classes eager to enjoy the best of local and imported music and dance.

Musical life blossomed accordingly and profited especially from being a "safe" form of cultural expression in an environment tense with growing nationalism and despotic censorship. Carpentier (chap. 8) relates how, from the first decade of the nineteenth century, wealthy patrons began hosting regular public performances of chamber music, and musical instruments—especially pianos—began to be imported in quantity. Publication of local compositions—including the contradanza "San Pascual Bailón"—started by 1803, well in advance of most other Latin American cities. "Academies" of music sprouted from the next decade, and visiting Spanish and Italian music-theater troupes, supplemented by local talent, commenced staging one-act *tonadillas* and *sainetes* and more elaborate operas, of both Continental and local origin, especially in the Tacón theater built in 1834. Lapique Becali's (1979) volume *Música colonial cubana en las publicaciones periódicas (1812–1902)* focuses on the great vogue—from the early 1800s, but especially from around 1830—of publishing piano scores of local compositions—primarily contradanzas—in newspapers, penny broadsheets, and (often ephemeral) music journals. The music editions of the publishing house established in 1838 by Juan Federico Edelmann (d. 1848), and maintained by his sons Carlos and Ernesto, also played a particularly important role in disseminating local compositions throughout most of the nineteenth century. Such publications, together with contemporary accounts of island life, indicate a lively and colorful world of amateur and semi-professional composition and performance, not to mention the nightly dances for which Havana was famous. Carpentier is worth quoting at length:

> In 1798, the chronicler Buenaventura Ferrer estimated that some fifty public dances were held daily in Havana. The enthusiasm was "almost crazed." Open to all, "young lads of idle occupation were accustomed to spending all night there." . . . The party started with a minuet, for which the bastonero (caller and master of ceremonies), wielding his cane, would size up the dancers. . . . Once the serious dancing concluded the contradanzas began, being the latest fashion since the arrival of the French in Santiago. By the third contradanza, "the dancers had cast aside all notion of reason and good judgment." . . . To keep limber, during intermissions they danced *zapateos*, *congos*, boleros, and guarachas. When those attending the parties were not very distinguished, everyone sang slum songs . . . rich in puns and libidinous allusions. (Adapted from Carpentier 2001: 155)

José García de Arboleya, a Colombian visitor to Havana in the nineteenth century, echoed these observations: "The dominant passion is dancing; everyone in Havana dances, regardless of age, class, or condition; from the child who can barely walk, to the elderly, from the captain-general to the lowest menial."[8] Another chronicler wrote in 1859, "Our dances take the name 'society dance,' 'theater dance,' etc., according to where they take place. They call it a *baile de ponina* if a few friends pay for it themselves; and they call *cuna* the gathering of low, immoral people, in which whites, blacks, and mulattos dance together. There are also dances of *escuelita* [little school], which are those periodically given classes for the poor, who each pay a *peseta* for each dance in which they take part."[9]

In Havana, a dance could take place, with varying sorts of instrumental ensembles, in a private home; in the elegant Tacón Theater; in a club, such as the Centro Asturiano and Casino Español; or in a *baile de cuna*, where well-to-do playboys could cultivate the acquaintance of mulatto women (Galán 1983: 130; León 1984: 251).

Havana was by no means the sole center for music and dance. The nearby city of Matanzas, gracefully straddling a picturesque bay, was a cultural center in its own right; for its part, Santiago de Cuba, near the other end of the island, has always rivaled the capital in terms of cultural vitality and was enlivened in particular in the 1800s by its "French connection." The English chronicler and painter Walter Goodman, who lived in Santiago from 1864 to 1869, penned in his 1873 *The Pearl of the Antilles* a colorful portrait of the lively music and dance scene there, centered around the contradanza and danza, which could be heard in various contexts. In formal concerts, and in the free matinees and soirées of pianist-composer Laureano Fuentes Matons (1825–98), one might hear piano or violin renditions of popular danzas, along with Cuban-inspired pieces by foreigners, such as the habaneras of Jean Henri Ravina, Pablo de Sarasate's "Capricho español," and Gottschalk's "Ojos criollos" (Goodman 1873: 120). The ideal context, however, was a night-long dance, in which a top ensemble, such as that of Lino Boza (brother of Antonio), would play the popular hits of the day (such as "El cocoyé," "La francesita," "La sopimpa," or "El merenguito"). As Goodman relates of a ball (1873: 154), "The famous 'danza criolla' is the favourite dance of the evening: indeed, with the exception of a vagrant polka and a mazurka or two, this dance occupies the entire programme." An Epicurean party-lover like Goodman could choose between a formal event at an elite venue or a more plebian mulatto affair, which would sooner or later be enlivened by a brawl. If one had not yet mastered the current dance figures, in order to avoid making an embarrassing literal *faux pas* at a society ball, one could learn them at a mulatto dance or at early morning sessions offered at the Sociedad Filarmónica, whose bar and restaurant were also outstanding (Goodman 1873: 154–155). The definition of "danza" (the more modern term for "contradanza") in Esteban Pichardo's 1849 erudite dictionary of Cubanisms attests to the degree to which the genre's popularity extended throughout the island and its diverse social classes: "The favorite dance of this Antillean isle, generally used everywhere from the most solemn function in the capital to the most indecent *changüí* [dance party] in a remote corner of the island" (in Galán 1983: 126).

While danza composers freely incorporated popular songs and opera hits into their pieces, their own compositions, if sufficiently catchy, were immediately taken up by the "informal sector" of the local music scene. García de Arboleya wrote, "As soon as any new danza is debuted—which happens all the time—it is incorporated in the repertoire of the ambulatory organ-grinders who play in the street day and night."[10] Similarly, Colombian visitor Nicolás Tanco Armentero wrote, "The same danzas are done in the palace as in the shack of a negro, and even the cripple who can no longer hop will content himself nodding to the music. One hears danzas being played all day long, whether in private halls or by the organ-grinder in the street, inspiring those around to dance" (in Balbuena 2003: 24). Often, as Goodman relates, a catchy danza tune would be spontaneously fitted with a whimsical text: "You have heard it [an 'irresistible' new tune of Boza] played all over the town to-day, and to-morrow you will hear it sung with a couple of doggerel rhymes in creole Spanish, which fit into the music so well as to 'appear to be the echoes of the *melody*'" (1873: 139). Such refrains set to danza tunes were sung especially zealously by street processions (*comparsas*) during Carnival. Thus danzas at once borrowed from and fed the popular street music of the day.

Although the contradanza was primarily dance music, amateur pianists could amuse themselves playing the pieces published in the newspapers, and professional pianists also played them during intermissions at theatrical performances (Lapique Becali 1979: 37). Contradanzas could also be performed on the concert stage, whether as piano solos or as chamber pieces, perhaps featuring a renowned soloist (see León 1984: 275). As mentioned, they also figured in the repertoire of the ambulatory ensembles of harp, flute, and clarinet that circulated in city cafes and parks. As Goodman (1873: 146) relates, they were also played, alongside airs from operas and zarzuelas and other favorites, by military bands at evening *retretas* (promenades) in town squares. Most characteristically, they were performed by a clarinet- and horn-dominated *orquesta típica* of six to twelve members. These ensembles served as conduits between the realms of art music and popular dance music; their musically literate and formally trained wind and string players brought a classical polish to the assorted popular tunes they included in their repertoires while also introducing these songs to elite salon audiences. An instrumentalist such as clarinetist Lino Boza could achieve special renown for his ability to animate dancers (Goodman 1873: 138). In general, with the contradanza as the core of their repertoire, these musicians epitomized the fluidity of the continuum between classical and vernacular music worlds in contemporary Cuba.

A distinctive and important feature of the contradanza's milieu, and especially of the creolization process, was the input of Afro-Cuban music and musicians. There is no need to romanticize colonial Cuba as a racial paradise, as Gilberto Freyre did with Brazil ([1936] 1987), for white Cuban racism could be profound and in some respects even intensified as blacks were eventually emancipated and theoretically enfranchised. However, the predominance of black and mulatto professional musicians and the fluidity of sociomusical exchanges between the races were marked features of colonial Cuban culture and contrasted dramatically with, for example, the racial polarization of the contemporary southern United States.

Blacks and mulattos were disproportionately numerous in the ranks of professional and semiprofessional musicians well into the latter nineteenth century. Contemporary whites did not regard music as a prestigious occupation, while for free blacks, who were denied access to law, medicine, and administrative jobs, music could constitute a presentable avocation that even offered a certain sort of access to elite society, albeit through the servants' entrance. Nor did blacks need to be free to acquire and use formal music education; in 1828 Abiel Abbott described a plantation owner who had forty of his slaves trained as an orchestra to perform at various functions (1965: 217). Such were the conditions that led an alarmed observer to comment, in 1832, "The arts are in the hands of people of color. Among the greatest evils this unfortunate race has brought to our soil is to have distanced the white population from the arts" (in Carpentier 2001: 153).

Many contemporary whites, however, would have questioned whether this situation constituted an "evil," since some accounts suggest that white audiences and dancers generally preferred black musicians over whites.[11] While white musicians tended to stick to the written score, black and mulatto ensembles—like their swing big band counterparts in the United States a century later—were celebrated for the inimitable interpretive and especially rhythmic flair with which they enlivened contradanzas and other pieces (Carpentier 1946: 141).[12] Moreover, people of color distinguished themselves not merely or even primarily as illiterate percussionists but as formally trained trumpeters, clarinetists, pianists, and violinists. Several, such as Tomás Buelta y Flores, were composers of contradanzas, and others were prominent soloists, such as Claudio Bríndis de Salas (d. 1911), who enjoyed stardom in Europe and Latin America as a virtuoso violinist; Lino Boza, of Santiago, was not unusual in being renowned as a clarinetist, composer, and bandleader. Still others worked as dance instructors and instrument makers. Meanwhile, many Afro-Cubans, far from restricting their tastes to rowdy rumbas, were ardent lovers of contradanza; Goodman, writing of the enthusiasts listening through windows to the soirées held by Fuentes in Santiago in the 1860s, relates, "Negroes and mulattoes of all shades are among the spectators of the pavement; but with the exception of a few coloured musicians, only white people are admitted within the building" (1873: 119). And yet, black and mulatto artists, despite their celebrity, were perpetually vulnerable to persecution; as Carpentier (chap. 7) notes, in the repression of the anticolonial Escalera Conspiracy of 1844, white plotters were pardoned, but black participants—such as Buelta y Flores, Bríndis de Salas (father), and others—were tortured (fatally, in the case of Buelta y Flores), and many more were executed.

While black performers were being alternately lionized and persecuted, several contemporary accounts attested, whether with bemusement or shock, how black influences percolated into white dance styles. One observer wrote in 1872, "The danza, as it is danced—and may its admirers forgive us for saying—has much in it of the African dances; the dance recently introduced by the name *coreada* [literally, the sung part] gives it an aspect quite similar to a *cabildo* of Ethiopians . . . and such indecent movements have been introduced in the danza, one of them being the so-called *infanzón*."[13] Another commentator wrote in 1837, "Who doesn't see in the movements of our young men and women, when they dance contradanzas and waltzes, an imitation of the blacks in their *cabildos*? Who doesn't know that the bass parts in the danza bands are an echo of the drum of the tangos [Afro-Cuban dances]?" (Félix Tanco, in Galán 1983: 135).

Given the popularity of the contradanza among diverse races and classes, and the concomitantly growing sense of pride in Cuban identity, it is not surprising that by the 1830s the genre was already being explicitly celebrated as an emblem of local creole culture, with its distinctive sensuousness and "melancholy voluptuousness."[14]

The contradanza occupied a central place in Cuban music culture, overlapping and interacting with a broad range of diverse musical genres and their sociomusical milieus. Neo-African music and dance styles flourished in the slave plantations, and especially in the urban *cabildos* (mutual-aid societies, often founded on African ethnic bases) where free and enslaved blacks could congregate. As we have seen, both rhythms and dance movements from these contexts found their way into contradanza styles. On the more Hispanic end of the continuum was the *zapateo*, an "open" (non-touching) couple dance, somewhat akin to such dances as the Mexican *jarabe* and Venezuelan *joropo*, which, though most characteristically a "folk" genre of farmers, could be danced at some of the same urban functions as the contradanza.

Closer to the contradanza in style, format, and status were the strictly European-derived social dances. These included the Lancers, the gavotte, the stately rigodón (rigadoon), the archaic allemande, the Spanish fandango (in both courtly and rustic versions) and the bolero/boleras (open couple dances with often arched arms and statuesque *bien parao* cadences), and, through the early 1800s, the minuet (*minué*). The latter, as discussed in this book's Introduction (Chapter 1), was the premier dance of the European Baroque and, to some extent, of the colonial Caribbean aristocracy in the 1700s. An open couple dance with elegant and restrained movements that required training, the minuet was an overt mark of social distinction. Hierarchy was also embedded in its performance format, with the opening figures being executed by the most distinguished participant (ideally, some periwigged prince). Many Cuban dance soirées of the early 1800s would open with a ceremonious and by then archaic minuet before proceeding to the more convivial and informal contradanzas.[15] As mentioned above, blacks, whether in Haiti or Cuba, might also dance minuets, and Afro-Caribbean influence was evident in the "minuet congo" that reached even the Parisian salons. However, on the whole, the minuet, with its relatively codified figures and elitist associations, neither lent itself to creolization nor cohered with the egalitarian sensibilities of the contemporary bourgeoisie.

More congruent with such attitudes were—aside from the contradanza—various related nineteenth-century dances, such as the quadrille (*cuadrilla*), rigodón, and Lancers (*lanceros*), all of which consisted of suites of sections with different figures, most typically danced by "squares" of two or four couples. All were popular in Cuba during the heyday of the contradanza itself, although they were not as extensively creolized or cultivated as were local compositional genres. Also popular was the waltz (*vals*), which revolutionized choreography in forsaking the collectively executed figures in favor of independent couple dancing. The contradanza, as it developed into the danza and eventually the danzón, paralleled this innovation and hence was often likened to the waltz. Finally, lower-class festivities, including those attended by "slumming" bourgeois young men, featured a variety of creole vernacular dances, such as the *chinchín, congo, tumba-Antonio, papalote, guabina, caringa, toro, dengue, culebra*, and others (León 1981: 9). While little is known of these, they presumably constituted informal couple or group dances whose ephemeral popularity could be likened to that of the "Macarena" of the 1990s. Despite their familiarity, these dances were all secondary in appeal to the contradanza, which lent itself well to creolization in terms of composition, musical performance, and choreography, and which accordingly soon came to be cherished as an icon of cultural nationalism.

## Choreography, from Contradanza to Danza

The danza and contradanza have not been actively danced for nearly a century, and our understanding of their choreography is impeded by the paucity, ambiguity, and often contradictory nature of contemporary descriptions, not to mention the absence of labanotations or video recordings from that era. Hence many aspects of the genre's choreography remain ambiguous, despite the energetic and erudite efforts of Cuban scholars—especially Galán—to reconstruct its form and evolution.

Seen teleologically, the development from contradanza to danza embodies the fundamental choreographic transformation to independent couple dancing, represented by the waltz in Europe and also evident in the evolution of the Dominican merengue and the Puerto Rican danza. In Cuba from the early 1800s, the contradanza was evidently danced both in the French style, with its *cuadrilla* format of two or four couples, and in the style derived from the English longways country dance, in which couples, initially arranged in a basic formation of two lines of men and women, executed sequential figures directed by a caller (bastonero). In the mid-1800s this collective contradanza format gradually gave way to the more modern danza in which individual, loosely embracing couples danced independently.

In the eighteenth-century European suite comprising the branle, courante, gavotte, and minuet, each dance was ideally initiated by a distinguished couple who went down the two rows of men and women and was then followed by the subsequent couples.[16] Two contemporary descriptions of the Cuban contradanza relate how this custom was perpetuated, with the added proviso that all had to imitate the figures set by the first couple. The first description is from Pichardo's *Diccionario* of 1849:

> To *poner una danza* [set a dance] is the privilege of the couple which took the first place, to obtain which men and women run immediately, forming two files by sexes; it is not polite to improve one's location after that and much less so to seize the first place. All are obliged to imitate the figures successively. . . . Any variation introduced by another couple is considered disrespectful. Only he who has set the figure, after he goes down [the rows] and comes back—that is, after he has danced alternately with each couple—is entitled to change the figure. Therefore, he should set easy figures so that others will not get mixed up, which would be called *perderse* [getting lost]. (In Galán 1983: 132–133)

Cirilo Villaverde's famous *costumbrista* novel of 1839 (expanded and revised in 1882), *Cecilia Valdés*, offers a similar description, differing only in portraying the lead couple as setting challengingly complex figures:

> In vogue during the period to which we refer [the 1830s] was the contradanza of figures, some of which were difficult and complicated, such that it was important to learn them before attempting to execute them, since one would be exposed to the ridicule of the public if one fumbled, which would be called "getting lost" [*perderse*]. He who positioned himself at the head of the dance "set the figure," and the other couples had to duplicate them or else retire from the lines. In every *cuna* [dance club] there was generally some maestro who assumed or was granted the right to set the figure, which he could alter at whim. Whoever set the most rare and elaborate figures gained the most credit as an accomplished dancer, his distinction extending also to the woman fortunate to be his partner.[17] (Villaverde [1839, 1882] 1971: 111)

As suggested in other accounts, the cane-wielding bastonero, if not actually calling the figures, would serve as a master of ceremonies, perhaps announcing the sequence of figures to be danced by all, controlling the duration of the piece, and arraying the dancers before beginning, including selecting the couple skilled and fortunate enough to *romper la danza*, or open the dance. In some contexts in Puerto Rico as well as Cuba, no bastonero would be present, such that the dancers would either repeat a standardized simple sequence (typically, *paseo*, *cadena*, and *cedazo*) or be obliged to remember a lengthy series of figures, typically as learned in the dance schools (*academías de baile*; see, e.g., Balbuena 2003: 26–27; Alonso [1849] 2002: 17). Clearly, the contradanza was performed in several styles and formats, depending on the skills and inclinations of the participants. Most descriptions, including those by Pichardo, indicate that the dance, once commenced, consisted of a series of collectively executed figures, which might be simple or intricate, familiar or new, and dainty or, alternately, provocative enough to be denounced by purists.

Some contemporary accounts indicate that the most conventional format came by the 1840s to comprise three or four familiar figures: *paseo* (promenade), *cadena* (chain), and *cedazo* (sieve), with a *sostenido* (literally, sustained) sometimes inserted before the *cedazo*. Local chronicler Gaspar Betancourt Cisneros ("El Lugareño") wrote in 1838 that while the contradanza formerly had many figures, these had been reduced to merely four: "Now it has become a complete bore; twenty contradanzas are danced in the same style and with the same figures" (in Lapique Becali 1979: 67). Each figure would be executed in the space of eight bars of music, after which it could be repeated. A standard procedure was to dance the *paseo* during the first A section, the *cadena* during its repeat, and the *sostenido* and *cedazo* during the first and second renditions of the B section, respectively. (This format, however, would last less than two minutes.) Pichardo and other sources also describe (with varying degrees of consistency) diverse other figures, some of which involved the entire assembly, while others were better executed with a smaller set—quintessentially, a *cuadrilla* of two couples (the format sometimes used in the specific dance of that name, corresponding to the "minor set" of Anglo-American contra dancing), of which several could be formed from the larger group. Throughout all figures, as in salsa dancing (starting from different beats) and, for that matter, the waltz, the basic foot pattern remained the same, with the first step of each bar being taken by alternate feet—for the man: right, left, right, slide-left, left, right, left, slide-right, and so forth (see, e.g., Balbuena 2003: 25–26; Fernández 1981). In the days before amplification, the sliding of the dancers' feet added an audible supplement to the music.[18]

As Pichardo notes (1849: 87), the division of a large group into two or more *cuadrillas* spared dancers from having to wait while others "set the danza" and brought the event closer in form to suite "square" dances, such as the *lanceros*, rigodón, and quadrille itself, with which it competed in popularity. The practice can also be seen as a step in the direction of independent couple dancing.

Most of the contradanza's figures corresponded to namesakes extant in Spanish salon dances of the eighteenth century. Galán (1983: 142), after Pichardo, describes the *ala* (wing) as the formation of the two male and female lines, with its central *calle*, or street.[19] In the *paseo*, the couples, one by one, proceed down the *calle* and back, or around the circle, whether as an opening figure or a relaxation between figures.[20] The *cadena* resembles its counterpart in the country dance and modern contra dancing: Man and woman, facing each other, pass each other to their right while taking the right hand of the other, and then each partner does the same with the left of the next person, proceeding in an "S" format, whether down the two adjacent lines (as suggested by Pichardo, in Galán 1983: 143) or around the circle formed by a few couples (as described by Fernández 1981: 35). In *molino* (mill, like the country-dance "star"), two couples (a *cuadrilla*) join their right hands in the center and walk in a clockwise circle (or left hands, walking counterclockwise). In the *latigazo* (whiplash), a man and two adjacent women hold hands in a trio (omitting the remaining man); the man and one woman raise their joined hands in an arch, under which the other woman passes, and then the first woman passes under the bridge formed by the other two. In the *lazo* (lasso, knot), which also involves a threesome, the trio forms a circle holding hands, and the man passes below the arch formed by the women's raised arms, which now intertwine in a "knot" that is then undone by his return to his original position. Other optional figures include the *ocho, tornillo, rueda* (Galán 1983: 164–165), *rodeos, alemanda*, and *puente* (Fernández 1981: 26–34). Each figure would generally last eight bars of music. Enthusiasts would attend *academías de baile* to learn diverse figures so that they could easily execute them on the ballroom floor.

Some of the figures—including *paseo, ocho, caja*, and *cedazo*—were retained in the danzón and casino dancing of later generations and even in the ring-formation *salsa de rueda* of today (Balbuena 2003: 29). Similarly, Galán (1983: 164) notes that *latigazo* and *lazo* persisted in the danzón, where a couple could invite a woman of an adjacent pair to form a threesome.

Of particular importance was the *cedazo*, typically reserved for last, in which the longways format would be abandoned and each couple would embrace ballroom-style to dance independently, such that Pichardo and others likened it to a waltz set to duple rather than triple meter (in Galán 1983: 146). Like the waltz, the *cedazo* represented a clear break from the collectively executed figures and the commands of the imperious bastonero and was accordingly controversial in its way. (The *cedazo* also corresponded to the French Caribbean couple dance variants, such as the biguine, which were used as the last movement of the quadrille.) In Galán's reconstruction (1983: 146–154), the transition to couple dance took the form of a gradual extension of the *cedazo* at the expense of the other figures. Closed couple dancing had already been extant in the form of the waltz and, on the more local level, the *sungambelo* documented from 1813 (Balbuena 2003: 28). Villaverde's *Cecilia Valdés* of 1839 seems to describe dance parties in which the collective figure contradancing would eventually give way to more informal and intensely intimate couple dancing.[21] When in the 1840s the contemporary Cuban danza/contradanza was adopted in San Juan, Puerto Rico, and, subsequently, Santo Domingo, it was denounced vehemently by moralists, presumably because of its intimate couple dancing. For the same reasons conservative elites of Santiago de Cuba in the 1850s were scandalized by the sensual dancing called "sopimpa," named after a popular dance (Goodman 1873: 155). In class terms, couple dancing came from both above and below, being associated at once with the cosmopolitan waltz and with the local clubs where young playboys could socialize with women of color.

Galán (1983: 151) asserts that by the 1830s it had become standard practice (at least in some dances) to quickly run through the *paseo, cadena*, and perhaps *latigazo* in the first sixteen-bar A section of the music, such that the B section could be devoted entirely to the *cedazo*, which could be prolonged. By the 1860s and 1870s—the heyday of the danza per se—the opening figures could be reduced to a brief *cadena* (Galán 1983: 170), and the bastonero's role was reduced to merely signaling the start of the dance. With the advent of the danzón around 1880, the transition to independent couple dancing was complete, and the collective character only remained in the group's alternation of relaxing *paseo* sections and ballroom-style, *cedazo*-like dance sections. However, as mentioned, the danzón—like the *son* and casino popular dancing that subsequently evolved—retained the basic step (*paso básico*) and some occasional specific figures of the contradanza.

Galán devotes many pages to discussing how the choreographic transition accompanied a name change, from "contradanza" to "danza." The terms were certainly used inconsistently; for example, as early as 1836 Pichardo called "contradanza" an archaic term for "danza" (in Galán 1983: 119), but music publishers and others continued using the former term through the 1870s. Saumell's pieces of the 1850s–60s, for instance, are all labeled "contradanzas," as are a few pieces of Cervantes published by Edelmann in 1875. Villaverde, in *Cecilia Valdés* ([1839, 1882] 1971), and Goodman (1873) use the terms essentially interchangeably. In general, musicians and publishers tended to preserve the older, more formal term "contradanza," but by mid-century the term "danza" was increasingly favored to distinguish the new style, emphasizing independent couple dancing, in contrast to the older, collective contradanza.[22]

## Musical Features

If many aspects of contradanza choreography remain enigmatic to us today, reconstructing the genre's musical features involves its own challenges. Notations fail to indicate how pieces were accompanied, interpreted, enriched with improvisation, or extended for dancing, and modern attempts to reconstruct ensemble renditions of pieces are inherently imaginative. Nevertheless, there is no doubt that the existence of notated scores, from "San Pascual Bailón" on, together with other contemporary descriptions afford us a vision of colonial musical practice in many ways more clear than can be obtained regarding dance.

The essential contours of the early efflorescence of the creole contradanza in Cuba are fairly clear. The first documented Cuban contradanza is "San Pascual Bailón" (see Figure 2.1), published in 1803, of unknown authorship, which illustrates features basic to the genre as flourishing over the next seventy years.[23] These include the following:

Binary form, consisting of an eight-bar A section (the *prima* or *primera*), repeated, followed by an eight-bar B section (the *segunda*), affording a thirty-two-bar AABB form, which could be repeated several times to accompany dancers

**Figure 2.1** "San Pascual Bailón," 1803.

Relatively simple diatonic melodies, structured in clear four- or eight-bar phrases, with little or no modulation or harmonic complexity
Use of the "habanera" (or "tango") rhythm as an accompanimental ostinato, especially as a bass (and presumably percussion) ostinato in the B section of the contradanza
Notation as a piano score, which, however, could often be regarded as a skeletal basis for performance by a chamber ensemble—typically, a string- or wind-dominated *orquesta típica*

A rhythmically distinct category comprised the several contradanzas, perhaps around 10 percent of all, which are set to 6/8 or 3/4 meter rather than 2/4. To some extent these may be seen as holdovers from English country dances and the Spanish contradanza, and, more generally, as atavisms reflecting the lingering Spanish predilection for triple meter, which was increasingly overshadowed by the Afro-Latin binarization process. Several of these contradanzas, by Saumell and others, display the hemiola so abundant in Spanish and Latin American musics. However, unlike those in 2/4, they could be said to represent an evolutionary dead end and constituted less overt sites for creolization.

The essential evolutionary dynamic animating the Cuban contradanza as a musical genre was the process of creolization. As Galán (1983: 66) observes, if such creolization were taking place in a genre imported to Italy, the distinguishing transformations might occur in the realm of melody, but in Cuba (as elsewhere in the region), the crucial and distinctive input of Afro-Caribbean musicians determined that the primary developments would be in the realm of rhythm. These consisted primarily in the use of the set of interrelated cells shown in Figure 1.2 and discussed in the Introduction (Chapter 1):

The aforementioned "habanera" or "tango/congo" cell (which can be rendered as "ONE-and-TWO-AND-THREE-and-FOUR-and," repeated without pause).

The "amphibrach," which literally denotes a short-long-short figure, but in this context also implies the presence of two subsequent eighth notes, affording the figure: "ONE-AND-TWO-AND-THREE-and-FOUR-and" (or 1-2-1-2-2); a slight variant of the habanera pattern, it appears primarily as a melodic rather than accompanimental figure.

The *tresillo*, with its 3+3+2 subdivision, which can appear as another accompanimental variant of the habanera (sounding as "ONE-and-TWO-AND-three-and-FOUR-and," or "ONE-two-three-ONE-two-three-ONE-two," or 3-3-2).

The *cinquillo*, which appears in a number of mid-nineteenth-century contradanzas and from the 1870s pervades the danzón of Havana and Matanzas; it occurs most distinctively in a two-bar pattern consisting of the *cinquillo* itself followed (or, less often, preceded) by a measure of unsyncopated notes (typically in the pattern "ONE-and-TWO-AND-three-AND-FOUR-and-ONE-and-TWO-and-THREE-and-four-and," or 3-1-2-2-2-2-4).[24]

As discussed in the Introduction (Chapter 1), scholars have debated the origins of the habanera rhythm, the amphibrach, and the *cinquillo* as used in Caribbean music. The habanera rhythm, whether as a melodic figure or even as an accompanimental ostinato, can be found in such a wide variety of musics worldwide that it cannot be conclusively traced to any particular source. However, its prominence in the Antilles is probably best seen as a Congolese-derived Afro-Caribbean practice, variously disseminating thence to the conga processional drumming of Santiago de Cuba, the Dominican *palo corrido*, the Spanish theatrical tango, the languid habanera vocal song, the early Argentine tango, and other genres.[25] In Cuba from the 1830s it was commonly linked with the tango or "*tango africano*" and hence designated the "tango" or "congo" rhythm. For its part, the amphibrach, which can be seen as a slightly decorated form of the habanera, occurs prominently as a bell ostinato in West African Ewe and Dogon music. It pervades Cuban and Puerto Rican danzas from the 1860s on as a melodic figure and also recurs in the related ragtime compositions of Scott Joplin, Tom Turpin, and others. The *cinquillo* may also be of West African derivation and became especially prominent in Haitian music, from Vodou drumming (especially *banda* and *Petwo* rhythms) to creole méringue folksong. In a creolized, two-bar form alternating with a measure in even note values, it appeared in Cuban contradanzas of the 1850s and became common in Puerto Rican danzas and Cuban danzones from the early 1870s; its popularity in the Caribbean is especially marked in regions touched by the French Creole connection, although it also occurs in traditional musics, such as Santería *batá* rhythms, Puerto Rican *bomba*, and Jamaican Maroon drumming.

In terms of melody and harmony, little is distinctively creole or Hispanic about the typical Cuban contradanza, which generally conforms instead to eighteenth-century European conventions. Galán (1983: 45)observes that Saumell's contradanza "La quejosita" imitates a *zapateo* tune, but the repertoire as a whole shows no particular evocations of Andalusian "Phrygian" harmonies nor of the modal melodies typical of much Afro-Cuban music (Manuel and Fiol 2007). Hence Mikowsky (1973: 55–64) can compare "San Pascual Bailón" with a typical Mozart contredanse (also of two sixteen-bar sections, in 2/4), finding the only stylistic differences to be the jaunty habanera rhythm of the former's B section, the contrast it affords with the A section, and the Mixolydian flavor provided by the flat seventh in bar eleven—an atavistic hint of modality that is not characteristic of other Cuban contradanzas. Cuban composer Nicolás Espadero (d. 1909) concisely articulated the challenge of writing and performing creole contradanzas and related genres: "The principal basis of creole musical manifestation is melody, at times tinged with languidness and melancholy, at times flirtatious and voluptuous, indolently cooing over a backdrop of a tormentous accompaniment, but symmetric" (in Carpentier 2001: 201). The bipartite form of the contradanza also recapitulates that of the English country dance, and the often contrasting character of the two sections—the first typically "classical" and perhaps pompous, and the second more lyrical or lively—conforms to typical conventions of eighteenth-century European salon music.

In most Cuban contradanzas, the distinctive creole character resides in the rhythms, and especially the habanera pattern of the bass. The habanera rhythm in fact occurs in a few different forms, with distinct degrees and forms of syncopation. Perhaps the most common is that which we may call the "Carmen" pattern, shown in Figure 2.2a, with the initial note being the lowest. A different order of syncopation occurs when the second and fourth notes are the lowest, as in Figure 2.2b. This pattern, stressing the *tresillo*'s "one-two-three-ONE-two-three-ONE-two" beats, is markedly more syncopated and creole, and as a bass ostinato it is dramatically different from the idiosyncratic habanera-like patterns found in Playford country dances or North African meters. Depending on voicing and accentuation, in its effective elision of the downbeat it constitutes a remarkable precursor to (or anticipation of) the standard "anticipated bass" pattern of post-1950s *son* and salsa (shown in Figures 2.2c and 2.2d), with the distinction that it does not anticipate the harmony in the same fash-

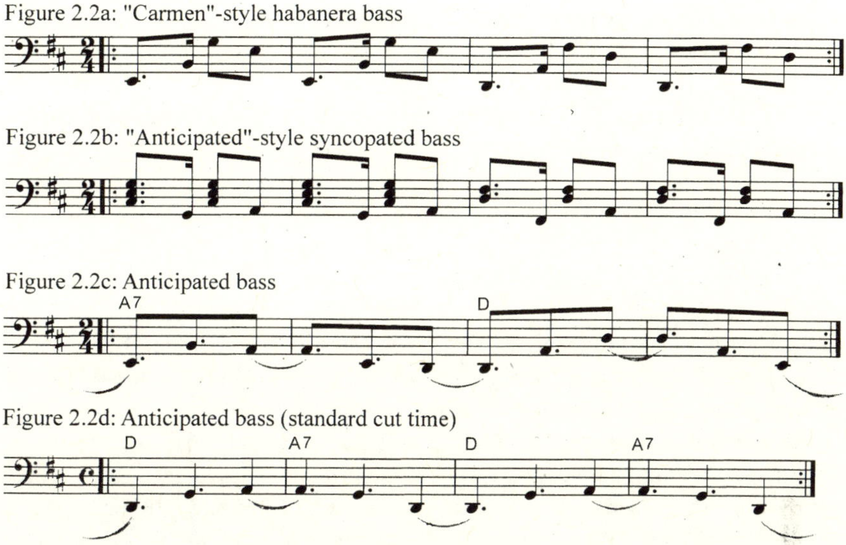


**Figure 2.2** Bass patterns in contradanza and popular song.

ion. Far from being a late development, this syncopated pattern occurs in "San Pascual Bailón" and is used in an even more distinctively creole fashion in 1850s–60s contradanzas, such as "Cambujá" (see Figure 2.4 below).

As mentioned, surviving published contradanza notations—from "San Pascual Bailón" to the works of Ernesto Lecuona—are all in the form of piano scores, as would be submitted to publishers. Accordingly, they certainly were played for entertainment by amateur pianists. However, in their mid-nineteenth-century heyday, many if not most were conceived as dance music, ideally to be performed by some sort of ensemble. In humble or informal circumstances, this ensemble might consist merely of a fiddle or flute accompanied by harp or guitar, but ideally it would constitute an *orquesta típica*, which might comprise two clarinets, four violins, a flute or piccolo (*flautín*), trombone, *figle* (ophicleide, a sort of bass bugle), contrabass, timbales (small kettledrum), and other percussion instruments, such as the *güiro* gourd scraper or even a *quijada* (jawbone of an ass, scraped like the *güiro*).[26] Larger ensembles also existed, such as the Matanzas *orquesta* of Los Hermanos Barani, which in 1848 counted twenty-two musicians (León 1984: 264). Published piano reductions might suggest instrumentation; thus, for example, the score of "San Pascual Bailón" indicates that its melodic parts are to be played by horns, thus allying it with traditions of minuets and regimental bands (Galán 1983: 107–117).The absence of notated parts leaves many aspects of accompaniment uncertain. Contemporary descriptions as well as composers' indications, such as Saumell's "*con sandunga*" ("with pep"), suggest a "ragged" and lively accompaniment style full of interpretive nuances, especially on the part of percussionists. One observer wrote in 1865, "Danzas may sound like an infernal cacophony to someone unaccustomed to hearing them, with every instrument seeming to go its own way" (in Galán 1983: 166). Accordingly, Odilio Urfé and others who have recorded reconstructions of danzas and danzones have clearly encouraged accompanists to play with a judicious amount of improvised flourishes. The compact disc accompanying this volume presents one such attempt to recreate the nineteenth-century style of ensemble playing, in the form of a contradanza of Saumell, "Los ojos de Pepa," performed by a latter-day Dutch *orquesta típica* under a Cuban baton. It is possible that percussionists in the 1850s–70s may have enlivened danzas with *cinquillos* in the creole, two-bar form that would later become standard in the danzón and bolero. The presence of such rhythms in danzas like "Cambujá" (shown below) shows that they were certainly familiar in Havana and Santiago from the 1850s.

While notated scores tend to be original compositions, contemporary accounts indicate that contradanza musicians freely interjected tunes, suitably enlivened with syncopations, from all manner of sources, including ephemeral popular songs of the day, along with themes from Verdi, Rossini, Bellini, and the other European opera and zarzuela composers who enjoyed great popularity in urban Cuba. The flexibility with which contradanzas could be performed was also evident in Edelmann's publication of a Gottschalk contradanza with simple and harder versions notated on the same page.

The melodic eclecticism of the danza was paralleled by the diverse and often colorful titles composers bestowed on them. Since titles did not need to bear any particular affective relation to the music, they could be as fanciful as the composer's imagination would admit. Hence, they could variously commemorate celebrities or friends (Saumell's "¡Toma, Tomás!" to composer Tomás Ruiz), celebrate notable current events ("El cable submarino" ["The Underwater Cable"], "La toma de Tetuán" ["The Capture of Tetuán"]), or, quite often, consist of colorful colloquial (and scarcely translatable) phrases of the time ("Dále pronto calabaza," "Fuácata," "Los bembitos"). Others reflected contemporary *siboneista* romanticization of Amerindian heritage ("La Indiana," "El Yumurí," "Los cantos del Siboney"), but many more invoked Afro-Cuban culture, which was seen in this context as colorful and exotic ("La Kalunga," "Los ñañigos," "Los negros catedráticos," and "Tu madre es conga" ["Your Mother Is Congolese"]).[27]

The profusion of contradanzas published in nineteenth-century newspapers, music journals, and elsewhere indicates a music scene enlivened by many dozens of amateur and semiprofessional composers, sustaining a veritable contradanza industry. As works of art, most such contradanzas may have been ordinary rather than sublime, but they serve in their way to highlight the distinction of the genre's most outstanding composers. Among the earlier of these was Nicolás Muñoz y Zayas, most of whose contradanzas were published between 1836 and 1845, illustrating how the style typical of subsequent decades was well established by his period. In the mid-century decades, prominent composers included José "Lino" Fernández de Coca (1830–?),

Tomás Buelta y Flores (1798–1851), Enrique Guerrero (ca. 1800–89), Nicolás Ruíz Espadero (1832–90), Tomás Ruiz (1834–89), Laureano Fuentes Matons (1825–98), and Manuel Saumell (1817–70); and of the subsequent generation, Cecilia Arízti (1856–1930), José Marín Varona (1859–1912), Ignacio Cervantes (1847–1905), zarzuela composer Jorge Anckermann (1877–1941), Miguel Faílde (1852–1921), and Raimundo Valenzuela (1848–1905)—the latter two being better known as danzón bandleaders and composers. Of all these, the reclusive and independently wealthy Espadero was the only one to achieve some recognition outside Cuba, despite never leaving the island and, for that matter, seldom leaving his home. Today, only the compositions of Saumell and Cervantes, who are discussed below, are likely to be heard or purchased in Cuba; published scores of the others merely gather dust and wormholes in archives.[28]

The contradanzas of all these composers tended to adhere to the conventions of the genre, with its regular eight-bar phrases, its concise bipartite form, and, as notated for piano, its general avoidance of virtuoso frippery, which would in any case have posed problems for ensemble and amateur renditions. Since the pieces were meant to be accessible to listeners and amateur performers, they also display none of the formal innovations in structure, texture, and harmony that characterized contemporary European pieces by Liszt, Chopin, or the late Beethoven; in spirit, they are closer to short, unpretentious works by Schubert or Mozart.

## The Contradance and Popular Song

Perhaps the most striking examples of truly Cuban creole flavor in the contradanza repertoire occur in the handful of pieces from the 1850s–60s whose B sections consist primarily of repeated, ostinato-like two-bar structures in which a syncopated, *tresillo-* or *cinquillo*-based measure alternates (in either order) with one in even notes. These passages constitute remarkable precursors of the composite ostinatos, called *montunos*, that form the basis of the second part of the *son* emerging in the early twentieth century and of the salsa that derived from it in the 1960s–70s, and that also pervade the mambo and chachachá emerging in the 1950s. Contradanzas displaying this feature include "El dedo de Landaluze" by Ruiz (1862), "Cambujá" and "¡Ave María Gallo!" by Lino Coca (ca. 1857), "Suelta el peso" by Juan de Dios Alfonso, "Suelta el cuero" (perhaps by the same author), "La expedición de Marruecos" (1860, by "P.B.C."), and "La Santa Taé" by Antonio Boza (1852). All these composers were based in Havana, with the exception of Boza, who was from Santiago de Cuba.[29] In the B sections of these pieces, the *cinquillo* or *tresillo* (sometimes in slightly altered form) alternates with a bar of more or less even eighth notes; this pattern strongly suggests and was possibly accompanied by the *clave* pattern that came to pervade the rumba and *son* as documented from the early twentieth century, with the *tresillo* itself falling on the "three" side of the *clave* beat, as shown in Figure 2.3.

Figure 2.4 presents "Cambujá," whose B section is based on a four-bar ostinato, repeated with a slightly different, cadential final two bars. As the section as a whole consists of a repeat of this four-bar ostinato, the standard two-fold repetition of the entire B section affords an eight-fold repetition of the ostinato. The ostinato itself (as well as the first section) strongly suggests "two-three" *clave*, in its two-bar pattern consisting of an unsyncopated bar followed by a (decorated or slightly altered) *tresillo*. The piece's B section thus acquires the character of a typical *montuno*, as would be especially apparent if the section were repeated a few times (rather than regularly alternating with the A section). Along with the harmonies and rhythms, also typical of the traditional *son* (along with bolero and *canción* styles) is the way the right hand strongly suggests the standard two-voice (*primo* and *segundo*) format of singing in thirds and sixths. Finally, as noted above, the syncopated form of habanera bass rhythm (in contrast to the less syncopated "Carmen" form) affords

**Figure 2.3** Correspondence of two-bar *cinquillo* pattern with *clave*.

**Figure 2.4** "Cambujá," by José (Lino) Fernández de Coca.

bass notes in the same pattern as that of the standard *son* and salsa bass—that is, the "anticipated bass" pattern, albeit without the harmonic anticipation. The overall effect is unmistakably, overwhelmingly, and charmingly Cuban. (This piece is also heard on this volume's compact disc, played on two guitars, with light percussion, in an attempted reconstruction of a typical informal performance format of the 1850s.)

The B section of Coca's "¡Ave María Gallo!" shown as Figure 2.5 (and also included in the compact disc) is similar in its quasi-ostinato structure, its "two-three" *clave* format alternating a bar in even notes with a *cinquillo*, and its *primo-segundo* treble voicing.

Galán suggests that such ostinato sections might be repeated indefinitely, treated as vamps over which a featured instrumentalist might improvise: "The two-part form of the contradanza became a theme and variations in the *cedazo* which constituted the final figure. The Cuban danza, in order to fill the time, could be prolonged in accordance with the imagination of the musicians, reaching thirty-six or more bars" (1983: 150).

Galán notes in particular how the score of "El dedo de Landaluze" by Ruiz specifically, if enigmatically, indicates how the two-bar ostinato, repeated once, could itself be repeated (once? indefinitely?), with its simple tonic-dominant harmonies being suitable for treatment as a *montuno* (1983: 166–169; see Figure 2.6).

Boza's "La Santa Taé," composed in Santiago, is similar in form, with the *montuno* section again suggesting "two-three" *clave* in a four-bar ostinato. (The relative simultaneity of all these pieces indicates a remarkable homogeneity of style in Santiago and Havana.)

These contradanzas, with their through-composed A sections and *montuno*-type B sections, their distinctively syncopated bass patterns, their implicit *clave* structure, and their *primo-segundo* treble voicings, constitute remarkable precursors to the *son*, which is generally regarded by musicologists as having

**Figure 2.5** "¡Ave María Gallo!" by José (Lino) Fernández de Coca, B section.

Figure 2.6 "El dedo de Landaluze," by Tomás Ruiz (1862), ostinato section.

evolved from the input of musicians and distinctive musical forms from rural Oriente in the early 1900s. As such, the existence of these Havana contradanzas calls for a revision of conventional Cuban music history (along with Carpentier's notions that the creole contradanza came from Oriente and that the *cinquillo* was absent in Havana salon music until the late 1870s). Insofar as they illustrate that most of the distinctive musical features of the *son* were already present in Havana in the 1850s, they suggest that whatever form of *son* was brought from Oriente would have constituted at most of a repertoire of refrains (*estribillos*, as in the simple *nengón* and *kiribá* format) and a syncopated *tres* style with characteristic eighth-note anticipations, coupled with the use of the bongó.

The *son*, of course, was a vocal song, whereas the contradanza was (primarily) instrumental. However, the links between the contradanza and vernacular dance songs were direct. First, contradanza composers borrowed liberally from popular songs of the day, such that compositions like "Cambujá" may have been stylized imitations of *guarachas*, *rumbitas*, or other aforementioned ephemeral entities enigmatically mentioned in nineteenth-century sources (see, e.g., León 1984: 274). A Cuban chronicler noted in 1852 that musicians composed danzas using "common ditties, and even street-vendor calls and songs of negros."[30] However, as mentioned above in reference to Santiago of the 1860s, it was also the custom to fit any catchy refrain with a short whimsical text, which, as Goodman noted, would then resound throughout the city. In Havana such refrains might be sung by dancers every time a new figure began (Martínez Rodríguez 2004: 27): "The 'Danza Criolla' is the patriotic music of Cuba, and every fresh carnival gives birth to a new set of these 'danzas.' When the air happens to be unusually 'pegajoza,' or catching, a brief song is improvised, and the words of this song chime so well with the music which suggests them, as to form a sort of verbal counterpart of the melody" (Goodman 1873: 121). Thus, contradanzas did not merely mirror and adapt popular dance songs—they inspired them. It is entirely conceivable, for example, that Coca wrote such a piece as "Cambujá" with the intention and expectation that dancers and other enthusiasts would merrily sing along with its tuneful *montuno* (perhaps something nonsensical along the lines of "Cambujá, te digo yo, Cambujá"). Some contradanza scores even indicated the text snippet to be sung. For example, the score of Coca's "Chichí pipí niní" indicates how those nonsense words are to be set to catch phrases of the B section (reproduced in León 1984: 257). As such, the roots of the *son* are perhaps best sought not in the hills of Oriente but in the contradanza salons of Santiago and Havana.

## The Question of Form

A contradanza, played at a moderate, danceable tempo with the indicated AABB repeats, totaling thirty-two bars, lasts under a minute—typically, about fifty seconds. However, several nineteenth-century accounts describe enthusiasts dancing for an hour, or even three hours, without stopping or separating (in Galán 1983: 151–153). The obvious question thus arises: How was the short notated contradanza extended for use as dance accompaniment? The often encountered standard description (e.g., in Pichardo) of the four figures each being performed for eight bars clearly raises more questions than it answers, and there are no notations or specific contemporary descriptions to resolve the issue. Galán is the only scholar to have addressed it in depth, and his interpretations, although plausible, remain speculative.

The Puerto Rican danza, for its part, could be extended by two means. First, as indicated in scores, the composer could write additional sections, extending the piece to 130 bars or more. However, Cuban danzas, from "San Pascual Bailón" to those written by Cervantes in the 1860s, adhered rigidly to the format of only sixteen bars of notated music (totaling thirty-two with repeats). Second, Puerto Rican danzas could be lengthened by having the bombardino player perform solos to the chord progression of the second section, as documented on early-twentieth-century recordings. However, since the Cuban danza declined before the advent of recording, no such discs exist to document such a practice therein.

One obvious extension technique was to simply repeat the danza indefinitely. This practice is standard in American square dancing and country/contra dancing, in which the merriment generated by the dancing overshadows the potential monotony of the music. León asserts that Cuban contradanzas would be repeated in this fashion, with instrumental variations for which featured soloists might receive tips from dancers (1984: 274). (Goodman, writing of Santiago in the 1860s, also mentions how an enthusiast might tip the bandleader to extend the piece [1873: 156].)

Another basic means of extending the music, also found in square and contra dancing, was to segue eventually from one piece to another, perhaps playing each for several minutes (in the form ABABAB . . . CDCDCD . . .). American contra dance musicians—for the sake of their own sanity as well as the entertainment of dancers—often use this medley technique, typically moving to another song after repeating one for a few minutes. Galán (1983: 153, 190) claims that danzas must have been played this way, as a suite (*tanda*), just as were waltzes, *lanceros*, and quadrilles in the same period.

As mentioned above, Galán (1983: 150, 168–169), echoing León, further claims that danzas could be extended by means of some sort of improvisation or theme-and-variation practice, especially in the repetitions of the B section during the *cedazo*. The resultant form would then resemble a rondo, as shown below, with the C, D, and E (and so forth) sections constituting fresh transformations over the harmonic material of the B section:[31]

AA BB AA B′B′ AA B″B″

Galán notes that if the A (*prima*) sections were devoted to the relaxing *paseo*, the resultant form would bear marked similarity to the contemporary Spanish bolero, which was certainly known in Cuba (1983: 189–190).[32] More significantly, its rondo form—with the recurring A section—foreshadows that of the danzón (e.g., ABACAD). As such, Faílde's innovation of 1878 would have consisted primarily of composing and notating the varied B and C sections rather than allowing musicians simply to improvise them as variations (Galán 1983: 169, 213).

The technique of extending the contradanza by variation may also have been employed by pianists performing them as solo items, whether in a salon, a concert hall, or as an *entremes* between theater acts. In the absence of documentation, we are obliged to wonder whether the pianist would simply play one short contradanza—lasting barely a minute—after another, or if it would be extended through repetition incorporating semi-improvised variations. If the latter were the case, it might seem surprising that Saumell and his Cuban contemporaries did not notate any such variations, even as suggestions to performers. However, a few danzas by Saumell's friend Gottschalk do in fact contain written repeats in which embellishments are introduced; an example is his popular "Ojos criollos" ("Creole Eyes") in ABA′B′A′ form. Such notations might be taken as indicators of contemporary performance practice, just as several of Gottschalk's pieces document various popular tunes and rhythms that he heard in Cuba and elsewhere. The technique of repetition with variation has been perpetuated by at least one modern interpreter, French-Martinican pianist Georges Rabol, who applies it to his renditions of Saumell's contradanzas.[33] However, Mikowsky, who studied piano in Cuba in the 1960s, relates that most Cuban pedagogues of that era discouraged such practices, sharing the contemporary Parisian disapproval of Romantic virtuosos whose performances obscured the intentions of the composer behind their own self-indulgent interpretations (pers. comm.).

## Four Composers

The abundant ranks of contradanza composers in nineteenth-century Cuba included men and women, whites and blacks, professionals and amateurs, and aristocrats and artisans of varying degrees of talent. Deservedly or not, most of these are forgotten today, and, indeed, only two—Saumell and Cervantes—are likely to be known by anyone except Cuban musicologists. These two, together with the singular figures of Gottschalk and Lecuona, stand out conspicuously from the multitude and deserve special consideration.

### *Manuel Saumell*

Manuel Saumell Robredo (1817–70) was the leading contradanza composer of the heyday of the genre and is regarded as the father of Cuban musical nationalism. Carpentier's description of him and his milieu is so evocative that it merits quoting at length:

> Born in 1817 into a destitute family, Saumell was destined to die relatively young, after leading a scattered life full of disappointments. An acceptable but not brilliant pianist, he knew the kind of turmoil experienced by those who try to live by their art in a meager milieu, where ubiquity had to make up for slim earnings. He went anywhere to play an instrument. Sweating, huffing and puffing, he ran from the Philharmonic to the Lyceum of Cristina; he would second Raffelin in the Academía de Cristina; he gave lessons; played indiscriminately at dances and concerts; or shuffled behind the stage of the Italian lyric company. He performed Beethoven trios with Toribio Segura and Enrique González; he played cello when an empty music stand had to be filled; he orchestrated and arranged pieces; he would leave the palace of the count of Peñalver, where he had sung parts of *Il pirata*, to take sheet music of a contradanza to Tomás Buelta y Flores, director of the dance orchestra at the Tívoli. When the organist at some church was sick, there went Saumell to run his worn-out soles over the pedals. And he still had energy left to work on the piano with [European immigrant] Edelmann—although not seriously—and study harmony, counterpoint, fugue, and orchestration with Mauricio Pyke. . . . He was . . . a truly hard worker, sensitive, generous with others, demanding of himself; he was eager to achieve great things, inspired to great projects, but he was the perennial victim of the lack of time to compose, affecting anyone who attempts to wed dignity and decency with the dearth of lucrative work. (1946: 180–181; see also 2001: 186)[34]

Saumell's primary "great project" was the composition of the first Cuban nationalist opera, with a melodramatic libretto depicting the interactions of Indians and Spaniards in the early colonial period. Although it foreshadowed the vogue of nationalistic zarzuelas that would culminate in Lecuona a century later, the opera was never completed. As such, Saumell is better known for his over fifty contradanzas.

Given the Cuban contradanza's prior evolution, it may be incorrect to celebrate Saumell, as has often been done, as the father of the genre or even as having innovated and standardized its distinctive features. Nevertheless, Saumell is regarded as the first whose contradanzas transcended mediocrity and the first to achieve an artful synthesis of Cuban musical creolisms and European sophistication.

The Cuban contradanza is certainly a "small" music genre, both in its brevity and in its general avoidance of the virtuoso effects and harmonic and textural innovations that characterized much Romantic-era music. Nevertheless, within this miniaturist format, several of Saumell's contradanzas are regarded as masterpieces of invention and variety. Melodies and textures are diverse and effective, and the B sections embody a skillful balance of creole syncopation and light-classical poise. Although displaying none of the formal innovations found in the music of such European contemporaries as Liszt, his pieces are in other ways prescient; "La Tedezco" (included on this volume's compact disc and presented as Figure 2.7) foreshadows the danzón quite explicitly in the way the A section alternates a four-bar eighth-note theme with a four-bar answer in sixteenths—a cliché of the danzón.

Serafín Ramírez (1891: 69–71) distinguishes two broad categories of Saumell's contradanzas. One set is characterized by a deliberate simplicity and grace, with relatively straightforward right-hand melodies and left-hand accompaniment; Ramírez cites "Los ojos de Pepa," "La suavecita," "La paila," "Sopla que quema," and "La María" as outstanding examples of this style. In others, while the harmonies remain fairly simple, Saumell avails himself of a richer pallet of rubato phrasing, more varied left-hand parts, and more capricious melodies, as in "Los chismes," "Recuerdos tristes," "Lamentos de amor," and "Soledad."

Cuban musicologist Hilario González (1980) points out the variety and ingenuity of Saumell's rhythms and the challenges some of them pose to interpretation by the solo pianist. As shown in Figure 2.8, "Tu sonrisa" ("Your Smile") combines left-hand passages in waltz meter with right-hand melodies in straight duple meter; in "Luisiana"—excerpted in Figure 2.9 and played on this volume's compact disc—the combination of ternary and duple meters is even more challenging. Similar complex rhythms pervade "La niña bonita," excerpted in Figure 2.10. All involve an intricate tension between the ternary rhythm of the left hand and the binary pattern of the right. As González illustrates, Saumell was very precise in his rhythmic notations, such that pianists should avoid, for example, rendering the bass in the "Tu sonrisa" excerpt in the form of the familiar and easy 3-3-2 *tresillo* syncopation or obscuring the syncopations in a fog of rubato (1980: 30–31). Such notational intricacies are not unique to Saumell but are also found in the contradanzas of Tomás Ruíz, and, in different fashions, in Puerto Rican danzas and Haitian salon méringues.

Several of Saumell's contradanzas, such as "Recuerdos tristes" ("Sad Memories"), "Lamentos de amor" ("Laments of Love"), and "¡Toma, Tomás!" ("Drink/

Figure 2.7 "La Tedezco," by Manuel Saumell.

Figure 2.8 Excerpt of "Tu sonrisa," by Manuel Saumell.

**Figure 2.9** Excerpt of "Luisiana," by Manuel Saumell.

**Figure 2.10** Excerpt of "La niña bonita," by Manuel Saumell.

Take It, Tom"), were clearly meant to be played as salon piano pieces rather than as dance tunes rendered by ensembles (Carpentier 1946: 187). Nevertheless, given their tuneful and distinctive characters, even these pieces, like his others, were probably played by contemporary dance bands. At present, of course, their heyday is long over, but most Cuban pianists and a few serious music lovers would certainly be familiar with Saumell, and in Cuba and elsewhere the interested listener or musician can find recordings and scores of his contradanzas.

### *Louis Moreau Gottschalk*

It may seem curious to discuss here a North American musician who spent less than four years in Cuba, whose musical output includes only a handful of contradanzas among dozens of other more ambitious works, and whose surname was consistently mangled both as pronounced and written by Spanish-speaking Caribbeans. Nevertheless, Louis Moreau Gottschalk (1829–69) played a significant role in Cuban as well as Puerto Rican "contradanza culture," as a composer, a performer, and an inspiring friend and supporter of local musicians, so much so that such writers as Ramírez (in his oft-quoted *La Habana artística* of 1891: viii) are proud to claim him as one of their own.

Gottschalk was born and raised in New Orleans, speaking French and English and inheriting a familiarity with Caribbean creole culture and music from his mother—a white refugee from the Haitian Revolution—from family domestics, and from the prevailing ambience in New Orleans, at that time a thoroughly French-Caribbean city. From 1842 he resided and studied piano in Paris, heard Liszt, was praised by Chopin, befriended Berlioz, and eventually achieved some recognition as a virtuoso pianist by European audiences, who particularly enjoyed the flamboyant exoticism of his creole-flavored composition "Bamboulá." Nevertheless, the European concert scene was then in a difficult period of transition from courtly patronage to public stage shows, and Gottschalk's career soon became conditioned by a lifelong struggle to support himself and his numerous dependents. After returning to the United States in 1853, he departed for Havana in 1854 and spent much of the next six years in Cuba, Puerto Rico, and other Caribbean islands. In Cuba he quickly endeared himself to Saumell, Espadero, and other local musicians and became a celebrity on the concert circuit, performing works of European contemporaries alongside his own compositions. While most of the latter were for solo piano, others were Berlioz-inspired extravaganzas that could require hundreds of musicians; an 1860 concert presented in Havana involved an arsenal of forty pianists and a *tumba francesa* drum ensemble brought from Santiago. Audiences especially appreciated Gottschalk's fondness for incorporating local music into his repertoire, whether in the form of such genres as the danza, settings of popular tunes (such as the Santiago *comparsa* song "El cocoyé"), or even the prominent incorporation of Afro-Cuban rhythms and drums—an innovation not to recur until the avant-garde works of Amadeo Roldán and Alejandro García Caturla in the 1920s.[35]

Gottschalk contributed to the contradanza scene in various ways. While Cuban audiences did not require the contradanza to be legitimized by a foreign stamp of approval, they clearly appreciated the enthusiasm with which this colorful European-trained artist cultivated the genre. Gottschalk also foregrounded his Cuban-style contradanzas in his North American tours, with "Ojos criollos" becoming a particular favorite. Further, Gottschalk, who was clearly an engaging and urbane individual, was a source of great inspiration and friendship to Saumell, Espadero, and other musicians, several of whom dedicated contradanzas to him (such as Saumell's "Luisiana" and "Recuerdos de Gottschalk"). He also served as a tutor and mentor to Cervantes, the leading danza composer of the next generation, and was a particularly important model for Lecuona.

Finally, of course, there are Gottschalk's contradanzas (or danzas) themselves, of which at least seven survive, with several others never having been properly notated or published. On the whole, these conform to the contemporary norms of the genre, in their bipartite form, their reiteration of the amphibrach and habanera figures in melody and bass patterns, and their relatively straightforward harmonies. However, such contradanzas as "Souvenirs de la Havane" and "Réponds-moi!" foreground a virtuosic style less characteristic of the more restrained—and often dance-oriented—Cuban composers. His "El cocoyé" (1854) and his "Danza" (Opus 33, written in 1857) contain extended passages of repeated right-hand *cinquillos*, presumably imitating the style of Oriente popular songs. (More reflective of subsequent conventions in the danzón and Puerto Rican danza were aforementioned pieces, such as Coca's "Cambujá," in which the *cinquillo* alternates, in *clave* style, with an unsyncopated bar.)

As mentioned above, Gottschalk did not strictly limit his scores to the standard thirty-two-bar AABB form. While most of his danzas display A and B sections of the standard repeated sixteen bars, pieces like "Ojos criollos" are extended by repeats of the A and B sections, with minor embellishments, as in the form AABBAAB′B′. In "Souvenir de la Havane," the A and B sections are considerably expanded, to 65 and 196 bars, respectively. "Di que sí" ("Say Yes"; 1859) presents three variations on the B part, and "La gallina" (1865) has four. "Danza" (Opus 33), one of his more ambitious and influential works, represents a different strategy of expansion, with the inclusion of a C section that recurs in increasingly embellished form, in the structure: A-B-(B′)-A-B-(B″)-C-(c′c″c‴)-A-B-(B″). "Danza" is generally regarded as relating less to the Cuban danza tradition than the Puerto Rican counterpart, both for being composed in the latter island and for its inclusion of the C section, which would become a standard feature in the music of subsequent Puerto Rican composers. (Accordingly, Puerto Rican writer Salvador Brau, in an influential essay, celebrated Gottschalk's sensitivity and contributions to the island's danza tradition [(1885) 1977: 11–12].)

Despite the tuneful charm of his danzas, their inclusion of liberal amounts of rhetorical fluff earned them the disparagement of later critics, such as Carpentier, who lamented how their manneristic embellishments were destined to become "synonymous with bad taste" (1946: 202). Indeed, while Saumell and Cervantes admired and learned much from Gottschalk, some aficionados might well regard their works as surpassing those of Gottschalk in poise, depth, and lyricism.

### *Ignacio Cervantes*

The cultivation of the Cuban danza as an independent piano work continued in the works of Marín Varona and reached its zenith in the music of Ignacio Cervantes Kawanagh (1847–1905). Born to a well-to-do and culturally sophisticated family, Cervantes studied piano as a youth from Gottschalk and Espadero, and at eighteen commenced three years of study in Paris, where he received prestigious awards, befriended Liszt, Rossini, and other luminaries, and was in a position to embark on a career as a virtuoso soloist. Nevertheless, he returned to teach and concertize in Cuba, with its smaller, though not hopelessly provincial, music scene. An outspoken and active supporter of the anticolonial cause, he was exiled from Cuba from 1875 to 1879, during which period he resided in the United States; he later left Cuba again to live in Mexico during the final Cuban War of Independence. During his extended exile in New York City, he collaborated with nationalist José Martí and donated most of the profits from his composing to the independence struggle.

With ambitions nurtured by his Parisian grooming, he wrote an unfinished opera, two zarzuelas, some waltzes, a symphonic overture, and a *Scherzo Capriccioso*—all of which, despite the merits found in them by Carpentier (chap. 12), remain essentially forgotten. Instead, Cervantes is remembered for his twenty-one published danzas, which he himself seems to have regarded as being of little importance, belittling them as "musical smiles." Favorites like "Improvisada" and "Ilusiones perdidas" ("Lost Illusions") are still performed in Cuba today in various contexts, even if published scores—like so many things in Cuba's "special period"—are hard to come by. His "Los tres golpes" ("The Three Blows") was the signature theme for a classical music program on the Cuban radio for many years. The danzas of Cervantes range from the lyrical, such as "Ilusiones perdidas," to the festive, such as "Los muñecos" ("The Dolls"), whose score at one point instructs the pianist to beat rhythmically on the top of the piano. "El velorio" ("The Wake") was intended to be accompanied by a whimsical dialogue about a deceased acquaintance.

Cervantes's danzas, composed primarily in New York between 1875 and 1895, adhere to the conventional form of two sixteen-bar sections, with the second featuring the syncopated habanera rhythm. Despite his own technical virtuosity and his mastery of the dazzling bravura pieces of Liszt, his danzas are restrained and lyrical rather than showy or bombastic. Hence, while Carpentier likens him to Chopin, it is the Chopin of the elegantly understated mazurkas rather than the grandiloquent scherzos and polonaises:[36]

> Cervantes expressed himself with sobriety, without saturating the staves. . . . His line is always precise, clear, bare, with great airy spaces between the notes. Without having to quote popular melodies, Cervantes managed to distill an artful, subtle Cuban creole character, in a way that could only constitute the culmination, and the end, of an era and a genre. . . . In his time, the contradanza was at the end of its rhythmic and melodic evolution—black rhythm, European melody—which had lasted more than eighty years. . . . When Cervantes appeared, this genre had reached the limit of its possibilities, having supported all of the rhythmic combinations that were admissible within a binary measure. (2001: 210–212).

Included on this volume's compact disc are two representative danzas of Cervantes, "Los tres golpes" and "Ilusiones perdidas." The former, shown as Figure 2.11, is typical of many contemporary danzas in its eight-bar phrases whose second halves—like the B section as a whole—are laden with amphibrachs, giving a slight hint of the jauntiness that would enliven the similarly syncopated ragtime of Joplin and others a few years later. The title refers to the three chords that recur in and conclude the piece. In "Ilusiones perdidas," a lyrical opening melody is accompanied by *tresillos* in the left hand and leads to a satisfying climax in the short space of thirty-two bars.

Both Cervantes and Saumell present the pianist with particular challenges of interpretation. Their initial editions—primarily by Edelmann—provide only minimal phrasing and no indications of tempo. Publishers of subsequent edi-

**Figure 2.11** "Los tres golpes," by Ignacio Cervantes.

tions of Cervantes have suggested widely divergent tempi and have generously adorned his scores with phrase markings (which a knowledgeable pianist might well choose to ignore).[37] Recorded versions have varied accordingly. French pianist Georges Rabol renders "Ilusiones perdidas" (shown as Figure 2.12) as a bouncy, Joplinesque rag, while most other pianists aim to express the sober

**Figure 2.12** "Ilusiones perdidas," by Ignacio Cervantes.

wistfulness suggested by the title. While titles of most contradanzas may simply consist of random phrases, Cuban American pianist Mirta Gómez (pers. comm.) points out that especially in the age of programmatic music, other titles give clear indications to the performer. Hence the title "Adios a Cuba" ("Farewell to Cuba")—written by the exiled Cervantes—naturally suggests a certain poignancy of interpretation, while Saumell's obliquely insurrectionary "El somaten" (in Catalan: "Som atents" ["On Guard!"]) calls for a martial rather than lyrical presentation.

Gómez also stresses the importance of playing Saumell and Cervantes with a strong sense of *sandunga*, implying not necessarily a blithe sauciness but a pronounced interpretive flair, to avoid the monotony that might result from an academic rendering of these pieces. A challenge for the pianist is to enliven the pieces with such expressivity while respecting their structure, just as the interpreter must also respect Saumell's rigorously precise rhythmic notations while rendering them with the rubato sometimes appropriate. Some indication of the remarkable expressive range of Cervantes's pieces is audible in unpublished recordings made by his daughter María (1885–1981), an extraordinary pianist, vocalist, and stage personality.

### *Postscript to the Danza: Ernesto Lecuona*

By the late 1870s the Cuban danza had largely exhausted itself as an original musical genre, and its fate as a popular contemporary dance genre was sealed when the danzón burst on the scene in 1879. Among the hundreds of records documented in Cristóbal Díaz Ayala's discography of early Cuban records, only a single danza appears, alongside dozens of danzones and *sones* (1994: 339). However, the history of the danza cannot be regarded as ending so abruptly. Danzas continued to be popular in the first two decades of the twentieth century; Emilio Grenet, writing in the late 1930s, attested, "Only twenty years ago it was the highlight which ended our dances" (1939: 31). Further, the genre had already given birth to another set of descendants, who flourished while preserving some of their progenitor's most traditional features. Its most immediate scion was the Puerto Rican danza, which, appropriately outliving its parent, thrived until the 1930s. Specific aspects of the Cuban danza were also perpetuated in other genres, as with the use of bipartite form in the theater *guajira* standardized by Anckermann around 1900. In Cuba, with the advent of radio in 1922 and the new opportunities it presented for crooning over varied accompanimental styles, a few *canciones*—romantic songs not intended for dancing—were set to danza accompaniments (Galán 1983: 206), more or less as happened contemporaneously with Puerto Rican and Dominican danzas. Further, as I discuss below, the derivative habanera took on its own life in the erstwhile metropole, Spain.

Meanwhile, a few Cuban composers continued to explore the danza as a piano idiom, with a self-consciously nationalistic, neotraditional orientation.

These included Rafael Pastor (1860–1943), Anckermann (1877–1941), the youthful Alejandro García Caturla, and María Cervantes, who authored six danzas in the style of her father. However, far better known and more distinctively original in style were the danzas of composer and concert pianist Ernesto Lecuona (1895–1963). Lecuona was the most internationally renowned Cuban musician of the first half of the twentieth century and was in his own way a titan of Cuban music. He was particularly celebrated as a keyboard virtuoso and as a composer of zarzuelas; even more popular than his zarzuelas per se have been their tuneful boleros and *canciones*, such as "María la O" and "Siboney," which took on independent lives as evergreens of Cuban popular song. His impressionistic tribute to Andalusian music, "Malagueña," must rank with Pachelbel's canon as one of the half dozen most popular classical or light-classical pieces of all time. While recording extensively and tirelessly touring Europe, the United States, and Cuba, he managed to compose prolifically, registering some 156 piano compositions alongside zarzuelas, songs, and other works. Lecuona's output abounds in stylized elements of Cuban creole music; during a period of intense racism in Cuba, many of his pieces explicitly foregrounded Afro-Cuban themes, as indicated in titles like "La danza negra" ("Black Dance"; 1925), "Danza de los ñañigos" ("Dance of the Ñañigos" [members of an Afro-Cuban society]; 1930), and his various "danzas afrocubanas."

While these pieces contributed in their own way to the legitimization of Afro-Cuban culture in Cuba and abroad, in their populist, accessible character they were antithetical in spirit to the avant-garde *afrocubanismo* of his contemporaries Roldán and Caturla, who seem to have regarded him with a mixture of scorn and envy; their collaborator and friend, Carpentier, accorded Lecuona not even a footnote in his otherwise exhaustive and even-handed *La música en Cuba*. Aficionados of classical music tended to regard Lecuona as having failed to develop his prodigious potential as a pianist and composer, devoting it instead to frivolous collaborations with Hollywood studios and the likes of bandleader Xavier Cugat. Nevertheless, in his day Lecuona enjoyed extraordinary popularity, both internationally and among Cubans, as what has been aptly called "a serious composer of popular music and a popular composer of serious music" (Jacobsen 1982: 6).

Of special relevance here is Lecuona's single-handed revival of the danza. Between 1910 and 1930 he composed over seventy piano danzas, which he presented as concert stage items, often for international audiences, rather than intimate salon pieces or dance accompaniment tunes. While several were never registered in any form, the rest were variously published for solo piano, multiple pianos, or piano with an added sung text. Lecuona's danzas reflect something of the Romantic-era spirit of his friend Ravel. His biographer Orlando Martínez writes, "In general, the danzas of Lecuona are picturesque and descriptive, but in many of them there is an inner world, an intimate world, subjectivism. They are like brief shreds of the inner life, artfully drawn with a light smile or a hidden tear" (1989: 80). Lecuona's best-known danzas are those in the three sets,

"Danzas Cubanas" (published in the 1920s), "Danzas Afrocubanas" (1930), and "Nineteenth-Century Cuban Danzas." The most popular in the first set was "La comparsa," composed when Lecuona was fifteen, set over a persistent left-hand altered *cinquillo.* A *comparsa* is a carnival procession with Afro-Cuban singing and drumming; accordingly, "La comparsa," while not imitating specific rhythms or tunes, is a programmatic piece whose soft beginning, vigorous middle section, and diminuendo conclusion are meant to evoke the sound of a rowdy street procession approaching and then moving out of earshot.

In terms of style, most of his danzas are conservative and even conventional, harmonically more suggestive of Schubert than of Scriabin and of 1830 rather than 1930, although at the same time more Romantic in flavor than those of Cervantes. Most—especially but not exclusively the self-consciously neoclassicist "Nineteenth-Century Cuban Dances"—adhere to the stock eight-bar phrases, diatonic melodies, and familiar, obvious harmonic schemes of the mid-nineteenth-century Cuban contradanza and even popular song. While Lecuona was a celebrated virtuoso at the keyboard, the danzas are largely free of showy display and in fact are rather tame and homogeneous in texture; some critics might opine that they lack the variety and concise lyricism of Saumell and Cervantes. Several depart from the conventional bipartite form: Those in the "Danzas Cubanas" set are in ABA form; among representative others, "A la Antigua" has an expanded B section; "Danza interrumpida" has only one section, which is repeated; while still others are supplemented by a third section. Several, like "¡No hables más!" have an improvisatory flavor or certainly give the impression of having been composed without excessive deliberation. Although scrutiny naturally reveals a fair amount of variety, several, such as "La comparsa," "Danza lucumí," "¿Por qué te vas?" or "Lola está de fiesta," reflect a somewhat standardized format, especially in the A section: The left hand opens with and maintains a syncopated ostinato, while the right plays a simple, diatonic melody in octaves, perhaps with an added tenth, set to an utterly conventional, tonic-dominant-based harmonic scheme (e.g., V–I–V–I–VI–ii–V–I); creole rhythms of *cinquillo*, amphibrach, and habanera abound in left- and right-hand parts.

## Cuban Contradanza contra Anglo-American Contra Dance: A Comparison and Contrast

At this point a brief digression might help contextualize Cuban contradanza culture, insofar as we can reconstruct it, by comparing it with the English country dance and contra dance as are cultivated today by networks of enthusiasts throughout the United States. (The primary distinction between country and contra dance, as practiced today, is that contra dancing is more vigorous and aerobic, especially involving partner swings, and more Americanized than the relatively staid English country dance.) The musical and choreographic affinities between the American and Cuban contradance traditions are numerous and overt. Musically, both feature instrumental thirty-two-bar compositions, in AABB form, with clear-cut eight-bar phrases, simple harmonies, and diatonic melodies. (Both are traditionally notated in the form of reductions, as piano scores, in the case of the contradanza, and as melodic "lead sheets" in the case of contra dances.) The composition is repeated indefinitely and, in a longer dance, might eventually segue to one or more other tunes to avoid monotony (especially as experienced by the musicians). In American country/contra dancing, as was presumably the case in the Caribbean, both old and new tunes from diverse sources are performed. Binary meter predominates, although jigs (in 6/8) and waltzes are also used in country/contra dancing, just as many Cuban contradanzas were in 6/8 time (and could themselves be interspersed with waltzes, rigodóns, and other items in a soirée). As in Cuban contradanzas, the instrumentation can vary depending on resources available, with a solo piano sufficing if need be.

Choreographically, both country/contra dances and Cuban contradanzas are based on the longways format, and many of the figures, as directed by the caller/bastonero, are the same, albeit with different names (e.g., "star" and *molino*). Several figures divide the two lines into smaller groups ("minor set," or, in Spanish, a *cuadrilla*). Finally, we can judge from colonial-era accounts that in the Cuban contradanza of the past, as in modern country/contra dancing, the general ambience was one of informal, unpretentious, and collective fun, in contrast, for example, to the hyper-refined and formal minuet or, for that matter, to the virtuoso pyrotechnics of salsa dancing.

Nevertheless, musical and sociomusical differences between the Cuban and American traditions are quite readily visible. The Spanish Caribbean contradanza, as we have seen, typically features more creole rhythms (the habanera rhythm or the *cinquillo*) in its second section, standardizing a contrast between A and B sections that is not characteristic of country/contra dance jigs and reels. Further, Cuban and Puerto Rican contradanzas were avidly cultivated as parlor piano pieces to an extent not typical of the English country and contra dance at any time during its history. In general, while the country dance constituted a significant aspect of English nationalism at times, it may be said that the Cuban contradanza as a musical genre enjoyed a prodigious prominence and even pre-eminence during its heyday, serving as a symbol of creole national culture, to an extent largely uncharacteristic of English and American country/contra dance. Accordingly, Cuban piano students today still learn light-classical contradanzas by Saumell and Cervantes, who have no particular counterparts in country/contra dance history. In that respect, the American country/contra dance scene bears greater resemblance to the Caribbean quadrille. Both country dance and quadrille have continued to the present primarily as folk or neo-folk traditions, with amateur musicians in ad hoc ensembles drawing freely from a set of conventional tunes and dancers who enjoy the conviviality and the pleasure of being able to dance in a style that is not especially demanding.

Meanwhile, the Cuban contradanza, for all its vitality in the nineteenth century, has fared poorly in comparison to the country and contra dance in the United States. As a social dance tradition the Cuban contradanza has been effectively defunct since the early 1900s. Revivalist clubs of contradanza aficionados in Cuba do not seem to exist. By contrast, the English country dance and the more Americanized contra dance—however "old-timey" they may be in character, and however marginal they may be to mainstream popular culture—are avidly practiced by networks of enthusiasts and clubs throughout much of the United States, with weekly dances at churches and social halls, and larger conventions every few months (sometimes overlapping with other folk-music revival circuits). Square dancing, a rural, predominantly nineteenth-century tradition incorporating quadrilles and contras, underwent an urban-based revival in the 1920s, and in the 1970s contra dancing experienced a fresh renaissance as an oppositional youth subcultural activity. As can be gleaned from attending a contemporary country/contra dance or even visiting the Web site of the Country Dance and Song Society (http://cdss.org), country dancing is a living tradition rather than a fossilized revival sustained by eccentric losers. Participants enjoy not only familiar tunes and dances but also new songs and especially new dances that are composed—usually by recombining familiar figures—by known individuals (typically with their own Web sites, booklets, and compact discs). Such performers and composers will not be seen on *American Idol*, nor will their works be reviewed in the *New York Times*, but collectively they animate a fairly dynamic contradance music and dance culture that has no analogue in the Caribbean.

## His Majesty the Danzón

In 1879—the year after the truce ending the decade-long First War of Independence—mulatto bandleader and composer Miguel Faílde debuted a tuneful piece, "Las Alturas de Simpson,"[38] which he called a "danzón," at a fashionable ball in Matanzas, inaugurating the heyday of that genre and the definitive eclipse of the danza as a genre of contemporary interest. In preceding years the Cuban danzón, by that name or not, had already become popular in local dances and was soon incorporated into the repertoire of Havana *orquestas* like that of Raimundo Valenzuela. The danzón (literally, a big danza) was the immediate successor to the danza, in terms of both dance and music. It constituted a vast genre, reigning as the national dance of Cuba for over fifty years, being avidly cultivated in Puerto Rico and the Dominican Republic, and enjoying a particularly distinguished career in Mexico, where it outlasted its Cuban counterpart. As such, it merits its own book-length treatment rather than a cursory review. Moreover, its inclusion in the present study is of arguable propriety, as the danzón's status in the contradance family is ambiguous and in some ways marginal. Hence this chapter provides only a brief and admittedly sketchy survey of the genre.

The danzón, in its classic form that crystallized in the 1880s, differed from the danza primarily in its rondo-like form (with repeating A section, as in the scheme ABACAD), its prominent use of the *cinquillo* in melody and accompaniment, and its independent couple dancing. However, as suggested above, neither did the danzón appear from a vacuum nor did it immediately eclipse the danza. Danzón dancers, for example, might indulge in the archaic *paseo* and an occasional *latigazo*. Further, as mentioned above, the genre's rondo format may have merely formalized a musical practice already embryonic in danza renditions. Moreover, the *cinquillo* in its two-bar *clave*-style format had appeared in aforementioned contradanzas like "Cambujá" and "¡Ave María Gallo!" and presumably had been a standard percussion accompaniment figure for danzas in the 1870s if not earlier. For some years the terms continued to be used inconsistently, with straightforward contradanzas of the 1890s being confusingly labeled "danzón" and, conversely, 1920s danzones in Santiago being referred to as "danzas."[39] Hence Galán (1983: 201) and a few other scholars regard the 1879 creation date as inaccurate and artificial.

In several ways, however, the danzón was novel, and its rapid ascent to popularity was dramatic. The collective figures were forgotten and the bastonero banished, as intimate couple dancing reigned supreme. The jaunty *cinquillo* (in its creole two-bar form) now emerged as a ubiquitous recurring ostinato. In general, the Afro-Caribbean tinge that had subtly enlivened the danza now became unmistakable and overwhelming, in the insistent *cinquillos*, the obstreperous percussion, and the sensually swaying hips of the dancers. Traditionalists fulminated, either denouncing the rowdy music or, like musicologist and composer Eduardo Sánchez de Fuentes, insisting that it had no African influence.[40] However, their battle was soon lost, and the danzón, as played primarily by black and mulatto musicians, became the new focus of dancers and listeners of all classes and races.

As we have seen, the danzón's sectional rondo form crystallized and elaborated a suite format already present in various other genres. Choreographically, the danzón's alternation of danced sections with relaxed strolling could be seen as perpetuating the danza's optional format of alternating *paseo* and *cedazo* sections, as well as the structure of the Spanish bolero. Cuban dancers and musicians were familiar with the four-part quadrille (*cuadrilla*) and five-part Lancers and rigodón. The rondo form can also be seen as an extension of the practice of repeating the bipartite danza with variations in the B sections, as in the featured instrumental solos in the sectional danzas of Tomás Ruiz. The danzón, in its classic form, overcame the potential monotony of the repeated danza by substituting fresh material in these sections, typically affording a formal scheme of ABACA.

From around 1910, as discussed below, it became standard to add a harmonically static, ostinato-driven coda, akin to the *montuno* of a *son*, typically resulting in an ABACAD form. The A section retained the character of a classical theme, like the *prima* of a contradanza of Saumell. It could be treated as an introduction, during which dancers would stroll arm in arm, in *paseo* style; however, its assertive, even pompous character also tended to give it the character of a refrain. Under Faílde's leadership, the new sections (which could generically be called "*otra*," or "other") soon acquired conventional formats, with the *primera* (B) typically featuring the clarinet, and the more placid *segunda* (C) the violins. As new melodic material was required for these sections, composers and arrangers helped themselves to whatever popular tunes were circulating. This predatory practice relieved the burden on the composer's muse and offered listeners the pleasure of hearing familiar melodies transformed into perky danzones. Hence the danzón soon became an omnivorous consumer of melodies. As one observer in Matanzas wrote, "These *danzones* based on melancholy African music, in an artistic hodgepodge most pleasurable to the ear, entertain us with passages of popular fragments of Italian opera, Spanish zarzuelas, French operettas, and Cuban *canciones*, all in the distinctive cadence and harmony [of the danzón]."[41] Themes from popular zarzuelas and operas, such as *The Barber of Seville*, were particular favorites, but the sources ranged widely, encompassing boleros, ragtime tunes, street vendor calls, *sones*, rumbas, Spanish *cuplés*, and pentatonic Chinese-Cuban melodies, such as that which opens José Urfé's familiar "El bombín de Barreto." Yet, as Carpentier (1946: 240) notes, despite such eclecticism the danzón generally retained an elegant classicism, with its Neapolitan passages in thirds, its common themes for trumpets in fifths, and phrases in strict eighteenth-century proportions. A more local sort of classicist cliché, foreshadowed in Saumell's "La Tedezco," consisted of an opening theme of four bars of 2/4 in eighth notes, followed by another four in sixteenth notes. Figure 2.13 shows the theme of the A section of "El bombín de Barreto," together with the standard rhythmic ostinatos that would be rendered on timpani or *güiro*:

> *cinquillo* / eighth notes / *cinquillo* / eighth notes /
> *cinquillo* / *cinquillo* / *cinquillo* / two eighth notes

Figure 2.13 "El bombín de Barreto," opening.

In subsequent sections of the danzón, the *cinquillo* would typically alternate in a more regular fashion with a bar of eighth notes; if in that order, the resulting two-bar pattern cohered with what modern Latin musicians would call "three-two" *clave* (as shown in Figure 1.2); if in the reverse order, it would suggest "two-three" *clave*. The *clave* sticks themselves occasionally sounded this pattern on early recordings. However, while in post-1950s recordings of *son* and salsa the same *clave* pattern (whether "three-two" or "two-three") is rigorously maintained throughout a song, in the danzón, as in contemporary *son* recordings, sections might alternate.[42]

Until the 1920s the danzón was generally played by an *orquesta típica* consisting of cornetín (carrying most of the melodies), two clarinets, two violins, valve trombone, an ophicleide, contrabass, *güiro* scraper, and one or two timbales or small timpani. This ensemble, while inheriting elements from military bands, is better seen as an updated version of the ensembles that typically performed danzas. It also bore significant affinities to the ragtime and early jazz bands of nearby New Orleans—a sister Caribbean city very much influenced by French Creole culture and sharing quadrilles and other repertoirial items. Most of the musicians were petty-bourgeois blacks and mulattos, many of them also pursuing the daytime profession of tailor traditional among many Caribbean musicians. In more humble circumstances danzones could also be performed by a *bunga* consisting of piano, flute, violin, and bass. Between 1910 and 1920—as the ten-piece *orquesta típica* found itself competing with the *son* septets and sextets—Antonio Romeu popularized a sort of enlarged *bunga* consisting of piano, wooden flute, two violins, bass, and percussion, which came to be called "charanga francesa," or merely "charanga." "Charanga" has long been a Cuban term for any sort of unpretentious ensemble. As Díaz Ayala (1994: 134) points out, there is nothing particularly French about the "French charanga"; rather, the "francesa" seems to have been added to dignify the name for this ensemble format, which soon became standardized. As Galán (1983: 203–204) notes, the presence of the piano liberated the flute and violins from outlining harmonies, enabling them to play more virtuoso melodic passages, in many cases of a classical flavor.

In the latter 1920s, pieces like Aniceto Diaz's "Rompiendo la rutina" popularized the *danzonete*, a danzón with a sung text, in a format that came to enjoy much greater popularity than the danza-style *canciones* that appeared in the 1920s (as well as ephemeral danzones of the 1880s featuring texts added to the finale). The *danzonete* could be seen as a means of competing with the increasingly popular *son* and as a way of using the radio format and recording media that enabled a gently crooning voice to be heard over instruments (even if amplification of the voice in live concerts did not come into common use until around 1950). The microphone and the incorporation of the *danzonete* into the new world of commercial popular song enabled crooners like Pablo Quevedo to become pop idols for a new generation of urban consumers.

Another sort of innovation was presented in José Urfé's aforementioned "El bombín de Barreto" of 1910, in the form of a final section that consisted of a montuno—that is, a harmonically static vamp, emphasizing rhythmic ostinatos played by all instruments. Galán (1983: 205) suggests that such codas might have been freely appended in earlier years, but it is certainly Urfé's still-familiar piece that popularized and codified the practice. In the 1920s, instrumental solos began to be inserted in this coda, and a distinctive "Latin" style of piano improvisation began to evolve, especially as cultivated by Romeu (see Manuel 1998: 131). By the 1940s the composite rhythm used in the coda had dispensed with the *cinquillo* and evolved into a distinctive, *son*-influenced set of interlocking ostinatos that Antonio Arcaño and Orestes López called "mambo." In the early 1950s, Enrique Jorrín's addition of sung texts over through-composed harmonic progressions set to this rhythm inaugurated the chachachá. Around the same time, Pérez Prado, Machito (Frank Grillo), and Tito Puente popularized the big band mambo, which can be seen as adapting the same rhythms of the danzón coda, in greatly accelerated form, to a swing jazz-style big band, using standard techniques of sectional arrangement.

Included on this volume's compact disc is a representative early danzón, "El biberón de Benitín" ("Benitín's Nursing Bottle"), recorded by the Orquesta of Enrique Peña in 1918.[43] The form is ABACA with a coda. The theme of the A section displays the conventional, if not clichéd structure foreshadowed in Saumell's "La Tedezco," consisting of a four-bar melody followed by a four-bar sixteenth-note run. The theme of the coda, resembling the familiar "Peanut Vendor," is taken from "Punto de Nano." Variety is provided, as usual, by altering the instrumentation of the sections, with the trumpet leading the first section, the clarinet leading the second, and so on.

## Habanera, Tango, and the Return to Spain

In 1841 a café in Havana's Plaza de Armas featured the debut of an innovative item: a vocal song, "El amor en el baile," set to the subdued but sultry creole rhythm of the contradanza. A few months later, a newspaper published the piece, designating it a "*canción habanera*" (i.e., "Havana-style song"). The item evidently enjoyed some popularity, and the new genre, like the European waltzes with sung lyrics that were coming into vogue just then, soon ceased to raise eyebrows. Unlike the odd *contradanza cantada* or sung contradanza that had occasionally surfaced, or the aforementioned practice of singing ditties to the catchy tunes of danza B sections,[44] the new form of *canción* was intended for listening rather than for dance and went on to be cultivated, somewhat marginally, either as a sort of urban folksong for two singers and guitar or as a salon item for voice and piano (Martín 1999: 32).

While it never came to rival subsequent vocal idioms like the bolero or *canción* in Cuba itself, the genre inspired the muse of Basque composer Sebastian Yradier (formerly Iradier; 1819–65), who may have visited Cuba in the 1850s. Sometime around then he published a song in Madrid, "La paloma," whose tuneful strain, set over the gently lilting rhythm of the danza's B section, went on to become one of the most familiar tunes worldwide (see Figure 2.14). In 1864 he published in Paris—as a "*chanson havanaise*" (again, Havana-style song)—another composition, "El arreglito," similar in style, tunefulness, and subsequent popularity. Both songs, and others composed in their wake, became known outside Cuba as "habaneras," the latter term evidently arising as an abbreviation of "*canción habanera*" or "*contradanza habanera*" (i.e., "Havana-style contradanza").[45] Opening phrases of both tunes contain the figure of an eighth-note triplet followed by two eighths—a sort of rubato-style amphibrach that recurred in many contradanzas. Bizet, thinking "El arreglito" was a folk song, adapted its tune for his famed "habanera" of *Carmen* (1875). Emilio Grenet, reflecting on the ambiguous status of Yradier's songs, wrote, "We, the Cubans, do not know what nationality to assign to 'La Paloma,' and if we wish to consider it as Cuban, considering that Yradier resided in Cuba some time, we could only do so by virtue of naturalization" (1939: 23).

**Figure 2.14** "La paloma" commencement, by Sebastian Yradier.

In Cuba itself, the term "habanera"—rather as happened with "salsa"—was only adopted subsequent to its international popularization, coming in the latter 1800s to denote a languid, romantic, and melancholy song, whose quintessential exemplars are José White's "Bella cubana" and Sánchez de Fuentes's "Tu" of 1892. (Cuban musicologists have been accordingly reluctant to speak of the "habanera" rhythm, generally preferring to call it the "tango" or "conga" rhythm.[46]) Habaneras also became popular in Cuban zarzuelas (light operas), as in their peninsular Spanish counterparts, which flourished in the decades around 1900. Salon habaneras also came to be cultivated in Venezuela, Mexico, Argentina, and elsewhere in Latin America (Martín 1999: 57). In Europe, the habanera went on to be cultivated as a lesser, slightly exotic concert piece, by Debussy (e.g., in *La puerto del vino*, 1913), Ravel (in his *Rapsodía española*, 1898), Chabrier (*Habanera para piano*, 1895), Saint Saens (for solo violin, 1887), and other French late Romantics. However, the habanera's true vogue as a living vernacular genre occurred in Spain. In fact, the habanera flourished in Spain in at least three entirely different forms. One of these was as a song form in the Spanish zarzuela, which thrived primarily from the 1850s to the 1930s. Alongside *seguidillas*, *romanzas*, paso dobles, and other contemporary popular song forms, many zarzuelas featured tuneful songs variously labeled "tango," "tango americano," or "habanera."[47] On the whole, these terms were used more or less interchangeably to denote a song with a short introduction and an accompaniment based on what had come to be known as the "habanera rhythm." The instrumentation, style, and texture are those of light opera rather than a Havana nightclub. Several habaneras, even before the advent of the mass media, became—and remain—as familiar as pop hits, such as "¿Dónde vas con mantón de Manila?" ("Where Are You Going with That Shawl from Manila?") from Tomás Breton's *La verbena de la Paloma* (1894), or, for that matter, the Neapolitan habanera "O sole mio."

Meanwhile, in the decades around 1900 quite a distinct kind of habanera took root in Spanish port towns in Cataluña, Valencia, Murcia, Asturias, Galicia, and elsewhere. Like other lyric song forms associated with maritime cities (such as the Lisbon fado), these habaneras sang of the longing and pangs of separation generated by sea travel. More specifically, they sang of Cuba, which so many thousands of Spaniards had visited in those decades, whether as soldiers, sailors, merchants, or migrant workers. For many thousands of Catalans, Galicians, and others, Havana was a more familiar and inviting city than Madrid. Hence despite the sufferings endured by so many soldiers in the War of Independence, the habaneras, like the flamenco-style *guajiras* popular at that time (see Manuel 2004: 147–148), idealized Cuba as a land of palm trees, flowers, sea breezes, and lovely *mulatas* left behind:

> Tropical nights, full of perfume, that invade my being
> The silvery moon that shines in the sea
> The nightingale sings its love over the murmuring of the sea.
> The gentle breeze caresses the palm tree, while the moon illuminates a flower. . . .
> I feel in my heart the pain of knowing that you'll never be with me again.
> (In Lafuente Aguado 1990: 290)

Once this lyric tradition was established, it took on its own life and affective significance, such that it was no longer necessary for a poet to have actually visited Cuba in order to sing wistfully of it; Cuba had become a sort of exotic Orient for Spain.[48] Depending on locale, lyrics could be in Castilian, Catalan, Galician, or even Basque. Despite the genre's name and the lyrics' frequent invocation of Cuba, such habaneras are seen as thoroughly Spanish rather than imported, and many songs have passed into oral tradition, such that their place of origin—whether Cuba or Spain—is no longer known (see Martín 1999: 70).

Most such habaneras were written by amateur or semiprofessional tunesmiths and were sung by amateurs at family gatherings, as sidewalk serenades, or at formal or informal musical soirées. Despite the decline of some of these contexts under the impact of modernization (Lafuente Aguado 1990: 11–22), habaneras continue to be actively performed, especially by amateur groups at formal concerts, most typically by two, three, or four vocalists, accompanied variously by accordion and/or stringed instruments. The tradition remains particularly strong in Torrevieja. The songs are rendered in languid tempo, with the softly swaying habanera rhythm pervading melody and voice. As in the other habanera styles described here, melodies also typically featured the closely related amphibrach, *tresillo*, and triplet eighth-note patterns, as in the commencement of Yradier's "La paloma," which also constitutes an evergreen in this tradition.

A third habanera tradition in Spain has been that of the "concert" habanera (or "tango"), cultivated as a nineteenth-century light-classical idiom especially by Isaac Albeníz and Manuel de Falla, and in the twentieth century by Cristóbal Halffter, Xavier Montsalvatge, and others. The habaneras of Falla and Albeniz, while identified as Cuban in inspiration, were included in sets devoted to distinctively Spanish music (such as Albeniz's *Suite española*), reflecting how thoroughly Cuba and its habanera were identified as Spanish before 1898 (see Nuñez 1998: 194). For their part, the habaneras of Halffter and Montsalvatge are short works, typically for piano with or without voice, set to the gentle habanera ostinato, and perhaps, as with Montsalvatge, artfully adorned with neoclassicist "wrong" notes and late-Romantic harmonies.[49] In spirit they are somewhat akin to the aforementioned habaneras of Debussy, Ravel, and their French impressionist contemporaries.

As a footnote to the history of the habanera and its trademark ostinato, mention must be made of the remarkable persistence of this pattern in the Cuban-derived bolero, an offspring of the habanera that became a pan–Latin American genre from the 1930s, and in the chachachá of the 1950s onward. The habanera rhythm, whether deriving from that genre, the contradanza itself, or an older common source, also figures prominently in the Mexican danza, the Paraguayan *canción*, the Brazilian *maxixe*, and the Argentine *milonga* and early tango. More recently, the pattern has resurfaced again as an up-tempo percussion ostinato in Trinidadian soca and, lastly, in reggaetón, which exploded on the music scene in the years after 2000 (see Figures 2.15–2.16).

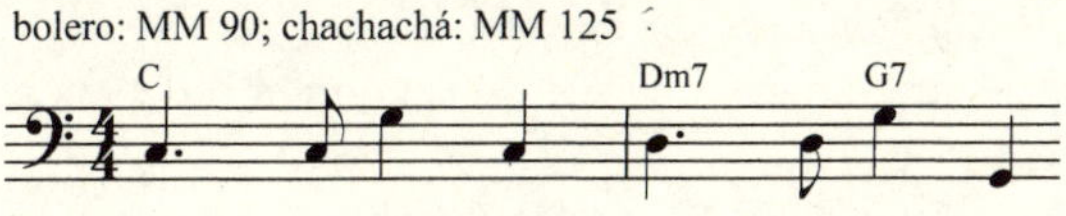


**Figure 2.15** Bolero and chachachá ostinatos.

**Figure 2.16** Soca and reggaetón ostinatos.

## *Tumba Francesa*

If the elegant, slightly "precious" habaneras of Montsalvatge represent the most distilled, Europeanized branch of the Cuban contradanza family, at the other end of the gamut lies the *masón* dance of the *tumba francesa*, in which contradanza choreographic figures are accompanied by thunderous neo-African drumming. The *tumba francesa* appears to be a product of the more than fifteen thousand Afro-Haitians who immigrated, along with Frenchmen and creoles, to eastern Cuba during the Haitian Revolution, primarily in 1802. (Another fifty thousand immigrated between 1913 and 1921.) Haitian slaves had for decades enjoyed imitating their masters' contradanzas and minuets, often in creolized forms. In Santiago de Cuba, Guantánamo, and surrounding towns, free and enslaved descendants of the Afro-Haitian immigrants, typically bilingual in Spanish and French Creole, recreated and creatively transformed many aspects of their traditional culture. In the 1880s, they formed recreational clubs (like the *cabildos* of Havana and Matanzas) that came to be called *sociedades de tumba francesa*, taking their name from the dance fiesta that constituted their central activity (see Alén 1986: chap. 1). Three of these clubs remain active today, performing dances for their own entertainment and in various quasi-folkloric contexts.

*Tumba francesa* dances are remarkable combinations of the European and the African. The latter elements are most conspicuous in the second section of the *yubá*, called *frenté*, in which a man dances solo in front of percussionists who pound out 12/8 polyrhythms, in typical West African–derived style, with the lead drummer straddling his Congolese-derived *premier* (or *mamomier*) drum on the floor. It is particularly in the first section of the *yubá masón* dance ("Masonic," presumably, or perhaps from *maison*, [the slave master's] "house") that such neo-African musical features are conjoined with contradance figures of clear eighteenth-century derivation. In the opening section of the *yubá*, the dancers are arrayed in longways format, in two lines. In the *masón*, directed by the shouts and whistles of a *mayor de la plaza* (the caller) and accompanied by vigorous drumming in duple meter, dancers execute a fairly standardized suite of figures, typically including circle, double circle, *molinete* (cf. the *molina* described above), *cadena* with "S" figure (also described earlier), "tunnel," and, finally, as in the contradanza's *cedazo*, a section of independent couple dancing (Armas Rigal 1991).

While nineteenth-century accounts of Afro-Caribbean dancing and even of related creole dances like the *tumba dominicana* often remarked on their perceived lewdness, there is nothing particularly suggestive or even distinctively Afro-Caribbean about the *masón* dance, which resembles instead various contradance variants. The Afro-Caribbean element is more overt in the central *masón* ostinato, which is the amphibrach or *cinquillo* drummed on the *catá* log idiophone, and in the *yubá*, in which the *catá* plays a triple-meter variant of the *cinquillo* (2-1-2-1-2-1-1-2). As we have seen, while these rhythms are almost undoubtedly of African derivation, they are also basic to the Cuban contradanza and its derivatives. The vocal parts are equally syncretic, combining European-style diatonic melodies with lyrics in Creole/patois. Further in keeping with the mincing contradanza choreography, women carry fans and hankies and wear long, elegant dresses, with finely woven frills and lacework, all presumably patterned on the slave owners' attire in the decades before the Haitian Revolution.

The *tumba francesa* can be seen as a legacy of the cultural explosion that occurred when exiles from the Haitian Revolution scattered throughout the Caribbean, bringing with them their music and dance traditions, both French and Afro-Haitian. Hence, for example, the use of the word "*tumba*" to denote dances in nineteenth-century Santo Domingo and Puerto Rico (where it was an archaic name for a *bomba* dance [see Sublette 2008: 278]). Meanwhile, in Haiti itself, the contredanse (*kontredans*) has persisted, however marginally, to the present, and the *mazoun/mazonne* dance also survives as a dainty creolized minuet accompanied by percussion.[50]

## Concluding Perspectives

A particularly distinctive and oft-noted feature of colonial Cuban culture is the permeability, if not outright absence, of boundaries between the realms of art music and vernacular music. Such sociomusical fluidity stands in marked contrast to the increasing polarization then taking place in European music culture, as art music became increasingly esoteric and detached from any vernacular moorings. As Theodor Adorno (1988: 22) noted, Mozart's *Magic Flute* represented a kind of apotheosis—and concluding climax—of a felicitous union of the popular and the cultivated, a union that was inexorably unmade by the innovations of the late Beethoven and his followers.

In Cuba, there was, to be sure, a vast gulf between the aristocrat attending an opera in Havana and the slave on the rural plantation dancing to the *yuka* drums. And yet between them lay not an unbridgeable sociomusical chasm but an organic tissue of music and dance styles, whose sinews consisted of the contradanza, in all its varieties. The contradanza complex, indeed, not only constituted the dominant music and dance of its era but also served as a shared medium through which musical features as well as participants could move. Black and mulatto musicians were the primary agents of such mobility and transmission, often moving fluidly between contradanza ensembles and Afro-Cuban rumbas and Santería ceremonies.[51] Accordingly, while a rowdy *tumba francesa* party might seem radically different in style, instrumentation, and mood from an elite contradanza soirée, both events could share dance figures and even specific musical features, such as the amphibrach, just as the *cinquillo* could animate both a Santería rhythm and a piano composition by Gottschalk.

Corresponding to the musical heterogeneity of the contradanza complex was the diversity of associated ideologies and aesthetic sensibilities it could accommodate. The Cuban contradanza itself, as an instrumental genre, could naturally lend itself to various affective associations (or to none at all). Carpentier speaks of it as being essentially loyalist—that is, pro-Spanish—as might be suggested by such titles as "La nueva cañonera" ("The New [Spanish] Gunboat"). But such an assessment seems questionable. A number of composers were ardent *independentistas*; Lino Coca was a colonel in the rebel army, Cervantes was exiled for his links to the independence movement, Antonio Boza was killed for sedition as he tried to flee the island, and Buelta y Flores was tortured to death for alleged participation in the insurrectionary Escalera conspiracy. The military bands of the *mambí* rebels of 1868 played contradanzas like "La caringa" (Díaz Ayala 2006: 75). As Galán notes (1983: 178–179), in contexts such as the Teatro Villanueva in 1869 the contradanza could be explicitly linked to the anticolonial struggle, with pieces like "¡Viva la libertad!" presented amid speeches vilifying the Spanish rulers. As such titles invited harsh persecution by the authorities, other titles expressed their sympathies more indirectly, as may have been Saumell's intent in his aforementioned "El somatén," homonymous with "Som atents" ("On Guard!"), the name of a Catalonian *independentista* journal. Other titles, such as "La filabustaera," advocated annexation to the United States. Meanwhile, on a more general level, the contradanza, despite or because of its Afro-Cuban elements, had become a symbol of creole cultural nationalism; hence Goodman, writing of Santiago in the 1860s, described the "creole danza" as "the patriotic music of Cuba" (1873: 121).

The racial dynamics of the contradanza are as complex and contradictory as are the relations of Cuban nationalism to Afro-Cuban culture. The black and mulatto presence in the contradanza was overt in the demographic makeup of musical ensembles and in the sensuous moves of dancers; it was equally essential, in however diluted and camouflaged a form, in the rhythms that distinguished the genre. Indeed, it was precisely these Afro-Cuban elements that lent the genre its creole and distinctively Cuban flavor. And therein lay the essential contradiction that the contradanza presented: The genre was a symbol of creole cultural nationalism, and its creole elements were Afro-Cuban contributions, but Afro-Cubans and their culture were by no means unproblematically accepted in Cuban political and cultural nationalism. Many white Cubans were as racist as they were anticolonialist, and many brutal slave-owners might well enjoy a danza and celebrate it as national, while having somehow to rationalize its Afro-Cuban aspects. The contradanza was, indeed, the first genre to pose this fundamental contradiction—between racism and the Afro-Cuban presence in creole culture—that was to become acute and unavoidable in the early twentieth century (see Moore 1997).

Cubans adopted a range of attitudes regarding this conundrum as presented by the contradanza, although an explicit *afrocubanismo*—overtly celebrating the Afro-Cuban presence in national culture—would not emerge until the 1920s. As we have seen, some negrophobes denounced the Afro-Cuban influences in danza music and choreography, some commented on them with evident bemusement, and still others mentioned them in what seems a matter-of-fact manner. Probably many contemporary Cubans would have tended to regard the habanera rhythm, the amphibrach, and the syncopations added by black musicians simply as "creole" elements rather than Afro-Cuban ones. As the Afro-Cuban character of such elements became overt in the danzón of the 1880s, so did the controversy regarding their implications erupt in full.

Meanwhile, in Spain and elsewhere in Europe, the choral habanera bore its own evocations, romanticizing Cuba as a land of tropical breezes, languid afternoons in the hammock, and sensual *mulatas*. The associations of the zarzuela habanera/tango, for its part, might naturally vary in accordance with the lyrics, but the sensuous, sultry rhythm established its own expressive mood, and Bizet's habanera, like the choral habaneras, set the Orient in Andalusia, with the olive-complected gypsy Carmen as the seductive and dangerous Other (see McClary and Wagner 1992).

On a more general level, the rise and fall of the contradanza can be seen as part of the metanarrative of dance in Western culture in the last three centuries. The bourgeois culture that emerged in Europe in the eighteenth century demanded a popular dance form that was democratic, informal, and free from the hierarchy and rigidity of the minuet. The country dance, rearticulated as a bourgeois dance in various national efflorescences, represented one expression of the new spirit, while retaining the collective character of older plebian circle and line dances. However, collective dances like the country dance were themselves undermined by the triumph of bourgeois individualism, rooted in capitalism's sundering of premodern social bonds and its new emphasis on the individual as socioeconomic unit. Hence the corresponding triumph of the waltz in Europe and, a generation later, of the danza and danzón in Cuba, with their couples dancing independently, even intimately. As a dance form, the contradanza thus served as a transitional genre—as a bridge not only between social classes and races but also between historical eras—in which the socioeconomic transformations of the age were literally danced. In recent years—perhaps reflecting the new economic independence and power of women—even the couple dance seems to be declining, as timba and reggaetón dancers often gyrate alone, or perhaps only in the general vicinity of their partners. Musically, ostinatos, of obvious Afro-Cuban derivation, have become the dominant structural feature, encompassing not merely rhythm (as in the habanera) but melody and harmony as well. And although the contradanza may seem to grow ever more remote in spirit as well as in years, its seminal character continues to resurface, as in the throbbing habanera rhythm that underlies reggaetón, now resounding throughout much of Latin America.

## Notes

1. While journalistic and scholarly attention in recent decades has tended to focus on modern commercial popular musics, and on Afro-Cuban musics in general, Cuban musicologists have published significant and rigorously scholarly studies of the contradanza. Particularly outstanding are works by Argeliers León (1981), Solomon Mikowsky ([1973] 1988), Zoila Lapique Becali (1979, 1995), and especially Alejo Carpentier (*La música en Cuba* [1946]) and Natalio Galán (*Cuba y sus sones* [1983]); the Carpentier and Galán works are masterpieces of style as well as erudition, representing the best in Cuban literary culture. Unfortunately for the Anglophone reader, the works of Galán and Lapique Becali are untranslated and poorly disseminated, and Mikowsky's study exists only in the forms of an unpublished English-language master's thesis and an obscure Spanish-language Cuban edition.
2. As discussed in this book's Introduction (Chapter 1), the *cinquillo*, presumably of African origin, became a fundamental recurring ostinato in Banda and Petro Vodou drum patterns and in folk and salon versions of the Haitian mereng/méringue, and it surfaces prominently in various other Caribbean genres—such as calypso—animated by the French/Haitian connection. It also appears in Louis de Moreau Gottschalk's 1854 setting of "El cocoyé," a street song from Santiago. In Havana-area Santería drumming, it appears in *toques* (standard rhythms) of Obatalá, Ochún, and Olokún.
3. "La sombra," a popular danza composed by Vicente de la Rosa in 1853, contains only a single *cinquillo*, in the left hand; "Los lamentos," of 1852, has no *cinquillo* (in Fuentes Matons [1891] 1981: 180–181). In "La sopimpa," the melody and bass part each contain one passing *cinquillo* (in Bacardí [1893] 1972: ii, 472). This piece was composed in 1847, according to Danilo Orozco, who kindly provided it to me. None of the three employs the habanera rhythm. The *cinquillo* is also absent in "Ensueños," a contradanza of Santiago-based composer Silviano Boudet (1828–63), published by Edelmann in Havana (in León 1984: 259).
4. The Havana-based periodicals that regularly published contradanzas do not appear to have had counterparts in Santiago (Lapique Becali 1979: 56).

   The Havana contradanza appears to have relied more on the habanera rhythmic ostinato (discussed below and in the Introduction [Chapter 1]), often with the similar amphibrach in the melody. While such pieces as "Cambujá" (discussed below) show that the *cinquillo* was certainly familiar to mid-century composers such as Saumell—not to mention later ones, such as Cervantes—they may have tended to avoid it out of a sense that combining it with the habanera rhythm afforded a somewhat jumbled sound.
5. See Lapique Becali (1995a: 139–140), who also argues that the presence of the habanera rhythm in one of Minguet's contradanzas indicates a Spanish peninsular, rather than creole Cuban, origin for this rhythm. However, as noted in the Introduction to this volume (Chapter 1), that rhythm also occurs in several of the English country dances notated in Playford's *The Dancing Master* (1651–1728); nevertheless, its prominence in the Caribbean is best attributed to African influence.
6. Eighth-quarter-eighth-eighth-eighth-quarter (1-2-1-1-1-2), in place of the more characteristic creole eighth-quarter-eighth-quarter-quarter (1-2-1-2-2). Guadeloupe had been taken by the British in 1759.

7. Mikowsky 1973: 50, quoting citation in Carpentier 1946: 106.
8. Nicolás Tanco Armentero, quoted in Balbuena 2003: 24, from Pérez de la Riva 1981: 126–127. All translations in this chapter are mine unless otherwise indicated.
9. José García de Arboleya, *Manual de la isla de Cuba*, quoted in Linares 1998: 119.
10. Quoted in Linares 1998: 118. In *Cecilia Valdés*, Villaverde writes of the contradanza "Caramelo vendo," "After resounding in dances and fairs [*ferías*] for the rest of the year and the winter of the next, it went on to become the most popular song [*canto*] of all classes of society" ([1839, 1882] 1971: 118).
11. E.g., Villaverde, in *Cecilia Valdés* ([1839, 1882] 1971: 118). Similarly, Serafín Ramírez (1891: 156–157) quotes a contemporary observer: "The music of the contradanzas is celebrated even by foreigners; and when it is composed by people of color, the creoles [Cubans] enjoy it more." However, Ramírez insisted that musicians of color were hired not because they were preferred to white people but because they were the only musicians around.
12. Villaverde, for example, writes of a mulatto band in *Cecilia Valdés*, "Every time a woman of any note entered, the violinists would invariably honor her by intensifying their bow strokes, the flute or [guitar-like] *requinto* would perforate one's ears with their high-pitched tones, the *timbales* [timpani] player would deliver a flourish, the double bassist—the subsequently celebrated Bríndis [de Salas]—would arch his body and extract the most resonant tones from his instrument, and the clarinetist would execute the most difficult and melodious variations" ([1839, 1882] 1971: 101–102).
13. The *infanzón*, as cited in other contemporary accounts, was evidently an Afro-Cuban dance style. This quote, from *La Tertulia*, was shown to me by Zoila Lapique Becali.
14. See, e.g., *Cecilia Valdés* (Villaverde [1839, 1882] 1971: 102, 108, 240) and Lapique Becali 1979: 141.
15. See, e.g., the 1830s dance party described in *Cecilia Valdés* (Villaverde [1839, 1882] 1971: 108).
16. Sachs relates, "In all four dances the court society formed a column in couples; the King with his partner performed the first dance and went to the ends of the line; the other couples did the same" ([1937] 1965: 396).
17. Villaverde continues, "The maestro himself, whose position *per se* might on occasion be disputed, also enjoyed the security of not having to worry about getting lost and thereby encountering the unhappy need to sit without having danced, after having earlier taken his place in the lines of the danza." Resuming the narrative, Villaverde then relates how a "maestro" set a particularly challenging series of figures, reserving the most intricate for last. The man in the sixth couple, despite having had the opportunity to observe the previous five couples dance, realized with great consternation that he could not perform them and looked in despair at the bandleader. His partner Cecilia, seeing his plight, was even more mortified by the thought of the malicious delight the other women would derive from her public humiliation. The bandleader, sizing up the situation and taking pity on Cecilia, of whom he was enamored, signaled the ensemble to stop, eliciting a sigh of relief from the man and a celestial smile from her ([1839, 1882] 1971: 111–112).
18. Villaverde writes in *Cecilia Valdés* ([1839, 1882] 1971: 110), "Above the sound of the ensemble, with its boisterous timbales, could be heard, in perfect time with the

music, the incessant *chis-chas* of the feet, without which those of color think that the rhythm of the *danza criolla* could not be properly maintained."

19. Fernández (1981: 31–33) describes *ala* as a more specific figure in which man and woman, while lightly joining their right hands above their heads, circle each other on their right while remaining facing in the initial direction. *Sostenido* was a standard figure in the Spanish contradanza (Ocampo López n.d.: 87).
20. Goodman (1873: 155) describes a different sort of relaxation section common in Santiago in the 1860s: "The step of la danza is distantly related to a slow valse; but being accompanied by certain graceful movements of the limbs—vulgarly termed, in creole vernacular, 'la sopimpa'—the excitement is far greater than it is with the fastest 'trois-temps' on record. So great, indeed, that after every other 'round' the couples pause and perform a kind of lady's-chain in quadrille groups of six or eight. Each dancer gives his or her favourite version of this remarkable step. Some appear to glide around as if propelled on wheels; while others define the step by hops, backward skips and short turns, now to the right, now the left; but all preserve the same graceful movements of the body."
21. Villaverde [1839, 1882] 1971: 119, 240. His description of the intimate, sensuous abandon of the couple dancing echoes Goethe's eulogy of waltzing: "The man always carries the woman as if up in the air, as while his right arm circles her waist, his left hand holds her hand gently. This is not mere dancing, with the body just following a rhythm, it is swinging as if in a dream to the sound of the moaning and voluptuous music, it is the intimate conversing of two lovers, the mutual caressing of two beings in love, in which time, space, situation, and convention are forgotten" (Villaverde [1839, 1882] 1971: 240).

    The term "*cedazo*" persisted until the early 1900s in eastern Cuba as connoting any couple dance, as in a gentleman's request of a woman, "Dáme un cedazo?" ("May I have this dance?" [Lapidus 2008: 38]).
22. Caution must be used in interpreting the term "danza," which also simply means "dance." See Mikowsky 1973: 95–98 for further discussion of the nomenclature change.
23. While the original published version of "San Pascual Bailón" has not surfaced, the piece is reproduced, with the dating of 1803, in Ramírez's *La Habana artística* of 1891.
24. "*Cinquillo*" is better translated by the ambiguous "five-let" rather than "quintuplet," which would imply five notes of even value.
25. Robert Farris Thompson claims that the Bakongo Congolese call the rhythm *mbila a makinu* and use it as a "call to dance" (2005: 115).
26. *Cecilia Valdés* describes a smaller ensemble consisting of three violins, contrabass, clarinet, flute, and a pair of timbales drums (Villaverde [1839, 1882] 1971: 98).
27. See Lapique Becali 1979: 38–42. Kalunga is a Congolese-derived deity (also worshiped in Dominican *vodú*); a *ñañigo* is a member of the Calabar-derived *abakuá* brotherhood; a "*negro catedrático*" was an Afro-Cuban urban dandy, of foppish attire and affected diction; the Siboneys were Amerindians who had shared the island with the Taínos.
28. However, quite a few contradanzas of this "ordinary" caliber are reproduced in Lapique Becali's *Música colonial cubana* (1979).

29. "Suelta el cuero," "Cambujá," "Suelta el peso," and "La expedición de Marruecos" (whose ostinato is based on the habanera pattern rather than the *cinquillo*) are reproduced in Lapique Becali 1979: 39, 175, 183. "¡Ave María Gallo!" and the ostinato of "El dedo de Landaluze" are reproduced and discussed in Galán 1973: 362–363 and Galán 1983: 167. "La Santa Taé" is found in Sanjurjo 1986: 204. See also Mikowsky 1973: 118–119.
30. "Las hacen sobre . . . cantos inventados por el vulgo, y aún de los pregones de los vendedores y las canciones de los negros" (in García de Arboleya 1858: 263–264).
31. Galán presents the scheme, in a manner that may strike some as less clear, as follows: A, B (a-b), A, C (c-d), A, D (e-f). . . .
32. The eighteenth- and nineteenth-century bolero was an Andalusian suite dance, not to be confused with its Cuban namesake. Treating the recurring A section as a *paseo* would naturally work better with danzas whose first section was of a more relaxed character than the B section; in most danzas, however, the A section is no more relaxed than the B.
33. See, e.g., his recording *Cuba and Louisiana* (Opus 111). His adornment of Saumell's "La niña bonita" with virtuoso runs might be regarded variously as enlivening or desecrating the piece; it is presumably not inconsistent with the relatively flexible approach to rendering scores that prevailed in the nineteenth century, as opposed to the dry and fetishistically "correct" purism of the present.
34. This seems to be a popular passage, as it is plagiarized at length in a few publications on Cuban music.
35. The music of Gottschalk, as a veritable musical ethnographer, brims with details of interest to the music historian. His usage of the *clave* rhythm in "La nuit de tropiques" (1857) may be the first notation of that subsequently ubiquitous feature of Afro-Cuban popular music. His "Souvenir d'Andalousie" (1852) may also represent the first documented appearance of the flamenco/Málagan folk ostinato later internationally popularized in Lecuona's *Malagueña* (//:e-g#-b-e-g#-b-a-c-b-a-g-f://).

    Gottschalk's life and times are admirably documented in Frederick Starr's engaging and exhaustively researched *Bamboula! The Life and Times of Louis Moreau Gottschalk.*
36. See Mikowsky 1973 for a more detailed discussion of Cervantes's danzas.
37. The score of "Los tres golpes," shown in Figure 2.11, is drawn from that published in *The World's Best Music* (de Vore 1921: 1301; several of the danzas are given incorrect titles). Other editions, such as the 1963 Havana edition by Olga de Blanck, differ quite markedly from each other and from the original Edelmann versions, which are believed to contain several errors.

    Commercial recordings containing contradanzas by Saumell and Cervantes come in and out of print; the interested reader may check Amazon.com for current examples. For ensemble reconstructions of some of these pieces, see *Cuba: Contradanzas & danzones*, Rotterdam Conservatory Orquesta Típica (Nimbus NI 5502).
38. Simpson Heights, a black barrio of Matanzas.
39. See García 1972: 63 and the scores reproduced in León 1984: 267–268. Even Faílde's renowned and seminal "Las Alturas de Simpson" appears to have had only two sections in its initial form, such that Borbolla (1975: 155) refers to it as a danza.

40. For example, one incensed writer in an 1881 periodical denounced the "degenerate" and "foreign" (from where?) danzón and even the danza, insisting that the legitimately Cuban national dance was the neo-Hispanic *zapateo* (in Martínez Furé 1991: 31). Ramírez, in his *La Habana artística* of 1891, accepted the dancing but urged substituting the music with contradanzas of Saumell and his contemporaries. The negrophobic Sánchez de Fuentes adopted the different tactic of accepting the music as national and legitimate, while insisting that Faílde invented it "without any intervention of African elements" (in Galán 1983: 194–195, 199).
41. Dolores María de Ximeno, cited in Lapique Becali 1979: 47. What might seem to be the curious characterization of Afro-Caribbean music as "melancholy"—rather than wild, lascivious, and so forth—recurs in various other sources of the epoch.
42. That is, a salsa song, for example, might alternate a section in "three-two" with one in "two-three," but only by inserting a single transitional measure at some point so that the two-bar *clave* pattern (whether actually sounded or not) would be maintained metronomically throughout. A "history of *clave*" in Cuban music and salsa would document how, among other things, this "rule" came to be established only in the 1960s.
43. Taken with permission from *Hot Music from Cuba 1907–1936* (Harlequin HQ CD 23).
44. Pérez Sanjurjo, for example, refers to danzas with texts mentioning various local public personages in the latter 1860s (1986: 206).
45. In Mexico the term "contradanza habanera" had been used since an 1836 edition to denote an instrumental contradanza in Cuban (as opposed to French or English) style.
46. To further confound matters, many Anglophone authors and editors established a thoroughly incorrect tradition of calling the genre "habañera."

    Meanwhile, the ambiguities attending the term "tango" and its designations are particularly acute. While the word itself may be of European origin (e.g., from Latin *tanguere*), a Kikongo origin (as with so many other "ng" words, such as *changüí, nganga, bongó, conga,* and so forth) is more likely, as suggested, among other things, by its documented usage from as early as the 1780s to designate an Afro-Caribbean dance (see Sublette 2008: 122–123). Moreover, in the nineteenth century the term came to be applied to several duple-metered genres. These included the zarzuela tango/habanera discussed here, the Argentine tango (whose early form clearly reflected the habanera/*ritmo de tango* ostinato), and the flamenco-style tango and the tangos of the *chirigota* groups of the Carnaval of Cádiz (which have no particular rhythmic affinity to the others, aside from being in 4/4).

    For further discussion of the habanera/tango in Spanish zarzuela, see Eli Rodríguez and Alfonso Rodríguez 1999: 33–45 and Linares and Nuñez 1998: 187–205. For more regarding the habanera in general, see Galán 1983: chap. 7 and Martín 1999.
47. If, in accordance with the plot, such a song featured an Afro-Cuban singing in "*bozal*" pronunciation, it would likely be called a "tango," or if the lyrics waxed nostalgically about Havana, it would be labeled "habanera." *Bozal* (fresh-off-the-boat slave) pronunciation omits "d" between vowels and skips or aspirates preconsonantal and final "s"; hence, "estados" becomes "ehta'o," and "pez espada" (swordfish) can become "peh-pá." However, far from being a distinctively "black thing," such pronunciation is typical of informal speech throughout Andalusia and the Spanish Carib-

bean. It stands out as distinctive only when appearing in a more formal context, such as a light-classical *villancico* or zarzuela song.

48. As in the flamenco *guajira* (see Manuel 2004: 148), the naively racist fantasies expressed in some habaneras might remind one why so many Afro-Cubans fought so gallantly against the Spaniards: "I want to live in Havana . . . to pass my life in a hammock, and to have a negro boy (*negrito*) fan me" (in Lafuente 1990: 254). For further discussion of the maritime habanera tradition, see Linares and Nuñez 1998: 197–205 and Lapique Becali 1995b.
49. One compilation of such pieces is *De Cuba a Catalunya: Habaneras de concierto* (Picap 90 0121-03).
50. See McAlister 2002: 29–30, 33 and Courlander 1960: 136.

    Ortiz (1924: 339–340; [1952–55] 1995) traces the word "*tumba*" to West Africa and the Congo, although given other possible sources, such as Indo-Aryan *tambor* and the French Renaissance dance "tombeau," its use in the Caribbean may be a case of Ortiz's "convergent etymology." In the Caribbean context it generally connotes "drum" and by extension the dance and social event in general—hence the related "*tumba dominicana*" of nineteenth-century Santo Domingo. Goodman witnessed a devotional dance by black slaves in Santiago de Cuba in the 1860s performed by two (non-touching) couples at a time, accompanied by an ensemble of *güiro*, cowbell (*cencerro*), and *tumba* drum(s), lain on the floor and straddled (1986: 194).
51. Danzón composer and bandleader Miguel Faílde, for example, was known to be a Santería devotee.

## References


Abbott, Abiel. 1965. *Cartas.* Havana: Consejo Nacional de Cultura.

Adorno, Theodor. 1988. *Introduction to the sociology of music.* Trans. E. B. Ashton. New York: Continuum.

Alén, Olavo. 1986. *La música de la sociedades de tumba francesa en Cuba.* Havana: Casa de la Américas.

———. 1991. "The tumba francesa." In *Essays on Cuban music: North American and Cuban perspectives.* Ed. Peter Manuel, 75–86. Lanham, MD: University Press of America.

Alonso, Manuel. [1849] 2002. "Bailes de Puerto Rico" (from *El Gíbaro*). In *Music in Puerto Rico: A reader's anthology.* Ed. and trans. Donald Thompson, 14–20. Lanham, MD: Scarecrow Press.

Aparicio, Frances. 1998. *Listening to salsa: Gender, Latin popular music, and Puerto Rican cultures.* Hanover, NH: Wesleyan University Press.

Armas Rigal, Nieves. 1991. *Los bailes de las sociedades de tumba francesa.* Havana: Editorial Pueblo y Educación.

Bacardí, Emilio. [1893] 1972. *Crónicas de Santiago de Cuba.* Madrid: Graf. Breogan.

Balbuena, Barbara. 2003. *El casino y la salsa en Cuba.* Havana: Editorial Letras Cubanas.

Borbolla, Carlos. 1975. "El son: Exclusividad de Cuba." *Anuario Interamericano de Investigación Musical* 2:152–156.

Brau, Salvador. [1885] 1977. "La danza puertorriqueña." In *Ensayos sobre la danza puertorriqueña.* Ed. Marisa Rosado, 1–13. San Juan: Instituto de Cultural Puertorriqueño.

Carpentier, Alejo. 1946. *La música en Cuba.* Mexico City: Fondo de la Cultura Económica.

———. 2001. *Music in Cuba.* Translation of *La música en Cuba,* by Alan West-Durán, ed. Timothy Brennan. Minneapolis: University of Minnesota Press.

Courlander, Harold. 1939. *Haiti singing.* Chapel Hill: University of North Carolina Press.

———. 1960. *The Drum and the hoe: Life and lore of the Haitian people.* Berkeley: University of California Press.

de Vore, Nicholas, ed. 1921. *The world's best music.* New York: University Society.

Díaz Ayala, Francisco. 1981. *Música cubana del areyto a la nueva trova.* San Juan: Editorial Cubanacán.

———. 1994. *Discografía de la música cubana: Volumen I: 1898–1925.* San Juan: Fundación Musicalia.

———. 2006. *Los contrapuntos de la música cubana.* San Juan: Ediciones Callejón.

Eli Rodríguez, Victoria, and M. de los Ángeles Alfonso Rodríguez. 1999. *La música entre Cuba y España: Tradición e innovación.* Madrid: Fundación Autor.

Esses, Maurice. 1992. *History and background, music and dance.* Vol. 1 of *Dance and instrumental diferencias in Spain during the 17th and early 18th centuries.* Stuyvesant, NY: Pendragon Press.

Evora, Tony. 1997. *Orígenes de la música cubana: Los amores de las cuerdas y el tambor.* Madrid: Alianza Editorial.

Fernández, María Antonia. 1981. *Bailes populares cubanos.* Havana: Editorial Pueblo y Educación.

Freyre, Gilberto. [1936] 1987. *The mansions and the shanties: The making of modern Brazil.* Berkeley: University of California Press.

Fuentes Matons, Laureano. [1891] 1981. *Los artes en Santiago de Cuba,* and Abelardo Estrada, *Estudio de un libro, su autor y la órbita de ambos.* Havana: Editorial Letras Cubanas.

Galán, Natalio. 1973. "Ocho contradanzas ochocentistas." In *La enciclopedia de Cuba, vol. 5: Artes, sociedad, filosofía,* 348–367. San Juan: Enciclopedia y Clásico Cubanos.

———. 1983. *Cuba y sus sones.* Valencia: Pre-Textos.

García, Juan Francisco. 1972. *Canciones dominicanas.* Santo Domingo: Universidad Autónoma de Santo Domingo.

García de Arboleya, José. 1858. *Manual de la isla de Cuba: Compendio de su historia, geografía, estadística y administración.* Havana: Imprenta del Tiempo.

González, Hilario. 1980. "Manuel Saumell y la contradanza: Órbita de la contradanza." In *Manuel Saumell: Contradanzas,* 5–38. Havana: Editorial Letras Cubanas.

Goodman, Walter. 1873. *The pearl of the Antilles or an artist in Cuba.* London: Henry S. King.

Grenet, Emilio. 1939. *Popular Cuban music.* Havana: Carasa.

Huertas, Eduardo. 1989. *Teatro musical español en el Madrid ilustrado.* Madrid: Lavapies.

Jacobsen, Gloria Castiel. 1982. "The life and music of Ernesto Lecuona." Ph.D. diss., University of Florida.

Lafuente Aguado, Ricardo. 1990. *La habanera en Torrevieja.* Torrevieja: Ayuntamiento de Torrevieja.

Lapidus, Benjamin. 2008. *Changüí and the roots of the Cuban* son *in Guantánamo.* Lanham, MD: Scarecrow Press.

Lapique Becali, Zoila. 1979. *Música colonial cubana en las publicaciones periódicas (1812–1902)*. Havana: Editorial Letras Cubanas.

———. 1995a. "Aportes franco-haitianos a la contradanza cubana: Mitos y realidades." In *Panorama de la música popular cubana*. Ed. Radames Giro, 137–154. Havana: Editorial Letras Cubanas.

———. 1995b. "Presencia de la habanera." In *Panorama de la música popular cubana*. Ed. Radames Giro, 155–172. Havana: Editorial Letras Cubanas.

León, Argeliers. 1981. "De la contradanza al danzón." In *Bailes populares cubanos*, by María Antonia Fernández, 7–16. Havana: Editorial Pueblo y Educación.

———. 1984. *Del canto y el tiempo*. 2nd ed. Havana: Editorial Letras Cubanas.

Linares, María Teresa. 1998. "La ida." In *La música entre Cuba y España: Tradición e innovación*, by M. T. Linares and Faustino Nuñez, 45–184. Madrid: Fundación.

Manuel, Peter. 1998. "Improvisation in Latin American dance music." In *In the course of performance: Studies in the world of musical improvisation*. Ed. Bruno Nettl with Melinda Russell, 127–148. Chicago: University of Chicago Press.

———. 2004. "The guajira between Cuba and Spain: A study in continuity and change." *Latin American Music Review* 25 (2): 137–162.

Manuel, Peter, and Orlando Fiol. 2007. "Mode, melody, and harmony in traditional Afro-Cuban music: From Africa to Cuba." *Black Perspective in Music* 27 (1): 45–80.

Martín, Tamara. 1999. *Las habaneras son de La Habana*. Guatemala: Editorial Cultura.

Martínez, Orlando. 1989. *Ernesto Lecuona*. Havana: Unión de Escritores y Artistas de Cuba.

Martínez Furé, Rogelio. 1991. "Tambor." In *Essays on Cuban music: North American and Cuban perspectives*. Ed. and trans. Peter Manuel, 25–47. Lanham, MD: University Press of America.

Martínez Rodríguez, Raúl. 2004. *Para el alma divertir*. Havana: Editorial Letras Cubanas.

McAlister, Elizabeth. 2002. *Rara! Vodou, power, and performance in Haiti and its diaspora*. Berkeley: University of California Press.

McClary, Susan, and Richard Wagner. 1992. *Georges Bizet: Carmen*. Cambridge: Cambridge University Press.

Mikowsky, Solomon. 1973. "The nineteenth-century Cuban *danza* and its composers, with particular attention to Ignacio Cervantes (1847–1905)." Ph.D. diss., Teachers College, Columbia University. Published in Spanish as *Ignacio Cervantes y la danza en Cuba* (Havana: Editorial Letras Cubanas, 1988).

Moore, Robin. 1997. *Nationalizing blackness: Afrocubanismo and artistic revolution in Havana, 1920–1940*. Pittsburgh: University of Pittsburgh Press.

Nuñez, Faustino. 1998. "La Vuelta." In *La música entre Cuba y España*, María Teresa Linares and Faustino Nuñez, 187–318. Madrid: Fundación Autor.

Ocampo López, Javier. n.d. *El folclor y los bailes típicos colombianos*. Manizales, Colombia: Biblioteca de Escritores Caldenses.

Ortiz, Fernando. 1924. *Glosario de afronegrismos*. Havana: Imprenta El Siglo XX.

———. [1952–55] 1995. *Los instrumentos de la música afrocubana: Las tumbas*. Havana: Editorial Letras Cubanas.

Pérez de la Riva, Juan. 1981. *La isla de Cuba en el siglo XIX vista por los extranjeros*. Havana: Editorial de Ciencias Sociales.

Pérez Sanjurjo, Elena. 1986. *Historia de la música cubana*. Miami: Moderna Poesía.

Pichardo, Esteban. 1849. *Diccionario provincial casi-razonado de voces cubanas.* 2nd ed. Havana: El Gobierno, Capitanía General y Real Hacienda.

Ramírez, Serafín. 1891. *La Habana artística.* Havana: Imprenta del E. M. de la Capitanía General.

———. 1928. "La Habana de otros tiempos." In *Evolución de la cultura cubana, Vol. 18,* 132–133. Havana: Imprenta Montalvo y Cardenas.

Sachs, Curt. [1937] 1965. *World history of the dance.* Trans. Bessie Schönberg. New York: Norton.

Santos García, Caridad, and Nieves Armas Rigal. 2002. *Danzas populares tradicionales cubanas.* Havana: Centro de Investigación y Desarrollo de la Cultura Cubana Juan Marinello.

Starr, S. Frederick. 1995. *Bamboula! The life and times of Louis Moreau Gottschalk.* New York: Oxford University Press.

Sublette, Ned. 2008. *The world that made New Orleans: From Spanish silver to Congo Square.* Chicago: Lawrence Hill Books.

Thompson, Robert Farris. 2005. *Tango: The art history of love.* New York: Pantheon.

Villaverde, Cirilo. [1839, 1882] 1971. *Cecilia Valdés o La Loma del Ángel.* New York: Anaya.

EDGARDO DÍAZ DÍAZ *and*
PETER MANUEL

# 3 / Puerto Rico

## *The Rise and Fall of the Danza as National Music*

Present-day Puerto Ricans live in a world throbbing to the beat of reggaetón, salsa, *bomba*, *plena*, bachata, rock, Dominican merengue, Afro-Cuban music, and, at times, the romantic and fatalistic bolero that alternates with Latin American *baladas*. Quite rare today would be anyone who recalls hearing of the contradanza, the variant of the European figure dance that was practiced in the first half of the nineteenth century in Puerto Rico. However, most Puerto Ricans would certainly recognize a close relative and creolized derivative—that is, the local danza—especially in the form of Puerto Rico's national hymn, "La borinqueña," which is heard in innumerable contexts, including as wake-up music on early-morning radio programs. In fact, whenever the "The Star-Spangled Banner" is heard in this colony of the United States, it is invariably preceded by the official local anthem, "La borinqueña," which, unlike most anthems, is not a pompous march but a suave and romantic danza. Composed in 1868 as a symbol of resistance to Spanish colonial rule, the hymn serves as a unique but representative example of the genre that constituted the most popular dance music expression in Puerto Rico between 1850 and the 1930s.

The beginnings of a distinctly Puerto Rican danza circa 1848 are documented in various newspapers and books published around those years (such as Manuel Alonso's *El gíbaro* of 1849) and the later reminiscences of such chroniclers as Alejandro Tapia y Rivera ([1880] 1973) and Salvador Brau ([1885] 1977). While the traditional contradanza was a collective figure dance whose sequential group choreography was either dictated by a caller or fixed by convention, the danza was regarded as revolutionary in that, like the waltz, it liberated the couples to dance on their own, often in scandalously intimate embrace. The danza emerged musically and choreographically from the ashes of the duple-metered European contradance through the incorporation of local and regional rhythms that incited dancers to move in ways that eventually subverted whatever aristocratic and stately identity remained in this expression. Such transformations constituted creolization insofar as they represented the growth of new, indigenous forms generated by the mixture of foreign and local elements. Of potential confusion to the student of Caribbean music history is the fact that the Puerto Rican danza, in the 1840s–50s, was most commonly known as "merengue," a term more familiar nowadays as the name of the modern, up-tempo Dominican popular music genre; as discussed in Chapter 4, although the term "merengue" has denoted a variety of genres in the Caribbean Basin, the Dominican form is by no means unrelated to the Puerto Rican one and indeed probably constitutes to some extent an offspring of it.

The family of contradances, as performed in Puerto Rico in the mid-1800s, included quadrilles, rigodóns, Lancers, and Spanish contradanzas based on the "longways" style of English country dance, with its initial and recurring format of men and women in two lines facing each other. Most of these formats remained prominent in upper-class dances until the early twentieth century. Of them, only one contradanza type, with its form of two duple-metered repeated eight-bar sections alternated indefinitely, is seen by most observers as the principal tableau for the emergence of the local merengue, although chroniclers disagree as to the source of the contradanza in Puerto Rico as well as that of the variant that became the merengue.

This chapter draws from original research (including that published earlier in Díaz Díaz 1996, 2006, and 2008) and the work of other prominent Puerto Rican scholars, including Ángel Quintero-Rivera, and earlier chroniclers, such as Tapia y Rivera, Brau, Alonso, and José Balseiro. It seeks to elucidate extant knowledge of the antecedents and dynamics of Spanish, British, and French contradances in Puerto Rico, their rearticulation as merengue, and the latter's renaming and popularization as the Antillean "danza" that became not merely a dance music genre but arguably the most meaningful artistic expression of Puerto Rican culture in that period of seventy years. It may not be an exaggeration to assert that no other symbol during that period possessed the power—especially at key moments, such as the 1868 anticolonial insurrection in Puerto Rico and Cuba—to unite all social classes and mobilize Antillean social life. From its European antecedents—of which the introductory *paseo* constitutes the most outstanding residue—a hidden fairy-tale world of monarchic births, weddings, coronations, and funerals also reverberates in this saga.

## The Contradanza in Puerto Rico

As discussed in the Introduction, the country dance appears to have originated in rural England in the mid-1500s and went on to be adopted in stylized form in the court of Elizabeth I by 1600. Over the next century, it became a favorite recreational dance of the rising middle classes. Introduced to the Netherlands and France around 1685, from 1710 it came to be cultivated by the Bourbon rulers of Spain in Madrid. The bipartite, longways-style contradance variety that much later transformed into merengue was practiced in the Spanish courts alongside the more formal and elegant minuet (Sachs 1937: 421); as such, most nineteenth-century Puerto Rican chroniclers of the contradanza tended to think of it as Spanish in origin, ignoring the dance's English beginnings behind the imperial façade of the Spanish courts. Spanish, French, and British colonists, sailors, and visitors collectively introduced diverse forms of the contradance and its derivative, the quadrille, to the Caribbean Basin from the latter 1700s. From Madrid, the contradanza and quadrille reached the Spanish American colonies through royal festivities as well as interchanges among sailors and other common folk. In Puerto Rico, particularly important were celebrations of births, baptisms, confirmations, weddings, birthdays, or wakes—generally modeled, on a more modest sphere, after activities held at the Spanish courts. On a more official level, social dancing occurred in formal commemorations and festivities held on Catholic holidays and festivities.

In Puerto Rico, although dances were often linked to other events, they also were held for their own sake since the beginning of Spanish colonization.[1] Dances were held variously indoors or outdoors, in public buildings, in private upper-class homes, and in humble shacks at lower-class fiestas. Particularly in San Juan, events directly tied to overseas royal celebrations entailed a higher degree of cosmopolitan influence, especially if they were held by authority officials imbued with up-to-date ideas of modernity or by merchants whose networks effectively transcended the cultural and economic dependency on the Spanish metropole.

By the first quarter of the nineteenth century, any day of royal festivities featured afternoon events, such as parades, horse racing, games, marching band music, and fireworks, that prevailed as contemporary forms of popular entertainment. At the conclusion of the day, the program eventually changed as elegant indoor dance activities replaced the traditional nightly dramatic plays. At the margins of these events was the remaining portion of the population, for whom outdoor dances were sponsored by local authorities in newly illuminated public spaces. Festivities might also include *comparsas*, or street processions of revelers. Such groups of revelers as well as equestrian routines could be called "quadrilles" (*cuadrillas*), and some have speculated that these conventions constituted one sort of inspiration or source for the contradance derivative of the same name. Social stratification and economic development increased in the transitional period that culminated in the 1811 *Cédula de Gracia*, a provincial bill that offered economic incentives to foreign and local investors to establish their businesses in Puerto Rico. The greatest beneficiaries were planters and merchants engaged in sugar production; as a result, the insular economy came to be gradually integrated into the world market, at the expense of the subsistence economy formerly enforced by imperial prohibitions of free trade.

The immediate effects of these global trends among the island's urban population included the introduction of cultural artifacts such as pianos, band instruments, musical scores from Italian operas, and teachers of contemporary dance trends, including current European contradanza styles that were seen as more fashionable than rustic local traditions. Even in rural areas, as long as they were closer to sugar plantations, cultural patrons frequently adopted cultural models in vogue from cities like Paris, Vienna, and Hamburg. A favorite context was the *soirée* or *velada*, a kind of indoor chamber performance of discourse, poetry, concert pieces, and opera excerpts, which ended with a dance party. Contemporary accounts indicate how a typical event of the 1830s might feature waltzes and contradances in French and Spanish styles, performed to the accompaniment of a twelve-piece ensemble.[2] Smaller villages and towns in the interior held their own festivities, with outdoor dances on a kind of improvised wooden stage known as an *enramada*, for all people, regardless of class and race.

By these years, the "Spanish" contradanza—generally implying the British-derived longways format—contended with a French cousin, the stately rigodón (rigaudon, rigadoon), along with waltzes for nightly indoor activities (Tapia y Rivera [1880] 1973: 18), most of which still remained affixed to royal celebrations. Even where communities were barely exposed to foreign cultural and economic goods, local Catholic priests held the official festivities with dance parties at their homes.[3] Dances were even held at funerals in churches (Brau [1885] 1977: 1).

On August 9, 1820, the San Juan *Gaceta* reported a festivity in Cumaná, Venezuela, that featured a parade of Spanish cavalry and infantry and a military ensemble, the Granada regimental band, that accompanied twelve couples contradancing, evidently in longways style, on a stage.[4] At first, the report seemed irrelevant to Puerto Rican social life, but the convulsions in South America and their repercussions would have direct impact on the island's culture. In June 1821, anticolonial leader Simón Bolívar inflicted a major military defeat on the Spanish military forces led by Peruvian-born Spanish Field Marshall Miguel de la Torre in the Battle of Carabobo. The disaster provoked a massive exodus of Venezuelan civilians and Spanish officials, whose main destination was Puerto Rico. De la Torre then became Puerto Rico's governor until the mid-1830s. With Puerto Rico's prior population estimated roughly at three hundred thousand people (twelve to fifteen thousand of these residing in the capital), the arrival of several thousand immigrants from Venezuela exerted a significant demographic and cultural impact, especially since so many of the newcomers were highly skilled and educated.

The 1820 *Gaceta* account of longways-style contradancing, together with other contemporary Puerto Rican accounts (especially Tapia y Rivera [1880] 1973: 126; Alonso 1849: 58), suggests that it was this longways style that would evolve into merengue twenty-eight years later. In San Juan, the ubiquity of this same Granada regimental band—at parties, drama and comedy intermissions, church and dance activities, and, of course, official celebrations—constituted the kind of "community service" delegated by high Spanish army officials to similar military ensembles through the rest of the century.

The contradanza had probably been introduced to Puerto Rico well before 1820, just as it had been established in Haiti and Cuba several decades earlier by visitors—whether elite or plebian—from Spain, France, and England. However, the arrival of the Venezuelan refugees appears to have provided considerable input in Puerto Rico (perhaps comparable to that of Franco-Haitian refugees in eastern Cuban in 1801). Brau (1842–1912), in his oft-cited 1885 essay on the danza, writes, "Benefiting from a wealth of civilization that we lacked, those immigrants spread throughout the country, thus modifying the rusticity of our old customs while lifting our rudimentary prosperity with the remnants of their fortunes. These immigrants came to be *the main introducers of the Spanish contradanza* that—along with the minuet, *cachucha*, waltz, brittany, and rigodón, but dominating these—delighted the generation of youths among our forefathers" ([1885] 1977: 4; emphasis added by Díaz Díaz).

In earlier years, the island's musical environment had consisted primarily of diverse folkloric genres of various Spanish and African origins together with the European religious, military, and art music patronized by the Church and the small elite. Only the San Juan Cathedral was able to sustain an orchestra that would have met Continental standards of size and quality, though a few smaller towns, such as Mayagüez, also boasted presentable orchestras.[5] Residents of other small municipalities could also be exposed to contemporary European styles via events featuring contracted musicians brought from San Juan, mostly for church activities. Such local communities often lacked the personnel to staff ensembles in accordance with European standards—that is, in the format of a "well-balanced" combination of string, percussion, brass, and woodwind sections. Until the 1880s, such gaps were typically filled by hiring members of the existing military bands, whose members also became active as music educators and dance-band performers, especially in San Juan and Ponce (Callejo Ferrer [1915] 1971: 43; Coll y Toste 1921: 162). Thus rural *hacendados*—sugar plantation owners—would be able to bring professional ensembles from cities for their festivities. The diffusion of contradancing throughout the island was not simply a matter of hiring musicians from the principal cities but also demanded the presence of knowledgeable dancers. For many of these dancers, the contradanza constituted more than mere entertainment; it also served as a marker of social distinction through which dancers could demonstrate their refinement, elegance, and ability to keep up with the latest Continental trends.

Despite a dearth of documentation preceding the 1840s, various sources do offer accounts of the longways-style contradanza. Thus, for example, a letter of 1831 describes how in the western coastal town of Rincón, a *comparsa* of twenty couples of men and women dressed as gardeners performed in the streets "longways contradanzas that, without exaggeration, we can say were of the best taste." After street lamps were lit, the group roamed the streets with music, attended a light comedy and a pantomime performance, and held a night dress dance at the local authorities' building known as *Casa del Rey* (or king's house).[6]

During his 1822–35 tenure as governor, de la Torre oversaw cultural changes fostering an environment conducive to public entertainment, including the spread of European contradancing. Allegedly saying, "People that amuse themselves do not conspire," he presided over the various festivities and the erection of a well-endowed public theater in San Juan in 1832, specifically intended to uplift the cultural level of the island. As the most prestigious indoor venue for the arts in Puerto Rico, this theater markedly distinguished upper-class dance events in the capital from those of the rest of the island.

Church and military interests still permeated the theater's mission, but the city's population demanded fresh activities, such as *veladas*, concerts, and masked balls, as well as drama and opera. Together with the increasing involvement in the world of market commodities came an enhanced interest in European cultural and political trends, including Romanticism and Enlightenment values that, in the colonial context, constituted political radicalism. By directly or indirectly promoting socioeconomic progress and international contacts, de la Torre ironically helped intensify anticolonial sentiment. Meanwhile, the need to raise revenue for the theater's maintenance necessitated contracting private entrepreneurs sponsoring popular entertainment, which also served to indirectly undermine the principles of the church-state alliance that owned the theater.

In 1838, a rebellion involving officials of the Granada Regiment whose aim was restoration of the Spanish Constitution led to the dissolution of this regiment and the arrival of two others, with their military bands: One, the Iberia regiment organized by Tapia y Rivera's father, was from Spain; perhaps more significantly in terms of musical interactions, the other, the Catalonia regiment, came from Cuba. A third military group, the Asturias regiment, arrived in San Juan around 1842 (Tapia y Rivera [1880] 1973: 124–125).

The prevailing choreographic form of contradanzas before 1850 was that of a figure dance, in which couples would perform a sequence of moves. As Alonso noted, the figures "symbolize restraints to some (the young men) but safety to others (the young ladies)" ( 2002: 15). This standard format for the contradanza obliged dancers to follow the elaborate figures set by the first couple, risking embarrassment and ridicule were they to get lost or commit a literal *faux pas* (false step). Tapia y Rivera described the system of contemporary longways contradancing, which he noted was identical to that danced in Seville, Spain, as related to him by an acquaintance of that city:[7]

> [The contradanza] consisted of couples following one another in a long series, starting with the gentlemen and ladies facing each other.

> The first couple began the dance, with the gentleman and lady . . . setting the figures of their choice, which the rest were obliged to maintain unchanged. Such figures, with their respective names, were at times so ingenious, given the zeal of those who set them, that the others had to study them closely, and no other couple could dance until arriving at the head of the set. So, when the established figure was executed correctly by every couple down to that in the last position, the "burner" [*fogón*], as it was called in disdain, the result was charming and picturesque. ([1880] 1973: 126–128)

Brau's description of the figure format is also worth quoting at length:

> Every dance, even the most intimate, that was done by our fathers had to have a bastonero (dance caller), the exclusive director of the event, whose commands could not be challenged, and which designated the number of couples that had to enter in the contradanza and the position each occupied. To those selected he provided a dance card or *tag*, enumerating each dance and specifying which young woman was to be the partner of which gentleman, obliging the latter, as indicated, to initiate their perambulations of the salon in search of the maiden indicated by the inflexible number shown.
>
> Our modern dancers would have little patience for the inconveniences of such a system. And truly, those inconveniences did not fail to annoy people then. It was doubtless for this reason that the designation of the partner by the bastonero was falling into disuse, until it was forgotten altogether by 1839.[8] ([1885] 1977: 5)

Brau went on to describe, in terms similar to Tapia y Rivera, the format in which dancers were obliged to reproduce the intricate figures initially performed by the first couple and how failure to do so might provoke the wrath of the first couple, interruption of the dance, and an infelicitous confrontation "on the field of honor." The pressure and conflicts ensuing from such practices constituted one incentive to discard the complex figures and adopt the independent couple dancing already standard in the waltz and subsequently adopted in the Puerto Rican merengue/danza as well as in the Cuban danza. Tapia y Rivera continued, "Later, the contradanza or danza was simplified, disregarding the positions and figures, for which no one needs any more the previous study that made dance academies indispensable in the past" ([1880] 1973: 126).

The extent to which foreign expressions overwhelmed local styles or vice versa varied in Puerto Rico according to diverse factors, especially socioeconomic ones conditioned by the island's topography. In coastal sugar-plantation areas, slaves perpetuated neo-African *bombas* in their relative social isolation from European culture. After Emancipation in the 1870s, many settled near towns and incorporated European elements into their dances and customs. Meanwhile, in the mountains, *jíbaros* (white peasants) preserved much of the musical, poetic, and choreographic styles introduced by early conquerors. Over the generations, however, both *bomba* and *jíbaro* music adopted a creole identity, largely due to centuries of social integration and cross-fertilization. Material conditions were also influential, obliging instrument makers to create native versions of their original models, whether European or African.

Various sources indicate that by the 1840s this local contradanza choreography had already become distinct from that of its Continental counterpart. Alonso wrote in 1849:

> The contradanza is the Spanish dance of the same name, preserved much better in Puerto Rico than in Spain itself; its figures display the variety which originally marked the contradanza, while its steps acquire greater charm with the natural grace of the daughters of the tropics. It is impossible to follow with the eye the motion of one of those dark beauties of languid glance, slender waist, and tiny foot without feeling his heart expand to the point of leaping from his breast. The *contradanza americana* is the most expressive dance imaginable; it is truly a poem of passion and of beguiling visions: in a word, the story of a charmed love. (2002: 14)

As Alonso indicated, the Puerto Rican contradanza had become distinct in musical as well as choreographic terms: "The music which contributes not a little to the enchantment of the contradanza is a mélange of suggestions: now melancholy, mournful and sentimental; now cheerful, witty, and boisterous. This music is a product of the island itself, and composers sometimes use known folk melodies, finding a pretext in some more or less celebrated event to compose a piece which will then bear their name" (2002: 15).

Although only a few printed scores of contradanzas from the 1840s and 1850s survive to this day, the accounts of Alonso and contemporary newspapers clearly indicate a lively music and dance scene in the island based around the contradanza, with local composers and ensembles accompanying dances in diverse settings for different social classes.

Danza scholars in Puerto Rico agree that a two-part piece of eight measures in 2/4 comprised the musical form to which dancers performed the longways contradanza just before its evolution into merengue. Composer Amaury Veray recalls having seen an 1839 score of a contradanza performed that year in Aguadilla and describes its binary shape in the following words: "Each of the parts had a specific character. The first part was less rhythmic than the second, as it was also less accentuated. The second one, on the contrary, was more lively and lilting. Both parts consisted of four eights, frequently having repeated chord figures with a solid and equidistant rhythmic unity" ([1956] 1977: 24). This bipartite form corresponded to that current elsewhere in the region and also, in a more general sense, to that established in the 1600s in the English country dance.

Contemporary accounts also indicate conflicting attitudes toward the proper spirit and tempo of social dancing, where rigodóns, mazurkas, gallops, and contradanzas alternated with each other. While one chronicler complained of the slowness of the rigodón (obliging one to move as "if one were a Capuchin priest in a temple"), others protested that the sometimes strenuous figures of the contradanza were unsuited to the sultry local climate, especially in the inadequately ventilated San Juan municipal theater. In 1839, one local poet, "P," decried the chaos and confusion ("like a sort of ballroom horserace") involved in performing the figures (which evidently commenced longways style) of the danza (opting for the term currently gaining favor in Cuba):

> How could they call it "danza" when in a hallway are "figuring"
> a hundred couples face-to-face, all waiting to be trampled upon,
> or better put, awaiting some clumsy oaf who doesn't look where
>     he's going?

"P" goes on to lampoon the clumsiness with which locals dance the rigodón and gallop and concludes by asserting that the vigorous danza is unsuitable to the balmy tropical climate:

> I do not hate danza at all, on the contrary, yes sir,
> I love it with as much fervor as has anyone,
> I admire the costliest one with ambitious fondness,
> but I also prefer the calm one, for there is heat in this land.[9]

What emerged in such accounts can be seen as a tension between local rhythmic exuberance and the perspiration and fatigue provoked by the heat, especially during dancing's high season in the summer; this tension was later reinterpreted as the "ambiguous" character of local dances ranging "between lively and melancholic and, above all, cheerful and characteristic of our climate and styles of sentiment" (Tapia y Rivera [1880] 1973: 128). In the decades to come, arguments about danza's appropriate tempo shifted to encompass a variety of ontological views, sometimes condemning the lively Afro-Caribbean "tango" and asserting that Puerto Ricans, being perpetual colonial subjects, were "indolent and docile," as reflected in the danza's lethargic and languorous pace. The overtones of these dialectics can be traced in part to the contradictory aesthetics of European Romanticism. Much of the variety of later Puerto Rican danzas can be seen as embodying this tension between the opposing orientations of the "romantic" as opposed to "festive" danzas. A parallel tension could be said to exist between conceptions of danza as a means of displaying social order and propriety and, by contrast, as an occasion for innocent and unpretentious diversion.

Concerning other specific details of the pre-1850s contradanza, several sources report the activities of military bands, the sale of pianos and piano music, and the performances of operas, such as Donizetti's *Belisario*. These operas—some of which contained contradances—would have provided melodic material to local composers and would have exposed local musicians to more varied harmonies than were typical of the relatively simple and straightforward local contradanzas.

Nearly all danzas written in Puerto Rico featured a time signature of 2/4, although most of them reflected variants of a metric combination of three against two (or vice versa, for melody and accompaniment, respectively). Puerto Rican danzas, as in other parts of the Caribbean, have traditionally been celebrated for the distinctive rhythmic flair with which they were interpreted, especially in the case of dance-band renditions of the more animated sections following the *paseo*, with their accordingly lively dance styles. Various chroniclers stressed how foreign musicians unfamiliar with the creole aesthetic would be unlikely to interpret it properly. As Alonso wrote, "In order to really understand the contradanza I had to hear one played by someone from the Antilles" (1849: 60). Some chroniclers used the word "*jaleo*" to describe this rhythmically kinetic aspect of contradanza renditions, which was also an essential trait of danza and merengue performances. In 1836, Cuban chronicler El Lugareño wrote, "A Cuban contradanza arrives in Europe; the European performer plays it, but never reproduces that feeling, that *jaleo*, that flavor which a creole performer shows" (in Galán 1983: 128). The term "*jaleo*" (which might otherwise loosely translate as "hubbub" or "boisterous noise") went on to denote both the rhythmic dynamism of the second sections as well as those sections themselves (as the term is still used in reference to the modern Dominican merengue's call-and-response section following the verse passage). Thus, for example, in April 1848, the *Gaceta del gobierno de Puerto Rico* reported that organizers of a dance gathering had included "one of those magic contradanzas with that Havana-style feeling that involuntarily make even the most serious people move their feet, with its staccato tones, its seductive rhythms, and its vivid and very special *jaleo*."[10]

It is not possible for us to ascertain for now the specific nuances that provided the sense of *jaleo* to nineteenth-century danza renditions. Conceivably, however, they may have had some relation to a rhythmic phenomenon that has been much discussed in literature on the Puerto Rican danza—the "elastic *tresillo*" (*tresillo elástico*). The term was coined, albeit with somewhat ambiguous meaning, in a 1915 book by bandleader Fernando Callejo Ferrer (1862–1926; see Rivera-Guzmán 1993: 9–15). Subsequently, the elastic *tresillo* has often been claimed to be a unique feature of the Puerto Rican danza. Eventually the term came to refer to the rhythmic pattern notated as a triplet in either of the two contexts shown in Figure 3.1 (A and B). (Note that the Puerto Rican use of *tresillo* to mean "triplet" differs from the Cuban use of that term to denote a 3-3-2 pattern, e.g., dotted-eighth–dotted-eighth-eighth.) As Callejo

Ferrer wrote, “The word ‘elastic’ means that the measure of a triplet must not be precise, but involves enlarging one note over another in order to make the accompaniment’s creole rhythm” ([1915] 1971: 54). Most typically, and especially among piano performers, the A pattern shown in Figure 3.1 tends to be played as an amphibrach, while the B pattern tends to be rendered as a *cinquillo* (see patterns C and D, respectively). These two rhythmic patterns themselves, of course, are scarcely unique to the Puerto Rican danza but rather are basic, typical, and even defining rhythms of creole Caribbean music.

The abundance of triplets in scores like “La mulata” (Figure 3.2), composed during danza’s formative period around 1850, reveals the signature of

**Figure 3.1** Elastic *tresillo* forms.

**Figure 3.2** “La mulata,” danza from circa 1855.

an old 6/8-metered contradanza from Spain introduced, as Tapia y Rivera and Brau stated, via educated immigrants, aristocrats, and military bands fleeing the Venezuelan revolution since 1817. Fernando Callejo Ferrer, one of the most distinguished composers and band leaders during the last two decades of the nineteenth century, asserted that these triplets appeared in the old "danzón" ([*sic*]; danza) imported from Venezuela in 1821 (Callejo Ferrer [1915] 1971: 244). But Callejo Ferrer added that these rhythmic cells, unlike the elastic triplet of latter-nineteenth-century danzas, consisted of quarter-note triplets "one measure . . . but not the next" ("un compas sí y otro no"), thus suggesting the pattern known as *sesquiáltera*—that is, "a 6/8 metrical feel alternating with a 3/4 emphasis" (Sheehy 1999: 41).

Pedro Malavet Vega (1992: 158) questions this assertion on the basis of Callejo Ferrer's misleading term "danzón," which he used to refer to this form. But traces of what is known as *sesquiáltera* are seen in "La mulata," on bars 2 and 8 (Figure 3.2), respectively, thus giving credence to Callejo Ferrer's thesis. The score for the right hand shows two syncopated triplets with a 6/8 feel, while the left-hand triplet for the entire 2/4 measure suggests instead a 3/4 one. A rhythmic and metrical feature prominent among mestizo populations (in countries like Mexico, Guatemala, Nicaragua, Argentina, Chile, Venezuela, and Colombia),[11] the inscription of *sesquiáltera* patterns in "La mulata"—along with the 6/8 feel—shows (in the opinion of Díaz Díaz) the degree to which imported South American contradances bridged the evolution from the old Spanish contradanza to the merengue emerging in San Juan twenty-seven years after the first significant Venezuelan migration in 1821.

In addition to the 6/8 feel in the 2/4 structure and the 6/8 and 3/4 metric combinations of the *sesquiáltera*, a third and definite rhythmic factor is the one that helps set the stage for the creolization of contradanza in Puerto Rico in those years: the so-called "habanera" rhythm that is prominently inscribed in the second section of local contradanzas like "La mulata." In piano scores, this distinctive pattern was generally assigned to the left hand. Otherwise, composers wrote them for instruments at the lower register. Beyond the musical implications of these habanera rhythms lie contradictions of a rather sociopolitical character observed during the formative period of the late 1840s. The adoption of this pattern into the pre-existing form of the local contradanza imposed a new impetus to the dance in ways that epitomized how creole Puerto Ricans responded musically and choreographically to the prevailing social and political environment.

## The Advent of the Merengue

In Puerto Rico, notions of "inner creole" and "outer creole" make sense as subcategories of identity for a process not constrained to the insular sphere. By the mid-1800s, a movement for the independence of Cuba and Puerto Rico was underway in which such intellectuals as Ramón Emetario Betances, a

French-educated Puerto Rican physician, visualized an integrated region of autonomous islands, regardless of language. With compatriot Eugenio María de Hostos, Dominican intellectuals and political leaders like Gregorio Luperón envisioned an Antillean danza as a shared expression of the region. A champion of the tenets of abolitionism and the Paris Revolution of April 1848 (Ojeda 2001: 22), Betances had arrived from Paris just at the time when merengue was documented in Puerto Rico. The abolitionist spirit that Caribbean slaves shared with many mulattoes and poor white laborers constituted a predisposition to the ready-made Afro-Caribbean rhythms that would enliven a new form, known as "merengue," which was about to become Puerto Rico's first "*baile del país*," or national dance.

The social dances of the mid-1800s were not merely idle recreation but physical embodiments of aesthetic and social sensibilities and ideologies. The courtly and over-refined minuet had increasingly come to be seen as stuffy and archaic, but the still-popular rigodón retained much of that earlier dance's formal solemnity. For its part, the contradanza could be executed in a spirit of fun and relative informality, but, as we have seen, it was often highly structured by the bastonero and the obligation to follow the first couple's figures. It also had a thoroughly collective, "family fun" orientation that prevented intimacy of any sort between couples.

By the end of the 1840s, a clearly local Antillean sensibility was spreading in Cuba, Puerto Rico, and the Dominican Republic in ways that invited dance couples "to merengue" (*merenguear*) sensually, embracing each other tightly, whispering intimately, and even undulating their hips in a manner suggestive of slave dancing. This new sensibility signaled a fundamental shift from the affective relationships once dominated by conventional conceptions of morality and good taste prevalent in European colonial regimes.

In Europe in the years around 1800, the revolutionary adoption of independent couple dancing had come in the form of the waltz and, to a lesser extent, the polka. The waltz had enjoyed some subsequent popularity in the Caribbean, including in Puerto Rico, where it had been documented as a stage dance since the 1820s and came to often be paired with the danza in ballrooms. But on the whole, the waltz did not lend itself to the same sort of creolization and the incorporation of a voluptuous character possible among creole Caribbean dances.

The arrival around 1845 of a group of youths said to be from Havana may have inspired what Tapia y Rivera ([1880] 1973: 126–128) called "a horde of undistinguished musicians who devoted themselves to composing danzas by the dozens, among whose ranks were distinguished those of Francisco Santaella." The names of danzas of this period reflect their unpretentious character, rooted in vernacular culture and colloquial phrases, such as "Ay, yo quiero comer mondongo" ("Oh, I Want to Eat Mondongo") and "Zabaleta, rabo de puerco" ("Zabaleta, Pork Tail"). Tapia y Rivera also noted that in contrast to the evident Cuban style of repeating the short contradanzas indefinitely, Puerto Rican composers like Aurelio Dueño began extending the second part of the dance piece in such compositions as "La sapa" of 1848. However, due to the absence of publishers comparable to Juan Federico Edelmann in Cuba, scarcely any surviving examples of Puerto Rican danzas predate the early 1850s. The earliest local danza found so far is the piece examined above, "La mulata," which Brau cites as enjoying particular popularity in 1855. Both it and "La hortensia" of 1865 (discussed below), although of historical interest, would fall into the category of the unpretentious and ordinary ditties [*"obritas"*] described by Tapia y Rivera. "La mulata," shown as Figure 3.2, resembles a typical Cuban contradanza of the period in several respects. Its formal structure consists of two sixteen-beat parts, with the first, in this case, consisting of a repeated eight-bar *prima* and the second being undergirded by the standard habanera ostinato. However, its melodic rhythms, at least as notated, are more typical of subsequent Puerto Rican danzas than of Cuban counterparts, as discussed above. The two forms of elastic *tresillos* (eighth-note triplets followed by two eighth notes) might in other pieces be "rounded off" to conventional duple-metered *cinquillos* and amphibrachs, but their combination in this piece with left-hand triplets suggests more deliberate and rhythmically intricate alternations and superimpositions of duple and ternary patterns with remnants of *sesquiáltera* patterns.[12]

In 1847, Puerto Rican newspaper clips began reporting the popularity of the "contradanzas habaneras" (Havana-style contradanzas), alternately known locally as "contradanzas del gusto habanero" (Havana-flavored contradanzas). Tapia y Rivera and Brau agree that "merengue" constituted musically a bipartite form. Unlike its Cuban counterpart, this new style of contradanza evolved into a multisectional genre consisting of *paseo* and two or three parts. Choreographically, it began to show the features of an independent couple dance under the circumstances described below.

The enthusiastic adoption of the sensual merengue in the 1840s and the fondness with which some contemporary writers praised it signaled a contemptuous rejection of the rigodón, which became associated, explicitly or implicitly, with European hegemony. To Puerto Ricans, their own "seductive" merengue came to be enjoyed precisely for its celebration of values as opposed to colonial ideals of decency and propriety.

One night in 1848, the Philharmonic Society in San Juan hosted a welcome party in honor of the recently installed governor from Spain, Juan de la Pezuela. The cultural get-together was designed to attract ordinary people who did not necessarily have interest in any sort of concert music. In order to assure a good turnout, organizers scheduled social dancing to follow the initial music performances. However, the attendants neither hid their impatience during the poorly rehearsed choral music nor concealed their disapproval in the presence of the sanctimonious governor when his wife, the marchioness of Moncayo, played a piano noticeably out of tune in the high register. The governor must have been further annoyed when the orchestra finally "revolutionized" the evening by providing a lively dance piece for the attendees (as related in an anonymous letter published in the *Gaceta de Puerto Rico*).

The "revolution" alluded to by the chronicler was not the one that Karl Marx and Friedrich Engels had incited that year in Paris, but was instead the introduction of a dance genre, the merengue. The anonymous writer to the *Gaceta* went on to declare with defiant intention that the merengue "will undoubtedly spread in Europe as soon as it is known and, in my judgment, its destiny is to replace the grave and boring rigodón."[13]

Pezuela had just arrived from a turbulent Spain, where the event known as the Paris Revolt had already left a profound sociopolitical imprint. He regarded Puerto Ricans as lazy and boorish, but rather than seek to improve their education, he rejected a proposal for a secondary school, stating that education was injurious and unnecessary. In his role as captain general of Puerto Rico, he had the responsibility of reading and overseeing the official government newspaper. As if intending to provoke the colonial overlord, the *Gaceta* writer went on to test the limits of the colonial regime's patience in more provocative and clearly confrontational lines: "Don't you believe like I do, my friend, that the rigodón seems to be more like a dance expressly sent by superior authority, instead of being the spontaneous product of happiness and well-being? I can only tell you that, once having seen people dance merengue, I find in the cherished rigodón nothing else than a rehearsal of courtesies."

Quite probably, Pezuela had these statements in mind when he released, several months later, a decree banning merengue, imposing a fine of fifty pesos on party hosts and eight days of jail on any musician that played it.

In Cuba, an isolated account circulating during this period indicates the existence of a type of "merengue" among various ephemeral dance styles that included the *ley brava* and the *sopimpa*. The account, found in an 1847 verse from Havana, depicts a mulatto woman dancing:

> *Porque su cuerpo se ciñe, se estira, encoge y doblega*
> *igual que la goma elástica, lo mismo que la gacela,*
> *Y "noramala el jaleo, el fandango y las boleras*
> *—dice ella—, cuando yo bailo la sopimpa de mi tierra,*
> *el merengue y la ley brava, danzas para mi compuestas."*
>
> Because her body gets pressed and stretched, gets pulled and gives in
> like a rubber band, just like a gazelle,
> And she says, "At bad times the jaleo, the fandango, and the boleras,
> when I dance the sopimpa of my land,
> the merengue and the ley brava ['wild law'], dances composed for me."[14]

As of today, this fictional lyric provides the first documented reference to the merengue as a dance-related expression, although one should hesitate to assume that this Cuban merengue was identical to or even directly related to that reported in Puerto Rico a year later. If this Cuban verse seems to describe the merengue only as a dance, the earliest documents in Puerto Rico clearly tie the term "merengue" with the contradanza—that is, as both a music genre and a dance—as analyzed above. Moreover, the merengue mentioned in the Cuban poem likely takes place in the realm of the local underworld of sailors and prostitutes, not like the merengue reported in Puerto Rico, which was centered in activities sponsored initially by liberal, educated groups. Furthermore, the Havana poem refers to a style of body movements with no reference, in any way, to any kind of sound or to any place of origin.

In 1885, Brau (b. 1842), a toddler living a hundred miles away during the events in question, wrote that in the early 1840s, a new musical and dance expression called "merengue" was introduced from Havana that revolutionized Puerto Rico's dance culture. With no other source but him and with no first-hand reference at hand to sustain such arguments, subsequent authors like Veray ([1956] 1977: 24) and Hector Campos Parsi (1976: 83) reproduced similar statements. But in the opinion of Díaz Díaz, the views by these and other writers who trace the origins of the merengue only to Cuba seem, so far, unsubstantiated and unreliable. In fact, none of the contemporary publications at the time indicate that the Cuban contradanza, as a musical form, was introduced from Cuba to remain as the exclusive or prevailing form. Yet, with the inspiration of voluptuous Havana-style rhythms, a stream of dance styles imported from Cuba helped subvert the old stately and solemn protocol in the name of a freer and voluptuous style, adopted by the same young members of the highly educated liberal elite advocating the liberty of Cuba and Puerto Rico.

The three styles referred to in the above-cited poem are also reported by Tapia y Rivera. After residing in Havana between 1858 and 1868, he commented that "merengue" denoted "the exaggerated style of dancing the *jaleo*, or second part of the danza, giving it some of the impudence of the Havana-style *lopimpa* [*sic*; sopimpa] or *ley brava*" ([1880] 1973: 128). The form of these dance styles, or whatever they seemed to be, is unclear, given the paucity and ambiguity of contemporary descriptions. But Tapia y Rivera, who supervised the 1848 party in honor of Governor Pezuela, refers to the merengue as a stylistic dance gesture (an "exaggeration") customary among dancers, as musicians played the second section of local contradanzas that bore the name "*jaleo*." The "impudence" referred to by Tapia y Rivera denotes more of an aspect relative to body movements likely imported from Cuba than that of a musical style or form. As for sopimpa, Tapia y Rivera's phrase "*lopimpa* [*sic*; sopimpa] or *ley brava*" may suggest that he was referring to one and the same dance style. John Chasteen reproduces a nineteenth-century description suggesting how Cuban dancers, as in Puerto Rico, conspired in using this style to subvert the pompous European modality of dancing contradances:

> Cuban musicians gave contradance a gently syncopated rhythm. Cuban dancers made their own variation by moving away from European bounciness, with more lateral movement to their hips. We can

"see" this in the evidence because hip motion implies a lower center of gravity, and lowering one's center of gravity tends to produce a shuffling sound of the feet—the same we "heard" in Buenos Aires dance halls. Cubans call called these sounds *escobilleo* or sopimpa. (Chasteen 2004: 157)

In Puerto Rico, local merengue composers, such as Aurelio Dueño and Francisco Santaella, enthusiastically adopted the habanera rhythms, although they continued to use and develop the old Spanish format. A piece like "La mulata," a 2/4 contradanza with a feel of 6/8 and traces of *sesquiáltera,* hardly falls into the category of the Cuban contradanzas, even if the voluptuous spirit that came to prevail was that of the Cuban habanera.

## The 1849 (Non-)Prohibition of Merengue

As cited above, Brau affirmed categorically that the contradanza was introduced by Venezuelan immigrants, a statement that explains why Brau may have confused "upa" as a dance style, with "merengue," as a contradance-related musical form. A survey of Cuban scholars by Dominican writers Catana Pérez de Cuello and Rafael Solano reveals that the "upa" was never reported in Cuba before the 1850s (Pérez de Cuello and Solano 2003: 223). Among the scholars interviewed in Cuba for this inquiry are prominent musicologists Maria Teresa Linares, Iliana García, and Jesús Gómez Cairo.

In fact, the abundance of references concerning this period indicates no evidence concerning "upa" before the August 1849 merengue prohibition by Governor Pezuela. It was precisely during the period of his incumbency (1848–52) that various references revealed the existence of "upa" for the first time. It is likely that the term "upa" was used strategically as a euphemism after Pezuela issued the ban on merengue in 1849. As Tapia y Rivera noted ([1880] 1973: 127), "The ban generated many epigrams, but failed to achieve its goals, because one cannot cure an established habit with remonstration or advice." One result of the ban may have been the tendency to disguise the dance by referring to it as "upa" and, more lastingly, as "danza."

Shortly after Pezuela departed Puerto Rico for Cuba in 1852, the term "merengue" was again cited in Ponce as a new dance, where it went on to provoke a lively debate from the first edition of newspaper *El ponceño* in July 1852 until its last edition in 1854.

Socorro Girón (1984: 211) has illustrated how ingrained merengue was by then in Ponce among ordinary people, who shouted out songs on its melodies. Due to the lack of an adequate ballroom, the list of places merengue dancers resorted to attending includes a center known as La Sonámbula, a house at Isabel Street, a site known as "Madame Fagot's home," and an improvised room in the so-called "Meat-market Street," as well as other numerous private homes, such as those of Catalonian merchants José Vilaret and Joaquín Balaguer.

The scarcity of notations of actual 1850s merengues is partially offset by the abundant accounts of it, which come mostly in the form of polemics against it. Detractors deplored in particular the sensual intimacy with which couples danced and the way that it put an end to the contradanza's group-oriented, asexual recreation that could unite young and old in the collective execution of the lively figures.

One objectionable feature, denounced in an editorial of *El ponceño,* was evidently the hip-swaying that the new dance accommodated: "The invention of that dance must be a product jointly combined by a poet, a musician, a crazy man, and the devil. What a contrast! The woman inclines her head on his shoulder, adopts a stance of humiliation, or fixes her eyes on St. Cecilia. Whereas the upper half of their bodies makes them look like saints . . . but then . . . the lower half of their bodies . . . heck, it all seems like the day and the night together, the joint of glory and hell, of truth and lie. Ah, merengue! [You are a] distant cousin of venial sin, and so parents must be blamed for your existence."[15] Another critic called for the invention of a new national dance to oust the merengue from that position it already occupied only a few years after its supposed banning: "Ask parents to assist the establishment of a decent society, if they fear the consequences of grave abuses; then, with the creation of a new *national dance* [emphasis added by the authors], merengue shall be eliminated, not by its roots, as these are many and deep, but gradually and by means of modifications which are not hard to effect in such a dance. . . . Establish a social organization and expel the merengue; but as long as it is barely sustained by a mere handful of youngsters, they will make it triumph."[16] The merengue's romantic and potentially erotic rather than family-oriented nature was bewailed by another critic, who in an 1853 letter to *El ponceño* denounced the events in which well-to-do young men, "forgetting their obligation to us, their mothers, their sisters, and their relatives," attended dances to socialize with other young women. That such women might be of lower social classes added yet another dimension to the merengue's harmfulness. As the writer elucidated, "Society can be compared to the steam engine on Father's plantation, whose various parts, each functioning separately, are never hindered in their respective motions except for the contact and the friction necessary to attain the general result. [. . . Accordingly,] each rank and class of the society in which we live, each circle of our social sphere, moves within determined limits beyond which the individual should not and indeed cannot venture without risking a clash with unknown bodies" (in Thompson 2002: 58). To the dismay of this aristocratic stuffed shirt, young men were evidently not only risking but actively seeking "clashes with unknown bodies" by attending merengue dances. Indeed, despite the fire and brimstone spouted by the merengue's enemies, the dance's supporters were clearly in the majority, expressing their enthusiasm either with their feet and hips or in letters and essays, such as this one from 1858:

> The music of these dances, that bears the sweet and revealing name "merengue," is itself quite unique and delicious, in its distinctive composition, particular harmony, and the melodies and modulations of its sections and phrases. It is certainly true that *upon hearing the danza, everyone dances*, because even people who, because of their age or other reasons do not wish to enter the dance floor, or even move their bodies gently, sway their heads, or at least tap their canes on the floor to the music—even they not only enjoy the music but find their nervous systems affected and moved by the special character and particular naturalism of its chords, cadences, and consonances. (In Brau [1885] 1977: 9; emphasis in original text)

## Merengue in the Military Bands

By the early nineteenth century, advances in design of musical instruments at once facilitated and responded to the proliferation of brass-dominated bands, especially associated with the military. Two of the most outstanding contributors in these trends were the Frenchmen Adolph Sax, inventor of the saxophone, and Hector Berlioz, genius of orchestration. These profound transformations were reflected as well among Spanish colonial regiments in the Antilles and in Puerto Rico by 1854.

As mentioned, many aspects of public musical life in the nineteenth-century Spanish Caribbean were tied to centers of colonial rule, in particular the Church and the military. These institutions provided the primary vehicles for many musicians and composers to fulfill their artistic aspirations. A case in point is that of regimental bands.

Regimental bands were an effective means to disseminate contemporary music, whether Continental European, local, or from other Caribbean islands. Informed by such sources, native composers and performers in the Caribbean worked under the continuous influx of incoming musical scores along with newly invented instruments. In most cases, the military administration was willing to pay, however dearly, for these items in its interest to maintain a prominent space within the musical environment of colonial society.

After 1852, to the extent that people no longer feared Pezuela's anti-merengue decree, the term "merengue" recovered its prominence as connoting dance music with some sort of repetitive rhythmic patterns. However, in their evening *retretas*, army officials tended to prefer the more elegant and less controversial terms "danza" or "contradanza."

"*Retretas*" were evening public concerts generally held twice a week by Spanish regimental bands—usually on Sundays and Wednesdays at eight, in open spaces, such as town squares. As seen in the following program for a *retreta* scheduled to take place on Sunday, March 8, 1857, Spanish regimental *retretas* were occasions where the public became acquainted with the latest musical styles from Europe and other parts of the Spanish and French Caribbean, including Louisiana:

1. The "March of the Coronation," from the opera *Il profeta*
2. Cavatina for *tiple*, from the opera *Lucia*
3. "*Tambulé*," contradanza
4. Obbligato aria for saxophone ("a newly invented instrument")
5. "*La bordonúa*," contradanza
6. "*Jota*," from *Postillón de la Rioja*
7. "*Cocoyé habanero*"
8. "*Para usted*," contradanza

During the months that followed, the Cádiz Cazadores band followed a format whose beginnings and conclusions consisted of local danzas or Spanish paso dobles, thus suggesting a preference among *retretas'* organizers to feature locally popular pieces along with peninsular Spanish ones.

One influential musician in the military and dance band milieu was a Frenchman named Carlos Allard, a flutist, bandleader, and brother of a distinguished Parisian violinist. Allard was probably a member of the delegation that accompanied Pezuela as the latter disembarked from Madrid. Subsequently, after his arrival in Ponce with the governor in April 1850, he figured prominently in the Peninsular Iberia Infantry Regiment No. 2. In March 1857, he became the band director of the Cádiz Cazadores's Regiment No. 1. In these and subsequent outdoor concerts, Allard introduced saxophone obbligatos, which—as more typically played on the euphonium, a brass instrument similar to the alto horn, referred to in Spanish as the "bombardino"—went on to become distinctive and important features of the Puerto Rican danza style, as we discuss below.

In 1857 at St. Thomas, Allard met Louisiana-born and European-trained pianist-composer Louis Moreau Gottschalk and singer Adelina Patti, then a fourteen-year-old girl. After all three of them arrived in Ponce, they gave several concerts with the Cádiz regimental band serving as accompaniment. Whenever the military band was not available, Gottschalk, the pianist, resorted to having Allard perform as flutist and Patti as singer (Starr 1995: 262). In 1858, after Patti's parents demanded her return to New York City, Allard joined Gottschalk in a tour of several Caribbean islands.

In Allard's absence, the Cádiz Cazadores's band came to be directed by the Spaniard Joaquín Montón, a danza composer who specialized in bombardino. In *retretas*, Montón maintained the tradition of saxophone obbligatos introduced by Allard and also applied this style to the bombardino.

## Manuel Tavárez and the Efflorescence of the Danza

Puerto Rican musicologists have typically divided the history of the danza into three periods: (1) an early stage, comprising roughly 1840–80 and culminating in the figure of Manuel Gregorio Tavárez; (2) a zenith of vitality and popularity, encompassing the 1880s–90s, represented especially by Juan Morel Campos; and (3) an autumnal period stretching to the 1930s, comprising the work of José Ignacio Quintón and his contemporaries.

By the 1840s, as noted above, local composers were avidly penning danzas and imbuing them with local flavor by incorporating elements of contemporary popular songs. From 1844, as we have seen, visitors from Cuba sparked the vogue of a dance style of independent couple dancing, most commonly called *jaleo*, which evidently constituted an especially lively and sensual way of dancing the second part of a danza/contradanza. As a musical idiom, this merengue, like the Cuban danza, would have been distinguished by a pronounced use of the habanera syncopation in the latter sections. In evident merry disregard of Governor Pezuela's ban of 1849, it is clear that by the 1850s the new merengue and independent couple dancing had effectively replaced the older Spanish contradanza, and presumably a more syncopated and creolized musical style had become standard. After 1852, with Pezuela gone and his ban evidently a dead letter, the term "merengue" and the dance itself could flourish without official censure; however, that term—which may have denoted a specific dance variant—increasingly gave way to the rubric "danza," which was at once more dignified and less controversial. (The term "merengue" hence came to refer to the individual parts of the danza that succeeded the introductory *paseo*.)

Strikingly, one of the first self-identified surviving "danzas" composed on Puerto Rican soil is the 1857 piece "Danza" (Opus 33), by Gottschalk (1829–69). As discussed in the previous chapter, Gottschalk spent much of the period between 1853 and 1860 touring the Spanish and French Caribbean, where he befriended, encouraged, and inspired local musicians and thrilled audiences with his colorful performances. Some of these were orchestral extravaganzas, but most were piano recitals in which he performed contemporary European classics alongside his own flamboyant compositions, many of which incorporated elements of local Caribbean vernacular music. In 1857, as previously mentioned, Gottschalk arrived from Cuba to Puerto Rico, where he collaborated with influential brass-band leader Allard. The same year, he presented a few new compositions of his own at packed concerts in Ponce and San Juan; one was "Marcha de los gíbaros" ("March of the Jíbaros"), which incorporated elements of *jíbaro* music and the Yuletide song "Si me dan pasteles"; the other was "Danza" (Opus 33), which can be heard on the compact disc accompanying this volume.

As mentioned in Chapter 2, Gottschalk's "Danza" (Opus 33) may have been inspired to some extent by Cuban music, as reflected in the insistent *cinquillos* typical of popular songs in Oriente, where he had recently resided, and the use of the term "danza," which was standard in Cuba as well as Puerto Rico. In at least one significant respect, however, the piece was more aligned with Puerto Rican practice than Cuban tradition. Cuban contradanzas and danzas, as discussed earlier, invariably comprised only two sections, which were presumably repeated ad infinitum in the dance context, perhaps with some improvised variations. By contrast, as mentioned, Puerto Rican danzas from the 1860s—and perhaps earlier—generally used a different extension technique, in the form of additional sections, such that they most typically consisted of a short introductory *paseo* followed by two or more sections popularly known as "merengues." "Danza" (Opus 33) can be seen as an idiosyncratic precursor or variant of this practice, with a C section segueing to a concluding return to the initial A and B sections. As performed to great success in his recitals, Gottschalk's "Danza" (Opus 33) further helped legitimize the danza as a genre fit for concert events and earned him the appreciation of intellectuals like Brau ([1885] 1977: 11–12) for his contribution to island music culture. (Composer Campos Parsi went so far as to call Gottschalk "the father of Puerto Rican national music," but most scholars would regard this assessment as an exaggeration [see Malavet Vega 1992: 246].)

In the 1860s, Puerto Rican musical life blossomed somewhat, aided by the construction of several theaters and social centers in San Juan, Ponce, and Mayagüez. Contemporary accounts attest to the popularity and vigor of the danza in this decade and also to its thorough creolization. The rustic *güiro* scraper, introduced as early as 1853, had become standard in ensembles, and composer Braulio Dueño Colón (1854–1934), in an influential 1913 essay, seemed to be writing of the 1860s in his denunciation of the more Afro-Caribbean, populist style of danzas preceding the genre's supposed rescue at the hands of Tavárez and others:

> We can't deny that there was a time during which our danza sadly degenerated due to the poor artistic taste of certain composers and bandleaders who used the African bomba [an Afro–Puerto Rican music and dance genre], imposing on the danza a grotesque and thus anti-aesthetic rhythm.
>
> Fortunately the exquisite taste of artists like Tavárez, Ramos [Heraclio] and [Morel] Campos imposed itself, and the creole danza recovered the suave and charming rhythm that always characterized it.
>
> In the epoch to which we referred, which was deadly for the development of our regional music, were written hundreds of danzas of detestable taste, of which only two or three survived the shipwreck, and which were composed by the likes of Santaella, a prolific author of dance music. ([1913] 1977: 13)

As it is, few danzas from this decade survive, although we have record, via Dueño Colón and others, of their colorful colloquial titles and their standard ensemble formats. One of the first documented pieces of the decade is "La hortensia" ("The Hydrangea"), composed by Ginés Ramos in 1865 (reproduced in Muñoz 1966: 53–54). "La hortensia" is in many ways typical of subsequent danzas. It opens with an unsyncopated eight-bar *paseo* in sixteenth notes (repeated once), an eight-bar B section (also repeated), and an eight-bar C section (repeated), with a final four-bar coda. The B and C sections could be regarded as comprising the "merengues" or body of the piece. Elastic *tresillos* permeate the right-hand melody of the B and C sections.

Despite its historical interest, a work like "La hortensia" is trivial compared to the series of sublime danzas that flowed a few years later from the pen of Tavárez. Born in San Juan in 1843 to a French Creole father and a local mother, Tavárez studied piano as a youth and in 1857 moved to France to further his training at the Paris Conservatory, becoming the first Puerto Rican musician to pursue such Continental grooming. In 1860, he suffered a stroke that impaired his hearing and the use of one of his hands and obliged him to return to San Juan, where he eventually commenced teaching, concertizing, publishing piano reductions of operas, and composing danzas, along with a few waltzes and other works. His first surviving danzas are "La lopita" (ca. 1861) and "Como me mira el viejo" (1863). In 1867, he shifted to Ponce, which enjoyed a livelier and more cosmopolitan ambience especially hospitable to the creole danza. There he became mentor to Morel Campos and others and composed his most famous danzas, including "Margarita," "Ausencia," "La ondina," and "La sensitiva," performing them at local theaters and private salons. In 1883, he died at the age of forty, being survived by his four children, including his daughter Elisa (1879–1960), who went on to become a distinguished pianist and pre-eminent interpreter of her father's oeuvre.

Prior to Tavárez, Puerto Rican danzas had flourished primarily as dance-band items, even if they were originally notated, like contemporary Cuban counterparts, as piano scores. Tavárez, however, was well familiar with Gottschalk's "Danza" (Opus 33) and presumably with some of the more pianistic 1850s and 1860s contradanzas of Cuban composer Manuel Saumell. Moreover, his Parisian training steeped him in the music of Chopin, Schumann, Liszt, and their contemporaries. It was his singular mission and contribution to elevate the danza to the level of a sophisticated light-classical salon and concert piano music while retaining its creole character. Although the danza predated Tavárez's input, he is regarded to some extent as the father of the local danza in that, like Saumell, he was the first to transform it from a quaint and provincial dance-music form into a sophisticated art form. Subsequently, of course, his danzas became widely popular and were easily absorbed into the island's vernacular music culture, being performed not only in formal piano recitals but by the most humble accordion-and-guitar ensembles. Most, like "Margarita," were also fitted with sentimental romantic lyrics, such that as slow, romantic songs, they enjoyed a status akin to that of the popular Cuban bolero from the early 1900s. Like his student and successor Morel Campos, Tavárez gave his danzas elegant, often wistful titles ("Absence," or dedications to society ladies) in contrast to the colloquial, saucy titles in vogue during the 1850s–60s.

"Margarita" can be heard on this volume's accompanying compact disc. The piece's Chopinesque and pianistic rather than dance-band orientation is evident from its first bars. The subsequent body of the piece epitomizes the languid and romantic voluptuousness for which local writers have celebrated the danza. Figure 3.3 shows the melody's first phrase (following the *paseo* introduction), with its accompaniment alternating *cinquillo*-like patterns and 3-3-2 *tresillos*. As discussed above, dance bands and even many pianists tend to play the two eighth-note triplets (with their tied inner notes) more or less as *cinquillos* (eighth-sixteenth-eighth-sixteenth-eighth; see Chapters 1 and 2); in her well-known recording of this piece, Tavárez's daughter Elisa retains the *cinquillo* pattern only in the most languorous rubato (as imitated in the compact disc's recording). They can be seen as the most sublimated, rarefied distillation of the same *cinquillo* that thunders insistently in vodun and *bomba* drumming and that, in more moderate tempi and alternating with bars in straight eighths, constituted a hallmark of the Antillean danza and Cuban danzón.

The assessment by Campos Parsi of Tavárez's role in island music culture merits quoting at length:

> It is with good reason that Manuel Gregorio Tavárez has been baptized "father of the Puerto Rican danza," as it was in his hands that the crude form of the Cuban habanera [*sic*; contradanza] was transformed into a personal vehicle of great finery and exquisite construction. The

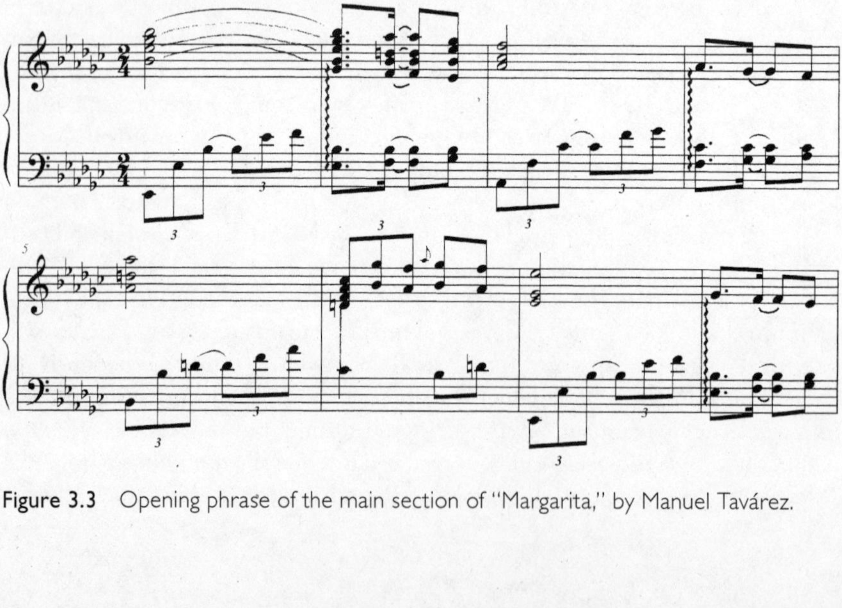

**Figure 3.3** Opening phrase of the main section of "Margarita," by Manuel Tavárez.

> danzas, which previously were played by humble ensembles for dance, were adapted to the fluid language of the piano. The composer not only created melodies of Romantic breadth, but also explored the distinctive sonorities of the instrument. It was Tavárez who linked the danza to the piano, elevating it to the characteristic form of his century. The danza returned as a messenger of profound and intimate emotions. It became the vehicle of the confession of longing, the disconsolate lament, or the expression of a felicitously requited love. In creole society these short pieces occupied the place which in Romantic-era Europe were held by the "musical moments," "songs without words," or "pages of an album" of Schubert, Mendelssohn, or Schumann.
>
> Tavárez created the prototype of the composer of danzas: the cultured and sensitive man, who while lacking an environment which would enable him to express himself completely, focused his energies on the creation of small, flexible works, which, though written as piano works for listening, easily lent themselves to being used as dance accompaniment.[17]

## Nationalism, Ponce, and "La Borinqueña"

By the 1860s, Puerto Rico and Cuba had the unenviable distinction of being the last remaining colonies of Spain in the Americas—in the words of Puerto Rican poet Lola Rodríguez de Tió, the "twin wings of the same bird" that was unable to fly. Spanish rule continued to be supported by various Hispanophilic reactionaries, employees of the colonial regime, and others fearful of potential domination by subaltern people of color. Yet in both islands, nationalist sentiment was growing, especially as a bourgeois phenomenon fueled by Enlightenment notions of democracy and progress, by imperial Spain's parasitic and backward economic policies, and by the despotic rule of arrogant governors sent from Spain who busied themselves with decrees like the bans on merengue and, for a period, on wearing beards. With governors like Pezuela actively opposing public education, the island's literacy rate was below 12 percent in 1860; colonial rule was also detested by the thousands of day laborers (*jornaleros*) required to fulfill quotas of forced labor on plantations under penalty of imprisonment.

Cuba, if for no other reason than its greater size, sustained a vigorous independence movement from the 1830s and armed insurrection in 1868. Such overt rebellion was less feasible in smaller and heavily garrisoned Puerto Rico, but by the 1860s anticolonial sentiment was strong and widespread, including among otherwise conservative hacienda owners frustrated by imperial restrictions on commerce. A popular nationalism increasingly came to manifest itself in the 1860s, whether via open political anticolonialism—however vigorously repressed—or in the more subtle, safe, and oblique form of a pride in creole culture, including the danza.

The capital city of San Juan enjoyed prominence as the hub of various forms of popular celebrations with its carnivals, diverse bands and orchestras, Afro-Caribbean ensembles from nearby sugar plantations, military and church events, and other formal ceremonies and celebrations sponsored by the colonial administration. By the 1860s, however, the southern city of Ponce emerged as a rival economic and cultural center especially hospitable to ideals of European liberalism and local creole arts, such as the danza. With its substantial communities of German, English, French, and Corsican immigrants, Ponce had a more cosmopolitan ambience than San Juan, whose religious life was dominated by reactionary and bigoted forms of Catholicism. As Quintero-Rivera and others have noted, Ponce's independent and progressive cultural ambience was linked, whether directly or indirectly, to its socioeconomic milieu. Ponce was the main commercial center for the fertile, plantation-dominated, south-central part of the island, where merchants and landowners felt particularly frustrated by Spanish mercantilist tariffs imposed on imports and exports. Progressive political activism extended to working classes and petty-bourgeois artisans, who published their own newspaper from 1874. Meanwhile, the town administration promoted cultural activities in its own way, as by the 1864 installation of lamps around the town plaza to encourage and enhance public open-air concerts (Quintero-Rivera [1986] 2002).

With the participation of slaves and lower-class mulatto artisans, Ponce's ambience proved especially hospitable to the creole danza as it flourished from the 1860s. While most composers and bandleaders remained in San Juan, those living in Ponce became the most prominent. As mentioned, Tavárez shifted to Ponce in 1867 to take advantage of its cultural climate, and the city went on to host his student, Morel Campos, the most outstanding composer of the 1880s–90s. Moreover, it was especially in Ponce and its surroundings that the danza became a more properly "national" genre in that it was celebrated as such by locals and its appeal extended to diverse social classes. Quintero-Rivera insightfully attributes this broad social popularity in particular to the "contradictory" socioeconomic orientation of the *hacendados*—capitalist slave owners who were at once linked to but frustrated by colonial rule—and their economic and cultural links to local artisans, from whose ranks danza performers came. Even today, Ponce retains some of its attractive colonial flavor, with its elegant balconies, plazas, and gardens. For composer and essayist Veray, Ponce's cultural charm was quintessentially expressed in the danzas of Tavárez and especially Morel Campos: "The danza of Morel Campos is saturated by the atmosphere of Ponce, and displays the defining qualities of that austere, provincial, sober, and defiant Ponce society of the 1880s" ([1977] 2002: 65).

The closest Puerto Rico came to hosting an open anticolonial revolution occurred in the provincial town of Lares, where in 1868 local conspirators proclaimed independence and seized the town in what was supposed to be the first spark in a broader insurrection; unfortunately, colonial militias soon snuffed out the uprising. Although abortive, the event—commemorated as the "*grito* [cry] *de Lares*"—intensified anticolonial patriotism, precipitated a liberalization of imperial rule, and promoted the popularity of a serenata that soon became the island's unofficial anthem, "La borinqueña." While the origin of this piece is contested, as a musical composition it appears to have been a song of anonymous authorship that surfaced in various parts of Latin America, including Peru. In Puerto Rico, its composition, or alteration, has been generally attributed to guitarist and composer Francisco (Paco) Ramírez Ortiz and his acquaintance, Catalonian immigrant Félix Astol; Ramírez at the least may have endowed the tune with the typical creole rhythmic touches that essentially transformed it into a danza. Astol is believed to have composed for Ramírez's melody a romantic text, eulogizing a lovely local mulatto woman. Verses similar to those attributed to Astol have surfaced in Peru and elsewhere. Astol's slightly precious lyrics commence:

> Lovely mulata, image of candor of the garden of Borinquen,
> pure and fragrant flower—
> dumbstruck is every person who beholds your genteel and gracious countenance
> and your dainty foot.[18]

In 1868, when anticolonial fervor flared into insurrection, nationalist poet Rodríguez de Tió composed a new, explicitly militant set of verses to the already popular song:

> Awake, Borinqueño [Puerto Rican], the signal has been given!
> Rise from this dream, the hour to fight has come!
> Doesn't your heart burn on hearing this patriotic call?
> Come, our companion will be the roar of the cannon.
> See how the Cuban will soon be free, the machete will give him his liberty.[19]

"La borinqueña," whether with the lyrics of Astol or Rodríguez, went on to enjoy extraordinary popularity and dissemination on the island that continue to the present. While the official anthem of Puerto Rico must by fiat remain "The Star-Spangled Banner," "La borinqueña" retains a special and more immediate patriotic appeal and in 1952 was declared the "National Hymn" of the island, as refitted with lyrics by Manuel Fernández Juncos (which such commentators as Malavet Vega deem rather bland [1992: 515, 265–276]). What is particularly significant for the present study is that the song is not a pompous martial air but a rather typical, if especially melodious, danza, with the characteristic creole syncopations of the 1860s. As such, the song provides another illustration of the extent to which the danza constituted a national genre and a quintessential expression of island cultural identity.

## Juan Morel Campos and the Danza in Its Prime

It would be a mistake to conceive of the history of the danza as a unidirectional evolution from a rustic dance music into the light-classical, rarefied piano idiom of Tavárez. In some respects, the culminating heyday of the genre involved not such a stylized purification but rather its vigorous flowering as a national dance music enjoyed by rich and poor, embodying a Caribbean creole character in a way that became distinctively Puerto Rican and, as such, a symbol of a truly national music. While Tavárez's unique achievements constituted a precondition for this efflorescence, ultimately the most important figure in this process was Juan Morel Campos, whose danzas were at once more broadly popular than the salon-oriented works of Tavárez while displaying a variety, tunefulness, and originality that distinguished them from earlier dance pieces and exhibited an ineffably Puerto Rican character.

Born in Ponce in 1857, Morel Campos undertook formal training in most of the standard instruments of contemporary ensembles, including bombardino, cornet, contrabass, and piano. With the French-trained Tavárez and Spanish-trained Antonio Egipciaco, he went on to study composition, harmony, counterpoint, and piano. During his obligatory military service, he served as featured bombardino player in the regimental band of the Madrid Cazadores. His professional career commenced in the latter 1870s, shortly after leaving the military, when he formed his own ensembles and began composing in earnest. Meanwhile, he worked on occasion as an orchestra conductor in South America and the Caribbean and as an arranger for itinerant Cuban theater troupes and Italian opera and Spanish zarzuela companies. His facility at playing several instruments was accompanied by a prodigious gift for producing ad hoc arrangements as were needed for performances of orchestral works in town ensembles lacking proper instrumentation.

Morel Campos was gifted with a Vivaldi-like fecundity and facility enabling him to compose music virtually as fast as he could write it down. Until his death from a heart attack at age thirty-eight in 1896, he composed around 550 pieces, including waltzes, paso dobles, mazurkas, polkas, church music, and zarzuelas; but he is remembered almost exclusively for his 283 danzas, especially such favorites as "Maldito amor," "Alma sublime," "Laura y Georgina," "Felices días," "Ten piedad," "No me toques," and others. Through two decades of regularly performing these pieces in ballrooms and public plazas, Morel Campos succeeded in popularizing them at diverse social levels, such that they entered the repertoire of ballroom ensembles, salon pianists, and humble street musicians. Morel Campos inspired several eloquent encomiums that celebrated his unique status in island culture. Campos Parsi noted how Tavárez had refined the unpretentious local merengues and danza tradition, elevating the danza to a sublime light-classical art. Morel Campos pursued a more democratic path:

> Morel Campos revitalizes it, inserts in it large doses of the popular, he reworks it, explores and molds it to his whim. He found in the danza the perfect form to express all his artistic, personal, and political needs. Fernando Callejo insightfully comments that in the danza, Morel Campos condensed the state of the popular Puerto Rican conscience agitated by the ongoing struggle for political freedom. Further, he used the danza as a great social leveler bringing to high society the picaresque rhythms of the people and to the people the rich harmonic conception and formal complexity of the salon danza. He was the great synthesizer of all the musical currents of the age in his island. (Campos Parsi 1976: 93–94, in Malavet Vega 1992: 317–318)

Veray also penned an expansive tribute to Morel Campos, similarly eulogizing how his danzas simultaneously symbolized the aristocratic bourgeoisie of the era and depicted "an entire generation, and an entire epoch" ([1977] 2002: 68).

As Balseiro observed in his informative discussion of the composer ([1960] 1977), Morel Campos notated his danzas for a variety of formats. Seventy-five were notated for piano, as was customary for contemporary Puerto Rican contradanzas, danzas, and danzones and enabled them to be sold as sheet music for local pianists. However, it is generally assumed that he intended most to be performed by dance bands in ballrooms. Some were fitted with romantic lyrics and written for voice and piano, while a few notations call for whimsical words or phrases to be shouted out. A few were penned for four-hands piano. From the 1940s, they became staples of the repertoire of renowned piano virtuoso Jesús María Sanromá (1902–84), who recorded many of them. In his lifetime, Morel Campos performed most of his danzas primarily as ensemble pieces for dance, in which he might take the role of featured bombardino player. Such ensembles would typically consist of three or four violins, two clarinets, two bombardinos, a cornet, a *güiro*, and a *timbalito* kettledrum. Since then, as mentioned, the danzas have been freely performed as rearrangements for various ad hoc combinations of instruments, and such favorites as "Maldito amor" might even be encountered in the repertoire of a humble *jíbaro* guitar-and-*cuatro* duo. As discussed in the next chapter, the danzas of Morel Campos (more so than Cuban danza and danzón composers) also became standards in the salon music of the Dominican Republic and constituted models for local composers there.

Campos Parsi and others have celebrated the prodigious variety of Morel Campos's danzas, many of which, like other Puerto Rican danzas, tend to fall into either "*afectiva*" (lyrical) or "festive" categories. In the first set are melancholy works, such as "Ten piedad," "Mis peñas," and "Vano empeño." Lighter and more festive are such pieces as "Anita," "No me toques," and "Sí, te toco."

Most of the danzas might be said to fall into an expressive and formal range that is in some respects homogeneous, finite, and not hostile to generalized description. The typical Morel Campos danza adheres to a form that was standard not only for the Puerto Rican danza but also for its derivative danza forms in the Dominican Republic and Curaçao. The danza traditionally commences with an eight-bar *paseo*, repeated once, often in straight, unsyncopated eighth or sixteenth notes, with a sort of annunciatory character, half-cadencing on the dominant. Then follows the true body of the piece, in the form of two "merengues," leading to a trio, and then a return to some material of the first merengue, and possibly a brief coda. In some cases, the harmonies are in a conventional early-Romantic, perhaps Rossini-like mode, and the melodies conform to familiar eight-bar patterns, always in 2/4. The merengues are enlivened with the by-then familiar creole rhythms—especially the habanera pattern, and the amphibrach and *cinquillo*—the latter two alternating, as in Cuba, with unsyncopated measures in even-note values. The *cinquillos* are typically notated in the form of elastic *tresillos*, suggesting and perhaps actually occasioning distinctively distended note values. As he expanded the traditional *paseo*-merengue structure of the danza, Morel Campos endowed the genre with melodic and harmonic sophistication with modulations into remote tonalities, while maintaining the austere, sober, and provincial character of his native city of Ponce. Traces of Italian cantabile are clear in danzas composed in the 1880s, such as "Alma sublime," "Tormento," and "Influencia del arte." Chromaticism is especially marked in danzas like "Noche deliciosa" (date unknown). His danza "Felices días" (1894), a piece that received an award in Florence, is considered a masterpiece of creole Caribbean popular music. Such pianists as Julio Arteaga, Gonzalo Nuñez, Anita Otero, and Elisa Tavárez brought Morel's danzas to international concert halls, alongside works of Chopin, Schumann, and other Europeans. Many were recorded in the 1940s by pianist Sanromá under RCA's Red Seal label devoted to classical music.

The compact disc accompanying this volume contains two renditions of "Laura y Georgina," one of the most popular danzas of Morel Campos. The first is a piano solo modeled on that recorded by Sanromá. The second was recorded in 1909 by the horn-dominated Orquesta de Cocolia (formerly the Juan Morel Campos orchestra). The piece opens with a *paseo* redolent of an Italian operatic introduction; the subsequent merengue nicely illustrates Morel Campos's gift for melody. The bass/left-hand accompaniment does not follow the standard creole forms of elastic *tresillo*, *cinquillo*, or amphibrach, but it can be seen as a sort of variant, providing, with passages of the melody, an ongoing and expressive ambiguity as to whether the piece is in 6/8 or 2/4.

Contemporaneous with the Ponce-based Morel Campos and others was a different set of composers and bandleaders who were active in San Juan, whose styles bear enough similarities as to be regarded as constituting a "San Juan school." The leading figures in this category included Julián Andino; regimental clarinetist Casimiro Duchesne (1850–1906); and versatile instrumentalist, conductor, and essayist Dueño Colón. None of their music is easily available today. Veray contrasts the two schools:

> The San Juan danza is more rowdy and frivolous. . . . It lacks the sentimental flight and daring of the Ponce danza. It is a danza of academic spirit . . . though at that time it was more tropical and legitimate than the Ponce style, evolving directly from the Spanish contradanza. It didn't have, like the Ponce style, that spirit of the French salons. It was thus more pure in essence. The Ponce danza of Tavárez was adorned with finery imported from Europe. The San Juan style insists on short, equidistant phrases. The Ponce style is more lyrical, querulous, and passionate. As it is more spontaneous, it enters our inner world more easily. ([1956] 1977: 30)

## The Mainstream Danza: Form, Style, and Structure

One distinctive feature of the danza, contrasting in particular with its Cuban danza and danzón counterparts, is its extended formal structure. As discussed in the Introduction, Cuban danzas—lasting barely a minute if played through only once—would typically be extended for dance accompaniment by being repeated numerous times or perhaps by reiterating, with some variation, the ostinato-like B section. The Cuban danzón popular from around 1880, by contrast, adopted a rondo format, with a recurring A section, and from the early 1900s could feature a vamp-like, harmonically static coda informed by *son* rhythms. Puerto Rican danzas as early as "La hortensia" of 1865 illustrate a different approach, in which the traditional two sections of the contradanza could be supplemented by further sections; as mentioned, the danzas of Morel Campos typically contained two or three such "merengues" after the introductory *paseo*. Further, the individual sections might extend far beyond the customary eight- or sixteen-bar lengths. As Brau notes, "Originally limited to sixteen bars, in 1854 it grew to thirty-four, and in an ever-ascending progression has stretched up to 130 measures" ([1885] 1977: 8). Particularly characteristic was the technique of extending a merengue by means of a passage featuring an obbligato on the bombardino or, less often, the saxophone.

An "obbligato" is a melody ranking in importance just below the main melody, typically with an independent rather than contrapuntal character. Earlier, obbligatos had been added to such frameworks as Bach's fugues and Baroque opera arias. (An obbligato familiar to North American ears is the flute melody that accompanies the primary theme of "Stars and Stripes Forever.") Eventually, upon its arrival in America, the obbligato was introduced in vernacular

(continued on next page)

**Figure 3.4** "Laura y Georgina," by Juan Morel Campos.

forms by saxophonists and *bombardinistas* in Puerto Rico and the Dominican Republic, and by flautists in Cuban danzón orchestras. In the danza, the obbligato typically consists of arpeggios outlining the through-composed (rather than recurrent ostinato) harmonies, while rhythmically adhering to an ostinato, most often a *cinquillo*, in the standard creole two-bar form alternating with a bar of even eight notes. In Figure 3.4, the bombardino obbligato would consist of the bass ("left-hand") pattern. The more typical creole *cinquillo* bombardino

(continued on next page)

**Figure 3.4** *Continued*

obbligato can also be heard on the piece "Impromptu," available on this volume's compact disc. This piece, a danza by Luis Rodriguez Miranda recorded in 1909 by the Puerto Rico Regimental band, also illustrates the style known as "canto de bombardino," in which the bombardino plays an extended precomposed solo.

**Figure 3.4** *Continued*

## The Danza and Its Cuban Counterparts

Except for its significant formal expansion and its idiosyncratic treatment of triplets as discussed above, the Puerto Rican danza, in its heyday roughly spanning the years 1850–1930, bears obvious links and evolutionary affinities to its counterparts in Cuba. In the latter nineteenth century, dance-band styles of both islands' danzas would have been similar in various respects. Further, in the salon piano idiom, the danzas of Tavárez and the Cuban Ignacio Cervantes are not dramatically different in style (and it would be pointless to argue for the superiority of one over the other). At the same time, after the advent of the merengue in 1848, the Puerto Rican danza followed what is better viewed as a parallel rather than derivative trajectory in relation to Cuban music.

As discussed above, most Puerto Rican chroniclers attribute the 1840s–50s flourishing of the merengue/danza to the "spark" provided by the importation of the habanera rhythms via exposure to the Cuban contradanza/danza between 1845 and 1848. However, it is clear that even by the 1850s the Puerto Rican danza was following an independent path. As we have mentioned, even in the 1840s–50s composers and bandleaders were basing pieces on local popular songs (as did their Cuban counterparts). Other formal distinctions of the local danza also arose.

One of these, also described above, pertained to the formal structure of the danza, in particular the practice of extending the piece not by endless repetition of the traditional A and B sections but rather by composing additional sections or extending them with parts featuring obbligatos, especially on the bombardino. The first part was reduced to an eight-bar (repeated) *paseo*, during which dancers would stroll about the floor arm in arm before embracing ballroom-style in the subsequent merengues. In contrast, the Cuban danza retained its two-part form until morphing into the rondo-structured danzón around 1880.

On the other hand, neither the bombardino nor the performance of extended obbligatos and solos on it appear to have been adopted in the Cuban danza. However, as we recall, the obbligato is given the role of a subaltern melody along the entire Puerto Rican danza. The joint contours of melody and countermelody led, in Díaz Díaz's opinion, to a form of counterpoint vernacularly known as "*contracanto*," a vocal style popular among Cuban *trova* groups. In Puerto Rico, the first signs of *contracanto* were registered in the danza "Alondra en los bosques," by tobacco worker Carlos Padilla (d. 1902; Limón de Arce 1925: 131). Much is to be inquired concerning the exchanges Puerto Rican tobacco workers had with their Cuban counterparts during the nineteenth century. However, in his memoirs, Sindo Garay, one of the founders of the *trova cubana*, attests to his exchanges with danza composer Morel Campos during the former's visit in Puerto Rico (De León 1990: 75).

We have also mentioned how several popular danzas of Tavárez, Morel Campos, and others were fitted, whether by the composer or a poet, with romantic lyrics, such that they circulated not only as instrumental works but as sentimental songs, somewhat akin to Cuban habaneras or early-twentieth-century boleros. Aside from the Cuban habaneras themselves, some Cuban danzas also acquired such vocal texts, but on the whole it appears that the sung aspect of Puerto Rican danzas enjoyed a greater prominence and popularity than did their counterparts in Cuba, where *canción* and bolero were the prevalent romantic vocal idioms.

By the 1880s in Cuba, the danzón had largely replaced the danza, such that the Puerto Rican danzas of Morel Campos and his contemporaries are better compared not with earlier contradanzas but with danzones, which, indeed, were popular in Puerto Rico and often played and danced alongside local danzas. Both the danzón and the Puerto Rican danza were typically played by similar ensembles, with similar persistence of the *cinquillo* ostinato (in its creole two-bar form, however notated), such that in listening to excerpts of either genre it might be easy to mistake one for the other. However, the different formal structures are again notable: The danzón used a rondo form (e.g., ABACAD)—often, from the early 1900s, with an ostinato-based, vamp-like coda—while the Puerto Rican danza, meanwhile, adhered to its multisectional form. Further, each genre had its own stylistic conventions and clichés; for example, nearly ubiquitous in the A theme of the danzón was the eight-bar rhythmic structure previously outlined in Chapter 2 and the cliché of following a four-bar melody with a four-bar sixteenth-note run. Such conventions were wholly uncharacteristic of the danza. On the whole, one might also generalize that an Afro-Caribbean percussive flavor was also somewhat more pronounced in the danzón than in the danza—perhaps in accordance with Puerto Rico's whiter racial demography. In extant early-twentieth-century recordings of ensemble danzas, such as those on this book's compact disc, percussion parts are barely audible, such that the pieces sound generally European except for the pervasive amphibrachs and *cinquillos*. Finally, the two genres have enjoyed—or suffered—different sorts of fates in the twentieth century. The Cuban contradanza and danza are extinct as dance idioms and survive at all only insofar as the works of Saumell and Cervantes are played and studied by some pianists. The danzón may be a bit more familiar to modern Cuban listeners, but its lasting historical importance may reside in the way that it evolved directly into the 1950s chachachá and big-band mambo—itself a precursor of salsa.

The trajectory of the Puerto Rican danza, which is discussed further below, has been in some ways distinct. On the one hand, it cannot really be said to have contributed directly to the evolution of the salsa and reggaetón that dominate modern dance music on the island. Nevertheless, even if the danza's era as a focus for composition passed in the 1930s, the genre has gone on to retain a certain niche in island music and dance culture that accords it a greater afterlife than the Cuban danza has had.

## The Danza in the Twentieth Century

Veray and other music historians generally regard Morel Campos's death in 1896 as marking the end of the danza's most dynamic period. As Veray comments, "With Juan Morel Campos closed the grand tradition of our nineteenth century; upon his death, the world of the danza seemed to lose its orbit" ([1956] 1977: 32). However, the danza enjoyed another three decades of prodigious popularity and compositional activity, while the island shifted from Spanish to North American colonial rule in 1898. Some of the leading composers during this period were of the generation of Morel Campos, although they outlived him and can be said to have perpetuated the fin de siècle idiom in their individual styles. Among Ponce-based followers of Morel Campos were Juan Ríos Ovalle, Jaime Pericas (1870–?), the Spanish-born Arturo Pasarell, and bombardino virtuoso and regimental bandleader Ángel Mislán (1862–1911); of the San Juan school were composer and essayist Dueño Colón (1854–1934) and violinist Andino. Most of these musicians composed danzas along with other works, while performing in dance bands and other contexts.[20]

Of the next generation, the most distinguished figure was José Quintón (1881–1925), who is generally regarded as closing the cycle of the genre. Quintón was a prodigious and prolific talent, composing Masses, concertos, and other works aside from danzas, few of which have been published. His danzas are themselves diverse in character; some incorporate elements of *jíbaro* music, while others showcase virtuoso display or impressionistic harmonies redolent of Debussy and contemporary European music (see Veray [1956] 1977: 34; Balseiro [1960] 1977: 57). Certainly Quintón sought greater vistas for the genre, promoting the idiom of the "concert danza" and introducing colorful cadenzas in some of them. In a different vein is his popular "El coquí" of 1901, whose playful arpeggiated octave leaps mimic the sound of the frog once unique to the island (and now annoying Hawaiians with its nocturnal ruckus); "El coquí" can be heard on the compact disc accompanying this book. Like Tavárez and Morel Campos, Quintón died young, at age forty-four. Also of Quintón's generation, but longer lived, was Simon Madera (1875–1957), whose best-known danza, "Mis amores" (composed at age eighteen), is also presented on this volume's compact disc. Since Quintón, production of danzas has not ceased entirely, but the spirit of subsequent compositions in this ultimately archaic genre has inevitably been either neoclassicist and impressionistic (as with Narciso Figueroa), self-consciously modernist (William Ortiz), or even postmodernist (Díaz Díaz).

In his oft-cited essay of 1885, Brau presciently foresaw the inevitable decline of the danza, steeped as it was in the sort of Romantic languor that could not survive modernity ([1885] 1977: 13). Indeed, by the 1930s the world of aristocratic *hacendados* and curtseying, fan-wielding *señoras* was disappearing under the advent of agribusiness, Cuban rumbas, and Yankee pop culture. For Antonio Pedreira, author of *Insularismo*, a widely read 1934 rumination on his island's culture, such developments were anathema, and he called for a revival of the danza as a quintessentially Puerto Rican product. Like other essayists of preceding generations, in his nostalgia for the era of the hacienda, he hailed the danza as ineffably languid, melancholy, soft, voluptuous, and thus "feminine," ideally suited to his island's climate and its people's endearingly mild and anemic disposition (Pedreira [1934] 1973: 152–165).

Perhaps because of its genteel eloquence, Pedreira's ode became standard reading in Puerto Rican schools, but its underlying obscurantism, Hispanophilic racism, and patriarchal essentialism—so glaringly obvious to modern readers—were trenchantly critiqued the very year after its publication by liberal essayist Tomás Blanco in his "Eulogy to the Plena" (1935). Blanco celebrated rather than lamented the black and mulatto presence in his island's culture and counterposed the earthy, feisty dynamism of the proletarian *plena* songs to what was by then the quaint prissiness of the danza. While acknowledging the beauty of many danzas, he wrote:

> The danza is a greenhouse plant. Transplanted and acclimated, its regional modifications were acquired by being grafted on; the leaves and flowers were nurtured at the expense of the roots. . . . Its gist, its substance, is the product of an epoch more than of a people. For this reason it has been accused of being foreign. . . . Very much of the nineteenth century, it has become disjointed from our present reality. See, if you disagree, how affected and precious appear to us today the lyrics of the most famous of our danzas, which undoubtedly, in their own time seemed charged with grace and emotion. [He quotes the lyrics of "La borinqueña," with its eulogy to the "genteel countenance" and "pretty and delicate foot" of the dainty lass on the balcony.] Such a woman suits the vulgar sensuality which romps through the measures of the danza. Lachrymose supplication and plump metaphors lent a Romantic prestige to the false ambience which cradled the aristocratic gallantry of the epoch. Today there scarcely exist examples of such women. Abundant, in their place, are sinewy, muscular mulatto women, whether slim or heavy, young or mature, but with calves and armpits instead of feet and countenances. (Blanco 1935: 42)

In his 1960 essay, Balseiro commented similarly on the anachronistic nature of the danza in the age of televisions and airplanes: "When we harness nuclear energy and atom bombs, it is foolish to hope that this dynamic can be kept on a par with the sweet, slow, and harmonious dance music of the last century" ([1960] 1977: 60). Like the mazurka, he noted, the danza lives on as a concert idiom rather than the social dance it once was.

Meanwhile, as for the essentially "feminine" (that is, soft and passive) character of the danza and Puerto Ricans as a people, one might well counterpose the insurrectionary stridency of Rodríguez de Tió's lyrics to "La borinqueña" and the activism of such a woman as proindependence militant Lolita Lebrón, celebrated in Vitín Calderón's danza "Lolita" (Aparicio 1998: 24–25).

Although no longer a focus of compositional interest, the danza has continued to occupy a place in Puerto Rican culture.[21] Through the 1960s, various sorts of ensembles and singers continued to record evergreens like "Laura y Georgina," which acquired the status of bolero-like vernacular popular songs. A period of patriotic revival in the 1970s became the opportunity for composers like Antonio Cabán Vale ("El Topo"), Eliado Torres, and Rafi Escudero to cultivate short danzas with unrepeated sections and straightforward harmonies. The most emblematic of these danzas is El Topo's "Verde luz" ("Green Light"), which has become an obligatory standard in family parties and festivities. School bands still perform danzas, and the works of Tavárez and Morel Campos remain strong in the repertoire of local pianists in conservatories and concert halls. Lastly, danzas may even be danced on occasion, especially at weddings, when the first song the band plays may be a chestnut of Morel Campos, during which the bride dances with her father.

## Notes

1. An exhaustive survey of several hundred historical documents by Díaz Díaz makes it possible to discuss with some accuracy the transformation of the contradanza into a native genre. Research also profited from the valuable annotated bibliography of Donald Thompson and Annie F. Thompson (1991). The present chapter includes revised versions of passages from earlier publications by Díaz Díaz (1990, 1996, 2008).
2. See, e.g., the letter by War Lieutenant Esteban Cambreleng to Captain General Miguel de la Torre, Ponce, February 16, 1831, in Colón 1971: 50–53. A useful source is Emilio Colón's edition of *Relación de las Fiestas Públicas de 1831*, a compilation of fifty-nine letters by military representatives of the island's population.
3. An early case of a dance celebration at a Catholic priest's home is found in the northern coastal plain of Vega Baja, to celebrate the Spanish Constitution of 1811 with an orchestra from San Juan, according to *La gaceta del gobierno constitucional de Puerto Rico*, August 8, 1821, p. 251.
4. *La gaceta del gobierno constitucional de Puerto Rico*, August 9, 1820, pp. 109–110.
5. *La gaceta del gobierno constitucional de Puerto Rico*, June 20, 1821, p. 196.
6. Letter dated February 16, 1831, by Jaime Cedó to Miguel de la Torre, in Colón 1971: 109.
7. However, Tapia y Rivera also relates how members of a recently arrived Spanish garrison, "ignorant of these customs," clashed provocatively with some local youths, occasioning the subsequent intervention of Governor López.
8. The carnet system is further discussed in Díaz Díaz 1990.
9. *Boletín Instructivo y Mercantil de Puerto Rico*, August 3, 1839, p. 358. "¿Cómo podrán llamar danza / figurando un corredor, / cien parejas frente á frente / todas en expectación / esperando una pisada, / ó mejor dicho una cos, / del que viene atolondrado / sin mirar alrededor? . . . No aborrezco yo la danza, / al contrario, sí Señor; / la amo con tanta gana / como otro cualquier la amó; / admiro la más costosa / con ambiciosa afición, / mas la escojo sosegada / que en esta tierra hay calor."
10. *La gaceta del gobierno de Puerto Rico*, February 24, 1848, pp. 3–4.
11. For relevant references to uses of the *sesquiáltera*, see Romero 1999: 383–422 regarding Peru, and Gradante 1999: 302–382 regarding Colombia.
12. This transcription was made from the faded and, in parts, barely legible manuscript copy found by Díaz Díaz in the Archivo General de Puerto Rico; among other ambiguities, the treble b's in m. 18 may be flat.

13. "Folletín," *La gaceta del gobierno de Puerto Rico*, September 19, 1848, pp. 2–3. (The *Gaceta*, Puerto Rico's leading nineteenth-century newspaper, changed its full name a few times in the course of that century.)
14. Bartolomé José Crespo, *Las habaneras pintadas por sí mismas* (Havana: Imprenta de Oliva, 1847), cited in Linares 1970: 20 and Quintero-Rivera 2005: 114. See Galán 1983: 245–256 for discussion of "*la ley brava*." The sopimpa is also mentioned in various other chronicles from Santiago, but no certainty exists concerning its specific nature. The fandango and *boleras* (bolero) were Spanish-derived dances. The verse resists translation into fluent English.
15. From *Boletin Mercantil de Puerto Rico*, as cited in *El ponceño*, May 6, 1854, p. 16; also cited in Girón 1984: 214.
16. *El ponceño*, May 13, 1854, p. 6.
17. In "La música en Puerto Rico," in *La gran enciclopedia de Puerto Rico* (Madrid 1976: 93–94), cited in Malavet Vega 1992: 318–319.
18. "Bellisima trigueña, imagen del candor, del jardín de Borinquen, pura y fragrante flor / Por ti se queda extático, todo el mortal que ve, tu aire gentil, simpático, tu breve y lindo pie." According to one version, after the dissemination of Rodríguez de Tió's fiery lyrics, Ramírez, fearful of persecution by the colonial regime, attributed the melody's authorship to Astol, who, as a Spaniard, would have been relatively immune to prosecution.
19. "¡Despierta borinqueño, que han dado la señal! ¡Despierta de ese sueño, que es la hora de luchar! A ese llamar patriótico, ¿no arde el corazón? Ven, nos será simpático el ruido del cañon. Mira, ya el cubano libre será, le dará el machete su libertad."
20. Andino, concertmaster of opera, theater, and cathedral orchestras, has the distinction of composing a subgenre of *jíbaro* music, the *seis andino*, which became standard in a repertoire otherwise accumulated in oral tradition.
21. Unfortunately, various parties, whether motivated by capitalist greed or bureaucratic obduracy, have done their best to lock up the national patrimony of Morel Campos and Tavárez.

## References


Alonso, Manuel. 1849. *El gíbaro*. Barcelona: Juan Oliveres.

———. 2002. Excerpt from "Bailes de Puerto Rico" (from *El gíbaro* [1849]). Trans. Donald Thompson. In *Music in Puerto Rico: A reader's anthology*. Ed. and trans. Donald Thompson, 14–20. Lanham, MD: Scarecrow Press.

Aparicio, Frances. 1998. *Listening to salsa: Gender, Latin popular music, and Puerto Rican cultures*. Hanover, NH: Wesleyan University Press.

Balseiro, José. [1960] 1977. "La danza puertorriqueña." In *Ensayos sobre la danza puertorriqueña*. Ed. Marisa Rosado, 46–61. San Juan: Instituto de Cultural Puertorriqueño.

Blanco, Tomás. 1935. "Elogio de la plena (variaciones boricuas)" [Eulogy to the Plena (Puerto Rican Variations)]. *Revista Ateneo Puertorriquenno* 1 (1): 97–106.

Brau, Salvador. [1885] 1977. "La danza puertorriqueña." In *Ensayos sobre la danza puertorriqueña*. Ed. Marisa Rosado, 1–13. San Juan: Instituto de Cultural Puertorriqueño.

Callejo Ferrer, Fernando. [1915] 1971. *Música y músicos puertorriqueños*. San Juan: [Ediciones Borinquen] Editorial Coquí.

Campos Parsi, Hector. 1976. *Música*. Vol. 7 of *La gran encíclopedia de Puerto Rico*. Madrid: Ediciones R.

Chasteen, John Charles. 2004. *National rhythms, African roots: The deep history of Latin American Popular Dance*. Albuquerque, NM: Dialogos.

Coll y Toste, Cayetano. 1921. "Consecuencias de la batalla de Carabobo en Puerto Rico (letter to Mr. L. Gonzalez Pacheco, Consul of the Republic of Venezuela)." In *Boletín historico de Puerto Rico, Vol. 8*, 161–163. San Juan: Tipografia Cantero, Fernandez.

———. 1924. *Boletín histórico de Puerto Rico, Vol. 11*, 144. San Juan: Tipografia Cantero, Fernández.

Colón, Emilio, ed. 1971. *Relación de las Fiestas Públicas de 1831*. San Juan: Editorial Coquí.

De León, Carmela. 1990. *Sindo Garay: Memorias de un trovador*. Havana: Letras Cubanas.

Díaz Díaz, Edgardo. 1990. "La musica bailable de los carnets: Forma y significado de su repertorio en Puerto Rico (1877–1930)." *Revista Musical Puertorriqueña* 5 (5): 2–21.

———. 1996. "Puerto Rican affirmation and denial of musical nationalism: The cases of Campos Parsi and Aponte Ledée." *Latin American Music Review* 17 (1): 1–20.

———. 2006. "El merengue dominicano: Una prehistoria musical en diez pasos." In *El merengue en la cultura dominicana y del caribe*. Ed. Darío Tejeda and Rafael Emilio Yunén, 179–209. Santo Domingo: Instituto de Estudios Caribeños.

———. 2008. "Danza antillana, conjuntos militares, nacionalismo musical e identidad dominicana: Retomando los pasos perdidos del merengue." *Latin American Music Review* 29 (2): 232–262.

Dueño Colón, Braulio. [1913] 1977. "Estudio sobre la danza puertorriqueña." In *Ensayos sobre la danza puertorriqueña*. Ed. Marisa Rosado, 14–22. San Juan: Instituto de Cultural Puertorriqueño.

Galán, Natalio. 1983. *Cuba y sus sones*. Valencia: Pre-Textos.

Girón, Socorro. 1984. "Ramon F. Caballero, 'Recuerdos de Puerto Rico,' y la polémica del merengue." Ponce: Unpublished manuscript.

González, Hilario, ed. 1980. "Manuel Saumell y la contradanza: Orbita de la contradanza." In *Manuel Saumell: Contradanzas: Estudio introductorio, selección y revisión técnica*, 5–38. Havana: Editorial Letras Cubanas.

Gradante, William J. 1999. "Andean Colombia." In *Music in Latin American culture: Regional traditions*. Ed. John M. Schechter, 302–382. New York: Schirmer Books.

Limón de Arce, José. 1925. *Trovadores populares de Arecibo (1839–1898)*. Mimeograph.

Linares, María Teresa. 1970. *La música popular*. Havana: Instituto del Libro.

Malavet Vega, Pedro. 1992. *Historia de la canción popular en Puerto Rico (1493–1898)*. Ponce: Self-published.

Muñoz, María Luisa. 1966. *La música en Puerto Rico: Panorama histórico-cultural*. Sharon, CT: Troutman Press.

Muñoz de Frontera, Nélida. 1988. "A study of selected nineteenth century Puerto Rican composers and their musical output." Ph.D. diss., New York University.

Ojeda, Felix. 2001. *El desterrado de Paris: Biografía del doctor Ramón Emeterio Betances, 1827–1898*. 1st ed. San Juan: Ediciones Puerto Rico.

Pedreira, Antonio. [1934] 1973. *Insularismo*. Rio Piedras: Editorial Edil.

Pérez de Cuello, Catana, and Rafael Solano. 2003. *El Merengue: Musica y baile de la Republica Dominicana*. Santo Domingo: Codetel.

Quintero-Rivera, Ángel. [1986] 2002. "The danza: A sociopolitical view" [Ponce, la danza y lo nacional: Apuntes para una sociología de la música puertorriqueña]. Trans. Donald Thompson. In *Music in Puerto Rico: A reader's anthology*. Ed. and trans. Donald Thompson, 71–84. Lanham, MD: Scarecrow Press.

———. 1994. "The camouflaged drum: Melodization of rhythms and Maroonage ethnicity in Caribbean peasant music." In *Music and black ethnicity: The Caribbean and South America*. Ed. Gerard Behague, 47–66. Miami: University of Miami.

———. 2005. "El merengue y la danza: Orígenes sociales del baile en pareja en el Caribe." In *El merengue en la cultura dominicana y del caribe*. Ed. Darío Tejeda and Rafael Emilio Yunén, 105–152. Santo Domingo: Instituto de Estudios Caribeños.

Rivera-Guzmán, Félix. 1993. "A rhythmic riddle: A guide to the performance of rhythms in the piano *danzas* of Juan Morel Campos." Ph.D. diss., University of Miami.

Romero, Raúl R. 1999. "Andean Peru." In *Music in Latin American culture: Regional traditions*. Ed. John M. Schechter, 383–423. New York: Schirmer Books.

Sachs, Curt. 1937. *World history of the dance*. New York: Norton.

Schoenrich, Otto. 1918. *Santo Domingo: A country with a future*. New York: Macmillan.

Sheehy, Daniel. 1999. "Popular Mexican musical traditions: The mariachi of West Mexico and the conjunto jarocho." In *Music in Latin American culture: Regional traditions*. Ed. John M. Schechter, 34–79. New York: Schirmer Books.

Starr, S. Frederick. 1995. *Bamboula! The life and times of Louis Moreau Gottschalk*. New York: Oxford University Press.

Tapia y Rivera, Alejandro. [1880] 1973. *Mis memorias, o Puerto Rico como lo encontré y como lo dejó*. Rio Piedras: Edil.

Thompson, Donald, ed. and trans. 2002. *Music in Puerto Rico: A reader's anthology*. Lanham, MD: Scarecrow Press.

Thompson, Donald, and Annie Thompson. 1991. *Music and dance in Puerto Rico from the age of Columbus to modern times: An annotated bibliography*. Lanham, MD: Scarecrow Press.

Veray, Amaury. [1956] 1977. "Vida y desarrollo de la danza puertorriqueña." In *Ensayos sobre la danza puertorriqueña*. Ed. Marisa Rosado, 23–37. San Juan: Instituto de Cultural Puertorriqueño.

———. 1960. *Manuel Gregorio Tavárez, soledad y plenitud*. San Juan: Ateneo Puertorriqueño.

———. [1977] 2002. "The danza: A traditional view" [La misión social de la danza puertorriqueña de Juan Morel Campos]. Trans. Donald Thompson. In *Music in Puerto Rico: A reader's anthology*. Ed. and trans. Donald Thompson, 64–71. Lanham, MD: Scarecrow Press.

PETER MANUEL

# 4 / The Dominican Republic

## *Danza and the Contradanced Merengue*

In 1890 Puerto Rican poet Lola Rodríguez de Tió wrote the oft-quoted lines, "Cuba and Puerto Rico are the twin wings of the same bird; they receive flowers or bullets in the same heart." Rodríguez de Tió was referring to the close cultural and political ties between the two islands, which remained sister colonies of Spain until 1898, many decades after the rest of Latin America had broken free. For its part, the Dominican Republic (or Santo Domingo, as it was called prior to 1844) in 1797 fell out of Spanish sovereignty, which was only intermittently and ineffectually restored later. In other respects, including its geographical location between Cuba and Puerto Rico, the Dominican Republic did seem to cohere with Rodríguez's simile, as the body that once linked the two wings but was later lacerated by bullets, in the form of the violence and instability of its history. Such convulsions occurred primarily in the nineteenth century, which was precisely the period of the contradanza's heyday elsewhere in the Spanish Caribbean. Hence, if the contradanza enjoyed a distinguished and colorful career in Cuba and Puerto Rico, in the Dominican Republic it struggled along as a poor, if feisty, handmaiden, which did, however, play some role in generating the rambunctious merengue of twentieth-century fame.

Corresponding to the perversities of nineteenth-century Dominican social and cultural history is the woefully inadequate amount of documentation of the contradanza and related genres. If the student of Cuban music history can explore a relative abundance of musical scores and contemporary accounts dating from as early as 1803, the relevant Dominican materials predating 1900 comprise a mere handful of enigmatic musical notations and generally ambiguous and often contradictory descriptions. Reconstruction of the contradanza's history, as we shall see, is further impeded by confusion surrounding the meaning of the more commonly used terms "merengue," "danza," and "*tumba*."

The exiguity of source materials has not, however, led to a corresponding dearth of modern scholarship, as researchers—primarily Dominican—of recent decades have done their best to reconstruct aspects of their country's nineteenth-century history, especially in poring over the few useful historical accounts.[1] This chapter draws in particular on the work of Dominican writers Catana Pérez de Cuello, Fradique Lizardo, José Guerrero, and Bernarda Jorge; that of Puerto Ricans Edgardo Díaz Díaz and Ángel Quintero-Rivera; and that of North American ethnomusicologist Paul Austerlitz. However, the attention of most of these investigators has been focused on the history of the Dominican merengue, with the local version of contradanza being significant only insofar as it contributed to that genre. For the purposes of this chapter, while the merengue of the 1850s constituted a contradanza variant of clear interest, the Dominican and especially Cibao-style merengue that subsequently evolved is largely out of the orbit of the contradance family. However, the salon merengue of the 1920s–1940s, ephemeral and marginal as it was, can be seen both as a revival of the *merengue contradanzeado*—the "contradanced merengue"—and as a local flowering of the Puerto Rican danza; accordingly, it is relevant to this study. Moreover, the Dominican Republic did host a local version of the danza, which was modeled on but not entirely identical to its Puerto Rican counterpart. If this *danza dominicana* did not flourish as vigorously as its Cuban and Puerto Rican siblings, it nevertheless constitutes a distinctive and under-documented entity in its nation's music history and in the history of the contradance family in the Caribbean.

## Early History to the Rise of the *Tumba Dominicana*

European colonization of the eastern portion of Hispaniola—"Quisqueya" to the Indians, "Santo Domingo" to the Spanish colonists, and the "Dominican Republic" after 1844—got off to an early and auspicious beginning, with the island being the focus of Christopher Columbus's interest and exertions from the 1490s. The city of Santo Domingo was the first to be established in the New World and was the leading port of the 1500s; by the 1530s a dynamic creole society had also emerged in the northern region of the island (the *banda norte*). However, in the eighteenth and nineteenth centuries the island's economic and cultural development stagnated in comparison to that of Cuba and Puerto Rico, in ways that limited the efflorescence of the contradance. Spanish colonial interest shifted to mineral-rich Mexico and the Andes from the 1530s, and one of the few imperial projects energetically undertaken in Santo Domingo was the complete destruction in 1603 of the *banda norte* settlements, which Madrid resented as a smugglers' haven. In the 1700s, French colonists turned the western part of the island—Saint-Domingue, subsequently Haiti—into an economic dynamo based on sugar plantations.[2] Santo Domingo, the

Spanish-speaking eastern sector, remained a relatively underpopulated, undeveloped, pestilential, and hurricane-ridden backwater, with a local economy based on cattle ranching and subsistence farming, and its pirate-infested ports neglected in favor of Havana. As Haiti exploded in revolution from 1791, Santo Domingo was repeatedly swept up in violence and served as a battleground for Haitian and French armies between 1801 and 1805. Nominal rule by bankrupt and remote Spain resumed from 1809 to 1821 but was so ineffectual and useless that the period is dubbed that of "España Boba"—foolish Spain. The Haitian occupation of 1822–44 brought little socioeconomic progress, and the political independence finally achieved with the expulsion of the Haitians was interrupted in 1861 by an ignominious return to Spanish sovereignty, itself concluded with the War of Restoration in 1865. In the subsequent decades the independent country of the Dominican Republic was repeatedly wracked by violent struggles between thuggish regional *caudillos* (strongmen). Economically, demographically, and culturally, nineteenth-century Santo Domingo lagged well behind Cuba and could barely sustain the kind of stable urban bourgeois society in which something like the contradanza could flourish.

Despite such vicissitudes, a distinctive Dominican society did emerge in this period, whose most outstanding feature was its pervasively creole character. If sugar plantations—such as those of Saint-Domingue and western Cuba—tended to foster a society polarized between white owners and black slaves, Santo Domingo's cattle ranches generated a more fluid and even homogeneous continuum in which whites, mulattos, and blacks—whether free or technically enslaved—often worked and lived side by side while intermarrying and developing shared creole music and dance forms. Moreover, importation of African slaves to Santo Domingo dwindled after 1800 and ended altogether in 1820—unlike in Cuba and Puerto Rico—such that neo-African practices tended to blend with Hispanic ones, and the country's population became prevailingly (though not entirely) mulatto.

Travelers' chronicles of early colonial life in Santo Domingo, like those regarding Cuba, attested to the contemporary fondness of the locals for dancing. Around 1698 R. P. Labat wrote, "Dancing is the favorite passion in Santo Domingo, and I do not believe there is any population in the world more fixated on it." Another observer wrote, "The passion for dancing is beyond imagination; the elderly, the young, the children—all seem to have been dancing since they were in their mothers' wombs" (in Nolasco 1948: 102). In subsequent years, although being repeatedly overrun by foreign invaders may not have been conducive to socioeconomic growth and stability, it did contribute to the diversity of music and dance forms that existed in Santo Domingo in the nineteenth century. The Spanish heritage was perhaps naturally predominant among these. Hence, contemporary accounts indicate the popularity of the fandango and bolero, which were solo or couple dances typically accompanied by guitar-like instruments, featuring graceful hand and arm gestures and statuesque *bien parao* ("nicely stopped") pauses at cadential points.[3] Also flourishing was the creolized Afro-Caribbean calenda, described in Santo Domingo by Labat and a century later by Médéric Louis Elie Moreau de Saint-Méry (henceforth Saint-Méry) as a line dance in which men and women faced each other in two rows; both Labat and Saint-Méry indicate how this dance, although originally associated with blacks, was avidly adopted and danced by Spaniards on social occasions and even church functions.[4] As elsewhere in the Antilles, the presence of the neo-African calenda must have contributed to the easy adoption of the longways-style contradance, with its similar basic choreographic configuration.

The contradance itself would have been introduced both from the Spanish and French sides, with the French style, as in Cuba, more extensively flourishing and being creolized. The contradanza, whether in the longways Anglo-French style or the *cuadrada* (square) Spanish format, would have certainly been imported in the eighteenth century from Spain, where the French-style contredanse had taken root under Bourbon influence since the early 1700s. Hence the presence of the contradance in Santo Domingo was noted as early as 1747, when locals and Canary Island immigrants danced it in honor of the coronation of Fernando VI (in Guerrero 2006: 82). In the 1790s Frenchmen and their entourages of slaves fleeing the Haitian Revolution brought their own dances, including the minuet, waltz, and especially the contredanse. The creolization of the latter had already commenced, as Saint-Méry had commented in 1783 how blacks in Puerto Príncipe were fond of dancing minuets and contredanses in imitation of whites. Such influences were reinforced in the "French Era" of 1801–5, when the island was nominally unified under Franco-Haitian control, and contemporary sources attest to the balls and dances held in Santo Domingo by the French forces under General Charles Leclerc (see Guerrero 2006: 82). Meanwhile, the Englishman William Walton, relating his travels in Santo Domingo around 1810, mentions how the local populace, while occasionally dancing fandangos and the like, preferred the waltz and the "Spanish country dance," which he describes as slower yet less monotonous than that of his own countrymen.[5] Franco-Haitian influences would again intensify during the 1822–44 Haitian occupation. According to Haitian author Jean Fouchard (1973), one creolized dance introduced by Haitian soldiers around 1805 was the *carabiné* (*carabinier*), which he claims to be a contredanse derivative that generated the Haitian méringue.

Dominican writers on the subject tend to concur in assuming that by the 1820s the contradance, having been imported in various forms, was becoming a local, distinctively creolized entity (e.g., Pérez de Cuello 2005: 169). One indication of this process is the name by which the genre became known, the *tumba* or *tumba dominicana*. The origin of the word "*tumba*" (like that of other key words, such as "merengue," "*zarabanda*," and "tango") is disputed, with some writers linking it to an Andalusian dance of that name, and others—especially Cuban ethnologist Fernando Ortiz—tracing it to various West African and Congolese words meaning "drum" (1924: 339–340; 1995). For that matter, the word is not remote from *tombeau*, the name of a French Renaissance dance. Most likely "*tumba*" is an instance of what Ortiz calls a "convergent etymology" (1985: 475), fusing similar words of diverse origins. In creole and Afro-Caribbean contexts, the term came to connote a drum and associated dance or song. Hence the *tumba francesa*, discussed in Chapter 2, is a recreational dance of descendants of Afro-Haitian immigrants in eastern Cuba. While the vigorous, ostinato-based drumming of the *tumba francesa* is overwhelmingly Afro-Caribbean in character, one of its two dances, the *masón*, derives its figures from the contredanse. It is safe to assume that both the *tumba dominicana* and the *tumba francesa* derived primarily from related Franco-Haitian dances and eventually acquired their national suffixes to help distinguish them from each other in certain contexts.

The *tumba dominicana*, unlike the *francesa*, no longer survives, nor are there any transcriptions or recordings to enlighten the scholar. What survives instead is a single, albeit informative, contemporary account, written by visiting Frenchman Paul Dhormoys in 1859:

> The Dominican dances are a singular spectacle. The quadrille, waltz, and polka are not unknown to them. The flower of Dominican youth is allowed even a *mazurka de fantasia*: but their favorite dance, to which they give themselves over with frenzy, is the tumba. It is that which constitutes the national dance. All the dancers arrange themselves in a line, two by two, like schoolchildren taken out for a walk, the men on one side, the women on the other. As soon as the orchestra gives the signal they wheel about and face each other. In certain moments indicated by some clarinet variations, the man dances with his partner, or the two, facing each other, indulge in poses and undulations which in one of our own public dances would make the moustaches of the municipal guards stand on end and place the executants in the *violón* [contrabass; the meaning is unclear]. Ending the first figure this way, each youth leaves her partner to take the adjacent one. When every woman has danced successively with all the men present, the tumba has ended, by general agreement, unless it repeats, that is, unless the whole sequence is done again. Each figure lasts at least a minute. If there are forty-some couples, one can imagine the state of the dancers at the end of the tumba. Sweat runs down their faces; dust ground from the brick paving fills the air. Fortunate is he who has brought a flask of cologne to such a Dominican dance.
>
> In France they say that dancing has no opinion. Such is not the case in the Dominican Republic. Every intimate dance is a political demonstration. One is invited to dance in honor of this or that person (to congratulate so-and-so), and it is for this reason, no doubt, that no invitation is needed in order to be admitted to a dance. Anyone passing in the street can enter to dance, have a refreshment, if there is such,

and depart without even having greeted the owners of the house. (In Pérez de Cuello 2005: 248–249)

Dhormoys's description, while far from exhaustive, is informative in its own way. The 1850s *tumba* he describes was clearly a version of the longways-style contradance, which existed alongside various other European dances. It was evidently cultivated by the urban bourgeoisie (presumably among others) and could be accompanied by an ensemble Europeanized enough to include a clarinet. In that sense its music seems to have been less overtly Afro-Caribbean than, for example, the *tumba francesa*, which, now as in the nineteenth century, uses a thunderous battery of three drums. Dhormoys's failure to comment further on the music suggests that it was unremarkable to him and presumably consisted of relatively straightforward renditions—likely instrumental—of familiar contradance tunes, rendered by an ad hoc salon dance ensemble (clarinet, violins, assorted guitar-like instruments, *güiro* scraper, tambourine-like *panderos*, and so forth), conforming to what at that time might have constituted a sort of standard "mainstream" creole Caribbean style. At the same time, some of the figures and postures were evidently more suggestive than would be acceptable in France. In contrast to some, but not all, forms of the contradance, past and present, no cane-wielding bastonero caller was present; rather, it seems that a single figure would be repeated with different partners.

A different sort of description of the *tumba* is presented in the historical novel *La conspiración de los Alcarrizos*, by Dominican writer Max Henríquez Ureña (1885–1968), published in 1941.[6] As Pérez de Cuello (2005: 260) notes, Ureña may never have witnessed an actual performance of a *tumba dominicana*, though he might have seen one of *tumba francesa* in Cuba. Nevertheless, he clearly took a scholar's interest in the subject, as can be gleaned from the rather didactic nature of his description that he inserts, somewhat digressively, in his novel. Although far from authoritative, his description (or recreation) of the *tumba* is certainly plausible and merits reproduction here:

> The melodic phrase was of a native flavor, although it certainly betrayed, as is typical of creole music, an echo of musical expressions of other places in the world, often of Spain, and via Spain, of the Arabs. But imitation is not copying; and if creole music imitates, it modifies as it does so, adapting the melodic phrase to the native sentiment, giving it a new musical feeling. The rhythm of the tumba had syncopated, African-style aspects and thus could be marked clearly by the *güiro*.
>
> From the point of view of choreography, the dance could be seen in its origins as a derivation of the minuet. Not lacking were aspects of imitating this dance of the French *gallant*, although neither the music nor the rhythm was copied from France. It retained, then, a certain choreographic affinity with the French contredanse, which was the immediate antecedent to the quadrille. In the French part of the island,

> the tumba was conserved in this form, with time acquiring the name of tumba francesa, to distinguish it from the tumba danced in the Spanish part of the island, where the figures tended to become simpler, and the innovation introduced in other dances—like the waltz, which was by then already in vogue in the Americas—resulted in the couples dancing *enlazadas* [embracing ballroom-style] from time to time. Thus, the *tumba dominicana* was soon transformed into a couple dance, in keeping with the current fashion, although with some vestiges of the figures that it had in its early form. The same happened with the contradanza: faced with the French contredanse, a figure dance, emerged the creole contradanza, a couple dance, and antecedent of the *danza antillana* [Caribbean *danza*]. (In Pérez de Cuello 2005: 264)

Ureña's portrayal of the *tumba* eventually evolving into a couple dance is credible, although in Dhormoys's account of 1859 it was clearly still a longways group dance. Yet a more conspicuous development is the effective disappearance of the *tumba*, which essentially vanishes from the historical record in the latter 1800s, although folklorists, as we discuss later, documented a form of it in the early 1970s. In the salons, it is clear that the *tumba* and the collective longways-style contradance were effectively replaced by independent couple dancing, starting in the mid-1800s.

## Enter the "Merengue"

The eclipse of the *tumba* by new couple dances was part of a broader process occurring in the mid–nineteenth century throughout the Spanish Caribbean, as discussed elsewhere in this volume. Evidence suggests that this process commenced in Cuba, spread thence to Puerto Rico, and from there to the Dominican Republic. In each locale the old collective figure dances—whether fixed by convention or directed by a bastonero—came to be seen as backward, artless, and lacking the romantic intimacy and "naturalness" afforded by the waltz and, more importantly, the new creole contradance variants. In each place, the new dance styles—as happened with the European waltz around 1800—provoked ultimately unsuccessful campaigns by critics who saw them as indecent and asocial. Accompanying the choreographic transformation was a process of rhythmic creolization, pithily described by Dominican musicologist Julio César Paulino: "As those dances sustained the hurricane-like blow of the waist of the *mulata*, they started incorporating syncopations, dotted rhythms, polymeters, and polyrhythms" (1994: 30).

The historian's attempt to reconstruct these transformations is impeded by a general shortage of documentation coupled with persistent ambiguity in nomenclature, with one term denoting different genres and, conversely, different terms designating a single genre, which itself might be identified either by choreographic or musical features. Hence, in Cuba, the terms "contradanza" and "danza" were used inconsistently, although the latter name gradually came to connote the independent couple dance of the 1840s–70s. In Puerto Rico, "contradanza" generally referred to the old-style Spanish group dance, with the couple dance that emerged in the 1840s being initially known as "merengue" and, subsequently, "danza." In the Dominican Republic, a fundamental ambiguity has involved the relation between the "merengue" of the 1850s—a contradance-related couple dance—and the familiar popular genre of the next century known by the same name. To some extent this conundrum affects less the focus of this chapter—that is, the contradance—than it does the historian who seeks to reconstruct the history of "the" merengue, by which is generally meant the familiar modern genre. As it is, by the 1870s in the Dominican Republic the term "merengue" had come to denote the rural, accordion-based, folk predecessor to the modern merengue, which was quite distinct from any contradance variant and thus out of the sphere of interest of this book (with the exception of the salon merengue of the 1920s–40s). However, the "merengue" of the mid-1800s—which might be retrospectively labeled the *merengue contradanzeado* or "contradanced merengue"[7]—does constitute a significant stage in the trajectory of the contradance in the Dominican Republic.

The origins and early history of the merengue in the Dominican Republic have been debated extensively by scholars and admirably summarized by Austerlitz (1997).[8] As discussed in the preceding chapter, the first reference to the merengue as a Spanish Caribbean music and dance idiom is from Cuba in 1847; subsequent sources relate how in the early 1840s, under Cuban influence, a dance called "merengue" took root as a contradance variant in Puerto Rico and soon attained sufficient popularity for it to be explicitly banned by an 1849 decree of the colonial ruler Juan de la Pezuela y Ceballos, who regarded it as indecent. However, the Puerto Rican merengue not only survived but also evidently spread to the Dominican Republic. Nevertheless, some Dominicans have argued for an essentially indigenous origin of the genre. According to one oral tradition, the genre was created in the form of a song mocking a cowardly Dominican general at the 1844 battle of Talanquera against the retreating Haitians. Another tradition attributes its invention to composer Juan Bautista Alfonseca (1810–65), who is regarded as the father of Dominican national music, having effectively asserted its individuality as the nation emerged in 1844 from Haitian occupation.[9] Alfonseca is not known to have labeled any of his compositions "merengue," nor do any of his manuscripts survive, and even an 1879 elegy referred to his pieces as "danzas" rather than merengues (in Rodríguez Demorizi 1982: 77). Nevertheless, such writers as Dominican folklorist Flérida de Nolasco claim that he was composing merengues, implicitly from the 1840s. Attributed to Alfonseca are the opening lines of an alleged merengue, "Juana Quilina," sung in 1938 by an elderly informant to Nolasco (1948: 166). Although we know nothing of this song's larger form, its accompanimental patterns, or the way it might have been danced, the melody does seem like a typical creole song in its prominent amphibrach rhythm and eight-bar phrases. The lyrics are, "Juana Quilina va llorando, porque la llevan merengueando" ("Juana Quilina is weeping, because they are taking her merengue-ing").[10]

The titles of Alfonseca pieces like "El sancocho" (a local stew) and "Mangulina" (a folk dance) are also typical of merengues (or Cuban and Puerto Rican danzas and contradanzas) in their evocation of local vernacular culture. However, it is ultimately impossible to make much of Alfonseca's alleged role in the merengue's evolution, since documentation is so scanty, and since terms like "merengue," "*tumba*," and later "danza" were used so interchangeably and inconsistently throughout the latter nineteenth century. Even if one were to acknowledge that Alfonseca popularized or created some creole dance song genre called "merengue," the distinguishing features of that genre and its relation to the imported merengue of the 1850s would remain unclear.

As such, merengue scholars have tended to focus greater attention on the first documented local references to the merengue, which appeared in 1854–55 (four years after the Puerto Rican decree against it) in the form of a four-month-long polemic waged against the genre in a Santo Domingo literary weekly called *El Oasis*. The fomenters of the brouhaha were young intellectuals of a culturally conservative sensibility, notably Manuel de Jesús Galván (1834–1910) and Eugenio Perdomo (1836–63)—respectively twenty and eighteen years old at the time. Perdomo fired the opening salvo against the merengue, which had evidently become widely popular in the city's bourgeois dance salons, in a paragraph in an article denouncing the alleged shallowness, pedantry, hypocrisy, and moral decline of his fellow city-dwellers—especially the young women. Writing like his colleagues, under a pseudonym, Perdomo stated, "And when the merengue begins, dear God! One man grabs the woman opposite him, another runs around, knowing not what to do, and then tugs on a señorita's arm to ask her to merengue, while yet another shoves aside some woman who's in his way—in a word, even the most elegant person bungles some dance figure and then blames his partner, and everything is a confused mess, a labyrinth lasting until the piece ends."[11] In a response a few weeks later, one "Ismenes" asked why Perdomo did not direct his ire against the parents of children who get in the way of other dancers and continued, "Finally, why don't you criticize that cursed merengue, which is already being danced as indecently as in the country where it was born?" Perdomo replied the next week by urging Ismenes and his friends to imitate those who dance the new style with decency, lest parents disallow their daughters to attend such dances and the men end up having to dance with each other. In the same issue, "Eliodoro" lamented that even educated people of high society danced the "ridiculous" figures of the merengue, disturbing other dancers in an unpardonable offence to decorum: "Nor can it be claimed that it is the most comfortable manner of dancing, because it requires some exertion for the partners to hold each other so closely, the arms raised higher than the head, the woman putting her hand on the man's shoulder" (in Pérez de Cuello 2005: 124). The affair then stimulated the poetic muse of Galván, future author of the "Indianist" novel *Enriquillo*, to pen a lengthy ode, "Complaint of the Tumba against the Merengue," which commences:

*La tumba, que hoy vive desterrada*
*por el torpe merengue aborrecible;*
*que en vil oscuridad yace olvidada,*
*llorando su destino atroz, horrible . . .*

The tumba—today exiled
by the clumsy and contemptible merengue—
which lies in dismal obscurity, forgotten,
bewailing its sad and horrible fate . . .

On top of suffering the cruel sting of Galván's alliteration and synecdoche, the merengue was then subjected to further literary abuse in the form of a poem in another journal, *Folletín*, in which the author fantasized that the vile dance, depicted as a passenger on a ship, drowns when the vessel is lost at sea. And then, in mid-1855, the polemic ended, either because the authors had largely succeeded in banishing the genre from elite ballrooms, or, more likely, because their campaign had failed and they had spent themselves in their literary exertions.

The polemic itself, although revealing in its way, is on the whole frustratingly enigmatic. About the merengue as music, it tells us almost nothing, although this very lack of commentary does suggest that the music was not in itself so controversial as was the dance and perhaps resembled that of the *tumba* (about which we also know little or nothing). However, one of the polemicists mentioned dancers hastening to the floor as soon as the ensemble began playing a merengue, suggesting that the music was in some way recognizably distinct. Quite possibly it featured, like the Cuban contradanza of the time, more of the creole syncopations—especially the "habanera rhythm"—than did the *tumba*. Presumably it was performed by the typical ad hoc dance ensemble of the time, which could include clarinet, flute, violin, guitar-type instruments, and assorted percussion instruments like *güiro* scraper and timbal.

Scarcely more clear is what precisely inspired the vitriol of the "Oasists." Austerlitz (1997: 19–20) attributes Galván's stance to the "anti-African, pro-European sentiment that prevailed within his social class," noting that the eighth stanza of Galván's anti-merengue poem inveighs against the way women swing their hips in dancing—a vice presumably acquired from Afro-Caribbean dancers. Galván, Austerlitz observes, went on to support his country's re-annexation to Spanish colonial rule in 1861–65, and his popular novel *Enriquillo* celebrates a historically dubious Amerindian basis of Dominican culture while contributing to the marginalization or even demonization of Afro-Dominican culture and Haitians. Nevertheless, Pérez de Cuello notes that the polemicists did not specify any racial aspect to their argument and contends that if the merengue had actually been seen as Afro-Dominican or, worse, as Haitian, they certainly would have mentioned that fact in their diatribes. Further, Pérez de Cuello notes, the Oasists themselves were of diverse political leanings, with Perdomo going on to be executed by the Spaniards for his militant opposition to their rule. Even folklorist Fradique Lizardo, an indefatigable critic of Dominican negrophobia, opines that the Oasists' campaign shows no evidence of being motivated by racial factors (1974: 220, 226).

One possible explanation, aside from favorite academic themes of race and class dynamics, is that the Oasists were merely lovers of *tumba*, which after all generated its own unique sense of collective merriment. Or were they simply young nerds, who could neither master merengue nor find any girls homely or sympathetic enough to attempt to dance it with them? For whatever reason, despite their youth they were evidently archconservatives who regarded the merengue as unruly, vulgar, and licentious.

While sources like the *Oasis* debate are ambiguous on the issue, the general assumption among interested scholars is that the controversial merengue was an independent couple dance. The contemporary merengue of Puerto Rico was described in those terms by reliable informants, and certain comments of the Oasists suggest the same. Hence, "Eliodoro" contemptuously describes the ballroom-style embrace of the genre. Similarly, Perdomo's description—complaining that when the merengue begins, "one man grabs the woman opposite him"—suggests that the dancers had been arrayed in two lines, as if ready to dance a longways-style *tumba*; upon hearing the strains of the merengue, they broke formation and somewhat chaotically formed couples. The references to the clumsiness of the figures suggest that the merengue was not merely a shapeless shuffling but included certain contradance-derived patterns. Probably the hip-swinging that offended Galván was the sort that became basic to Caribbean independent couple dances, such as *son*, salsa, and the modern merengue, and for which there was little scope in the collective figures of the contradanza. Further, for the Oasists one objectionable aspect of the merengue was that, like the waltz, it seemed disorderly, with individual couples gyrating about the floor and colliding into each other, unguided by any bastonero.[12] Most palpably, the independent couple dancing of the merengue would have put an end to the *tumba*'s spirit of collective "family fun," in which fathers, mothers, aunts, uncles, children, and friends could enjoy themselves together in an asexual ambience of clean, wholesome diversion.

If the *Oasis* polemic sheds relatively little light on the style and structure of the merengue as dance and music, it is equally enigmatic regarding the genre's origin. The sole reference to its source is that of "Ismenes," who, as noted above, laments that it was "already being danced as indecently as in the country where it was born." His statement would seem to contradict the notion that Alfonseca had earlier created the merengue on Dominican soil; unfortunately, Ismenes does not mention the alleged country of origin, and there is more than one contender for that distinction.

One candidate would be neighboring Haiti, which is the possible source for several Dominican music genres, such as the *carabiné*. As discussed in Chapter 2, Haiti appears to have constituted one source for the Cuban contradanza. Franco-Haitian origin is also suggested by the possibility that the term "merengue" may derive from the French "méringue," which, as meaning whipped egg whites and sugar, is documented in the French lexicon from 1739 (Pérez de Cuello 2005: 147); the culinary term, with its connotations of sweetness and physical vigor (in the whipping process) might have easily been applied to the dance.[13] However, others have claimed an African etymology, from a Mozambican dance called "mouringue" (Fouchard 1973: 106) or a couple dance called *maringa* from the West African island of Fernando Po. (As discussed in the preceding chapter, the first reference to merengue as a dance music genre is from the aforementioned Cuban song lyric of 1847; describing the sensual gyrations of a mulatto woman, who speaks of dancing *jaleo*, fandango, and *boleras*, along with the merengue and *sopimpa* "of her own land.")[14] Quite possibly the adoption of the term constitutes yet another case of Ortiz's aforementioned "convergent etymology," in which African and French words combine to generate a new meaning. Haitian lawyer Fouchard devotes most of his 1973 book *La Méringue* to arguing for a Haitian origin not only of his country's méringue, a popular creole dance song of the nineteenth and early twentieth centuries, but also of the Dominican merengue. Both, he argues, derived ultimately from the contredanse and its Afro-Haitian variant, the calenda, described in the late 1600s by Labat. By the time of Haiti's independence, these had given birth to creolized dance genres, including the *chica*, *gragement*, and, subsequently and most importantly, the *carabinier*, which he considers the immediate parent of the méringue and merengue.

Fouchard's thesis, although not implausible, is hypothetical and suffers from a lack of documentation, especially of such entities as the Haitian méringue prior to (or even after) the 1850s. Nevertheless, as Guerrero and others have suggested (2006: 91), it is entirely conceivable that in the mid-1800s, contradance-related versions of the creole *carabinier/carabiné*, the emergent Haitian meringue and Dominican merengue, and related genres like the Dominican *mangolina* all interacted and cross-fertilized, leading to a general confusion or laxity of nomenclature. In the Dominican Republic, as in Cuba and Puerto Rico, terminological distinctions would have been further obfuscated by the omnivorous way in which the contradanza, or its local variants, incorporated tunes and other features from all manner of sources, be they Italian operas or local creole songs. (The *carabiné* is discussed in the conclusion to this chapter.)

Despite the likelihood of some Haitian input, direct or indirect, into the evolution of the Dominican merengue, the argument for a primarily Haitian origin is weakened by the essentially nonjudgmental manner in which Ismenes refers to the alleged foreign origin of the merengue. As Dominican scholars have noted, given the intense anti-Haitian sentiment prevailing among urban

Dominicans in the 1850s, if the merengue were of evident Haitian origin, Ismenes and other anti-merengue polemicists would certainly have denounced it as such. Instead, Ismenes merely mentions the foreign derivation of the genre in a matter-of-fact, parenthetical manner, suggesting that the country of origin was not a hated foe but an essentially neutral entity. That is, implicitly, the source was neither savage Haiti, despotic Spain, libertine France, nor blasphemous England. Rather, the likely suspect is Puerto Rico.

Although Puerto Rico can hardly be said to have prospered under Spanish colonial rule in the eighteenth and nineteenth centuries, it was untouched by the constant upheavals and military campaigns that stunted the growth of an urban bourgeoisie in neighboring Santo Domingo. Hence urban musical life in Puerto Rico, although provincial and insular in its way, may have flourished more vigorously than in its violence-wracked neighbor to the west. The Spanish contradanza, a collective dance with figures guided by a bastonero, had been well established in the island since the early 1800s, being introduced both from the metropole as well as by elite Venezuelans fleeing Bolívar's liberation wars. One may assume that the Spanish contradanza flourished alongside a Cuban-style creolized contradanza that derived more from the French contredanse, whose final section consisted of independent couple dancing. In the mid-1840s, presumably inspired by Cuban developments, these group dances were rapidly giving way to a waltz-like dance that dispensed with the initial collective figures and the dictatorial bastonero; instead, it commenced directly with independent dancing by couples embracing intimately in ballroom style, accompanied by a creolized version of the contradanza, with its syncopated dotted rhythms (the 3-1-2-2 "habanera" or "tango" rhythm). By the end of that decade, this new dance and music style had variously come to be called "danza," "contradanza," or, most commonly, "merengue," although that term was never widely used in Cuba itself. As elsewhere in the Caribbean, the merengue—again denoting a "*merengue contradanzeado*"—was sufficiently intimate and sensual as to provoke the ire of conservatives, most notably colonial governor Pezuela, who officially banned it in an 1849 decree. However, the merengue evidently continued to flourish in Puerto Rico, whether under that name or, increasingly, under the more elegant title "danza,"[15] in accordance with the usage of that term in Cuba to denote the modernized couple dance that replaced the local contradanza. (Pezuela himself departed the island in 1852.)

Whether or not the Dominican Republic qualified as the torso between the two wings of Puerto Rico and Cuba, the 1840s saw intensified travels and migrations between Puerto Rico and Santo Domingo, especially as motivated by political upheavals. In 1843 many Dominicans fled to Puerto Rico in fear of impending attack by Haitian President Charles Herard, while in 1849 the fall of Dominican President Juan Jimenes induced many exiles to return from Puerto Rico (Rodríguez Demorizi 1982: 81). Alfonseca, the legendary father of Dominican music, himself visited Puerto Rico during this period, returning in 1855 and bringing with him the merengue, according to Dominican scholar Paulino.[16]

Amid so much jockeying for power, military bands played a particularly important role in disseminating music and dance. Such brass bands not only played pompous and formal marches for parading troops but also gave frequent public performances in town plazas for the general entertainment of local citizenry, during which they would play a pot-pourri of contemporary popular genres. Díaz Díaz has documented the repertoire of a typical mid-nineteenth-century Puerto Rican band, which consisted of arrangements of pieces from operas and zarzuelas (Spanish light opera), rigodóns, paso dobles, and danzas by contemporary Puerto Rican composers (2006: 198–201). As he notes, the bands, which often traveled from island to island, would vary their repertoire to include local items. Thus, he continues, in 1858 even a military band from Cádiz, Spain, stationed in Puerto Rico included in its repertoire a merengue, less than a decade after that genre had been officially banned by the Spanish governor Pezuela. In the years 1863–65, when the Spanish were struggling unsuccessfully to repress rebellion in the Dominican Republic, several military regiments converged on the northern part of the country, bringing their brass bands from Cuba, Puerto Rico, and Spain itself. While the merengue and Cuban-style danza had already become popular in Santo Domingo by then, the presence of such bands—including the Cádiz batallion—would have reinforced the popularity of the Cuban and Puerto Rican-style contradanza variants, whether under the name "danza," "contradanza," or "merengue." Meanwhile, regimental musicians might moonlight with local civilian ensembles, or defect altogether.

## A Digression: The Birth of the Dominican Merengue

For everyone except scholars of nineteenth-century Caribbean music history, the word "merengue" connotes not an extinct 1850s variant of the Dominican and Puerto Rican contradanza but either pie topping or else the sprightly commercial popular music and dance genre that has pervaded Dominican entertainment culture since the 1930s. As this genre has little in common with any form of the contradance, it is effectively outside the purview of this volume. Nevertheless, because of the modern merengue's prominence and its alleged derivation from its nineteenth-century namesake, the theories regarding its evolution may merit brief consideration here.

The modern merengue bears so little resemblance to the *merengue contradanzeado*, insofar as we can reconstruct that entity, that it is difficult to imagine an evolutionary relationship between them. The mid-nineteenth-century merengue was presumably a through-composed (rather than ostinato-based) instrumental composition in medium tempo, with a prominent recurring habanera rhythm. The modern merengue, by contrast, is an almost frenetically fast vocal song with accompaniment, whose larger portion typically reiterates a tonic-dominant chordal ostinato, often with call-and-response vocals, with no particular prominence of the habanera rhythm.[17] The ensembles of the genres also differ dramatically: While the *merengue contradanzeado* could be rendered by groups of mixed string and wind instruments, the modern merengue would either be played in an accordion-based *típico cibaeño* format or by a trumpet-and-saxophone-based *orquesta*.

Despite these conspicuous differences, most Dominican and Puerto Rican scholars argue that the *merengue contradanzeado* was the primary source for the modern merengue. According to them, after the merengue was banished from the bourgeois salons of Santo Domingo, it took root in the lower-class communities of the north-central town of Santiago de los Caballeros and the surrounding countryside (the fertile valley called the Cibao), and then in the 1870s it underwent a dramatic transformation. A sung text was added, in the same manner that light, often whimsical verses were set to the tunes of catchy Cuban contradanzas from the 1860s on; just as these refrains became core elements of the Cuban *son*, so did their Dominican counterparts become basic features to the evolving merengue rather than informal addenda. The adoption of the button accordion as the preferred melody instrument occasioned a drastic simplification of the harmonies, devolving to simple tonic-dominant ostinatos, as seems to have occurred with French Caribbean quadrilles. Free from the stuffy pretensions of the urban elite, the genre became more rhythmic, fast, and rustic in character, incorporating lively, perhaps military-derived rhythms played on the martial *tambora* and embellished by the humble *güira* scraper.[18] By the 1880s, the *merengue típico cibaeño*—the traditional merengue of the Cibao—was emerging into historical daylight, and its subsequent historical trajectory becomes fairly well documented.

The alleged transition that occurred in the 1860s–70s, like so many other aspects of Dominican musical history, is essentially undocumented. One of the very few useful citations from the post-*Oasis* era is the denunciation of the merengue in 1875 in a Santiago newspaper by patriotic author Ulises Francisco Espaillat. While his critique might seem to echo that of the earlier Oasists, it is clear from such details as his mention of the "insipid accordion" that the merengue he despised was already a different genre from the *merengue contradanzeado* and was instead the immediate precursor to the Cibao style soon to be codified by Nico Lora.

Given the striking differences between the two incarnations of the merengue, it is perhaps surprising that only one scholar, Guerrero (2006: 93), has questioned their presumed direct linkage. Guerrero suggests that the Santo Domingo salon merengue attacked by the Oasists in 1854 may never have had much diffusion in the countryside, such that the seminal merengue that emerged in the Cibao in the 1870s may have been an essentially unrelated genre to which the name "merengue" had come to be applied (perhaps because of the independent couple dancing). Unfortunately, verification of either Guerrero's hypothesis or the orthodox genealogy is inhibited by the sad lack of information regarding vernacular music in the Cibao in the latter 1800s. Espaillat's 1875 essay (in Rodríguez Demorizi 1982: 83) laments that the merengue had replaced the fandango (most typically, an open couple dance, accompanied by guitar-type instruments playing tonic-dominant ostinatos); it is possible that the Cibao merengue might be plausibly seen as emerging from the *fandango con estribillo* (fandango with sung refrain), while incorporating couple dancing from the salon namesake, the *tambora* rhythm from military bands, and vocal conventions from some creole song genre (such as those popularized by Alfonseca).[19] Certainly in its tonic-dominant ostinatos, the Cibao merengue closely resembles the creole fandango, such as the traditional one excerpted in Julio Arzeño (1927); if Arzeño's fandango were rendered on accordion in brisk tempo, supplemented with martial *tambora* rolls and verses or responsorial vocals, it would certainly be called a merengue today. Perhaps this hybrid genre emerged primarily from the creole fandango of the Cibao but was labeled "merengue" because it adopted the independent couple dance, in ballroom-style embrace, from the salon merengue/danza imported in the 1850s–60s.[20] Even if that *merengue contradanzeado* were to be seen as the most significant progenitor of the Dominican merengue, some of the most important structural elements of the genre would have to derive from such other sources. Some of these elements, especially the call-and-response *jaleos* set to rhythmic and chordal ostinatos, are clearly of Afro-Dominican provenance.

## The *Danza Dominicana* in the Latter Nineteenth Century

The fate of the "contradanced merengue" in the bourgeois salons after the Oasists' campaign is unclear, due to the lack of documentation about Dominican music culture in general in the latter (not to mention earlier) nineteenth century. Musicologists Pérez de Cuello and Paulino (pers. comm.) believe that the salon merengue tradition continued in some marginal and unverifiable capacity,[21] but even they join other scholars in asserting that the disreputable dance had been largely expelled from the bourgeois ballrooms. References from the 1860s indicate that the genre that took its place was the danza—a variant of what could be called the Caribbean danza that flourished at the same time in Cuba and Puerto Rico. The relation of this danza to the earlier controversial contradanced merengue is unclear; quite possibly, as seems to have happened in Puerto Rico, the salon merengue continued to flourish while being rebaptized with the more respectable (and Cuban-style) name "danza" (while the term "merengue" was taken up by the accordion-wielding bumpkins of the Cibao). More probably, the salon merengue was essentially assimilated into the emerging Dominican danza, which was largely, but not entirely, modeled after its Puerto Rican and, to a lesser extent, Cuban namesakes. Further, this genre must have been an independent couple dance, such that the Oasists—regardless of the fate of the merengue per se—had essentially lost their campaign to save the collective *tumba* and ban ballroom-style couple dancing.

While documentation of the salon music culture of the 1860s–90s is woefully inadequate, musicologist Bernarda Jorge paints a credible and evocative portrait of the scene, which is worth quoting at length:

> The empirical composer of the nineteenth century composed danzas, hymns, and music for specific occasions, of impoverished and often defective harmony, sometimes with errors of notation and failing to transcend familiar conventions and patterns. The ambience didn't require more.
>
> The dependence of Dominican society on the metropolitan centers throughout the century restricted the music, imposing forms, instruments, techniques, and habits, many of which remain in effect today. The backwardness, weakness, and academic inconsistency of the few musical "institutions" that existed, the dependency on European music, the feeling of inferiority and lack of confidence in terms of one's own creations and the absence of an academic musical tradition, drowned and frustrated the generation of Alfonseca . . . limiting their artistic ambitions and preventing them from crossing the threshold of the merely artisanal production.
>
> In accordance with a practice as well as a musical style itself, we have lived in a perpetual struggle against foreign influences. Our music culture, artistic and urban popular, has tended to be molded by what has been copied or borrowed. The composer, like the instrumentalist, had developed based on a foreign language, a practice, a material, and technique. The music teachers from Spain, Italy, and Puerto Rico, organizers primarily of instrumental ensembles in the nineteenth and early twentieth centuries, were only capable of orienting our musical development as a copy or extension of their own country of origin.
>
> The creole musicians imitated the models imposed, whether in dance music of little instrumental pieces (minuets, polkas, etc.) which circulated in the salons together with the serenades and Romantic fantasias.
>
> Colonization generated as a historical result a derivative music which duplicated the incidents of the metropolitan countries. Throughout the Americas, the predominant tendency among urban composers, most of whom had very modest musical training and were largely self-taught, was to write dance pieces in European style. But through the process of national cohesion and the integration of the bourgeoisie that occurred over the century, the distinctively national flavor began to insinuate itself. Depending on the level of professionalism, the colli-

> sion with the vernacular tradition gave birth not only to popular dance music but also to the incipient forms of "art" music.
>
> . . . The point of departure [for an aspiring bandleader or composer] was typically a demonstrated instrumental skill. After recognition as a good player of clarinet, flute, violin, etc., the next step was to organize one's own dance band. Such a recognized musician might also be engaged as a chapel master or director of a military band. . . . And from there to the creation of little pieces was but a small step. Juan Bautista Alfonseca, José María Arredondo, José Reyes, Luis Eduardo Betances and other composers of the first and second generation of the Republic set to composing and performing with only a very basic musical training, being largely self-taught, with scarce knowledge of the rules of harmony or the forms of music and the norms of composition. Even in the end of the century the same situation prevailed. (Jorge 1982: 49–51)

Extant documentation suggests that from the 1860s (the decade after the Oasist polemic), the dominant salon dance genre was the danza, consisting more specifically of Cuban and Puerto Rican pieces, together with a certain number of local compositions in basically similar style. Nolasco claims that the primary model was the Cuban danza, especially as brought to the country by José Agüero, who succeeded Alfonseca as director of the military band in the last administration of Pedro Santana (ending 1862; in Jorge 1982: 55). Accordingly, Díaz Díaz (2006: 199–200) notes that the Spanish lieutenant Adriano López Morillo, leading a regiment from Puerto Rico in Puerto Plata (in the Dominican Republic) during the 1863–65 War of Restoration, commented on the local popularity of the Cuban danza. Díaz Díaz, however, questions the accuracy of López's observation, and it seems evident that by the 1870s the primary model was Puerto Rico, which was only a day's sail away. Several of the professional bandleaders and music teachers of the era were Puerto Ricans, such as Ignacio Martí Calderón (1841–1903) in Puerto Plata, José Curbelo in La Vega (Jorge 1982: 50), and later José María Rodríguez Arresón (1875–1947) in Puerto Plata. Accordingly, from the latter decades of the century to the 1920s, the 1870s danzas of Puerto Rican composer Juan Morel Campos dominated the ballrooms and served as models for local composers.[22] Thus, most Dominican danzas followed what became a standard Puerto Rican formal structure of the 1870s: *paseo* (8 mm), first part (16 mm), second part (16 mm), third part (16 mm, featuring arpeggio-laden obbligato on bombardino), and a brief reprise of the theme of the first part, signaling the impending conclusion to dancers. This form could be represented as *paseo*-AABBCCA, or *paseo*-ABCA.

Nevertheless, by the 1860s Dominican composers were also penning danzas in a style that, rather than being entirely derivative, may have even exerted some influence on Puerto Ricans. Jorge (1982: 53–54) cites as particularly popular the 1864 danza, "El sueño" ("The Dream"), by Mariano Arredondo, which is presented as Figure 4.1 (and can be heard on this volume's compact disc). Jorge states that the piece is in Cuban style, and it does contain some left-hand habanera rhythms, but in other ways it is distinctive and closer to Puerto Rican models.[23] As transcribed by Jorge, it commences with a march-like eight-bar *paseo* (repeated); proceeds to a sixteen-bar A section (the first "merengue," repeated), then another sixteen-bar merengue (B, repeated); and then ends

**Figure 4.1** "El sueño," danza by Mariano Arredondo, 1864.

with a return to the *paseo*. Unlike the bipartite thirty-two bar Cuban form, this pattern is instead typical of Puerto Rican danzas from the 1860s.

One of the many curiosities found in mid-nineteenth-century danzas is the left-hand rhythm of the first merengue—essentially, the habanera pattern followed by three eighth notes and a rest. In Cuba, this rhythm appears in *batá* drumming, in popular songs, such as Arsenio Rodríguez's "Bruca manigua," and as an icon of Afro-Cubanism in zarzuela productions. Cuban and salsa musicians call it the "Afro" rhythm.

Danzas by composer, bandleader, and bombardino player Pablo Claudio (1855–99), the most distinguished composer of the generation after Arredondo, can be seen as representing variants of the standard Puerto Rican form. Most of the six in the Dominican national archives consist of an eight-bar *paseo* followed by four sixteen-bar sections (the "merengues"), each except the last being repeated, as shown here:[24]

*paseo* (8mm), repeated
A (16mm), repeated
B (16mm), repeated
C (16mm), repeated
D (16mm)
or: *paseo*-AABBCCD

While the manuscripts label the pieces "danzas," Jorge states that Claudio called them "dominicanas," perhaps to distinguish them from the Puerto Rican model (1982: 55). In their five-section form, they are certainly distinctive. The manuscripts show only the main melody, so we are unable to know if, for example, standard habanera rhythms were used in the bass. Nevertheless, creole syncopations abound, as in the ambiguously notated triplets and what are presumably habanera rhythms (with missing dots) in "El 1555," shown in Figure 4.2.

**Figure 4.2** Excerpt of "El 1555," by Pablo Claudio.

Claudio's *paseos*, unlike the A sections of Cuban danzas, resemble those that used to commence traditional merengues in their straightforward, unsyncopated, march-like rhythms. (See the Introduction [Chapter 1] for further discussion of the *paseo.*) A few pieces, such as "Josefita," are presented in different keys for different instruments (e.g., the guitar-like *requinto*). The score for "Las misas del pecado" indicates that the B section is to foreground the cornet, while the C section specifies "bomb. canta"—i.e., the bombardino (saxhorn, Claudio's instrument) is to lead in a *cantabile* style, as in Puerto Rico. Other local danza composers at the turn of the century included Manuel Martínez, Alfredo Máximo Soler (1859–1922), José Feliu, Emilio Arté, and Ramón Emilio Peralta (1868–1941). According to Nolasco, "The *danza dominicana*, which commenced following the Puerto Rican model, reached its peak around the end of the nineteenth century. Many of these danzas are not inferior to the best Puerto Rican ones. An example is the danza of José de Jesús Ravelo [1876–1951] dedicated to Flérida Otero Damirón" (1948: 149).

From the early decades of the twentieth century, a degree of political and economic stability allowed musical life in Santiago, Santo Domingo, and elsewhere to flourish (see, e.g., Hernández 1969: 8; Jorge 1982: 80–86). Danzas in Puerto Rican style continued to dominate the ballrooms; Enrique Deschamps, in his turn-of-the-century portrait of contemporary Dominican society, devoted five pages to the local danza milieu, discussing Morel Campos at some length while not mentioning a single Dominican composer (1906: 274–279). Nevertheless, whether derivative or distinctive, Dominican danzas continued to be performed and composed during these decades. As in Puerto Rico, and in Cuba of the early 1920s, many of the early-twentieth-century Dominican danzas were vocal songs—perhaps better regarded as *canciones* in danza style—such as a few of those included in the 1947 volume *Canciones dominicanas antiguas* (Holguín Veras 2001). These pieces are light, romantic songs, with extended through-composed melodies rather than distinct notated formal sections per se. Other danzas gained popularity even in the Rafael Trujillo period (1930–61); Austerlitz (pers. comm.) notes that the vocal danza "Era gloriosa" remains familiar to many Dominicans, however problematic may be its lyrics eulogizing Trujillo, who himself enjoyed dancing to danzas. Dominican danzas were composed and performed alongside other popular genres of the day, especially Puerto Rican–style danzas, Cuban-style danzones, and assorted other idioms. Jorge (1982: 93) notes that in 1916 the repertoire of the Municipal Band of Santiago included 176 paso dobles, 156 danzas, 100 waltzes, 84 mazurkas, 73 polkas, 14 danzones, and various schottisches, boleros, and the like. Around 1930, she continues, José de Jesús Ravelo (1876–1951) had composed ten danzas, seventeen paso dobles, nine waltzes, and three mazurkas, while in the 1920s José Dolores Cerón (1897–1969) was composing Cuban-style danzones, danzas in the mold of Morel Campos, and other pieces.

Salon composer Juan Francisco (Pancho) García (1892–1974) also penned a few danzas, such as "Contigo" and "Recuerdo grato," for piano or piano and voice. As he pointed out, in "Contigo" he departed from the standard Puerto Rican form in using rondo structure (specifically, *paseo*-ABCADA), again reflecting what could be seen as a tendency for structural variety in the *danza dominicana*. García also wrote vocal songs in danza style, to which he applied the neologisms "melodanza" and "criolla-danza." "Melodanza," as he explained, differs from a typical danza in having a *paseo* followed by two sections and a short coda, of which each is repeated thrice; for its part, the "criolla-danza" is a danza-like ballroom piece otherwise similar to the *criolla*, a serenade for singer with guitar (García 1972: 62–63). Ravelo's 1924 danza "Celeste Aurora," played by Angelina Tallaj-García on this book's compact disc, is closer to the mainstream Puerto Rican pattern, commencing with a march-like *paseo*, segueing to A, B, and C sections, and closing with a return to the A. Rondo-like structure is also evident in such pieces as "Danza" (Opus 74) by Luis Emilio Mena (1895–1964).

Jacob Coopersmith, writing in 1945 (215), observed that the danzas of Pablo Claudio were still being played then, yet by this period the heyday of the danza, as in Puerto Rico, was well over. Arzeño had noted even in 1927 that the danza never enjoyed popularity among Dominican *campesinos*, who preferred more lively music. (He went on to muse, "Perhaps Puerto Rico still has not become free and autonomous due to its enervating and lachrymose music" [i.e., the danza].[25]) At the present time, the Dominican danza is long dead as a compositional idiom and even in performance contexts has fared far worse than its counterparts in Puerto Rico and Cuba. Scores of the danzas of Claudio, Ravelo, and the later vocal danza composers could be categorized as collectors' items, except that hardly any collectors appear to be interested in them, and the works are seldom taught or heard even in the local conservatories, much less public concert halls or the mass media. Hence the recordings of some of these works by pianist Tallaj-García on the compact disc accompanying this book are unique.[26]

## Nationalism and the Re-emergence of the Salon Merengue

By the early twentieth century the Dominican merengue, as played primarily by accordion-based bands in the Cibao, had assumed its modern form in terms of basic style and structure. In spite of the amphibrachs and *cinquillos* that surface in its melodies, it had moved well out of the Caribbean contradance family and, accordingly, out of the scope of this book. However, in the 1920s a few composers and bandleaders, inspired by a new form of cultural nationalism, promoted idiosyncratic varieties of salon merengue that bore close affinities to the contemporary danza and danzón and hence can be regarded as bona fide members of the contradanza complex. Although ephemeral and limited in popularity, these merengues constitute an underacknowledged chapter in the history of Dominican music history and of the Caribbean contradanza family in general.

Dominican political and cultural nationalism can be seen to have gone through a series of stages, with different degrees of intensity, different contemporary factions, and different notions of national identity in accordance with the predominant hegemonic antagonist during a given epoch. In the 1840s, when Santo Domingo was struggling against Haitian occupation, local nationalism was defined in contradistinction to racially darker and supposedly barbaric Haiti. Hence, Alfonseca's "Himno nacional" addressed compatriots not as Dominicans but instead commenced, "To arms, Spaniards, rush to combat!"[27] However, after cynical and opportunist politicians engineered a return to Spanish colonial rule in 1861, Dominican nationalism perforce defined Spain as the primary antagonist during the bitter War of Restoration that finally re-established the independent republic in 1865.

Cultural attitudes toward Spain would have remained ambivalent in subsequent decades. Many Dominicans would continue to regard Spain as a cultural lodestar and would certainly prefer to trace their ancestry to Iberia rather than to Africa. However, many, like Puerto Ricans and Cubans, took pride in a creole Caribbean culture that was emerging as a shared patrimony of the three locales. Hence, Dominican musicians and audiences would be likely to embrace Cuban and Puerto Rican danzas as parts of a Caribbean creole patrimony rather than as objectionably "foreign" imports (just as Puerto Ricans could adopt and creatively adapt the Cuban danza, as well as later genres, such as bolero and *son*, without any sense of contradiction with nationalism [see Manuel 1994]). Accordingly, as we have noted, Puerto Rican musicians figured prominently in latter-nineteenth-century Dominican music culture, and local musicians readily accepted the danzas of Morel Campos as models for composition and performance.[28] Jorge, in the extended quotation presented above, laments the historical dependence of Dominican composers on foreign models, whose reasons, she continues, "must be sought in the ideology of the dominant class, manifested in a repudiation of the creole and an imitation of foreign modes. Our own was forgotten in favor of the European or Puerto Rican music then in vogue" (Jorge 1982: 52). The emulation of foreign models can also be seen more charitably as the logical stance of musicians who recognized the provincial and (literally) insular status of their local culture and the need to cultivate a broader artistic palette via incorporating the richer metropolitan and Puerto Rican traditions.

In the second and third decades of the twentieth century, a more acute and explicit sense of cultural nationalism developed, with overt effects on music culture. One stimulus for this development may have been the musical nationalism that inspired Romantic European composers, such as Isaac Albeniz and Manuel de Falla, to seek inspiration in their own countries' vernacular musics. Paradoxically, composers in peripheral countries could emulate metropolitan models by consciously rejecting mainstream Euro-American musics in favor of stylized versions of local genres—a strategy that further cohered with the avant-garde primitivism of Stravinsky or, in the 1930s, Cuban composers Alejandro García Caturla and Amadeo Roldán. A more immediate incentive to musical nationalism was provided by the occupation of the Dominican Republic by the U.S. military from 1916 to 1924. While the U.S. presence served as a vehicle for the popularization of Yankee genres like the fox-trot and Charleston, at the same time it generated among many Dominicans a fresh sense of nationalism as a form of ideological resistance to the foreign invader (see Austerlitz 1997: chap. 3; Alberti 1975: 32).

Hence a movement arose among trained and patriotic musicians to self-consciously seek inspiration in local musics, including the rustic merengue, which continued to be excluded from the bourgeois salons. Composers Pancho García (1972: 24–25) and Emilio Peña Morel and writer and composer Enrique de Marchena (1908–88) specifically called for the cultivation of a distinctively Dominican national music.[29] Peña Morel became the first to systematically research Dominican folk music, and in 1927 Arzeño published the first book-length study of the subject, in which he proclaimed, "We must abandon exotic rhythms and be Dominican musicians" (7; see Austerlitz 1997: 43). Leading the wave of musical nationalism was Santiago-based composer and bandleader García, who introduced themes from folk genres like *mangolina*, *carabiné*, and merengue into such works as his 1918 "Ecos del Cibao" ("Echoes of the Cibao") for chamber ensemble and his "Sinfonéa quisqueyana." Moreover, cultural activists—especially Peña Morel and Marchena—were exhorting colleagues to shake off emulation of the Puerto Rican model, which was finally coming to be seen as hegemonic rather than stimulating.

What is most relevant for the purposes of the present study is the way that the prevailing nationalistic fervor generated a new form of *merengue contradanzeado*, both in the ballrooms and the chamber-music salons. In some cases, the introduction of merengue melodies was hybridized with danza elements in order to disguise them, in a milieu where as recently as 1911 an attempt to play a merengue at a society ball had led to vehement protests and flashing of revolvers (Austerlitz 1997: 47). Hence García, fearful of such a reaction, presented his merengue pot-pourri in "Ecos del Cibao" as "*danzas típicas*." For a 1912 high-society ball, García adopted a different strategy, insinuating a merengue theme into the final section of a Cuban-style danzón, effectively hybridizing the two genres (Paulino 1994: 31). Cuban audiences, of course, were well accustomed to the fashion of incorporating into danzones themes from all manner of rustic rumbas, *sones*, stylized street-vendor calls (*pregones*), and even Cuban-Chinese ditties, so García's act could be seen as a localization of this familiar Cuban practice.

In García's wake, a number of musicians set to composing merengues primarily intended for the chamber concert rather than the ballroom. Pre-eminent among these artists was his protégé, Santiago-based Julio Alberto Hernández (1900–99). Some of Hernández's merengues were in an essentially popular idiom, with lyrics of a deliberately more sanitized nature than the often ribald folk merengues. Intended more for the concert salon were such pieces as his piano merengue, "Santiago," which sounds much like an idiosyncratic danza variant in its instrumental format and its abundant creole rhythms. "Santiago," which is heard on this volume's compact disc, commences with a *paseo*, using more sophisticated chromatic harmonies than would be heard (or even playable) from an accordion-led band. Then follows a section designated "*jaleo*" that does not function like the concluding, responsorial *jaleo* of a standard merengue but evidently represents Hernández's adaptation of a typical saxophone-led *jaleo*. The *jaleo* segues to a sixteen-bar repeated "merengue," whose abundant *cinquillos* lend it much of the flavor of a contemporary danza or danzón. A bridge section then leads to a similarly *cinquillo*-laden sixteen-bar "trio" and finally a return to the *jaleo*—this time in its proper concluding position. (For further discussion of this piece, see Austerlitz 1997: 43–44, 48.) The multisection format of the piece (*paseo*-ABCA) is reminiscent of the earlier danzas of Claudio and Arredondo. While not composed for dancing, it was recorded by a dance band in a style typical of contemporary danzas and danzones.[30] Such hybridization of danza and merengue was even more explicit in pieces like García's "Yo me enceleré," labeled a "danza-merengue," and "Dominicana," a "merendanza" by Luis Rivera, husband of folklorist, singer, and dance troupe director Casandra Damiron (1919–83).

Around 1920 bourgeois ballroom dancers, animated by the growing nationalistic fervor, were belatedly coming to accept and even embrace merengues, provided the songs were presented in a suitably dignified style rather than the rustic accordion/*güira*/*tambora conjunto*. Leading this development was composer, arranger, clarinetist, and bandleader Juan Bautista Espínola (1894–1923) of La Vega. Espínola was the director of a popular dance band that specialized in Cuban-style danzones, which he also composed himself. From 1920 he augmented his fame by performing merengues, such as "Terapéutica," "Mi entusiasmo," "Los agrarontes," and "Rubén." By 1928 he had become the first to record merengues, in the form of his "Rubén" and "Los agrarontes," released on Victor Records. "Los agrarontes" is included (courtesy of Austerlitz) on the compact disc accompanying this volume.

Espínola's recorded merengues are enigmatic in various ways. The degree to which they represent the performance style of his band is not clear, as the recordings were done abroad by a different ensemble (the "Orquesta Internacional"), which, Austerlitz (pers. comm.) opines, may have been a Cuban group or perhaps a New York–based pickup band. Nevertheless, the instrumentation resembles that of his standard group, which consisted of two clarinets, a saxophone, two baritone horns, tuba, string bass, and *timbaletas* drums (Austerlitz 1997: 47). This ensemble represents a standard danza or danzón *orquesta típica* rather than an accordion/*güira*/*tambora* merengue *conjunto*. The style of the recordings, as can be heard in "Los agrarontes," is also thoroughly distinct from that of the *merengue cibaeño* or any subsequent style; hence Aristides

Inchaustegui (1995: 302) characterizes them as "unrecognizable" as merengues. While the melodies are familiar early-twentieth-century merengue tunes, the accompaniment style, with its persistent *cinquillo* ostinatos, is that of a conventional danza or danzón.

In terms of formal structure, "Los agrarontes" commences with an introductory *paseo* and then segues to an A section, which might be called the first "merengue" proper. While the *cinquillo*-based accompaniment is typical of a contemporary danza or danzón, the melody, shown in Figure 4.3, is that of a familiar Cibao merengue and is very similar to that used by García in his "Ecos del Cibao" and other pieces and also by Hernández in a 1928 song (see Austerlitz 1997: 44–45). The tune is played four times, with a varied ending and instrumentation, and then segues to a second "merengue," and then a third. Whether one regards Espínola's pieces as merengues or danzas would depend on what one chooses to regard as the structural elements: the merengue tune and form, or the danza-style rhythm and instrumentation.

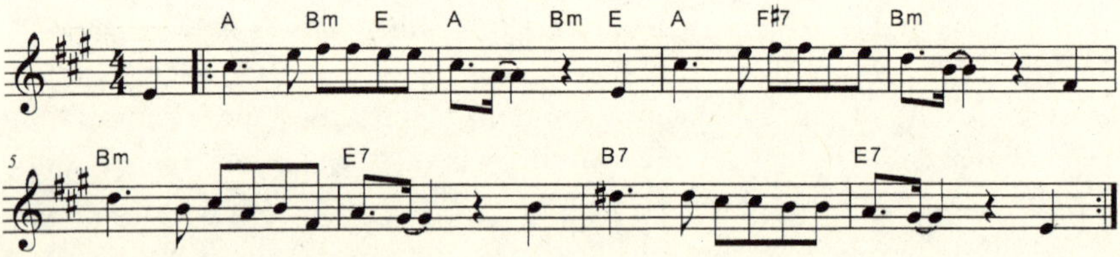


**Figure 4.3** Melody of first "merengue" in "Los agrarontes," by Juan Espínola.

Espínola's music, as a hybrid of danza and merengue, was in some ways a *sui generis* entity but in other ways a representative fusion, resembling other pieces by Mena, Marchena, Ravelo, García, and Hernández. Where García presented his merengue tunes as "danzas," Espínola, from one perspective, presented danzas (i.e., pieces in danza style) as "merengues." More specifically, he called these pieces "merengues de contradanza" (Austerlitz, pers. comm.); Dominican scholars have categorized them by the term used in this chapter, "*merengue contradanzeado*" ("contradanced merengue" or "contradance-style merengue"). As Paulino (1994: 31) argues, Espínola's salon merengues can be seen as a revival or continuation of the *merengue contradanzeado* tradition that was (allegedly) inaugurated eighty years earlier by Alfonseca, intensified during the 1850s, and then marginalized by the Oasists and their followers. Espínola must have known something of the salon merengue that, as suggested by Espaillat, may have survived a mere forty-some years earlier, as Austerlitz (pers. comm.) observes. However, in incorporating merengue into his repertoire and presenting it to his genteel audiences, Espínola evidently adorned it in the style of the genre he and his band knew best—the danzón.

Espínola, García, and Hernández deserve much of the credit for reintroducing merengue into the ballrooms, although this task would not be fully realized until the 1930s under the diktat of Trujillo and his "house band" of Luis Alberti. Ironically, in fusing their version of merengue with the danza and danzón, they also guaranteed its ephemerality, as those very genres would decline dramatically in subsequent years. In the 1930s, under the leadership of Alberti and the promotion of Trujillo, the merengue became entrenched in the urban ballrooms, not in the form of a revival of the archaic *merengue contradanzeado* but as a stylized and elaborated form of the Cibao-style folk idiom. At present, the salon merengue of Espínola and his contemporaries is thoroughly neglected, despite clearly meriting recognition as a colorful stage in national music history.

## Contradance and Quadrille in Dominican Folk Culture

While merengue and bachata are the only Dominican dance music genres to have become internationally known, an impressive variety of regional social dance forms have flourished in the country, some of which represent different syncretic hybrids of European- and African-derived elements. A few of these genres, such as the fandango, are extinct on the island. Others are seldom, if ever, encountered "in the field" but are regularly performed at various occasions by the dozens of amateur and semiprofessional folkloric groups that exist throughout the country.

In the early 1950s folklorist Edna Garrido de Boggs documented a folk dance called *tumba* in and around the town of Jarabacoa, in the hills to the southwest of Santiago de los Caballeros. The choreography and the name strongly suggested descent, in some form, from the *tumba* that flourished in urban salons and presumably elsewhere in the 1840s. As witnessed by Boggs, the *tumba*, like the longways-style contradance, featured a basic formation in which the men and women faced each other in two lines and subsequently executed figures and changed partners, to the accompaniment of a typical accordion/*güira/tambora* group ([1952] 2006: 154–155). Boggs reported that the dance was performed only by elders and was clearly in the process of disappearing.

A decade later Fradique Lizardo documented the *tumba* in the same two communities. Lizardo's description of the dance (1974: 239–250) is more detailed and slightly different; he evidently did not encounter the longways format but rather one in which the basic formation involved sets of two partners, who would collectively execute a series of figures, abounding in bows and curtsies. To Lizardo, such figures reflected an essentially courtly origin and a clear derivation from the nineteenth-century *tumba*. Lizardo also provided a transcription of the *tumba* melody, an eight-bar tonic-dominant arpeggiated figure played on the accordion with alternating *cinquillo* and amphibrach figures, shown in Figure 4.4 (from Lizardo 1974: 243). While Lizardo evidently attempted to rescue the dance by incorporating it into the repertoire of his folkloric group, at present it is no longer performed either by this group or others.

Figure 4.4 Tumba melody.

Lizardo also discovered a version of the quadrille (*cuadrilla*) danced during annual festivals of San Andrés, to the accompaniment of a marching band. The quadrille had been documented in Santo Domingo, as in Cuba, in the mid-1800s. Lizardo states that the quadrille he encountered "is a European dance which no one would claim to be Dominican" (1974: 65). The San Andrés quadrille, like other Caribbean quadrilles, is a suite, although of three movements rather than the four or five more common elsewhere in the Caribbean. Eight pairs of dancers form a square, with two couples on each side, and perform a fixed set of figures, including an initial salute, a *serrucho* (handsaw) in which they form lines moving in opposite directions, a "coronation" figure for each woman, a "chain" (*cadena*) pattern, and a closing salute. The accompanying music, presented as a piano score by Lizardo, consists of three simple march-like tunes, the first two in 6/8 and the last in 2/4 (1974: 65–72). While simply alternating tonic and dominant chords, they comprise European-style through-composed tunes rather than creole-style ostinato patterns. The quadrille, like the *tumba*, is evidently not danced anymore, whether by folkloric groups or unaffiliated enthusiasts.[31] Nevertheless, its persistence until the 1970s in the Dominican Republic constitutes the only documentation of this dance in the Spanish Caribbean since the nineteenth century.

As mentioned, the gamut of Dominican folk dances also includes several genres that are seldom, if ever, performed by ordinary enthusiasts but are nevertheless standard items in the repertoires of the numerous folkloric groups that exist throughout the country and perform in diverse contexts, from town festivals (*fiestas patronales*) to tourist hotels. Such dances would include *mangulina*, *carabiné*, *chenche matriculado*, *bamboulá*, and *sarambo*. The folkloric groups' choreographed, stylized versions of these dances could be regarded as "artificial," but these dances, now largely defunct in the field, could also be said to have taken on new sorts of lives in the folkloric context. Of interest in this chapter is the *carabiné*, which, as mentioned above, is argued by Fouchard to have been a Haitian contredanse derivative that itself gave birth to the Haitian méringue and Dominican merengue. Oral tradition, reiterated by several Dominican writers, traces the genre's origin specifically to the Haitian military encampment of Haitian leader Jean-Jacques Dessalines outside Santo Domingo in 1805, and the *carabiné* went on to flourish primarily in the western part of the country, with its strong and ongoing Haitian presence.[32] However, the region also hosted many Canary Island immigrants in the mid-1700s, and Lizardo (1974: 177–203) attributes several of the distinctive choreographic figures—such as that in which men form a circle around the women—to a dance called *isa* from the Canary Island of La Palma. This pattern is typical of other Canary dances as well, such as local versions of *seguidillas* and *malagueñas*. However, it also occurs in Caribbean quadrille dancing.

As in most forms of traditional contradanza, dancers in the *carabiné*, as led by a bastonero, commence in longways format and then execute a series of collective figures in which they alternately embrace ballroom-style and separate and change partners; the concentric circle formation is particularly distinctive. However, the *carabiné* as it exists today could be said to exhibit only a very general and partial affinity with the contradance family. Most folkloric groups tend to perform the same two or three songs (especially "Cara sucia"), which consist of simple, repetitive, *cinquillo*-laden responsorial tunes over tonic-dominant ostinatos, accompanied by a typical string- or accordion-based group with *balsié* drum.

In surveying the legacy of the contradance in the Dominican Republic, it remains to make parenthetical mention of an idiosyncratic form of collective figure dance, in the form of the stylized versions of merengues and *mangulinas* done by the folkloric groups. In their customary forms, the merengue and *mangulina* are independent couple dances, but the folkloric groups flourishing since the 1960s have inevitably turned them into collective dances in which the couples execute synchronized figures in order to make a pleasing spectacle. While it would be incorrect to regard the resulting format as a direct derivative of the contradance, it can nevertheless be seen as a curious reincarnation of the nineteenth-century dance's collective structure, albeit reoriented for presentation to an audience.

## Notes

1. Thus, for example, the eighteenth- and nineteenth-century accounts of Saint-Méry, Labat, Walton, Dhormoys, Bono, and others are quoted and discussed repeatedly in the more recent works of Pérez de Cuello (2005), Jorge (1982), Rodríguez Demorizi (1982), Coopersmith (1945), Lizardo (1974), Austerlitz (1997: chap. 2), and others. These books, aside from that of Austerlitz, are difficult to find even in the Dominican Republic, not to mention elsewhere. At present, Puerto Rican scholar Edgardo Díaz Díaz is preparing fresh perspectives on the history of the Dominican danza and merengue. In writing this chapter, I am indebted for exchanges with him, with Austerlitz, and with Dominican scholar and pianist Angelina Tallaj-García, who also provided me with valuable notations of Pancho García and other composers.
2. Saint-Domingue's prosperity did not, of course, extend to the slaves, who enjoyed an average life span of seven years after being imported.

3. Saint-Méry describes the fandango as a solo female dance (1797–98: 91). In the accounts of Walton and Francisco Bono, it is a couple dance (see Jorge 1982: 26–27). Elsewhere in Latin America, the term "fandango" came to be a general term for a wide variety of dances, which did not necessarily share any choreographic or musical features.
4. See the Introduction (Chapter 1) regarding Labat's and Saint-Méry's descriptions of the calenda.
5. In volume 1 of "Present State of the Spanish Colonies . . . ," (1810: 161–162), cited in Coopersmith 1949: 48. On the next page Coopersmith suggests, presumably erroneously, that this dance was a quadrille.
6. See pp. 252–254. The relevant passage is cited in Pérez de Cuello 2005: 260–265 and in Jorge 1982: 28–29. Jorge, however, does not note that the work is fictional and gives the date as 1841 rather than the correct 1941.
7. This is the clarifying term used by Paulino (1994: 31), among others.
8. See note 1. Pérez de Cuello (2005) provides the most exhaustive overview, although Díaz Díaz (2006) presents important subsequent perspectives.
9. This attribution is made in Nolasco 1948: 125, Rodríguez Demorizi 1982: 108, Paulino 1994: 31, and elsewhere. The Hispanophilic Nolasco, however, also attempts to trace the merengue to the thirteenth-century Cantigas de Santa María. See note 17 in the Introduction (Chapter 1).
10. For a transcription of this excerpt, see Austerlitz 1997: 23.
11. From *Oasis*, no. 1 (Nov. 26, 1854): 3. The most extensive discussion of the polemic is in Pérez de Cuello 2005: 115–141.
12. The Viennese waltz, however stately it may seem in retrospect, was criticized and lampooned for the same reasons.
13. See Pérez de Cuello 2005: 143–59 for a thorough discussion of the theories regarding the etymology of the word "merengue." Other culinary terms applied to dance music would include "salsa," Indo-Caribbean chutney, the Mexican *jarabe*, and Andean *chicha*.
14. Velázquez and Ureña (2004: 23) claim, without specifying their source, that merengue was the name of a dance performed by slaves marketed in Curaçao in the late 1700s.
15. Díaz Díaz (2005) suggests that the term "danza" was deliberately adopted as a stratagem for perpetuating the dance in the face of Pezuela's ban of the merengue. See Chapter 3 for further discussion of the merengue/danza in Puerto Rico. In the 1950s Flérida de Nolasco (1956: 41) also suggested a Puerto Rican origin for the Dominican "*merengue contradanzeado*."
16. In *El Caribe* (March 30, 2005), cited in Díaz Díaz 2006: 199.
17. Some Dominican scholars have argued for a structurally significant role of the variant of the habanera pattern played on the *tambora* and the occasional appearance of the *cinquillo* in vocal melodies, such as that of the familiar "Compadre Pedro Juan" and, in an obscure form, in the *tambora* pattern of the *pambiche* variant. (See Pérez de Cuello 2005: 303.)
18. Díaz Díaz (2006: 202–204; 2008: 249–231) makes an intriguing and persuasive case for the nineteenth-century military roots of the *tambora* and its characteristic drum roll preceding the downbeat.

19. While a few writers refer to the *fandango con estribillo*, Lizardo (1974: 280) seems to question whether any such genre ever existed. Velázquez and Ureña (2004: 18–19) paraphrase an 1875 description written by Pedro Francisco Bonó of a fandango with vocal lyrics.
20. Paulino, while accepting the attribution of the Cibao merengue to the earlier salon style, suggests, "The lower stratum of society started to imitate the [salon merengue], incorporating it as a genre of their own within the repertoire of the generic complex of the fandango" (1994: 31).
21. The 1875 quote by Espaillat suggests that the merengue may not have been entirely expelled from the salons, but, as mentioned, his reference to the "insipid accordion" indicates that the merengue of his time was already the rustic Cibao style, quite distinct from the earlier *merengue contradanzeado*. Espaillat wrote, "We would content [*contentaríamos*] ourselves with saying that, in the opinion of many, the merengue should be uprooted from respectable society; but I, who wish only the best for all classes, would argue that it should be expelled entirely" (in Nolasco 1948: 147 and Rodríguez Demorizi 1982: 83; Rodríguez Demorizi presents Espaillat as writing, "We *will* content [*contentaremos*] ourselves with saying").
22. See Deschamps 1906: 274–279. García (1972: 62–63) also describes the Puerto Rican and Dominican danzas as basically identical.
23. Her statement that the piece's rhythm is a variant of the *cinquillo* is not borne out by the score. Her transcription of Claudio's "Congojas de amor" is inconsistent with the manuscript I examined in the Dominican archives.
24. The pieces are "El 1555," "Josefita," "Congojas de amor," "Las misas del pecado," "Piang'io perle," and "Leonor," whose pages are mixed up. In "Piang'io perle," the final section is a repeat of the A section. The manuscript of "Congojas de amor" bears the unlikely date of "'64"—i.e., 1864, at which point Claudio would have been nine years old. As Díaz Díaz observes (pers. comm.), the only extant contemporary counterpart of the tripartite form used in Arredondo's "El sueño" would be Gottschalk's "Danza" (Opus 33) of 1857. Other well-known danzas by Claudio were "La silfide," "Tu mirada es el cielo," "Recuerdos bellos," and "Del paraíso hasta el cielo."
25. Arzeño 1927: 44. As Díaz Díaz (pers. comm.) pithily quips, by that time Arzeño had not even heard Rafael Hernández's "Lamento borincano" ("Puerto Rican Lament")!
26. Tallaj-García relates (pers. comm.) that she was able to acquire scores for these and other works only with difficulty.
27. "Al arma, españoles, volad a la lid." Anti-Haitian sentiment has remained an important aspect of Dominican nationalism, with its own ramifications in music culture, including long-standing attempts to deny or exclude the Haitian presence in national music.
28. See Díaz Díaz 2008 for further discussion of this phenomenon.
29. Peña Morel, from *Listín Diario* (Feb. 2, 1919), and Marchena, in *Blanco y Negro* 8 (371), cited in Díaz Díaz 2008.
30. This recording is included on the CD *Merengue: Dominican Music and Dominican Identity* (Rounder CD 1130), produced by Paul Austerlitz.
31. Pers. comm., Xiomarita Pérez, National Folklorist of the Dominican Republic.
32. One of the several links between Dominican dance-music culture and the dance-music culture of Santiago de Cuba is the practice in Santiago de Cuba—docu-

mented in the 1860s by Walter Goodman (1873: 146)—of referring to a dance as a *carabina*, as in a gentleman's request to a lady before a dance: "Would the *señorita* kindly grant me a *carabina*?"

## References


Alberti, Luis. 1975. *De música y orquestas bailables dominicanas*. Santo Domingo: Taller.

Arzeño, Julio. 1927. *Del folk-lore musical dominicano*. Santo Domingo: Imprenta La Cuna de América.

Austerlitz, Paul. 1997. *Merengue: Dominican music and Dominican identity*. Philadelphia: Temple University Press.

Boggs, Edna Garrido de. [1952] 2006. *Reseña histórica del folklore dominicano*. Santo Domingo: Dirección Nacional de Folklore.

Coopersmith, Jacob Maurice. 1945. "Music and musicians of the Dominican Republic: A survey (part II)." *Musical Quarterly* 31 (2): 212–226.

———. 1949. *Music and musicians of the Dominican Republic: A survey*. Washington, DC: Unión Panaméricana.

Deschamps, Enrique. 1906. *La República Dominicana: Directorio y guía general*. Barcelona: J. Cunill.

Díaz Díaz, Edgardo. 2006. "El merengue dominicano: Una prehistoria musical en diez pasos." In *El merengue en la cultura dominicana y del caribe*. Ed. Darío Tejeda and Rafael Emilio Yunén, 179–210. Santo Domingo: Instituto de Estudios Caribeños.

———. 2008. "Danza antillana, conjuntos militares, nacionalismo musical e identidad dominicana: Retomando los pasos perdidos del merengue." *Latin American Music Review* 29 (2): 232–262.

Fouchard, Jean. 1973. *La méringue*. Ottawa: Editions Lemeac.

García, Juan Francisco. 1972. *Canciones dominicanas*. Santo Domingo: Universidad Autónoma de Santo Domingo.

Goodman, Walter. 1873. *The pearl of the Antilles or an artist in Cuba*. London: Henry S. King.

Guerrero, José. 2006. "El merengue: ¿Cubano, puertorriqueño, haitiano o dominicano? La problemática antropológica de los origines." In *El merengue en la cultura dominicana y del caribe*. Ed. Darío Tejeda and Rafael Emilio Yunén, 69–104. Santo Domingo: Instituto de Estudios Caribeños.

Henríquez Ureña, Max. 1941. *La conspiración de los Alcarrizos*. Lisbon: Sociedad Industrial de Tipografía.

Hernández, Julio Alberto. 1969. *Música tradicional dominicana*. Santo Domingo: Postigo.

Holguín Veras, Miguel. 2001. *Acerca de canciones antiguas dominicanas*. Santo Domingo: Academía de Ciencias de Republica Dominicana.

Inchaustegui, Aristides. 1995. *Por amor al arte*. Santo Domingo: Secretariat de Estado de Educación.

Jorge, Bernarda. 1982. *La música dominicana: Siglos XIX–XX*. Santo Domingo: Editora de la Universidad Autónoma de Santo Domingo (UASD).

Lizardo, Fradique. 1974. *Danzas y bailes folklóricos dominicanos*. Santo Domingo: Taller.

Manuel, Peter. 1994. "Puerto Rican music and cultural identity: Creative appropriation of Cuban sources from danza to salsa." *Ethnomusicology* 3 (2): 249–280.

Nolasco, Flérida de. 1948. *Vibraciones en el tiempo.* Ciudad Trujillo (Santo Domingo): Editora Montalvo.

———. 1956. *Santo Domingo en el folklore universal.* San Cristóbal: Impresora Dominicana.

Ortiz, Fernando. 1924. *Glosario de afronegrismos.* Havana: Imprenta El Siglo XX.

———. [1952–55] 1995. *Los instrumentos de la música afrocubana: Las tumbas.* Havana: Editorial Letras Cubanas.

———. 1985. *Nuevo catauro de cubanismos.* Havana: Editorial de Ciencias Sociales.

Paulino, Julio César. 1994. "Contradanzas, independencia y merengues." *Cultura* [Dominican Republic] 1 (2): 30–31.

Pérez de Cuello, Catana. 2005. "Génesis del merengue: Raices, trayectoria y diffusion en el siglo XIX." In *El merengue: Música y baile de la República Dominicana,* 1–369. Santo Domingo: Verizon.

Quintero-Rivera, Ángel. 2006. "El merengue y la danza: Orígenes sociales del baile en pareja en el Caribe." In *El merengue en la cultura dominicana y del caribe.* Ed. Darío Tejeda and Rafael Emilio Yunén, 105–152. Santo Domingo: Instituto de Estudios Caribeños.

Rodríguez Demorizi, Emilio. 1982. *Artes dominicanas.* Santo Domingo: Caribe Grolier.

Velázquez, Cralos, and Alejandro Ureña. 2004. *De Santo Domingo al mundo: El merengue y la bachata.* New York: Galos Publishing.

DOMINIQUE O. CYRILLE

# 5 / Creole Quadrilles of Guadeloupe, Dominica, Martinique, and St. Lucia

On a late October evening in Laplaine, a village in southern Dominica, I was watching a quadrille performance during the selection rounds of the Heritage Festival, an annual contest that celebrates Dominica's culture. All contestants were members of cultural groups representing villages or communities from the southeast district that had been succeeding each other on stage in separate sets of adults and children to perform the quadrille, the *mazouk*, the bèlè, and other national dances. It was already late into the night when a new set of adult quadrille dancers came on stage. I was admiring the dancers' stances and smiling faces and marveling at the way the smooth, elegant movements of the ladies were emphasized by the traditional attire, the *wob dwiyet*, when someone in the audience exclaimed, "That's not quadrille, that is bèlè!"

Bèlè is the other national dance of Dominica. While quadrille is of European derivation, bèlè has kept obvious ties with West African dance styles. Whether danced by one or two individuals, the characteristic bèlè step patterns, the arm movements, and the bent contour of the dancer's body and knees could not be confused with the distinctive steps and erect body attitude required for quadrille dancing. Furthermore, like most Afro-Caribbean dance styles in Dominica, Guadeloupe, Martinique, and St. Lucia, bèlè is performed to the sound of a one-skinned, conical drum and responsorial singing. This format helps distinguish it from quadrille, which is played with bands that include at least one melodic instrument. In Dominica this ensemble is called jing-ping band. It consists of an accordion (the actual "jing-ping"), a frame drum called *tanbu bass*, a *shiyak* scraper, and a *boom-boom*, a four-foot-long end-blown tube traditionally made out of bamboo that is used to play bass pitches.

The man's incisive comment, insisting on maintaining the distinction between quadrille and bèlè, kept me wondering because it seemed to echo others that I had heard in Guadeloupe, Martinique, and St. Lucia, islands of the Lesser Antilles that are close neighbors to Dominica. There, too, quadrille is a vivid tradition, and when people dance it they must avoid too much swaying of their bodies or flailing of their arms. Should they fail to maintain a certain composure during their performance, someone will remind them that what they are dancing should be the quadrille, not bèlè—or *gwoka*, its counterpart in Guadeloupe.

Guadeloupe, Dominica, Martinique, and St. Lucia are islands of the Eastern Caribbean where people have been dancing quadrille for about two centuries. Just a few decades ago, most dancers in these islands were unaware that quadrille was a vital tradition in the neighboring islands as well. Antilleans did their dance, each in their separate community, because it was part of their local history. People danced the quadrille as a means to feel connected to their community and to their ancestors. Since the early 1990s, growing feelings of Creole identity have provided dancers from these islands with new incentives and opportunities to perform in front of each other. Because they all speak the French-based Creole language, quadrille dancers from Dominica, Martinique, and St. Lucia have been invited to perform during festivals that celebrate Creole diversity. However, as an unexpected outcome of these gatherings, the quadrille dancers found that instead of discovering dances distinctive of each community, the quadrille was recognized as a practice common to many people across the neighboring islands. Moreover, Antilleans who performed in these festivals became aware that they often agreed on the qualities that made a good quadrille dancer, and on the movements and gestures that were acceptable in quadrille as well. The dance, therefore, took on a new significance. It became an embodiment of their shared Creole culture and a link that pulled them closer to each other.

St. Lucia, Martinique, Dominica, and Guadeloupe share a common background as former French colonies, although they form separate political entities today. Although the English had claimed St. Lucia a few years earlier, the French began settling it in 1617 and acquired Guadeloupe and Martinique in 1635. The British tried to seize Dominica from the aboriginal Caribs in 1627, but it was the French who effectively colonized the island at the end of the seventeenth century (Honychurch 1984: 35). The French crown then appointed governors who administered the islands until the late 1750s. During the second half of the eighteenth century, constant feuding between the French and English for domination over the islands caused numerous transfers of power, until a set of peace treaties that France and England signed at the turn of the nineteenth century finally gave Martinique back to the French in 1802 and Dominica to the English in 1805. The following decade, in 1814, St. Lucia also became English. Guadeloupe had remained French during the last decade of the eighteenth century.

In all four islands many tradition bearers view the quadrille as resulting from this complicated past and give credit to the French for initiating practice of the dance in their country. They do not feel, however, that quadrille was simply passed on to them by the former European colonizer. Rather, Antilleans consider their quadrille a new creation, because although it was first introduced by Europeans, the dance was adopted and subsequently transformed by the people of African descent. Their contribution made quadrille the new Creole dance it has now become.

Martinique and Guadeloupe, located to the north of St. Lucia and Dominica, respectively, contributed greatly to the diffusion of French culture in the Lesser Antilles. Martinique was the most valued French colony during the entire slavery era, except between 1740 and the late 1780s when Saint-Domingue (present-day Haiti) temporarily took precedence. By that time, however, French settlers in Martinique had built comfortable theaters where French dancers and musicians touring the Americas came to perform excerpts of the same shows that were fashionable in Paris. During the prolonged periods of French administration, several planters from Martinique who sought to expand their domain established new plantations in St. Lucia. Dominica, on the other hand, seemed particularly appealing to poorer French planters. The island also attracted racially mixed couples, as well as free mulattos (people of mixed European and African ancestry) whose economic status would have placed them among the higher classes in the French islands of Martinique and Guadeloupe. There, however, strict local laws limited their civil rights and access to property. French settlers in St. Lucia and Dominica did not sever the links that tied them to the French islands. When these islands were conclusively transferred to the British, the French were not forced to leave. Rather, they were allowed to stay and contribute to the development of the agriculture (Davy 1854). For decades French settlers kept close ties with their relatives and friends who lived in Paris or in the other French colonies. The ones who could afford it also sent their children to Paris, France, or to Martinique in order to complete their education (Sturge and Harvey [1837] 1968: 127). Moreover, the proximity of these islands allowed for easy and frequent travel between them. When in the early nineteenth century England abolished slavery in its colonies, hundreds of runaways fled Martinique and Guadeloupe to find refuge in St. Lucia and Dominica (Sturge and Harvey [1837] 1968: 93). Some of the runaways were African-born, but most were creoles—that is, born in the Caribbean (Davy 1854).

Martinique remained French throughout most of the slavery era despite constant feuding with the English. According to early accounts by R. P. Du Tertre ([1671] 1973) and R. P. Labat, a few hundred aboriginal Caribs lived there in the beginning of European settlement. This population decreased rapidly within a few decades, and by the end of the seventeenth century the Carib population had disappeared from Martinique. The slave trade officially began there in 1640 and lasted until 1833. Forced African workers, nevertheless, continued to be brought to the colony up to the mid–nineteenth century (Nicolas 1996: ii, 56).

During the first decades of continuous French presence on the island a new group of people, the mulattos—offspring of European colonists with their African slaves—began to appear (Du Tertre [1671] 1973: ii, 152). A very small group at first, mulattos were granted civil rights by both the local usage and by law and did not seem to form a separate group or a special class in the colony. By the late eighteenth century, however, the mulatto group had grown significantly and formed an intermediary socioracial class between the French colonists and the enslaved people of African descent (Geggus 1996). They had also become a political force to be reckoned with (Moreau de Saint-Méry [henceforth Saint-Méry] 1791; Meignan 1878). Indeed, their mixed European and African ancestry gave them an ambiguous status in Martinique (Gautier 1985). In the late eighteenth century, many were either born free or were freed before their maturity by their white parents. Some had received a good education in Martinique, or the wealthiest, in Paris, whereas the white planters were poorly educated no matter how rich, according to most visitors (Girod-Chantrans 1785; De Rodellec du Porzic 1826; Granier de Cassagnac [1842] 1844) and to Saint-Méry as well ([1797] 1984: 36–37). Many mulattos were given a small piece of land by their white parents and even a couple of slaves in order to have an easier start in life.

In the 1780s mulattos danced the French contredanse, which they had learned from dance masters (Saint-Méry 1803). The French had introduced the contredanse in their colonies in the late eighteenth century as part of a nostalgic attempt to recreate aspects of the lifestyle they would have enjoyed on the continent (Saint-Méry [1797] 1984: 34). However, soon after its introduction in the Americas, the dance came to appeal strongly to all socioracial classes in the colonies and spread. By the early nineteenth century blacks, whites, and mulattos were all dancing the European court dances (Girod-Chantrans 1785; Saint-Méry [1797] 1984; Dessalles [1836] 1987). The late eighteenth century was a time when ideals of freedom and equal rights promoted by the French Revolution had intensified the mulattos' struggle for power and caused violent uprisings among the enslaved Africans. Many French colonists, however, regarded the French contredanse and quadrille as their prerogative. In this context, the European court dances became an arena where issues of race, ethnicity, and power were rediscussed and renegotiated.

## From the French Contredanse to the Creole Quadrille

The court dances from which the Creole quadrilles derive should not be confused with earlier styles of European dances introduced in the islands in the seventeenth century. These earlier contredanses had not come as the result of the nostalgia most planters felt for the country they had left behind, as was the case in the late eighteenth century. Rather, they were part of the French missionaries' efforts to replace African dance movements and gestures that they found lascivious with more restrained European attitudes. In fact, according to written sources, it was "in order to make them [the Africans] lose the habit of these infamous dances [that] they were taught others like the passe-pied and the courante so they [could] jump and entertain themselves at will with no indecent gestures" (Labat 1724: 2, 54).[1] Seventeenth-century dances differed significantly from the contredanses of the late eighteenth century, though they share the same names (Guilcher 1969). They did not impact the creole genres directly, or at least not in the same way as the quadrille. They did, however, greatly help the Africans become accustomed to Europeans' aesthetics. As a result, by the early eighteenth century numerous domestic slaves had been noticed for their musical aptitudes. According to Labat (1724: 2, 56), it was a source of pride if a planter owned a domestic musician who could also provide the musical accompaniment for his dance parties. In eighteenth-century France, as well, most musicians were domestics who added the practice of a musical instrument as a special skill. When French colonists used some of their talented domestic slaves as musicians in their functions, they were merely perpetuating common practices from their society of origin.

The French contredanse, which epitomizes the last period of the *ancien regime*, was a square dance consisting of a sequence of patterns (figures), using a variety of prescribed steps. Each figure is concordant with a segment of the music. In the French contredanse only four couples can figure at a time. There are two configurations for the contredanse; in the first one, the couples form two opposite lines, corresponding to the longways style of English country dance. The second configuration is the same one that characterized the eighteenth-century cotillion.[2] Each couple stands along one side of the square—hence the name "quadrille"—and all the dance moves and figures are performed within the square. Dance scholar Jean-Michel Guilcher indicates that between the early 1780s and 1792—during the golden age of the French contredanse in aristocratic receptions—cotillions were danced either as a single number or in sets of two and up to nine called *pot-pourri* (1969: 144–147).

The quadrille is defined in most sources as a dance that derived from the French contredanse and is performed by four couples in a square configuration. Typically it is a set dance composed of five elements called "figures," which collectively alternate duple and triple meter. In the first years of the nineteenth century, French society emerged from the post-Revolutionary "Reign of Terror" era (1793–94) with a new passion for dance. Contredanses in *pot-pourris* became the norm in public ballrooms where aristocrats and commoners danced together (Guilcher 1969: 148). Back then, each number of the set was in reality an old contredanse. The quadrille per se began to appear in the 1820s when musicians began to compose sets of contrasting contredanses instead of separate numbers. The number of pieces inside a set was fixed to five in the following years (Guillard 1988: 7–8).

The dance that is known as French quadrille took shape progressively in the first half of the nineteenth century. It consisted of an arbitrary assemblage of five French contredanses, four of which were fixed, and the fifth remained variable; the first four were "*le pantalon*" (trousers), "*l'été*" (summer), "*la poule*" (hen), "*la pastourelle*" (shepherd girl), and "*finale.*" Regarding the variability of the final movement, Raviart (n.d.) relates, "In the eighteenth century, people were especially attracted to creativity. . . . Everything changed after the French Revolution. From then on, dancers began reproducing steps that came from high dance, or ballet. In the beginning of Napoleon's era (during the Directoire, the Consulate, and the early Empire), *brisés, jeté-battus, flic-flacs, entrechats, balonnés, fouettés, mouchetés, sissonnes*, multi-turn pirouettes gave brilliance to the contredanse, and later to the quadrille. Correspondingly, the figures were simplified and made common."

Some of these figures became stereotypes, and were reproduced from one contredanse to another: "The *avant-deux*, which was originally part of a contredanse called *été*, became the signature pattern of all *étés*. By the same process various *poules, pastourelles, grâces, gigues*, and *trénis* would also appear, each one with its own special movement pattern, but performed on various music styles" (Raviart n.d.).

The French quadrille, which acquired its permanent shape in the early 1840s, strongly influenced the creole quadrilles that emerged in the French-dominated islands during the latter nineteenth century. These quadrilles are vivid traditions in the Caribbean and are continuously evolving.

The St. Lucian quadrille comprises four figures simply called figure one, figure two, figure three, and figure four. However, although tradition bearers in St. Lucia mention four figures when they describe their quadrille, few dancers in St. Lucia's capital seem to remember the fourth figure, because it is rarely performed today. Like the French quadrille, the St. Lucian dance is performed by four couples in a square configuration. They perform the same kind of step patterns that identify the figures of the French quadrille. Nevertheless, tradition bearers do not seem to know any French name for the figures they perform. In St. Lucia, the term "quadrille" is also a generic name for all dances of European origin that were re-created on the island during the colonial era.

In Dominica, while there are at least two dances that fall into the category of quadrille, one of them is not considered such by most Dominicans. This is the dance that they call "the Lancers," although it bears no similarity to the better-known Lancers said to be invented by John Duval around 1817. Rather, it closely resembles the creole quadrilles that exist today in the French islands of Martinique and Guadeloupe, both in music and dance style.

Like its St. Lucian counterpart, the dance that Dominicans call "quadrille" consists of four figures that in Petite Savanne, a village in southern Dominica, people also name "*l'été*," "*la poule*," "*la trinitèz*," and "*le pantalon*."[3] Nevertheless, most of the tradition bearers with whom I spoke simply call them figure one, figure two, figure three, and figure four. Unlike the St. Lucians, Dominican quadrille dancers always perform the fourth figure. It is in fact the most important element of the set and the one that helps juries evaluate the dance troupes that perform on stage during the yearly quadrille competitions organized nationwide during the Heritage Festival.

Guadeloupeans know and practice five different quadrilles. The first four emerged in the Guadeloupean archipelago[4] during the colonial era. They are the *quadrille au commandement* (with calls) of Grande Terre; the *quadrille au commandement* of Marie-Galante; the quadrille of Côte-sous-le-vent, in Basse-Terre; and the quadrille of Vieux-Fort, also in Basse-Terre. The fifth quadrille is not of creole origins but is the Lancers, which is the dance supposedly composed by Duval. Although the four Guadeloupean quadrilles are different from each other, they all derive from the French quadrille and comprise the standard five figures: *pantalon, l'été, la poule, la pastourelle,* and a variable finale. This can be a second *l'été,* as is often the case in *quadrille au commandement* from Grande-Terre, or a biguine, a *mélingué,* or any other couple dance that the accordionist sees fit.

In Martinique of the 1980s it was still possible to meet with people who remembered and danced at least four different quadrilles: the *lakadri* (from "*la quadrille*"), the *pastourelle,* and two variants of *haute-taille,* a quadrille with calls found only in southeastern Martinique. The name "*haute-taille*" connotes the old French "*danse haute*" or "*haute danse,*" whereas "*taille basse*" connotes "*danse basse,*" which meant unrefined dance. "*Taille*" in this context means "cut" or "pattern." *Haute-taille* is thus a dance of "high pattern" (Raviart n.d.). Today only one *haute-taille* that merges elements from the earlier styles appears to be thriving on the island. It consists of five sections and does not seem to derive from the French quadrille per se. This means that the step patterns that characterize each figure in *haute-taille* are not those of the *pantalon, été, poule,* and *pastourelle,* nor do they appear in that specific order. Rather, this *haute-taille* is closer to the Dominican Lancers, although the dancers are led by a caller. For its part, the Martinican *haute-taille* comprises five elements. Old tradition bearers also call the first three "contredanses" or "chains" (the ladies' chain, the side chain, and so forth), while the last two elements or figures are called *été* and *aimable*. The similar names used for the creole quadrilles of the eastern Caribbean and for the French quadrille of the mid–nineteenth century do not indicate that the dances are mere reproductions of a European original. Raviart (n.d.) observes that as people selected one element and rearranged another, simplified here and enhanced there, through amalgamation of the new contributions with their own traditional forms or mélange with new traits acquired elsewhere, they have effectively remodeled the dance. Like most creole forms, they were adapted and re-created while being adopted by the people of African descent. Yet, she continues, it is sometimes possible to see traces of the old French dance in the creole forms. For example, in the *haute-taille* of Martinique, dancers try to outdo each other with brilliant, adventurous, and spectacular jumping steps that are sometimes improvised.

Likewise, each island of the continuum possesses its own quadrille band. In St. Lucia it is a string band typically consisting of a violin, a banjo, a ukulele-like *cuatro* (sometimes two banjos or two *cuatros*), one or two shakers called *chac-chac*, and a tall drum. The Dominican quadrille is danced to the sound of an accordion-led jing-ping band. The small music ensemble to which Guadeloupeans do their quadrilles is very similar to the Dominican jing-ping. Traditional Guadeloupean quadrille bands include an accordion, a frame drum called *tanboudbass*, a scraper called *siyak*, and other handmade percussion instruments, such as a triangle and a *chacha*, which is a handmade shaker. A guitar contributes both to the harmony and to the polyrhythmic feel of the music. In the Vieux-Fort area the accordion is replaced by a violin. In Martinique, although the accordion has become more frequent these days, there is still a marked preference for melodies played on the violin.

In addition to the above-mentioned instruments, in Martinique and Guadeloupe bands playing the *haute-taille* and the *quadrille au commandement* also have a *commandeur* who intones his or her own rhythmic sequences as a means of calling the figures and steps and interacting with the dancers and musicians as the quadrille unfolds. The addition of a *commandeur* in some bands from the French islands sets apart their quadrille ensemble. In all four islands, however, whether or not a *commandeur* is added to the band, rhythm remains an important aspect of quadrille music. All the instruments contribute to it, even those that usually play melodic lines in European bands. (See Figures 5.1 and 5.2.)

## Dance and the Aristocrat of the Late Eighteenth Century

In a letter dating from 1782, Jacques Girod-Chantrans, a Swiss who visited Martinique and St. Domingue, wrote, "It is very untrue that the colonies are populated with the refuse of the metropoles" (1785: 323). Indeed, in the second half of the eighteenth century commoners no longer formed the core of the planters group in Martinique. The planters' society had become increasingly refined and wealthy. Many planters could claim some degree of aristocracy (CAOM Fm3: 159–160), although true nobility was rare on the island (Saint-Méry 1803). To French aristocrats of that time, dance, along with martial arts and horseback riding, was a noble art that denoted a fine education. As Jean-Philippe Rameau writes, dance "contributed to the pomp and to the magnificence of the shows that delight[ed] the people and sometimes entertain[ed] some of the greatest of the princes" (in Guilcher 1969: 21).

Rameau, of course, was speaking of France when referring to court dance as a symbolic representation of order and controlled nature. The concept of

**Figure 5.1** "Voici Reynoir," a typical Guadeloupe quadrille, excerpt of first figure (*pantalon*). *Siyak* and *chacha* not shown. Denis Clovis dit Boniface, *commandeur*. (From *Reynoir Casimir dit Négoce et Signature: Kadri Gwadloup* [Musique du Monde 3016972]; note ostinato form, syncopated *commandements*. Transcribed by Peter Manuel.)

**Figure 5.2** "Vous me faites plaisir—An kontan zot," Guadeloupe quadrille, opening of third figure (*la poule*), in standard 6/8 meter. (From *Reynoir Casimir dit Négoce et Signature: Kadri Gwadloup* [Musique du Monde 3016972], track 3. Transcribed by Peter Manuel.)

nature in need of human intervention to be perfected was still dominant in eighteenth-century France and was a fundamental notion for the aristocrats. "This is pure convention," Jean-Georges Noverre, a famous eighteenth-century French dance master explained. "In order to dance with elegance, walk with grace, and have a noble appearance it is absolutely necessary to reverse the natural order of things and force the limbs to take an entirely different position" (Noverre 1760: 316–317). As a reflection of the harmony that should exist between the enlightened mind and the educated body, dance was meant to express what the French call "*bon goût*," or refined taste.

The role of the dance master was therefore crucial in the eighteenth century, because it was through his lessons that young nobles could acquire perfect body positions, in order to move effortlessly and with elegance. The master also taught them the manners, postures, and curtseys needed at court. These were extremely important skills that could only be learned through years of practice under the careful eye of the dance master. Dance was "conceived as a syntax of the socialized body" Emmanuel Bury explains (1998: 198), "and any *faux-pas*—literally false step—denoted a lack of taste and became a factor of social exclusion." Economics additionally played a part in the capacity of court dance to express hierarchy. Only the wealthiest could afford years of lessons and regular practice with a good dance master. And, to Noverre, of course, white peasants and non-European people in general did not dance. Rather, "the Levantines, the Africans . . . jump and move their bodies without any principle" (Noverre 1760: 23–24). Thus in the eighteenth century, the French posed the specific code and aesthetics of their own court dance as universal principles with which all other practices were evaluated.

## Contredanse as a Signifying Practice

In the 1760s, French aristocrats began taking inspiration for new dance steps and figures from the choreographed ballets they saw at the opera, adapting them to the French contredanse in vogue at that time. Thus they began reproducing slightly simplified versions of staged contredanses in their receptions (Guilcher 1969: 93–94). The French contredanse had appeared in formal receptions during the first half of the eighteenth century. The aristocrats welcomed it as an elegant dance with relatively easy steps compared to the minuet, which had been the ceremonial dance that revealed education and rank in aristocracy for about a century. The strict etiquette of the ceremonial minuet indicated who should dance with whom and in what order. During the second half of the eighteenth century, the aristocrats felt in need of a less severe ceremonial dance, and the French contredanse in *pot-pourris* inspired by the staged ballets they saw at the opera appeared to meet their needs. As Guilcher explains, "The contredanse was made for a public of spectators as much as for the pleasure of the dancers themselves" (1969: 17–18). Dancers were fond of the quadrille format, in which each couple had for a few minutes the undivided attention of the audience while they performed inside the square. Cavaliers could demonstrate agility, strength, and their mastery of a dance that required much practice, while their partners displayed their economic status through jewelry, coiffure, dress, and, of course, knowledge of the dance. By the 1780s the French contredanse had become a favorite number at the queen's balls.

It is not surprising therefore that the planters and rich merchants in colonial Martinique developed the habit of hiring dance masters straight from Paris so that their children, too, could learn the subtleties of the contredanse without leaving the plantation (Saint-Méry [1797] 1984: 69). Martinican planters of the late eighteenth century wanted to be aristocrats (Archives, CAOM Fm/F3: 159–160). They did not want to be associated with uncivilized people, such as the aboriginal Caribs, for example, of whom Saint-Méry wrote, "They hold one another by the arms, two by two and they cackle some monotonous and lugubrious sounds while they alternately bend down and stand up for hours, and then they believe they were dancing" (1803: 56). To the contrary, the planters often had opera singers and ballet dancers come to St. Pierre, Martinique, to perform excerpts of the same shows that delighted the Parisian audiences.

But if the colonists' primary motive was to facilitate their children's integration into the high society of Paris if and when they traveled to France, they also felt a need to confirm the distance that separated them from the blacks. In the context of the plantocracy, as an expression of "the greatest feelings of the soul" (Saint-Méry 1803: 1) and an indicator of economic power, court dance—including contredanse—also served to represent the distinctiveness of the colonists' culture.

## Social and Political Background

From the colonial French standpoint, keeping a distance between themselves and the blacks was critical. The number of black people was at least six times larger than the number of whites in their colonies. For example, in 1788 there were a little over 11,600 whites for approximately 65,000 blacks in Martinique. In Guadeloupe in 1789 the total population counted 106,593 people, of which 89,823 were slaves. The French colonists, and especially the merchants whose fortunes were based on the forced labor of African workers, lived in constant fear of a rebellion that could put an end to their monopoly. In the 1780s the French planters had the example of Saint-Domingue, from which many planters were fleeing because of the increasing violence. It seems that in Saint-Domingue, as in Martinique and Guadeloupe, many of the uprisings were led by mulattos.

Consequently, most administrators and rich merchants viewed mulattos as a threat and did all they could to restrict their sociopolitical rights (Petit-Jean-Roget 1980: 125). But when it came to the mulatto issue, planters were often opposed to the merchants.[5] According to Pierre and Adrien Dessalles, who were Creole planters of Martinique in the late eighteenth and nineteenth century, all the male planters had black or mulatto mistresses with whom they often had children (Dessalles, in Gautier 1985: 81–82). Given their education and socioeconomic status, these young mulattos generally felt closer to the whites than to the blacks with whom they, indeed, had little in common (Geggus 1996).

As mentioned above, during the second half of the eighteenth century the number of mulattos and free blacks in general was increasing at a very rapid pace. Meanwhile the number of whites did not increase. Faced with growing numbers of free people of color, many of whom were light-skinned, educated mulattos willing to participate fully in the sociopolitical life of the colony, the

French decided to pass laws aimed at restricting the mulattos' freedom. These laws were not always strictly enforced in colonial Martinique, in part for the reasons mentioned above. Yet because the French colonists were afraid that if any privilege were granted to the mulattos all the people of African descent would feel entitled to the same rights, and the whites would lose control of the island's economy, there was constant friction between the two groups.

## The Shifting Meanings of European Court Dances

As a means to further humiliate the free-born mulattos, the French colonists had placed them in the same social class as the newly freed blacks, though the two groups were rather different from each other. Officially, and from the Europeans' point of view, there were three classes in the colony. At the top of the social ladder were the planters, rich merchants, and high administrators. The second social class comprised artisans, clerks, soldiers, and clergy people of European origin. All the free people of color—free-born mulattos as well as newly freed blacks—were placed together at the bottom of the social ladder. They had to show deference to all whites at all times as a general rule. The following quote, a 1789 answer to Governor Saint-Méry's enquiries about the status of mulattos in the English colonies, encapsulates the French colonists' concerns and defensive attitude about mulattos' civil rights:

> The English law does not make any difference between the free people of color and the whites, and on that matter the leeward islands cannot depart from the laws of the metropole. But the local usages have become as strong as law. In the English islands the people of color are not elected as representatives nor do they vote to be represented, although it is their legal right to do so. They are not called to take part in the local assemblies but if they came no one could deny them, the usage, however, prevails everywhere. There has been a very limited number of exceptions in favor of certain free men of color whose merit was exceptional and to whom the colonists in one island had all agreed to grant all the privileges of the whites, but such cases are extremely rare. Jamaica is the only island where the term "mulatto" was defined by law. Everywhere else there is no such thing as a mulatto. (CAOM F/3/91: 238)

In colonial Martinique, the enslaved blacks were not counted as humans but as disposable goods. They were not, therefore, part of any recognized social class. However, all groups, including the enslaved blacks, knew the ceremonial and educational value of the French contredanse. As mentioned above, many free-born mulattos were educated and had learned the contredanse through lessons taken with dance masters. According to Saint-Méry, they danced it as well as if not better than many whites (1803: 40).

The newly freed, on the other hand, had no formal training. However, many had lived close enough to the whites to know the dance and understand the value the colonists placed on it. Some were concubines of the French planters, others were parents of free mulattos, while others were skilled artisans who had bought their own freedom. The former domestics and concubines, for example, had served in their masters' houses during the planters' lessons. Some of them knew the music quite well because they were musicians in the planters' receptions. Consequently, despite their superficial knowledge of the dance, the newly freed also danced the contredanse and quadrille with which they were growing increasingly familiar. The whites generally showed much disdain and contempt toward black people, and especially the newly freed, who had appropriated the European court dances. Again, I turn to Saint-Méry: "It would also be necessary that they [the newly freed] be persuaded that performing similar movements is not a true reproduction, that one needs to study these balancements, these *petits-pas* and these scenes that the graces have created and only the graces can reproduce" (1803: 39).

Yet by the late eighteenth century the enslaved domestics, too, had appropriated the contredanse and quadrille. They performed them inside the planter's house to celebrate a wedding or a baptism, which was not a rare event during the first decades of the nineteenth century. During this period, to which historians refer as "the era of decline," many planters allowed their slaves to marry and even contributed money and food to the reception that usually followed, if the newlywed were house slaves. This was also a good occasion to invite other planters for a sumptuous supper before the slaves' reception could begin (Dessalles [1836] 1987). These domestics "who viewed themselves as an intermediary class between the field slaves and the freed blacks" also adopted the European court dances. To Saint-Méry, their rendition of the French contredanse was quite burlesque: "One would have to see these balls to seize their oddity fully, and Calot or Teniers [two famous French painters of that era] would have certainly be elated if they had to reproduce these grotesque scenes" (1803: 41).

## Dance as an Expression of Socioracial Difference

Many colonists were annoyed to see their dance appropriated by the blacks, whom they felt were inferior creatures, especially because until then they had often used African music and dance to create particularly negative images of blackness. Earlier accounts by Du Tertre ([1671] 1973) and Labat (1724), for example, depict clearly different dances for each group of Africans enslaved on the island. Such differences still existed in the late eighteenth century, though considerably attenuated (Girod-Chantrans 1785: 192–193). However, despite the existence of distinctive elements for each African tradition in colonial Martinique, the white colonists consistently used the same words in their descriptions of black dance and music. Black dance was depicted in many travelogues as "savage" (Saint-Méry 1803), "unrefined, repetitive" (Saint-Méry [1797] 1984), and "lewd" (Labat 1724: 53). In their chronicles black people dancing were making "awkward, grotesque contortions" (Du Tertre [1671] 1973: 491). To the Europeans, African traditions were especially crude because they were performed in open air, under a tree or in a clearing of the fields, by barefoot or scantily clad dancers. In addition, in the eyes of the French colonists, control and moderation were unknown to the blacks, who usually made music and danced until they were forced to stop (Du Tertre [1671] 1973; Saint-Méry [1797] 1984: 65). The following account by Adolphe Granier de Cassagnac, who visited Martinique in the early 1840s, provides us with a good example of the dominant European discourse about black dance and music:

> When she had been dancing for one hour, the ground was shaking under the regular hammering of her heels; her body violently arched backward was two thirds bent over and her haggard eyes were turned towards the sky. . . . After four hours the rage had communicated to the other negroes. The one on the drum was jumping on his instrument like a gnome spurring a ghoul; two or three brown women armed with shakers were raising them in rapture; the whole gang was dancing and singing; and in the middle of that pandemonium which swarmed under a tamarind tree, in the light of two torches, the negro woman was sitting on her legs that could no longer support her, her chin rested on the ground, her elbows lifted up like a wounded bird; she was still dancing with her head. ([1842] 1844: 214)

Whether knowingly or not, Granier de Cassagnac does not mention anywhere in this account intended for white readers in Continental France that the dance described was likely to be part of a religious event. To the contrary, everything suggests that it is an ordinary dance by enslaved Africans on a sugarcane plantation. Indeed, the aesthetics of African music, the instrumentation field slaves commonly used in the colony, and their drumming technique further contributed to create stereotypical images of the people of African descent. According to such descriptions, the music produced by these instruments was a monotonous sound of drums and rattles: "While one negro beats the skin of the barrel, another one armed with two wooden sticks hits the sides. The noise he produces is dry and uniform and results in nothing else than placing a noise next to another" (Granier de Cassagnac [1842] 1844: 217). To many colonists indeed the drums and rattles made a "rather disagreeable noise" (Du Tertre [1671] 1973: 526). Some, however, did find the African music somewhat harmonious, but other comments about the music or the dance usually undermined the positive aspects of their statements.

## European Dance as Performative Dialogue

It is not surprising therefore that in the last quarter of the eighteenth century, newly freed blacks and mulattos who were constantly submitted to the influence of the French colonialism chose the contredanse as a preferred form of entertainment. It fit their lifestyle and expressed simultaneously their difference from the enslaved blacks.

To mulattos, the performance of French contredanse and quadrille additionally aimed at demonstrating their economic superiority and higher level of education to the poor, uneducated white people to whom they were forced to be subservient. Indeed, mulattos dancing the contredanse also did it as a demonstration of their equality with the French, something the Europeans had been trying to avoid. The care mulatto people put in learning the appropriate dance movements was also intended to emphasize how different they were from the dark-skinned, newly freed blacks whom they did not invite to their receptions (Saint-Méry 1803: 37).

Newly freed slaves also wanted to express a distance from other blacks, perhaps especially the domestic slaves. In January 1834 Pierre "Adrien" Dessalles wrote an entry in his diary about the wedding of two of his domestic slaves. Freed blacks came to the wedding celebration, he wrote, and that night, the domestics danced the quadrille. The music was so lively, he added, that the newly freed *even* danced with the domestics. That Dessalles felt it necessary to stress the participation of the newly freed is significant. In another description of a ball organized by domestic slaves in Fort de France about ten years later, Granier de Cassagnac felt humiliated because these domestics were dancing the quadrille. Such a "profanation," he explained, only happens in the towns because black people in the countryside "remain faithful to the bamboula, the drums, kakois and legends with contortions, shirts, and bare feet. But domestics from the towns who study the good manners and receive the 'Journal des modes,' dance the quadrille just as it is done at court" ([1842] 1844: 220).

"Just as it is done at court" means that they knew the appropriate steps and body attitudes. It also means that dancers put specific efforts into the way they dressed for these events. It was particularly important because of the sumptuary laws that forbade the free blacks to dress in a manner that could be similar to the whites. Hence, instead of changing their outfit five times in the course of one dance event, as some of the planters' wives used to, the mulattos held balls where all the guests had to dress in the same specified fashion (Saint-Méry [1797] 1984: 76–77). Newly freed slaves also wanted to express their distance from other blacks, but in this case it was from the house slaves, a group that many of them had recently left. For their part, domestics saw in the performance of quadrille new opportunities to demonstrate the distance that separated them from the field slaves. According to Granier de Cassagnac domestics used to wear a profusion of gold, lace, and satin for their own receptions ([1842] 1844: 220–221). For a variety of reasons, they took great pleasure in displaying the jewelry and finer clothes that white planters had often offered them (Saint-Méry [1797] 1984: 34).

Yet, the colonists focused solely on the free blacks' legitimate desire to escape their inferior position that was expressed through the performance of contredanse and quadrille. As Saint-Méry stated, "It is not surprising that in places where all the privileges belong to one hue, the other individuals take pride in approaching it and consequently, mingling with the white blood inspires some idea of superiority" (1803: 38).

For all the reasons that I explain above, it seems to me that this was much more than a mere desire to demonstrate closeness to the whites. It was an act of rebellion; but the questioning of the entire slavery system it entailed could not be acknowledged by the colonists. Through the practice of contredanse and quadrille, blacks were stating that they were humans, not the disposable goods colonists had wanted them to be. If for a long time in colonial Martinique dance styles and musical traditions had helped to maintain a distance between the whites and the blacks, at the turn of the nineteenth century the European court dances were helping to close the gap.

## Creole Quadrille as a Language of the Politicized Body

When large numbers of mulattos, newly freed blacks, and domestic slaves began to perform the French contredanse in colonial Martinique, it could no longer serve as the distinctive dance of the French colonists; however, the notions of power and superiority Europeans had tried to convey through the dance remained attached to it. Further, the vogue of the quadrille in the first half of the nineteenth century coincided with the periods of decline, and abolition of slavery in all French and English Caribbean possessions. Performance of the contredanse and quadrille took on a new significance for the people of African descent, especially to the newly freed blacks whose rights to assemble for a dance had previously been limited by law (Saint-Méry 1803: 38). The dance became synonymous with upward socioracial mobility and access to freedom (Granier de Cassagnac [1842] 1844).

Today in the postcolonial Caribbean, decolonization has brought considerable change in the sociopolitical context. Martinique and Guadeloupe were integrated into the French nation as overseas *départements* (DOM) in 1946, nearly three hundred years after their acquisition. Twenty years after their integration as *départements*, the economic structure of the territories was undergoing radical change. This change, in turn, caused the dismantling of most rural societies. The late 1960s and 1970s marked an era of violent opposition to French culture, reaching a peak in Guadeloupe after the French army quelled a strike by firing bullets at workers during a 1967 street protest.

In the 1970s and 1980s, militants and intellectuals who belonged to nationalist parties and unions came to view quadrilles (and the biguine as well) as instrumental in the subjugation of Guadeloupe by France. Even in August 2006, I met with a Guadeloupean music teacher who asserted:

> When one dances quadrille one is a bit less Guadeloupean than when one dances *gwoka*. Because these [quadrilles] are melodies that were composed with a [specific type of] harmonic structure, therefore these are melodies that are no longer Guadeloupean in the sense that one can analyze the melody and as one sees the intervals, one can see that it is tonal music. This was not, in the beginning, our way of thinking about music. Therefore one can say that the music itself, with its melody, its harmony and so on, came from elsewhere. Even if it is accompanied with the drum, it came from elsewhere. Therefore, when one takes pleasure in that music it means that one has become creolized, that one has somehow moved away from Guadeloupean music. . . . In order to be a true Guadeloupean one must not be Creole. (F. Castry, pers. comm.)

Such disparagement of quadrille, in contrast to *gwoka*, used to be widespread in Guadeloupe during the second half of the twentieth century. In this nationalist view, the responsorial structure of *gwoka* songs, the frequent use of pentatonic scales, the overlapping rhythmic sequences, and, of course, the *gwoka* drums represented pure African culture, free from European influences despite centuries of slavery and colonization. These African retentions were seen as emblematic of the foundation of "authentic" Guadeloupean culture, which was best expressed in the lifestyle and customs of low-wage agriculture workers (*Ja ka ta* 3 [February 1978]).[6] *Gwoka* music, which many peasants knew and practiced, became presented therefore as the only repertoire that was truly Guadeloupean. Conversely, the Creole biguine and quadrille became the target of unrelenting attacks. This situation compares in many ways to that of Martinique, where quadrille was often disparaged in contrast to the more Afro-Caribbean bèlè. Arguably this criticism can be seen as a reaction to *départementalisation*, which many Guadeloupeans and Martinicans feared would cause their culture to dissolve into that of the metropole.

In the heady atmosphere of the 1970s and 1980s, when Guadeloupean nationalists and independentists engaged in violent confrontations with the French government, they also exhorted people to stop practicing non-Guadeloupean styles and to perform *gwoka* music and dance exclusively (*Ja ka ta* 3 [February 1978]: 14). Quadrille, however, had developed within the same peasant communities that knew and practiced *gwoka*. Until the early 1970s, quadrille was the dance style that was most practiced in Guadeloupe and served a factor of social cohesion, while performing *gwoka* was still a factor of social exclusion, in the sense that its practitioners were seen as lower class and less civilized. Promotion of *gwoka* became an important part of the nationalists' efforts to reverse the negative view of Africa.

Such a use of dance as political statement was not new in Guadeloupe. As suggested earlier, French colonists had made dance an important tool for socio-racial distinction (Labat 1724). In the late eighteenth century, the notion of dance as an expression of the connection that exists between the enlightened mind and educated body was still dominant in Continental France. Hence, when French settlers in the Caribbean colonies sought to make European court dances a praised embodiment of civilization and refinement, the contre-danse and quadrille became even more appealing to the blacks and mulattos engaged in a struggle for freedom and equal rights.

Today, quadrille continues to be frequently performed in the four islands. Although performance of the dance no longer implies socioracial upward mobility, some of the notions that were once attached to it have left a trace on the ways in which Antilleans read dance movements. As Jocelyne Guilbault points out in her 1985 study, "A St. Lucian Quadrille Evening," St. Lucian quadrille dancers see the square configuration of the dancers as a symbol of order and attach notions of self-control to the restrained body movements. Dominican dancers also appreciate the moderation with which a good quadrille dancer performs the dance; for example, I heard a dancer praised because he "can dance an entire night" but does not "perspire too much."[7] In Guadeloupe and Martinique quadrille is still viewed by some as a dignified activity that is compatible with the morals of a Christian lifestyle.[8] These notions are reflected in the movement sequences and postures that Antilleans view as distinctive of quadrille in all four islands. They are expressed in the restrained movements of the hips and lower torso, which seemed to play no part in the European court dances; in the placement of the arms that quadrille *cavaliers* keep along their waistline or folded in the back when they are not leading their partner during a figure; and in the smile that brightens the dancing couples' faces as they gaze into each other's eyes. These features cannot be confused with postures or movement sequences of the African-derived bèlè also danced in the same areas and by the same people who do the quadrille.

Today, although the old French notion of dance hierarchy has become obsolete, some Antilleans from older generations still have ambivalent feelings about the African-derived bèlè. While traces of the old stigma that still linger in the background have led some political activists to take a stand against quadrille, most Antilleans do quadrille for entertainment, because it has always been done in their community and because it allows them to feel connected to their ancestors and to regional history. In Dominica, for example, as a national dance quadrille is given pride of place in the annual Heritage Festival that celebrates the island's culture during the month of October. It is also a means of representing the nation abroad.

In St. Lucia, in addition to the biweekly quadrille nights that are organized in the suburbs of the capital city of Castries, quadrille is often performed to grace the receptions of foreign officials and is always included in the celebrations of independence. In Martinique and Guadeloupe, quadrille groups take turns to organize and host balls that bring together dancers of all ages and economic background. In the French islands, quadrille acquires an additional special value when it is danced on stage during festivals celebrating Creole culture. In the context of these Creole festivals, quadrille becomes a language of the body that tells a story many Caribbean people share. It is also a means to claim their difference from Continental French people.

As mentioned above, up to the 1980s Antilleans danced quadrille in their community and were generally unaware that comparable versions of the dance also existed in the neighboring islands. That same decade, a new awareness of the Creole culture prompted Antillean quadrille dancers to participate in the celebration of their diverse ethnic/cultural background in such festivals as Creole Day, a day-long festival held simultaneously in places worldwide where people speak the French-based Creole language. It was during such events that quadrille dancers from the four islands rediscovered each other's dance and became aware that they were interpreting the characteristic body postures and movement patterns of quadrille in much the same way, that they told much the same stories about the dance. As a result, quadrille became to many performers an equivalent to the creole language they all speak. It now embodies their common Caribbean experience. Entire festivals are now dedicated to the West Indian quadrille, particularly in the French islands.

Today performers from the Creole continuum who seek to harmonize their differences have taken to dancing quadrille as a means to claim belonging to the same community. It is an ambiguous dance form that straddles countries, social groups, and ethnic groups. It allows Antilleans to speak the unspeakable. They perform quadrille together as a means to relive and retell their story. They gather together in festivals celebrating their Creoleness and eagerly engage in animated conversations in the Creole language, further obliterating political borders. Performing quadrille together, they dance into being the community to which they claim to belong and thus deconstruct colonial discourses of subordination and of dispersion. This community that their dance celebrates and simultaneously brings into being transcends the geographic and political boundaries of their respective island nations.

## Notes

1. All translations are by the author.
2. According to French contredanse specialist Jean-Michel Guilcher (1969), it was at the dawn of the eighteenth century that an old French dance called *cotillon* became fashionable. At that point the *cotillon* was a specific dance for two couples of dancers, performed during the refrain sections of a popular tune also called "*Le cotillon.*" French dance documents from 1706 show that at the same period longways-style country dances from England were performed by an unlimited number of couples, with the basic format being men and women facing each other in parallel lines. Dur-

ing the first decade of the eighteenth century, the *cotillon* grew so much in favor that dance masters began creating new choreographies that allowed its performance by eight dancers instead of four. The dance aesthetic remained nonetheless in the style of the old *cotillon*. In the following decade, the "cotillion" became its own dance genre when choreographers introduced it to the theater stages. From then on and during much of the eighteenth century, the term "cotillion" was used to differentiate the French contredanse for four couples in a square configuration from longways-style country dances of English derivation that were often performed by an unspecified number of dancers in two lines, men on one side and women on the other.

3. Alan Moise (pers. comm.). The names of the figures that compose the creole quadrilles are given here in the Creole language.
4. Although people commonly speak of Guadeloupe as if it were one island, this overseas department of France comprises five islands or groups of islets. They are Basse-Terre (or Guadeloupe per se), which is separated from Grande-Terre by a shallow and narrow ocean channel; Les Saintes; La Désirade and Petite-Terre; and Marie-Galante. St. Barthélémy and St. Martin, which until 2006 were part of the Guadeloupean archipelago, now form a distinct administrative region of France.
5. During the summer of 1789, soon after the bastille or king's prison in Paris was taken over by the Parisian people, France became a republic. Two months later, in October 1789, the news that France was governed by both King Louis XVI and the new Convention assembly finally reached Martinique and caused the highest degree of confusion. For a few days the French colonists could not decide whether to celebrate the event or to take arms against it. Many colonists approved the advent of the Republic, but the members of the Convention were not in favor of slavery, which they associated with the *ancien regime*. While the merchants in Saint-Pierre denied the mulattos access to the official celebrations, in Fort Royal (present-day Fort de France), where many French Creole administrators and planters had residences, mulattos were given the cocard, which is a blue, white, and red bow that symbolized the newly unified nation (CAOM Box 29: 102–194). The following year, the decrees by which the Convention intended to grant equal rights to the mulattos caused their lynching in Saint Pierre (Chauleau 1989: 155).
6. *Ja ka ta* is a journal, consisting largely of untitled and unattributed articles.
7. Gilles Jno-Baptiste and Hillary Julien (pers. comm.).
8. Eric Seguin-Cadiche and Deloumeaux (pers. comm.).

## References

Bury, Emmanuel. 1998. "La danse et la formation de l'aristocrate du XVIIe siècle." In *Sociopoétique de la danse*, 191–206. Paris: Anthropos.

Chauleau, Liliane, with Bernard Lehembre. 1989. *La révolution aux Caraïbes.* Prologue by Aime Césaire. Paris: Nathan.

Cyrille, Dominique. n.d. "Alarèpriz, une étude des quadrilles guadeloupéens avec un aperçu historique par Naïk Raviart." Manuscript.

Davy, John. 1854. *The West Indies before and since emancipation.* London: Cash.

De Rodellec du Porzic, Amédé. 1826. *L'enseigne de Vaisseau Amédée de Rodellec du Porzic: Ses croisières en Grèce, aux Antilles et la prise d'Alger (1826–1827).* Société des Archives de Bretagne.

Dessalles, Pierre-Adrien. [1836] 1987. *La vie d'un colon à la Martinique au XIXe siècle. Correspondance.* Montrouge, France: Désormeaux.

Du Tertre, R. P. [1671] 1973. *Histoire générale des isles habitées par les françois (1661–1671).* Fort de France: Editions des Horizons Caraïbes.

Gautier, Arlette. 1985. *Les sœurs de solitude: La condition féminine dans l'esclavage aux Antilles du XVIIe au XIXe siècle.* Paris: Editions Caribéennes.

Geggus, David. 1996. "The slaves and free colored in Martinique during the age of the French and Haitian revolutions: Three moments of resistance." In *The Lesser Antilles in the age of European expansion.* Ed. Robert L. Paquette and Stanley L. Engerman, 280–301. Gainesville: University Press of Florida.

Girod-Chantrans, Jacques. 1785. *Voyage d'un suisse dans les différentes colonies françaises d'Amérique pendant la guerre.* Neuchâtel, Switzerland: Imprimerie de la Société Typographique.

Granier de Cassagnac, Adolphe. [1842] 1844. *Voyage aux Antilles Françaises, Anglaises, Danoises Espagnoles à Saint-Domingue et aux Etats-Unis d'Amérique: Première partie Les Antilles Françaises.* Paris: Dauvin et Fontaine.

Guilbault, Jocelyne. 1985. "A Saint-Lucian kwadril evening." *Latin American Music Review* 6 (1): 31–57.

Guilcher, Jean-Michel. 1969. *La contredanse et les renouvellements de la danse française.* Paris: Mouton.

Guillard, Yves. 1988. "Le quadrille tel qu'il se dansait à ses origines et son évolution au cours du XIXe siecle." In *Cahiers de recherche.* Le Mans, France: Fricassée.

Honychurch, Lennox. 1984. *The Dominica story: A history of the island.* London: Macmillan Education.

Labat, R. P. 1724. *Nouveaux voyages aux isles françaises de l'Amérique.* Paris: Delespine.

Meignan, Victor. 1878. *Aux Antilles.* Paris: Plon.

Moreau de Saint-Méry, Médéric Louis Elie. 1791. *Considérations présentées aux vrais amis du repos et du bonheur de la France.* Paris: Imprimerie Nationale.

———. [1797] 1984. *Description topographique, civile, politique . . . de la partie française de l'isle de Saint Domingue.* Paris: Société d'Histoire d'Outre Mer.

———. 1803. *De la danse.* Parma: Bodoni.

Nicolas, Armand. 1996. *Histoire de la Martinique.* 3 vols. Paris: L'Harmattan.

Noverre, Jean-Georges. 1760. *Lettres sur la danse.* Facsimile of the 1760 Stuttgart ed. New York: Broude Bros.

Petit-Jean-Roget, Jacques. 1980. *Le mémorial martiniquais.* Nouméa, New Caledonia: Société des éditions du mémorial.

Raviart, Naïk. n.d. "Le quadrille, origine et survie." Manuscript.

Sturge, Joseph, and Thomas Harvey. [1837] 1968. *The West Indies in 1837: Being the journal of a visit to Antigua, Montserrat, Dominica, St. Lucia, Barbados and Jamaica, undertaken for the purpose of ascertaining the actual conditions of the negro population of those islands.* London: Routledge.

MICHAEL LARGEY

# 6 / Haiti

## *Tracing the Steps of the Méringue and Contredanse*

The contredanse was the foundation of many of the social dances that emerged in the Caribbean in the nineteenth and twentieth centuries. The degree of cross-fertilization between different types of social dance that are separated by political and linguistic boundaries, however, makes the task of tracing the origins of specific dance musics difficult and ultimately, perhaps, futile. By seeing musical genres, especially music associated with couple dances, as related through a shared historical process (if not actual lineage) and set of traits that may or may not be present in all dance versions, it may be preferable to ask different questions about the significance of social dance music and how such music may be understood in specific historical contexts. For scholars of the Haitian music, the contredanse and especially its derivative, the méringue, have become focal points for discussions of several different social and political conflicts within Haitian society.[1]

As a genre that is most often traced to the contredanse of the eighteenth century, méringue (Haitian Kreyòl: mereng) has a long history that gives it cultural weight in discussions of Haitian culture. At the same time, méringue's links to other Caribbean dance genres—Dominican merengue, Cuban danza and danzón, and Puerto Rican danza—undermine efforts on the part of Haitian méringue chroniclers to posit a uniquely Haitian identity for the popular couple dance. Despite efforts on the part of Haitian writers to enshrine the méringue as the "national dance of Haiti" (Fouchard [1973] 1988b; Saint-Cyr 1981–82), the méringue and contredanse have remained classificatory "problems" for analysts of Haitian culture, precisely because they share so many characteristics with other Caribbean dance music forms.

Today, Haitians use the term "méringue" to refer to a variety of folk music styles, including but not limited to music that features the syncopated *cinquillo* rhythm so common in the Caribbean (see the Introduction [Chapter 1]). As has often been pointed out, it may be a mistake to assume that dance forms that share similar names are indeed the same dance. The méringue is one such dance that appears in the Haitian literature in many guises and contexts.

Rather than spill more ink on the question of the origins or ownership of the méringue and contredanse, this chapter outlines the history and modern forms of the Haitian contredanse and explores themes related to the development of the méringue from the late nineteenth to the mid–twentieth century. By tracing the historiography of the méringue in Haitian music sources, I hope to shed light on how Haitian audiences have worked out complex social and political issues through dance music.

## From the Calenda to the *Carabinier*: The Early History of Contredanse-Derived Music in Haiti

The earliest published descriptions of social dance in colonial Haiti (or Saint-Domingue, as it was then called) appeared in Médéric Louis Elie Moreau de Saint-Méry's *Description topographique, physique, civile, politique et historique de la partie française de l'isle Saint-Domingue* (1797–98), a tome that described many aspects of life in the colony. In his account of Saint-Domingue just before the beginning of the Haitian Revolution, Saint-Méry included descriptions of two dances that he claimed were of African origin: the calenda (or kalenda) and the *chica*. According to him, the calenda was of African origin but was danced in a manner that resembled the contredanse popular among the plantation masters of Saint-Domingue. He describes the dance as follows:

> Each man selects a woman before whom he will perform his steps. This is a dance which seldom varies. . . . It consists of a step wherein each foot is alternately extended and withdrawn, striking the earth hard, first with the toe and then with the heel. It is somewhat as is done in the Anglaise. The man turns either around in the same spot or around his partner, who also turns and changes her place, while shaking the two ends of a kerchief which she holds. The woman keeps lowering and raising her arms while holding her elbows close to her body and her fists nearly closed. ([1797–98] 1985: 55–56)

Saint-Méry compares the calenda to the "Anglaise," one of several names used during that period to refer to the "English" or "country dance," especially in its longways format of men and women arrayed in two lines (Schwartz and Schlundt 1987: 313). The English country dance had earlier been brought to France through Brittany. The earliest mention of the word "contredanse" in French sources was in 1684, when a diarist named Dangeau wrote that he danced the contredanse "for the first time with an English dance instructor named Isaac" (Guilcher 1969: 16). The importation of the English country dance is generally attributed, however, to a dance instructor by the name of André Lorin, who wrote several manuscripts on the proper execution of the dance (Guilcher 1969: 16n3).

The emergence of the country dance in England and its spread throughout Europe are summarized in the Introduction to this volume (Chapter 1). Several popular versions of the English country dance existed, including the round form, square-eight form, and the longways style. By the 1820s, the rough English country dance had been transformed by French enthusiasts into the "contredanse français," or French contredanse, most typically performed in a square formation of four couples. The contredanse was firmly entrenched in the French court by the early eighteenth century. As Guilcher (1969: 21–22) notes, French rulers saw dance "as indispensable to an aristocratic education." While French aristocrats of different social standing sponsored salon dances in which they tried the latest dance steps, the French king was responsible for hosting "*grands bals*" in which his authority as French ruler was demonstrated for the assembled dignitaries.

The French contredanse demonstrated the fluidity of class boundaries with regard to dance styles. From its origins as a humble entertainment for common people to its transformation into a highly stylized dance ritual that was enjoyed by the highest ranking rulers in France, the contredanse showed that despite their very different social positions, people of all social classes enjoyed the contredanse and used it for their own purposes.

As French businessmen traveled to Saint-Domingue and adapted their favorite entertainments to their new environment, the contredanse enjoyed a similar fluidity between social classes. Perhaps the most dramatic instance of this flexibility was in the adaptation of the contredanse by enslaved Africans, many of whom provided musical entertainment for their French masters. As Haitian music historian Jean Fouchard writes in his 1973 book on the méringue, minuets and contredanses were frequently danced to the "latest popular tunes in fashion" ([1973] 1988b: 91). While freed black slaves and light-skinned persons of color or *milat* (mulattos) who were offspring of French men and African women were prohibited from attending the many of the popular entertainments of the day as participants, they were allowed to observe whites dancing at large public gatherings (Fouchard [1973] 1988b: 95). Despite the ban on slaves and freed persons of color participating in public dances, both groups had ample opportunity to observe the steps of the minuet and contredanse and use such dances in their own private celebrations. According to Fouchard, women of color in the cities of Saint-Marc, Jérémie, and Les Cayes organized their own dances.

After Haitian independence in 1804, the political environment in which social dancing took place underwent a dramatic transformation. With the elimination of the white planter class either by exile or execution, *gens de couleur* (persons of color), mostly drawn from the light-skinned *milat* offspring of former slaveholders, asserted their control over the economic sectors of the newly emergent Haitian society. Black elites, also known as *lelit nwa*, asserted their own power, especially in the domain of the military, which had been one avenue of social advancement for dark-skinned people, particularly during the protracted struggle for independence. *Milat* and *nwa* audiences alike, however, retained their enthusiasm for social dance and organized their own dances during the early days of the new Haitian republic.

With the end of Saint-Domingue, the French colonial legacy of opera and musical theater disappeared from the Haitian musical stage. White and *milat* musicians fled in large numbers to the United States during the early to late 1790s. Such musicians were influential in the development of local musical life in Charleston, South Carolina, and New Orleans, Louisiana. Refugees from Saint-Domingue found responsive audiences for their musical talents, and many of the early theaters and music halls in New Orleans and Charleston had performers from Saint-Domingue in their casts (Cale 1971; Fouchard [1955] 1988a; Hunt 1988).

The Haitian entertainment market was forced to adapt to the mass exodus of musical talent from Saint-Domingue and the disruptive effects of the Revolution. One of the immediate effects of the political changes was the indigenization of former colonial institutions. The prosperous seaport of Cap Français was renamed Cap Haïtien, and the city's theater, formerly the Comédie du Cap, was reopened under the name Théatre Haïtien (Hunt 1988: 67).

The transformation of the former French colony into the modern Haitian state was a selective process, combining revolutionary ideas with the maintenance of the social and cultural trappings of French life. Members of the *milat* elite continued to pursue the entertainments they developed a taste for during the colonial period. Dances or *bals* were one source of entertainment for elites who were isolated on their plantations. The dances also served as vehicles for the new social order in Haiti. The first *milat* presidents, Alexandre Pétion and Jean-Pierre Boyer, racially segregated their official dances, allowing only those *nwa* elites of sufficient rank and power to attend.

With the disappearance of the French-run theaters and their imported musical productions from the French metropole, Haitian military bands, called "fanfares," became the principal groups that disseminated dance music to elite audiences. Fanfares generally consisted of brass instruments (including trumpets, trombones, baritone horns, and French horns), woodwinds (including flutes, clarinets, and, in the late nineteenth century, saxophones), and a drum battery (including snare, field, and bass drums). The repertoire of the fanfares ranged from the music necessary for drills, parades, and other official military functions to arrangements of popular songs from a variety of musical genres, including marches, quadrilles, waltzes, and polkas. Unlike the music of the French-sponsored theaters, the music of the fanfares was intended for a large and socially diverse audience. Fanfares regularly sponsored free outdoor concerts for the public.

While the French theater tradition crumbled during the last days of the colony, the demand for fanfares grew apace. Military leaders had their own fanfares to provide music for their official occasions as well as for their personal entertainment and prestige. Haitian jóurnalist and amateur music historian Constintin Dumervé reported that in 1798 Toussaint Louverture's military band of forty instrumentalists gave a concert in honor of the recapture of Môle St. Nicolas (Dumervé 1968: 32). The first Haitian president, Jean-Jacques Dessalines, established his own fanfares that provided musical entertainment for 1 January 1804—Haitian Independence Day—and for Dessalines's coronation ceremony making him Haiti's first emperor. César Télémaque wrote "L'ode à l'empereur" ("Ode to the Emperor") for the event, which was sung to a tune from Jean-Jacques Rousseau's *Le devin du village*, one of the most popular comic operas on the stages of colonial Saint-Domingue (Dumervé 1968: 33).

With the departure of French-born and -educated music teachers after the Revolution, Haitian fanfare musicians conducted most of the musical instruction in the country. Fanfare performers were among the few professional musicians who received the benefit of musical instruction. The large military fanfares were located in the cities of Port-au-Prince and Cap Haïtien. Smaller bands, usually consisting of keyed bugles, drums, and fifes, provided marches and drills for local troops as well as entertainment for local civilian audiences. These small bands were sometimes called "batteries" or "*batteries sonores*" in reference to the large numbers of drums they employed. Many of Haiti's thirty-eight military regiments had their own batteries.

Fanfares also participated in nonmilitary musical ceremonies, specifically in what were known as "serenades." Intended to honor or praise local officials, serenades were sponsored by the government and were vehicles for political promotion. Praise song lyrics often cast the political figure to be praised as a "bon Papa" (good father) to the Haitian people, a strong and competent leader worthy of the crowd's respect and devotion. Fanfares also occasionally joined forces with the *batteries sonores* for large political celebrations. One type of event called *coup d'jaill* (Kreyòl: *koudjay* or a "gushing, surging event") was intended to stimulate an atmosphere of enthusiasm and support for the government by "heating up" local crowds.[2]

Fanfare repertoire grew during the nineteenth century to include newer genres of music, including what many historians believe to be the precursor to the Haitian méringue: the *carabinier*. The *carabinier* (or *carabiné*) was a couple dance that gained popularity as early as 1805 when, according to J. M. Coopersmith (1949: 53), Haitian soldiers introduced the dance to soldiers from the Dominican Republic. According to one of Coopersmith's elderly consultants:

> Only this much is known: (1) that the carabiné was a group-dance directed by a *bastonero* or leader who did not participate in the dance, but who merely called the figure-changes; (2) that a promenade preceded the dance; (3) that the first figure consisted of a concentric

> circular-formation of men and women facing each other; (4) that the participants, moving in a counter-clockwise direction, danced such figures as dos-a-dos and "swing your partner" as it appears in the Virginia Reel, which were alternated with a native shuffling step, known as *escobillando*. (Coopersmith 1949: 54)

The *carabinier* was danced during Dessalines's presidency and came to be the pre-eminent social dance among elite Haitians until the emergence of the méringue in the mid–nineteenth century. The *carabinier*'s popularity during Dessalines's reign was due, according to Fouchard, to the skill of a woman named Couloute from the southern town of Jérémie. Fouchard identifies Couloute as one of Dessalines's mistresses who excelled in social dance. Her grace and dexterity on the dance floor were immortalized in a folk tune sung to the Haitian Kreyòl lyrics "L'empereur vini voir Couloute danser" ("The Emperor Came to See Couloute Dance"; Fouchard [1973] 1988b: 48).

The origins of the *carabinier* are not well documented, but some scholars point to the militaristic name of the dance and the predominance of militarism in the early Haitian republic as evidence that the dance was closely tied to the military music making in the Haitian republic. The noun "carabineer" means rifleman or sharpshooter, and the verb form of the word means "to skirmish." Coopersmith notes the martial association with "*carabinier*," stating that the dance's name derived from the carbine rifles, "which the Haitians swung on their shoulders as they danced" (1949: 53–54). The predominance of military fanfares during the early days of the Haitian republic may account for the martial associations with the dance. Certainly, the dance's name of "rifleman" did not dissuade elite audiences from embracing it with enthusiasm.

According to Fouchard ([1973] 1988b), the *carabinier* remained popular with elite Haitian audiences from the beginning of Dessalines's rule to the end of the Fabre Nicolas Geffrard regime in 1847, when it was allegedly supplanted by the méringue. Rural Haitians continued to dance the *carabinier* through much of the twentieth century; it was documented by Harold Courlander as late as 1941 as part of the rural dance repertoire (1941: 373n5). For elite Haitians, the méringue became an important social dance featuring couple dancing as early as the mid–nineteenth century until sometime in the mid–twentieth century. Among rural Haitians, méringues are still danced as part of the *fèt champèt* or country dances that feature the contredanse.

## Contredanse in Haitian Culture

The contredanse (Kreyol: *kontradans*) itself was common in both urban and rural society until the mid–twentieth century. Michel Lamartinère Honorat described its movements in some detail in his *Les danses folkloriques haïtiennes* of 1955, outlining a dance based on the French format of a square of four couples rather than the longways two-line format. The four male-female pairs of dancers began and ended each major section of the dance in their "home" position on one of the sides of an imaginary square on the floor. The movements of the dance emphasized smoothness and refinement; the couples' first action was to greet each other, "avec élégance" ("with elegance"; Honorat 1955: 115). Couples that faced each other on the northern and southern sides of the square engaged in steps that mirrored one another; once their movements were complete, the couples on the east and west sides of the square did the same movements.

Rural versions of the contredanse still exist in Haiti today, mostly as part of *fèt chanpèt* or "country festivals." Contredanses are also performed as part of larger community celebrations, including Vodou ceremonies. In 1988 I attended one such ceremony in which a contredanse was held outside the temple where religious dancing took place (see also Largey 2006: 231–233). The contredanse featured men and women, young and old, dancing in couples with upright posture, although several women and some men were displaying the fluttering shoulder movements more commonly associated with the *zepòl* (shoulder) dances of the Vodou ceremony. The music was provided by an ensemble consisting of bamboo flute, handmade field drum, and a hand drum called the *tambouren* (whose origins and construction are discussed in Averill and Yih 2000). The melodic and rhythmic organization of the music is considerably less complex than most Vodou ceremonial music. In Figure 6.1, the flute plays a repeated four-bar melody with the drums.

**Figure 6.1** Excerpt of rural contredanse.

A caller, called either a *konmandè* (commander) or *mèt dans* (dance master), shouted out the steps to the assembled dancers; he also occasionally berated dancers for incorrect steps or for dancing too close together. When one couple engaged in a close embrace more typical of *konpa*, the popular Haitian dance-hall style, the caller shouted "*Nou p ap danse konpa isit!*" ("We don't dance *konpa* here!") and insisted that the dancers maintain an appropriate distance for the remainder of the dance.

Contemporary rural contredanse music is most often performed by *kò mizik mennwat*. According to Gage Averill and Yuen-Ming David Yih, such ensembles derived their name from the military *corps de musique* and from the courtly French minuet. *Kò mizik mennwat* have repertoires that reflect the complex cultural history of Haiti. They provide music for the *bal lwa* (spirit dance) intended to honor the *lwa* or spirits of Vodou. *Kò mizik mennwat* also perform dance repertoire that is taken directly from the European social dances that were introduced to Saint-Domingue in the eighteenth century including *mennwat* (minuet), contredanse, quadrille, polka, valse, *à la visite,* and *les lanciers* (Lancers; Averill and Yih 2000: 282–283).

*Kadri,* a rural version of the contredanse-derived quadrille, also survives in contemporary Haiti as part of Vodou religious ceremonies. According to Louis Maximilien, who was writing in the 1940s, the Vodou initiation ceremony (*ousi kanzo*) called "*boule zin*" featured European social dances as part of the ritual. Maximilien writes, "Once the spirits leave, the drums perform the rhythm of the contredanse. The initiates arrange themselves in two lines, facing each other, and they perform the figures of the quadrille. In Vodou, it is the *crabignin* (carabiner) that closes the ceremony" ([1945] 1982: 113).

Contredanse can also be included in the repertoire of the rural cooperative labor team known as *konbit.* When independent farmers need help harvesting their crops or building a large structure, they enlist the help of their neighbors by sponsoring a *konbit*; neighboring farmers form a work brigade that includes musicians whose job is to keep the workers entertained and energized for their labors. After the work in the fields is complete, the workers gather at the home of the sponsor of the *konbit* for a *banbòch* or party. It is at this party that contredanses and méringues are often performed.[3]

Elite Haitians also enjoyed the contredanse as part of their social entertainments during the twentieth century. In his doctoral dissertation on the regional drumming styles in Haiti, Yih (1995: 442) notes that contredanses were danced at invitation-only dances until sometime after the U.S. occupation, when they were replaced by American dances, such as the two-step and fox-trot. Averill notes that public dance events also afforded people the opportunity to enjoy social dances that were derived from the eighteenth-century dance repertoire. He writes:

> At the dawn of the American occupation [of Haiti], the better-off residents of Port-au-Prince partied at private balls as well as at public dances called *bastreng* or *douz edmi* (twelve and a half, the entrance fee for me, in centimes). The instrumental accompaniment for these events typically included either a piano or a small, French-inspired string orchestra called *òkès bastreng* which comprised cello, bass, violin, clarinet and/or trombone. The repertoire included popular European couples and figure dances: mazurkas, polkas, waltzes, *lanciers* (lancers), *contredanses,* quadrilles, as well as *mereng.* (1997: 35)

Since the 1940s–50s, European-derived social dances, such as the contredanse, have also entered the repertoires of folkloric troupes and amateur organizations dedicated to the preservation of Haitian dance. In her dissertation on Haitian folkloric music in New York City, ethnomusicologist Lois Wilcken points out that while most Haitian folklore troupes concentrate on the dances most closely aligned with Haiti's African past, some of them also include dances from the eighteenth-century European repertoire. In the 1950s, for example, La Troupe Folklorique Nationale of Haiti included minuets and Lancers in its official repertoire list, according to Lavinia Williams Yarborough, an African American dancer trained by Katherine Dunham and former director of the troupe (Yarborough 1959; quoted in Wilcken 1991: 168). Wilcken describes the *younifòm* or costumes that were adapted from European-style dress and used by folkloric dancers during their performances: "Female dancers in folklore wear European style dress often embellished with lace. As tourism picked up in Haiti during the [1950s], further stylization was achieved by the use of satin or satin-like fabrics because they intensify color. In choreographies associated with the countryside, male dancers mimic peasant men by wearing the *varèz* (a denim blue tunic), blue jeans, a straw hat, and a satchel; female dancers wear dresses in the same blue. Women nearly always wear head scarves, as they customarily do in Haiti" (1991: 171). Frisner Augustin, a master drummer raised and trained in Haiti and artistic director of the New York–based Haitian folklore group La Troupe Makandal, relates that in groups like Makandal the contredanse is most typically performed as part of a suite, preceded by *rabòdaj* and *djouba* dances, which have their own rhythms, and segueing again to the more lively *djouba* for a finale. Wilcken points out that European-derived folkloric dance repertoire is much more popular in most other Caribbean and South American nations. She notes, "The near equation of folklore and the neo-African religion is strikingly evident in the repertoires of Haitian folkloric companies" (1991: 170). Although the European-derived dances of Haitian folklore troupes constitute a small part of their repertoires, they are recognized as an important part of Haitian dance history.

A rural contredanse might commonly be performed by an accordion or flute, and percussion instruments—often the standard Vodou ensemble of *manman*, *segon*, and *boula* drums. While these reiterate a basic ostinato, the melodic instrument typically repeats a four- or eight-bar pattern outlining a dominant-tonic ostinato, and the *konmandè* intones his calls to the dancers. The general structure closely resembles that of the Guadeloupe quadrille schematized as Figure 5.1. However, there are also a few familiar vocal songs in the contredanse repertoire. One of the most common of these, shown as Figure 6.2, was shown to Peter Manuel by Augustin.[4]

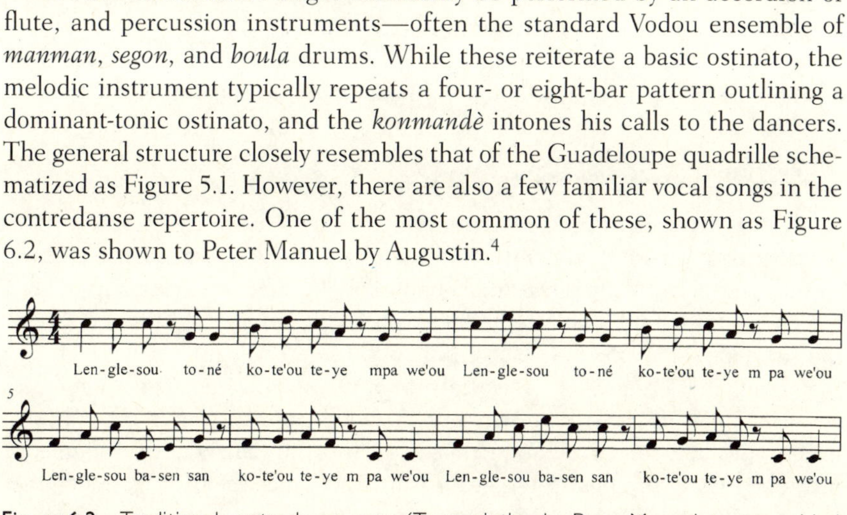


**Figure 6.2** Traditional contredanse song. (Transcription by Peter Manuel; text provided by Lois Wilcken.)

In Haiti contredanses are also performed by amateur groups that view their performances as part entertainment and part cultural preservation. Such groups often employ the costumes described above by Wilcken and perform their dances for select audiences, mostly in Port-au-Prince and its wealthy suburb, Pétionville.

Unfortunately, the contredanse tradition has tended to be neglected by researchers of Haitian music and dance, most of whom have concentrated on traditions more closely derived from African antecedents. For example, Harold Courlander, a novelist and amateur musicologist who wrote *Haiti Singing*, the first book published in English on Haitian music, admitted that he was especially interested in African survivals in Haitian music and therefore tended to ignore music from the Catholic Church and other "European" influences (Courlander 1939: 234). Courlander was following the lead of Melville Herskovits, his mentor and the author of the first English-language ethnography of Haitian rural life, titled *Life in a Haitian Valley* (1937). In his effort to valorize the study of Haiti's African-descended rural majority, Herskovits downplayed the contributions of European culture on Haiti and thus ignored many of the so-called creolized forms of Haitian culture, including contredanse.

Despite the lack of attention from academics in the mid–twentieth century, contredanse continued to interest Haitian audiences through its presence in the popular music industry. Several commercial recordings of contredanses were made by urban dance bands in the 1950s–60s, such as those by Nemours Jean-Baptiste, the legendary Haitian dance band leader who popularized the *konpa-dirèk* ("direct rhythm") style in the 1950s. Jean-Baptiste's pieces, such as "Contredanse #5" and "Contredanse #6,"[5] resemble rural counterparts in consisting of simple or varied repeated melodic patterns over tonic-dominant harmonies, albeit arranged for horn sections, with the vocalist intoning calls like a *konmandè*. They thus differ from the Haitian salon méringues or the nineteenth-century danzas and contradanzas of the Spanish Caribbean, with their repeated sixteen-bar sections and prominent *cinquillos* and amphibrachs.

## Méringue and Social Class

By the early twentieth century, the méringue—a creole song danced by independent couples—had become more popular than the contredanse in high society as well as among the general population. In the Haitian versions of both the contredanse and *lanciers*, the méringue could serve as the final dance of the set (Honorat 1955: 113). According to dance ethnologist Michel Honorat, the méringue was danced by all social groups: "There is a dance that dominates all of national life. It is the méringue. . . . In the countryside, in the suburbs, in the cities, it asserts itself and struggles against the exotic dances. Bourgeois, petits-bourgeois, urban proletariats, peasants, all dance the méringue such that it is recognized in all celebrations, in all the manifestations of joy and pleasure, in all amusements" (1955: 40). While all Haitians may have danced a version of the méringue, the difference between upper- and lower-class versions of the dance may have been significant. In addition to his description of upper-class Haitians dancing méringues at the conclusion of contredanses, Honorat also mentions a lower-class phenomenon in which méringues were sung during Carnival as part of a large procession. Eating and drinking their way along their route, these bands were made up of "veritable nomads who danced an irrepressible méringue adapted to the Carnival spirit" (Honorat 1955: 122). According to Honorat, these groups were the precursors of the contemporary *bann kanaval* (Carnival bands) that, in 1955, played pieces that were referred to as méringues. Although Carnival bands no longer play méringues in Haiti, the name "méringue" is still used to describe music played by itinerant musicians, many of whom can be heard at restaurants, hotels, and other tourist destinations. Elite Haitians also patronize the méringue today, but mostly in the form of folkloric dances that celebrate an imagined past in which the méringue was a ubiquitous symbol of Haitian identity.

Méringues have also often been used in ways reminiscent of the fanfare repertoire in the early nineteenth century. Some served as tools of political promotion by electoral candidates. Few of these overtly political méringues have survived, since many of them were taught by rote to lower-class Haitian citizens at political rallies. Local citizens were paid a small amount of money to sing political méringues, or, as Dumervé (1968: 293) claims, participants sang political songs for some *"gâteaux et grogs"* (cakes and beers) and engaged in energetic dancing in order to create an impression for onlookers that their political candidate was supported by local Haitians. This practice has remained popular among Haitian political candidates to the present and is often associated with the music of Carnival as well as Rara, a Lenten celebration with strong ties to the Vodou religious tradition and politics (cf. Largey 2000; McAlister 2002).

Such méringues are called *méringues coup d'jaill* (*mereng koudyay*) or *méringues de carnaval* (*méringue kanaval* or Carnival méringue). Averill describes *méringue koudyay* as "essentially indistinguishable from *méringue kanaval*" and having "evolved out of fast, celebratory songs of the early Haitian military sung on the occasion of a military victory, which were later adopted at carnival-like festivities" (Averill 1997: 220n41). Elsewhere, I have discussed one such méringue titled "Antoine Simon dit ça" ("Antoine Simon Said That") in detail (Largey 2006: 104–106). The song was subtitled a "sung méringue" and was written to commemorate Haitian President Antoine Simon's victory over his political predecessor, Nord Alexis, who Simon ousted in a political coup. Written in 1909, published in 1910, and sung in Haitian Kreyòl, the song praises Simon for his military prowess and criticizes Alexis for his lack of leadership qualities.

"Antoine Simon dit ça" was one of several *méringues coup d'jaill* published by Fernand Frangeul, an entrepreneur in Port-au-Prince who ran his own music publishing company. Frangeul's efforts to bring the fast-paced popular music of the street to the salons and parlors of elite Haitians shows that méringues enjoyed by working-class Haitians appealed to wealthy people, even if the performance of such méringues in Sunday recitals was only a vicarious way for elite Haitians to imagine what it was like to be a Haitian worker.

While lower-class Haitians enjoyed fast-paced *méringues coup d'jaill*, elite Haitians enjoyed their own form of the popular dance music genre. Several Haitian composers wrote *méringues lentes* or slow méringues, which were favorites of elite Haitians. Slow méringues were rarely used as dance music; instead, they were pieces for salon concerts, usually held on Sundays in people's homes.

One of the most popular slow méringues of the late nineteenth century was "Choucoune." Composed by Michel Mauléart Monton (1855–98) and based on a poem by Oswald Durand (1840–1906), "Choucoune" sings the praises of a young "*marabout*" woman with long, silky hair and white teeth. The song was originally called "Frè P'titt Pierr" ("Little Brother Pierre"); the poem tells of a poor young slave who is in love with Choucoune. As I have argued elsewhere, Durand's poem became an anthem for bourgeois Haitians interested in connecting themselves with their local culture (Largey 2006: 83). During readings of the poem, Durand himself dressed as a peasant, complete with clay pipe and straw bag, and recited the poem from the point of view of Little Brother Pierre (see Figure 6.3):

*Dèyè yon gwo touf pengwen*
*Lòt jou mwen kontre Choucoune*
*Li souri lè li wè mwen*
*Mwen di: "Syèl, ala bèl moun!"*
*Mwen di: "Syèl, ala bèl moun!"*
*Li di: "Ou trouve sa chè?"*

*Ti zwezo t ape koute nou nan lè*
*Ti zwezo t ape koute nou nan lè*
*Kon mwen sonje sa*
*Mwen genyen lapenn*
*Ka depi jou sa*
*De pye mwen nan chenn*

Behind a big yucca plant
The other day I met Choucoune
She smiled when she saw me
I said: "My stars, what a beautiful person!"
I said: "My stars, what a beautiful person!"
She said: "You think so, dear?"

Little bird that we can hear in the woods
Little bird that we can hear in the woods
When I remember this
I feel great pain

(continued on next page)

**Figure 6.3** "Choucoune," méringue by Michel Mauléart Monton, 1884.

Because since that day
My two feet are in chains[6]

Non-Haitian listeners would likely recognize the chorus of "Choucoune" as similar to that of "Yellow Bird," a melody most often attributed to a Jamaican origin. As Averill notes (pers. comm.), the tune to "Choucoune" also bears

**Figure 6.3** *Continued*

a striking resemblance to earlier melodies from Trinidad; Caribbean song composers often borrowed tunes from other sources and recast them for home audiences (Averill 1999). Averill is quick to note, however, that such musical borrowing was very common in the late nineteenth century and that it should not "diminish the compositional achievements" of the song-writing duo. In fact, the provenance of "Choucoune" has become a rallying point for Haitians who assert the méringue as a Haitian national music. Like other Caribbean musics that have been appropriated by foreign musicians—as in the case of Lord Invader's (a.k.a. Rupert Grant's) "Rum and Coca-Cola," which was published in the United States by Morey Amsterdam (Hill 1998: 86–87)—the melody of "Choucoune" was popularized by Jamaican American singer Harry Belafonte under the title "Yellow Bird" and became associated with its English-language adaptation in the United States. Many Haitians are vexed by the fact that Durand's poem and Monton's tune are sometimes thought to be arrangements based on "Yellow Bird" when, in fact, "Choucoune" predates "Yellow Bird" by several decades (Auguste 2005). "Choucoune" also features the five-note rhythmic pattern called *quintolet* (Spanish *cinquillo*) that, as discussed below, pervades Haitian folk, salon, and popular music as well as the Puerto Rican danza and Cuban danzón.

As "Choucoune" demonstrates, many Haitian elite artists struggled with how best to express their aspirations to be internationally respected artists while maintaining connections to local Haitian culture. One musician who exemplifies this position was Ludovic Lamothe (1882–1953), a composer of both slow méringues akin to Puerto Rican danzas and *méringues de carnival.* Born into a musical family, Lamothe studied piano in Paris on a scholarship and returned to Haiti to teach and perform in salon concerts. His best-known méringue was "La dangereuse," a work for solo piano, shown as Figure 6.4 and played on this volume's compact disc.[7] "La dangereuse" is typical of most slow meringues with its lyrical melody and its lack of dynamic markings.

Lamothe's efforts to write méringues that would appeal to different social classes in Haiti underscore the importance of méringue as a source of inter-class connection. Lamothe's most famous *méringue de carnaval*, "Nibo," was written for the 1934 Carnival celebration and won the best-song competition that year. Lamothe's endeavors appealed to working-class Haitians while giving elite Haitians a vicarious sense of connection with Haitians of lower social standing. As Averill (1994) has pointed out, Carnival is a celebration in which Haitian elite classes provide an opportunity for the lower classes to take to the streets and to express themselves without fear of elite reprisals. It is also a time when elite control of Haitian affairs is reinforced, since lower-class demonstrations of political power take place in a carefully scripted public display event that is controlled by elite Haitians.

Other composers tried in their own ways to bridge the class divide through their méringue compositions. Justin Elie (1883–1931), perhaps the Haitian composer best known outside the island, wrote *Méringues populaires*, a set of six méringues that was published in New York City by R. de la Rozière in 1920. The sixth méringue in the set was set to the tune of "*Totu pa gen dan*" ("Totu Has No Teeth"), a popular song composed by Auguste de Pradines, who went by the name Candio. By 1920, Pradines was an outspoken critic of the U.S. occupation of Haiti, and his topical songs were in high demand by people of all social strata in Haiti (Averill 1997: 47–50). According to Claude Dauphin, the first line of the melody is sung to the lyrics "*Totu pa gen dan, moun pa konen*

Figure 6.4 "La dangereuse," mm. 1–30, méringue, by Ludovic Lamothe.

*ke jan l fe mode*" ("Totu has no teeth, no one knows how he bites"), an elliptical reference to Candio's position as a person outside politics who, despite a disability due to a childhood bout with polio, is nevertheless able to make his songs "bite" those in power (Dauphin 1980: 56).

Elie's interpretation of Candio's song, however, relied on an unorthodox musical notation. All of the *Méringues populaires* were notated with alternating measures of 2/4 and 5/8 meter, giving the appearance that the songs added an extra half-beat every two measures. In practice, most Haitian performers play the 5/8 measure as a 2/4 measure, changing the five even eighth notes to a syncopated five-note rhythm that can be counted "ONE-and-TWO-AND-three-

AND-FOUR-and" (or 2-1-2-1-2). As noted in Chapters 1 and 2, this pattern—an icon of Haitian, Cuban, and Puerto Rican contradanza variants—is called *cinquillo* in Spanish and *quintolet* in Haitian musical parlance. Elie was not the first Haitian musician to try to establish a unique rhythmic notation for the méringue. His efforts to render the special qualities of the dance in notation followed at least forty years of debate, including in newspaper editorials, about how best to write the méringue rhythm.

## Notating the Haitian Méringue

As I have noted elsewhere (2006: 211–218), social and political issues are often the real focus of debates about musical orthography or the notation of sounds in written form. In the case of the Haitian méringue, musicians' attitudes toward the "proper" notation of the dance have often coincided with larger cultural debates about how best to present local culture to a wider cosmopolitan audience. The choice that Elie made to present his méringues in alternating 2/4 and 5/8 meter underscores a long-standing tension in Haitian society about how best to trace the roots of the Haitian méringue. For many Haitian composers in the twentieth century, the choice of duple or quintuple meter reflected the degree to which Haitian music should be interpretable to foreign audiences. Advocates of duple meter notation saw foreign, especially American, audiences as potential consumers of Haitian sheet music, but only if they could read the rhythms easily. Those who pushed for the use of 5/8 meter in compositions tended to view Haitian music as connected to African musical antecedents. Composers like Werner Jaegerhuber, who conducted fieldwork among Haitian peasants and saw rural Haitian music as linked directly to African culture, advocated the use of 5/8 meter for the transcription of Haitian folksong whenever possible. He believed, "It is quite evident that if we exclude irregular and varied rhythms and imprison them in a rigid 2/4 measure, it will result in a false and invariably deceptive syncopation in their modern usage that has no affinity with the ancient music of African folklore" (Jaegerhuber 1943: 53).

At the same time, most of the composers who experimented with different meters for dance music were not writing for the ballroom but rather for the concert hall (Dauphin 1980: 58). Experiments with musical meter demonstrated elite composers' desire to fashion a unique Haitian rhythm while maintaining their connections to upper- and lower-class culture.

The earliest notation of the rhythm of the méringue in print is in the *Petite grammaire musicale* (1882), a music primer coauthored by Occilius and Occide Jeanty, a father-and-son team of Haitian composers. Occilius Jeanty was a director of the Central School of Music in Port-au-Prince as well as a mathematics instructor at the Lycée Pétion. His son, Occide, was a gifted cornetist and composer who eventually became the director of the Musique du Palais, the military band of the Haitian president (Largey 2006: 77–81). In their textbook, the Jeantys provided two different notations for the proper execution

**Figure 6.5** *Quintolet* notation, from *Petite grammaire musicale*, by Occilius and Occide Jeanty.

of the méringue. The first notation consisted of five even pulses over a duple meter, as shown in Figure 6.5 and also as used in "Choucoune" (Figure 6.3).

The Jeantys called this five-note figure a "*quintolet*," a term often used as the French version of the *cinquillo* or five-note syncopated rhythm associated with the danza. The Jeantys went on to note that the *quintolet* could also be written in a more standard form, such as that used in notations of the Cuban danzón or, for that matter, in the left-hand patterns of "La dangereuse," as presented above as Figure 6.4. According to the Jeantys, the use of either notation was dependent on the individual composer, who was assumed to "follow their taste" (Jeanty and Jeanty 1882: 15). The Jeantys did not make any generalizations about the origins of the méringue. Their notation for the dance was adopted by many méringue composers, including the most prolific of méringue popularizers, Frangeul (Dumervé 1968: 183–190; Largey 2006: 103–104).

The performance practice of most méringues, at least by elite Haitian interpreters in the late nineteenth and early twentieth centuries, tended to shift between a rigid interpretation of the *cinquillo* rhythm—with its alternating eighth and sixteenth notes—and a smoother, more lyrical interpretation of the rhythm that evened out the syncopation and approached an even quintuplet. The Jeantys' alternate transcriptions of the *cinquillo* rhythm codified what Haitian salon pianists had been doing routinely since the nineteenth century: applying a rubato style to the méringue that was in line with some of the other *cinquillo*-based dance genres in the Caribbean, such as the Puerto Rican danza.

It was only in 1910 with the publication of Sténio Vincent's *La République d'Haiti telle qu'elle est* that the méringue received attention as an important aspect of Haitian social life. Vincent, a former mayor of Port-au-Prince who would eventually assume the Haitian presidency during the final years of the U.S. occupation of Haiti, called upon Théramène Ménès, a music teacher at the prestigious Lycée Pétion in Port-au-Prince, to write a section on the méringue for the book.

Ménès traced his history of the méringue to the *chica*, one of the dances that Saint-Méry cites in his description of colonial Saint-Domingue. However, Ménès also claimed that the *chica* was influenced by what he termed "the danza," a social dance of Spanish origin that likely originated in the colonial period before the French took control of Saint-Domingue in 1695 under the Treaty of Ryswick.

Like the Jeantys, Ménès outlined several possibilities for the correct rhythmic notation for the méringue rhythm. Ménès claimed that the practice of writing the *quintolet* as five even pulses over a duple rhythm, as the Jeantys advocated, was a distortion of the rhythm. He also claimed that dancers expected the syncopated version of the rhythm over a strong duple meter in order to do the dance properly.

Ménès had other reasons for supporting the duple meter version of the méringue. He wrote a laudatory méringue for Vincent titled "Magistrat Vincent" in which he praised the then Port-au-Prince mayor's accomplishments:

Magistrat Vincent, we are happy
Magistrat Vincent, you are doing well
When you do well, you do well
The people are always happy

(Vincent 1910: 222–279)

Vincent, a light-skinned elite Haitian, was eager to promote himself as a political candidate whose sympathies were in line with U.S. political interests.

Ménès's insistence on writing méringues that appealed to foreign audiences was accepted by many Haitian composers and critics, most notably Dumervé, whose history of Haitian music advocated writing the méringue in 2/4 time and stated that the dance itself "should be executed with a movement a little slower than that for the gavotte, since the méringue and the gavotte are danced exactly in the same fashion" (1968: 311).

The use of a 5/8 time signature for the méringue was revived by Haitian composer Jaegerhuber in the 1940s. Jaegerhuber's endorsement of the use of 5/8 rhythm for most Haitian folk music was based, in part, on his ethnographic work with Haitian peasants, who were seen by many elite Haitians as being culturally closer to their African ancestry than their upper-class compatriots (Largey 2004, 2006). Jaegerhuber thought that since most of Haiti's music was derived from African sources, it made sense to develop what I have termed a "musical orthography" or way to write specific musical ideas that visually demonstrates contemporary Haitian music's connection to its African past. Jaegerhuber's insistence on writing Haitian music, including the méringue, in 5/8 meter to demonstrate "an affinity with the music of African folklore" challenged other composers to reconsider the origins of the méringue to include more African influences on the genre.

The attempts by Haitian composers to notate méringue rhythms in a distinctive manner paralleled similarly idiosyncratic practices in Puerto Rico, especially in the much-discussed "elastic *tresillo*" discussed in Chapter 3. Both sets of practices and the debates around them were informed by a concern with establishing the relationship between local danza/contradance variants and related forms elsewhere in the Caribbean. In Haiti, debates over the etymology of the word "méringue" were also colored by nationalistic concerns (see., e.g., the different theories advocated in Dumervé 1968; Lassègue 1938; Lassègue 1919: 15; Fouchard [1973] 1988b: 79; Saint-Cyr 1981–82: 64). In an article titled "Can We Have a National Music?" Lamothe argued for the uniqueness of the contemporary Haitian méringue while acknowledging that the dance's origins were not strictly Haitian. Lamothe observed that "the méringue today, our national dance, in spite of the untimely intrusion of the vulgar foreign dances (one-step, foxtrot, etc.) is plainly of Spanish origin and is called the 'Habanera'" (1935: 11). Lamothe himself wrote numerous méringues, danzas, habaneras, and "Spanish dances," most of which employed similar syncopated rhythms (Lamothe 1955). Despite his acknowledgment of the affinities between the méringue and other dance forms favored in the Spanish-speaking portions of the Caribbean, Lamothe never composed any works that evoked the popular dance from Haiti's closest neighbor, the Dominican Republic. Although the Haitian méringue and Dominican merengue share similar names and origins, their positions as "national musics" of their respective countries have made it difficult to get a clear view of their historical connections.

## Notes

1. This essay uses the French spelling of the word "méringue" because of its consistent use in most of the historical sources and because this essay focuses on the use of the term among the upper classes in Haiti. The Haitian Kreyòl spelling "mereng" has been used only since the late 1970s, when the orthography of Haitian Kreyòl was standardized by the Haitian government.
2. See Averill 1997 for a discussion of "heating up" (*chofe*) Haitian music audiences in the twentieth century.
3. See, e.g., Wilcken 2005.
4. Wilcken translates the text as, "Lenglesou, damn! Where are you? I don't see you. Lenglesou, blood basin, where are you?"
5. On *Musical Tour of Haiti* (Ansonia HGCD-1280).
6. Several transcriptions of the lyrics of "Choucoune" list the first line of the chorus as "Ti zwezo nan bwa ki t ape koute." This transcription is adapted from Frangeul's arrangement of the song.
7. See Largey 1994 and Largey 2006 for more details on "La dangereuse."

## References

Auguste, Louis J. 2005. "Stolen legacy: The ordeal of Choucoune." Available at http://www.ludovicspeaks.com/2005/03/the_story_of_ch.html. Accessed June 1, 2007.

Austerlitz, Paul. 1997. *Merengue: Dominican music and Dominican identity.* Philadelphia: Temple University Press.

Averill, Gage. 1994. "*Anraje* to *angaje*: Carnival politics and music in Haiti." *Ethnomusicology* 38 (2): 214–247.

———. 1997. *A day for the hunter, a day for the prey: Music and power in Haiti.* Chicago: University of Chicago Press.

———. 1999. "#891: A review of the Choucoune material from Gage Averill." Available at http://www.webster.edu/~corbetre/haiti-archive/msg01015.html. Accessed May 31, 2007.

Averill, Gage, and Yuen-Ming David Yih. 2000. "Militarism in Haitian music." In *The African diaspora: A musical perspective.* Ed. Ingrid Monson, 267–294. New York: Garland Publishing.

Cale, John. 1971. "French secular music in Saint-Domingue (1750–1795) viewed as a factor in America's musical growth." Ph.D. diss., Louisiana State University and Agricultural and Mechanical College.

"Comment sauver la méringue haïtienne?" 1954. *Haiti Journal*, April 30, p. 1.

Coopersmith, Jacob Maurice. 1949. *Music and musicians of the Dominican Republic.* Washington, DC: Division of Music and Visual Arts, Department of Cultural Affairs, Pan American Union.

Courlander, Harold. 1939. *Haiti singing.* Chapel Hill: University of North Carolina Press.

———. 1941. "Musical instruments of Haiti." *Musical Quarterly* 27 (3): 371–383.

Dauphin, Claude. 1980. "Le méringue entre l'oralité et l'écriture: histoire d'un genre musical haïtien." *Canadian University Music Review* 1:49–65.

Dumervé, Etienne Constintin Eugène Moïse. 1968. *Histoire de la musique en Haïti.* Port-au-Prince, Haiti: Imprimerie des Antilles.

Elie, Justin. 1920. *Méringues populaires.* New York: R. de la Rozière.

Fouchard, Jean. [1955] 1988a. *Plaisirs de Saint-Domingue.* Port-au-Prince, Haiti: Imprimerie d'Etat. Reprint, Port-au-Prince, Haiti: Editions Henri Deschamps.

———. [1973] 1988b. *La méringue: Danse nationale d'Haïti.* Port-au-Prince, Haiti: Editions Lémeac. Reprint, Ottowa: Editions Henri Deschamps.

Gerstin, Julian. 2004. "Tangled roots: Kalenda and other neo-African dances in the circum-Caribbean." *New West Indian Guide [Nieuwe West-Indische Gids]* 78 (1–2): 5–41.

Guilcher, Jean-Michel. 1969. *La contredanse et les renouvellements de la danse française.* Paris: Mouton.

Hill, Donald. 1998. "'I am happy just to be in this sweet land of liberty': The New York City calypso craze of the 1930s and 1940s." In *Island sounds in the global city: Caribbean popular music and identity in New York.* Ed. Ray Allen and Lois Wilcken, 74–92. New York: New York Folklore Society and the Institute for Studies in American Music, Brooklyn College.

Honorat, Michel Lamartinière. 1955. *Les danses folkloriques haïtiennes.* Publication of the Bureau of Ethnology of the Republic of Haiti, series II, no. 11. Port-au-Prince, Haiti: Imprimerie de l'Etat.

Hunt, Alfred. 1988. *Haiti's influence on antebellum America: Slumbering volcano in the Caribbean.* Baton Rouge: Louisiana State University Press.

Jaegerhuber, Werner A. 1943. "Les origines de la musique folklorique haïtienne." *Cahiers d'Haïti* 1 (5): 53, 55.

Jeanty, Occilius, and Occide Jeanty. 1882. *Petite grammaire musicale.* Paris: Librarie Evangélique.

Lamothe, Ludovic. n.d. "La dangereuse." Hamburg, Germany: Musikalien-Druckerei.

———. 1935. "Pouvons-nous avoir une musique nationale?" *Le Temps* 9:11–12.

———. 1955. *Musique de Ludovic Lamothe: Valses, dances espagnoles, scènes de carnaval et autres.* Ed. Jean Antoine and Fernand Lamothe. Port-au-Prince, Haiti: n.p.

Largey, Michael. 1994. "Composing a Haitian cultural identity: Haitian elites, African ancestry and musical discourse." *Black Music Research Journal* 14 (2): 99–117.

———. 2000. "Politics on the pavement: Haitian rara as a traditionalizing process." *Journal of American Folklore* 113 (449): 239–254.

———. 2004. "Ethnographic transcription and music ideology: The music of Werner A. Jaegerhuber in Haiti." *Latin American Music Review* 25 (1): 1–31.

———. 2006. *Vodou nation: Haitian art music and cultural nationalism.* Chicago: University of Chicago Press.

Lassègue, Franck. 1919. *Ciselures, la musique à travers Haïti.* Albert, France: Libraire A. Crossel.

———. 1938. "La méringue: Danse nationale d'Haïti." *Le Temps* (April 27). Cited in Herrisé, Félix. *Etoiles haïtiennes.* L'Ecole Sainte Trinité Collection, Port-au-Prince, Haiti.

Maximilien, Louis. [1945] 1982. *Le vodou Haïtien: Rites radas-canzo.* Port-au-Prince, Haiti: Imprimerie Henri Deschamps. Reprint, Port-au-Prince, Haiti: Imprimerie de l'Etat.

McAlister, Elizabeth. 2002. *Rara! Vodou, power and performance in Haiti and its diaspora.* Berkeley: University of California Press.

Monton, Michel Mauléart. 1884. "Choucoune." Lyrics by Oswald Durand. Arranged by Fernand Frangeul. Port-au-Prince, Haiti: Fernand Frangeul.

Moreau de Saint-Méry, Médéric Louis Elie. [1797–98] 1985. *A civilization that perished: The last years of white colonial rule in Haiti* [Description topographique, physique, civile, politique et historique de la partie française de l'isle Saint-Domingue]. Ed., trans., and abr. Ivor D. Spencer. Lanham, MD: University Press of America.

Nolasco, Flérida de. 1939. *La música en Santo Domingo y otros ensayos.* Ciudad Trujillo (Santo Domingo), Dominican Republic: Editoria Montalvo.

Richardson, Philip J. S. 1960. *The social dances of the nineteenth century in England.* London: Herbert Jenkins.

Saint-Cyr, Jean Franck. 1981–82. "La méringue haïtienne." *Revista INIDEF* 5 (5): 62–74.

Schwartz, Judith L., and Christena L. Schlundt. 1987. *French court dance and dance music: A guide to primary source writings, 1643–1789.* Dance and Music Series. No 1. Stuyvesant, NY: Pendragon Press.

Vincent, Sténio. 1910. *La République d'Haïti, telle qu'elle est.* Brussels: Société Anonyme Belge d'Imprimerie.

Wilcken, Lois E. 1991. "Music folklore among Haitians in New York: Staged representations and the negotiation of identity." Ph.D. diss., Columbia University.

———. 2005. "Work and celebrate: The konbit, carnival, and rara." In *Vodou Music in Haiti.* Available at http://www.lameca.org. Accessed January 29, 2008.

Yarborough, Lavinia Williams. 1959. *Haiti-dance.* Frankfurt: Bronners Druckerie.

Yih, Yuen-Ming David. 1995. "Music and dance of Haitian vodou: Diversity and unity in regional repertoires." Ph.D. diss., Wesleyan University.

KENNETH M. BILBY *and*
DANIEL T. NEELY

# 7 / The English-Speaking Caribbean

## *Re-embodying the Colonial Ballroom*

> Suddenly the hush into which we were rapidly falling was ruptured by a series of disharmonic chords and squeaks and loud thumps of the game leg and the bow on the floor. There was a moment of tension, a sigh, a violent expectoration over the pavilion railing, and the fiddler had "cum round." First he warmed up a bit of this and that: improvisations, snatches of old English airs and Creole melodies. Meanwhile two lines formed, one of men, one of women. The men vied for partners, the women modestly looked down and fingered their dresses, and then as if by silent agreement, fiddler and dancers were under way. There was a great flourish of curtsies, and gradually it dawned on me that this was the Maroon version of the quadrille.
>
> —Katherine Dunham, *Journey to Accompong*

The relationship between people of African descent in the Anglophone Caribbean and Western dance reaches back into the eighteenth century, if not earlier. At any rate, this is when colonial writers first began taking note of slaves adopting the music and dances of European society. Since that time, European dances in this part of the Caribbean have received considerable attention, and perhaps none as much as the quadrille. In the literature of the Anglophone Caribbean, the quadrille is treated more frequently than any other colonial social dance as an index of European influence. However, its popularity—like that of any other expressive form—has ebbed and flowed with shifts in taste; one of the things most often overlooked by writers is that the quadrille was but one of a number of dances originally associated with the European ballroom that were popular among the colonists in the Caribbean by the late eighteenth century. In view of this fact, it is misleading to treat the quadrille as if it existed in isolation. In the following sections, we attempt to take this broader picture into consideration while placing the quadrille in the Anglophone Caribbean in historical perspective and providing some idea of the contexts with which it has been associated in more recent times.

## The Ballroom Complex

Throughout the nineteenth century, a range of social dances originally associated with the European ballroom found favor in the colonies and became the basis for subaltern adaptations.[1] These included round dances, such as the polka, the mazurka, the polka-mazurka, the varsovienne, the two-step, and the gallop; circle dances, such as the maypole; longways dances, such as the contradance and the country dance; solo dances, such as jigs and clogs; and square dances, such as the cotillion, the quadrille, and the Lancers.[2] Many of these included steps that functioned as interchangeable parts of dance suites; others, such as particular longways and square dances, were themselves suites that included as few as four (but generally more) individual "figures."

On the continent, individual and figure dances were highly prescribed affairs, characterized in their original forms by a lack of physical intimacy, though this eventually changed, particularly through the international popularity of the waltz.[3] In the colonies, not only did these dances become the bases for local and sometimes idiosyncratic choreographic interpretation but they were also sometimes reconfigured, recontextualized, and resignified to such an extent that the only obvious remaining connection to their Continental forebears was their names. As John Szwed and Morton Marks (1988: 29) state, "a European dance name may refer to an entirely different dance; or a native New World term may disguise a well-known European form; and the European name for a step may label a complex dance in its own right." This terminological slippage can lead to some confusion, since, as is shown below, specific creolized varieties often ended up displaying little real resemblance to their European namesakes. Jennifer Post's work on music and dance in New England demonstrates that similar processes occurred in North America, where common European ballroom styles also became the basis for creative local developments (2004: 93). Despite certain similarities with the North American case, however, Caribbean choreography tended to rely less strictly on Continental models—a fact that may help explain the relative paucity of scholarly work comparing the two.

It has been suggested that much music in the Caribbean represents a creolized fusion of European and African elements, and that this is one reason the Caribbean might be thought of as a "single musical region . . . in spite of tremendous local variation."[4] This local variation ranges from musical and choreographic forms that contain expressive formal and stylistic elements based on African traditions to those that have a close stylistic relationship to nineteenth-century European social dance practices. It is precisely this local variation, produced by a history of complex transformations, that can create difficulty when one attempts to compare the various dance forms in the region that are derived from European ballroom traditions.

Much as with music, the varying local manifestations of these ballroom dances can be accommodated within a model that represents the Caribbean as a single choreographic region. In discussing African influence in creolized Caribbean forms, Samuel Floyd (1999) outlines three musical "structures of feeling"—the *cinquillo*, *tresillo*, and *son* and calenda "complexes"—that help provide a pan-Caribbean framework for cultural comparison and interpretation.[5] These widely distributed musical elements, Floyd argues, function as symbols of diasporic unity among African descendants in the Caribbean. Similarly, one might speak of a "ballroom complex," based on both musical and choreographic criteria, through which similar symbolic meanings may be evoked.

Rather than interpreting "creolized" European forms of this kind as symbols of colonial assimilation—or as repositories of a simplified history that must remain, in the words of Michel-Rolph Trouillot (2002: 189), "one level removed from the concrete circumstances faced by the individuals engaged in the process" of constructing this history—we would like to suggest that ballroom-descended forms might better be examined and understood as products of a shared history of creativity, struggle, and adaptation among the colonized. Starting from this premise, the analysis of this ballroom complex becomes a study of how the subaltern responded to a kind of cultural and musical "globalization" in the nineteenth century not only in the Caribbean but also around the colonial world.

## Adaptation and Transformation

Today there is great variation in how the quadrille is realized in the Anglophone Caribbean. Of course, a few widely shared features cut across the local differences produced by varying processes of adaptation and transformation—for instance, the retention of multiple dance figures, a small range of generic dance formations, steps borrowed from peasant forms, and, as Szwed and Marks (1988) have noted, the frequent incorporation of a local form (e.g., mento), often for the fifth figure.[6] But a survey of contemporary practices reveals a broad range of variations and shows that local traditions are connected to earlier models in varying ways.

Some variants are based, for example, on the formal standards of the nineteenth-century quadrille. In the relatively strict Continental approach to ballroom dancing, the quadrille consisted of five figures, each of which carried a title based on its position in the suite; these titles were derived from the various contradances that first made up the standard quadrille. In order, these titles were *le pantalon* ("trousers"), *l'été* ("summer"), *la poule* ("hen"), *la pastourelle* ("shepherd girl"), and *finale*. Another named figure, *la trenise* (after the dance master Trenitz), sometimes replaced the *pastourelle*, but in certain contexts (as was the fashion in Vienna), it would simply be added to the suite. Some of the steps that commonly accompanied these dances included a *chaine* of various types, including cross over, *chassez*, *poussette*, and promenade, as well as fairly standard movements, including balance and the wheel (see, for example, DeGarmo 1870; Howe 1858; Wilson 1816). Of the variety of Continental quadrilles that have left a mark in the Western Hemisphere, the most common in the Caribbean are the Albert, Lancers, English, and French varieties (Miller 2005: 407; Guilbault 1985: 38).

Within the Caribbean, the degree to which local variants adhere to Continental standards varies widely. Jocelyne Guilbault (2002a: 842), for example, has shown that in addition to a local fifth figure (variously called quadrille, sharp, slow, *caristo*, French, Irish, or Polish), quadrilles in some parts of Dominica consist of four "compulsory" figures clearly related to the nineteenth-century Continental convention—*pastouwèl*, *lapoul*, *lété*, and *latrinitez* (to use Creole orthography). In these figures, the arrangement of the four pairs of dancers into squares similarly recalls the familiar choreographic pattern associated with square format quadrilles (Phillip and Smith 1998: 95–124). Several couple dances, many of which are based (in name, at least) on European forms—including the méringue (mereng), the Viennese waltz (*vals o vyenn*), the *mazouk* (a local form of mazurka), the schottische (*sotis*), the biguine (*bidjin*), and pure polka (*polka pil*)—may also be appended to the last of the square figures, furthering the sense of the quadrille's transformation and local specificity.

The number of figures in a quadrille varies widely across the Caribbean. Lorna McDaniel (1998b: 871) mentions six-figure suites in Carriacou. In Jamaica, there is no real consensus on how many figures a quadrille should have. The first commercial recording of a quadrille (1957) includes only four (Chin's Radio Service C1035 [to hear a portion of this recording, listen to this book's compact disc]), while later accounts describe them as having five (Smith 1981: 50–53) or six, with the sixth considered the *brawta* (extra) figure (Baxter 1970: 198).[7] Still another source describes one community's quadrille tradition having as many as eight figures (Lewin 2000: 132).[8] Contemporary musicians report that they are required to play five figures for official cultural events, but they also say that "at home" (or in the past), six or even seven figures would be more common. It is generally the case that where strict choreographic standards do exist, they are the product of cultural development programs, national festivals, and state-judged competitions.

The fact that few traditions have maintained the original French figure names may be a reflection of the quadrille's malleability. Today, many local versions identify dance figures simply by their numeric position in the suite. Guilbault notes this lack of original French names even in the *kwadril* of French Creole–speaking St. Lucia, where the figures are known simply as *pwémyé fidgi*, *dézyèm fidgi*, *twazyèm fidgi*, *katwiyèm fidgi* (Creole for "first figure," "second figure," and so forth, though the fourth figure is also sometimes called *avantwa* or *lanmen dwèt*), save for the final dance, which is a local take on the *gwan won* or "grand round."[9] This is the case on other islands as well; contemporary mento musicians in Jamaica, for instance, most often speak only of numbers when naming figures ("first figure, second figure"), while in Montserrat, figures are normally referred to as "number one quadrille, number two quadrille," and so on (Dobbin 1986: 70).[10]

When and how this particular change took place is not clear. In 1921, Helen Roberts made transcriptions and several recordings of dance sets in Jamaica that suggest that some of the older designations continued to be used well into the twentieth century. In a transcription of one quadrille she heard (she appears to have heard several), she included eight tunes, each given a particular name—a first figure called "quadrille," a couple of "reels," a "shay shay," one called "catch-me-time," and two with no names. The third piece in this set, however, which was in 6/8, was called "Lapool" (i.e., *la poule*)—a clear (and apparently unusually late) reference to earlier practice.[11] None of Roberts's other transcriptions of set dance music includes such an attribution, nor does a 1901 article in the *Daily Gleaner* newspaper that defines the word "mento" as a kind of dance suite ("a set of Lancers") and provides titles for its six dance figures. (These, however, appear to be no more than the titles of the songs to which each figure was danced.) Similarly, while Walter Jekyll's 1907 *Jamaica Song and Story* describes a "standard" five-figure quadrille and lists dozens of dance figures (by number according to their place in a set), he gives no indication whether the performers themselves had any other way of referring to them.

Some traditional European elements other than original titles for figures have been retained as well, notably certain nineteenth-century choreographic features. Many older step names and related expressions are still used, for instance, in Jamaica, including advancing and retreating, crossing (also called "fours" or "pass-through"), honoring, possette, promenade, figure of eight, the star formation, and the grand chain, as well as wheeling and balancing (Smith 1981: 25, 32, 35). Similarly, Rebecca Miller (2005: 407) has found the expressions "balancing" and "wheeling" in Carriacou; and according to Beverley Steele (1996: 44), the same terms occur in the Lancers of Grenada. "*Balansé*" is also a term used in the quadrille of Dominica (Phillip n.d.; Phillip and Smith 1998: 65). Similar terms are found across the Anglophone Caribbean, from the Bahamas to Grenada. Alongside these quadrille traditions, a wide range of other ballroom dance forms have also been retained. Mazurkas, polkas, and waltzes are widely distributed. In addition to the examples from Dominica and St. Lucia mentioned above, Molly Ahye (1978: 133) writes of the popularity of nineteenth-century ballroom styles in Trinidad and Tobago, as well as the continuing existence of the "heel and toe" dance (a polka, which has its own characteristic choreography), which is also danced in Carriacou and Grenada (e.g., Miller 2000, 2005; Steele 1996) and many other parts of the Anglophone Caribbean.

Although eighteenth- and early-nineteenth-century contact with British traders exerted intermittent influence on the earlier musical culture of the Caribbean coast of Central America, the popularity of quadrille-based suite dances and other ballroom forms in this area seems to have resulted primarily from later labor migration. Beginning in the 1870s and continuing well into the twentieth century, thousands of workers from around the Caribbean migrated to Panama, Costa Rica, and Nicaragua in search of work. Those who went to Costa Rica and Nicaragua worked mainly on banana plantations (Putnam 2002; Scruggs 1999), while those in Panama worked initially on a railroad project and later the canal (Cramer 1946). Many—but by no means all—of these people came from British territories; many of the latter were from Jamaica (Putnam 2002: 51; cf. Cramer 1946: 246–247).

Jamaica's influence on the quadrille's development along the Caribbean rim has been strong over the years. Carlos Fernandez, for example, suggests that it was Jamaican laborers who introduced the quadrille to Costa Rica, where it flourished as a local variant called *cuadrilla* and developed a repertoire said to include "more than fifty dances, each having up to five or six figures or movements, including *vals*, Colombian *pasillo*, Prince Albert, Caledonia, Lancers, Basquet Cotillion" (Fernandez 1998: 690). Ronald Smith states that quadrille and contradance were once very popular in Panamanian Antillean towns, which were inhabited by laborers from Antigua, Barbados, Guadeloupe, Haiti, Jamaica, Martinique, St. Kitts, and Trinidad and Tobago (Smith 2002: 773). Although the heterogeneity of the people who settled these communities might lead one to expect a musical picture reflecting this diversity, many of the songs documented in these locations are actually from Jamaica, where they have been used as figures in quadrilles (Cramer 1946). Jamaican influence is evident in other ballroom styles as well; T. M. Scruggs, for example, has described a close relationship between Nicaraguan *palo de mayo* (a musical style and circle dance based on the maypole) and Jamaican mento (a similar form used at times to accompany maypole dances in Jamaica; Scruggs 1999: 312). (It should be noted that on the nearby island of San Andrés [a Colombian department], mento is also performed, as well as a longways dance suite.)

Although relevant documentation is generally hard to come by, not all figure dances in English-speaking territories along the Atlantic rim are the result of Jamaican migration. For example, the Garinagu (also known as Garifuna, or formerly as Black Caribs), a mixed African and Amerindian ethnic group inhabiting parts of Belize, Guatemala, Honduras, and Nicaragua, dance a form called *gunjei* that resembles contradances and square dances and may reflect a different historical migration (Conzemius 1928: 192; Greene n.d.).[12] An early-twentieth-century account of this dance among the Garinagu in Honduras (Conzemius 1928: 192) suggests that it may have been based on a Haitian form called "*kujai*," introduced by a community of Haitians living in Trujillo, Honduras. Also interesting in this connection is a passage in the classic study *Slave Songs of the United States* (Allen, Ware, and Garrison 1867: 113), referenced by Lawrence Gushee (2002: 155), which suggests that a set of slave songs in French Creole dialect, collected in St. Charles Parish, Louisiana, were accompanied by "a simple dance, a sort of minuet, called the *Coonjai*."[13]

One of the most conspicuous ways in which quadrille and other figure dances vary across the Anglophone Caribbean—and this says much about the extent to which these European-derived forms were adapted to local circumstances—is in instrumentation. Even within a single island one may find tremendous variation. In Jamaica, for instance, the common string band consisting of fife or violin, banjo, guitar, rhumba box (bass lamellophone), and assorted percussion (represented on the track "Quadrille, Third Figure" on this book's compact disc) coexists with fife and drum ensembles that are normally identified with Yuletide masquerading but are often just as comfortable performing figures of the quadrille and a variety of other "set dances." (The latter, featuring homemade side drums played with two sticks and a single bass drum played with a padded beater, resemble British military fife and drum bands.) Some string bands include clarinet or saxophone, sometimes along with stand-up bass. In some parts of the island, quadrille is performed by stripped-down, percussion-heavy groups featuring drums, graters, maracas, and bass "trumpets" (or boom pipes), with melody handled by harmonica.

We find the same kind of variation elsewhere in the region. Like Jamaica, St. Vincent boasts string bands and fife and drum ensembles, both of which are known for their performances of quadrille and other ballroom music; the same can be said for St. Kitts and Nevis (Abrahams 2002). The quadrille (and broader ballroom) tradition of Dominica, in contrast, has its "jing-ping" bands, featuring *lapo kabwit* (flat, circular frame drums played with the hands and sometimes a stick), *siyak* (a kind of combined rasp and shaker), blown wooden or bamboo boom pipes, and accordion and/or banjo (Phillip and Smith 1998: 61–64; Bilby and Marks 1999). In Montserrat and Tobago, as well as Carriacou, the kinds of ensembles traditionally associated with quadrille make use of similar flat frame drums (and in some cases actual tambourines with jingles), along with violin (Dobbin 1986; Dewar 1977; Elder 1971; McDaniel 1998b, 1998c; McDaniel and Hill 1999; Miller 2005)—although Montserrat also has fife and drum bands similar to those of Jamaica, St. Vincent, and other Anglophone islands, and these perform quadrilles as well. And in the Bahamas, the "rake-'n'-scrape" bands that perform renditions of quadrilles and other ballroom genres typically consist of "goatskin drums" (large, single-headed barrel drums played with the hands), scraped carpenter's saws, and accordion, harmonica, or guitar (Wood 1998: 809).

## Country Dances and the Quadrille: A Historical Perspective

As early as 1774, when Edward Long noted that the enslaved had "good ears for music" (1774: 423), evidence exists from Anglophone territories to suggest that slave musicians were exposed to and incorporated aspects of European forms into their repertories.[14] But how extensive was this process during the slavery era? Although choreologist Hilary Carty argues that "the slave population learned and mastered the quadrille . . . [perhaps] as an escape from the harshness of everyday life" (1988: 47), there is little data to support this kind of claim (cf. Abrahams 1972). Too often absent from accounts of early musical creolization is a sense of how musical exchange occurred and why the quadrille (as a peculiar element of the ballroom complex) became one of the forms most common throughout the Anglophone Caribbean.

Most scholars are in agreement that before emancipation, slaves learned from and performed for the pleasure of the white colonial classes (Banfield 2007: 141–143; Lewin 2000: 131; Bilby 1985a: 185; Baxter 1970: 197; Lewin 1968: 1).[15] The music and dance performed for the colonists generally reflected Continental tastes, and none seems to have been as popular as the longways country dance, as suggested by John Stewart in the early nineteenth century: "Country dances are the greatest favorites; and the negro fiddlers, accompanied by the lively sound of the tambourine in lieu of the bass viol, often play, though not regularly taught, with wonderful accuracy and apparent taste" (1808: 178).[16] A bound sheet music collection in the National Library of Jamaica that once belonged to a "Mrs. Bland" lends support to this account; alongside a variety of dance music pieces of English and Irish origin, all of which date to around 1800, the only dance suite included is a country dance (consisting of four figures for a longways-based choreography).[17]

What role did slaves have at the social occasions where such music and dance were performed? It is widely assumed (although not often documented) that slaves—particularly house slaves—observed whites dancing on plantations and, copying their moves, transmitted these to other slaves (Mintz and Price [1976] 1992: 31; Marks and Szwed 1988: 31). Stewart's account is intriguing because it seems to suggest that the direct teaching of slaves may not have been common, contrasting with Errol Hill's claim that some estates kept "two or three expert fiddlers who would be required to provide music for the reels and country dances held at the great house" (1992: 220). In fact, both observations may be entirely valid; after all, the details of pedagogical practice are poorly documented at best, and practices may have varied from estate to estate. In any case, how faithful to colonial models ballroom-inspired dancing among the slaves themselves actually was is not known.

At any rate, by the early 1820s the picture appears to have grown more complex. The amount of musical exchange seems to have increased, and writers now commented specifically on the relationship between social status and musical preferences. Let us listen once again to Stewart:

> The drums of the Africans vary in size &c. according to the different countries, as does also their vocal music. In a few years it is probable that the rude music here described will be altogether exploded among the Creole Negroes, who show a decided preference for European music. Its instruments, its turns, its dances, are now pretty generally adopted by the young Creoles, who, indeed, sedulously copy their masters and mistresses in everything. A sort of subscription balls are set on

> foot, and parties of both sexes assemble and dance country dances to the music of a violin, tambarine [*sic*], &C. (1823: 272)

In this account, Stewart seems to be indexing changes occurring primarily among the interstitial Jamaican-born "brown" classes, who enjoyed some limited degree of legal and social privilege. In an oft-cited passage, another observer, Henry De La Beche, helps us enlarge this picture, telling us of an "old school" of "goombay and African dances" that likely reflected a pan-African performance aesthetic of the kind posited by Sidney Mintz and Richard Price; and, coexisting with this, a "new school" consisting of "fiddles, reels, &c" (De La Beche 1825) that maps easily onto Stewart's depiction of the musical tastes of the emerging middle stratum of slave society.

Later writers have used these passages as a window onto the larger historical processes of musical transformation that occurred across Jamaica during the early nineteenth century and as evidence of creolization from the slave perspective (cf. Stolzoff 2000: 31–32). What these descriptions also clearly suggest is the coercive nature of slavery and its impact on the expressive lives of the enslaved, whose musical practices and tastes were quickly becoming stratified along lines of color and positioning within the social hierarchy. (It is worth noting here how much these passages omit; they tell us next to nothing, for example, about indigenous recreational performance outside of contexts in which European social dancing was considered appropriate.) In any case, other written evidence from this era suggests that musical change was never unidirectional.[18] When we turn to the sheet music of the time, for instance, we see that European ballroom forms and the colonists who introduced them, for their part, were probably more deeply influenced by the musical practices of the enslaved than commonly thought.

One glimpse at this side of the story dates back to the period around or shortly before Stewart's and De La Beche's 1820s publications. Around 1820 (and perhaps as early as 1815) Philip Young, a pupil of English composer William Crotch and then a resident of Jamaica, published in London a collection of airs entitled *West India Melodies or Negro Tunes | Adapted for the Piano Forte | As Performed by the Negroes in the West-Indies with the Regular Negro Beat | Which Commences on the Weak Beat of the Measure*. In an attempt to "elevate" native expression into a commercial form, Young produced a mix of music that "imitated [the sounds] as made by the various African Instruments they use." The issue consisted of nineteen piano arrangements, fifteen of which had titles in an approximation of Jamaican Creole (or "patois"). The balance—consisting of three waltzes with titles specific to Jamaican places and a final piece, "Success to the Injured," that included directions for a longways dance—seemed to deviate from the publication's self-consciously African-oriented aesthetic.

Young's work set an example that others would later follow. Within a decade, a young composer living in Jamaica named J. F. Edelmann, together with Francis Egan, an Irish immigrant who would later become the bandmaster of the

West Indian Regiment and also the organist for the Kingston Parish Church, compiled and published *West Indian Pot Pourri in which are introduced several creole airs, as sung and danced by the Negroes of Jamaica* (ca. 1825).[19] Edelmann was born on February 17, 1795, seven months after his father was put to death for an "active and violent" role in the French Revolution (Edelmann 1830). As a teenager, Edelmann studied music at the Paris Conservatory. He left that city in 1815, ostensibly for the United States, but instead ended up traveling for the next several years through Mexico, parts of Central and South America, and the Caribbean (Benton 1964: 186). By the 1820s he was living in Kingston, Jamaica, where he struck up a relationship with Egan.

Although Edelmann moved to Cuba in 1832 (where, in 1836, he opened his own music publishing firm, described by Alejo Carpentier as "a longtime . . . haven of local composers" [2001: 185]), his influence on Egan was substantial and lasting. Over the next decade, Egan published at least five sets of "Creole" airs.[20] The music contained in these collections consisted of repetitive dance pieces suited to colonial tastes. Despite rather pedestrian arrangements (and the somewhat misleading use of the word "Creole" in the title), these pieces provide a fascinating glimpse of the heterogeneity of this particular slice of Jamaica's early musical culture (something that is not apparent from what we know of Edelmann's work). While some pieces are simply subtitled "Native" or "African," for example, others are labeled "Spanish" and "à la mode de Santo Domingo," suggesting a kind of cosmopolitanism that has yet to receive the attention it deserves in historical studies of Jamaican music.

What is most remarkable about Egan's work (and that of his predecessors) is how popular these publications proved to be among the colonial classes.[21] Following the publication of Egan's third set of creole airs, for example, the *Jamaica Watchman* (January 2, 1833) reported, "That the Creole airs enjoyed a wave of popularity is evident in the announcement by Prospere Robert that he had rented a house in the city to teach dance . . . [and] . . . as the Creole airs have become so fashionable and are sometimes introduced in the first circles (of quadrilles), regular Steps and Figures are arranged to each . . . with written information of all the figures in the English and French languages."[22] Despite their representation as "Creole" airs, there is nothing immediately obvious in the printed music for these "native" pieces that would suggest a musical aesthetic significantly different from Continental European practice at this time. These pieces are, in fact, rather unremarkable, featuring somewhat meager arrangements, and one wonders whether they were intended for performers with limited musical ability. Figure 7.1 presents a representative piece from Egan's second collection, dating from the 1830s. In a similar vein is Figure 7.2, from a collection entitled *West-India Melodies; or Negro Tunes. Adapted for the Piano-Forte*, published in London in the 1820s.

Nonetheless, both their titles and their popularity among the dominant classes suggest that something about these pieces (beyond what is evident from the printed melodies themselves) served to signify the local. The vogue for

**Figure 7.1** "The Black Taglioni's Favourite Sha Sha [African]," collected by Francis Egan, 1830s.

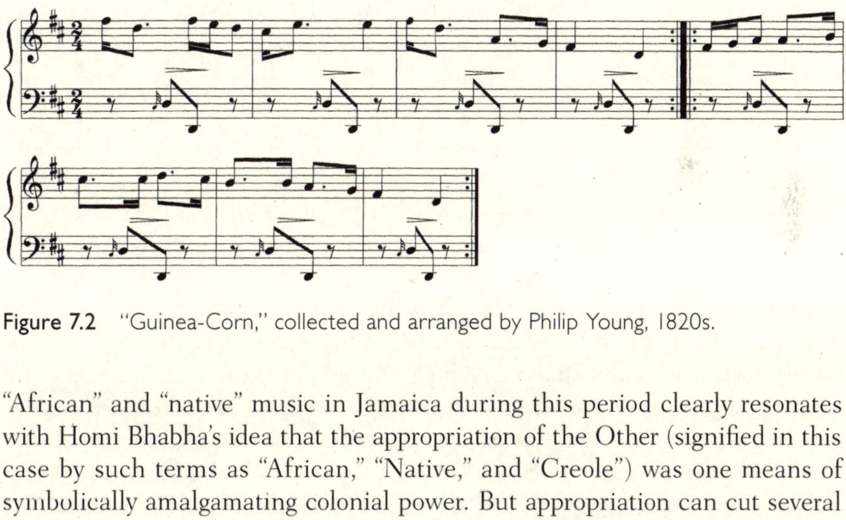

**Figure 7.2** "Guinea-Corn," collected and arranged by Philip Young, 1820s.

"African" and "native" music in Jamaica during this period clearly resonates with Homi Bhabha's idea that the appropriation of the Other (signified in this case by such terms as "African," "Native," and "Creole") was one means of symbolically amalgamating colonial power. But appropriation can cut several ways. One can speculate, for instance, that sparse arrangements such as these may have encouraged—perhaps even required—a certain amount of creative improvisation among local musicians in performance, and that this, along with other potentially "destabilizing" performative factors, such as participatory discrepancies (Keil 1987), might have gradually helped infuse genres introduced from "above" with new, clearly local qualities and sensibilities. Recognizing this possibility is an important prerequisite to a critical reappraisal of this period's printed music and to an understanding of how ballroom styles could be, and commonly were, resignified over time, not only in Jamaica but also in other parts of the Caribbean. It is important to keep such considerations in mind when thinking about the question of mimesis in this context—a topic we touch on in the next section.

What is of particular interest to us here is the relationship of these pieces to Egan's other body of published works, his quadrilles. Egan's publications contain the first known references to quadrilles in Jamaica. Beginning probably in 1828 with the *Belmore Quadrilles*, Egan capitalized on the dance's popularity in Jamaica; over the next decade he published at least two more collections. These pieces represent important elements of the ballroom complex's history, providing a perspective on intercultural and interclass expressive exchange—processes that remain poorly understood during this era.

The *Belmore Quadrilles* set was likely published to commemorate the arrival that year of Somerset Lowry-Corry, 2nd Earl of Belmore, who served as the governor of Jamaica until 1832 and whose term of office was probably contemporaneous with the initial popularity of the square-format quadrille as an alternative to the longways country dance in Jamaica. Although there are no dance indications in the *Belmore Quadrilles*, the inclusion of six named figures (*pantalon*, *l'été*, *poule*, *trenise*, *pastourelle*, and *finale*) and a waltz (perhaps as a page filler) suggests the Viennese fashion and its square choreographic format. It is interesting to note that each figure in this publication was named after a facet of the earl's ancestral home in Ireland, suggesting a historical moment when the quadrille was new to Jamaica and local adherence to metropolitan models stricter.

In contrast, Egan's subsequent quadrilles—"The Creoles" (ca. 1836) and "The Gleanings" (ca. 1840)—display a more local orientation. "The Creoles," for example, was dedicated to Sir Lionel Smith, who served as governor of the Windward Islands from 1833–36 and of Jamaica from 1836–39 (during which time he oversaw the emancipation of the slaves, in 1838). Although Smith presided over a watershed moment in Jamaican history, he performed his role in a way that ultimately reinforced the interests of the white colonists, including the locally born whites known as "Creoles." The title of the quadrille itself, "The Creoles," appears to have been a reference to the latter identity, which at the time suggested a simultaneous commitment to a Continental ideology and, as historian Christer Petley has argued, a local way of life (Petley 2005: 106–109); the use here of the word "Creole" as a signifier for the local is similar to that found in Egan's other publications. The idea also recurs in the names of some of the figures of this suite (of which there are six, again in the Viennese style), including "Creoles" and "Newcome"—both of which refer to a white, but specifically local, identity.

"The Gleanings," on the other hand, is far more cosmopolitan. This suite's figures lack any overt reference to the local at all, presenting us, rather, with a combination of trendy European steps gathered into a widely understood format; here, a German quick step ("An English Song") and the finale ("Love in a Tub") are paired against pieces that may or may not be local compositions ("The Sea," "The Bark," and an untitled fifth figure). Together they form a conspicuously motley assemblage that goes against strict European practice and represents the fashion in Jamaica at the time.[23]

Over time, the quadrille fell out of favor; by 1861, according to one source, "quadrilles [were] spoken of contemptuously; but waltzes, schottisches and polkas . . . pronounced glorious" (Sewel 1861: 173). As reflections of their time, Egan's pieces are invaluable. They are of particular interest because of their proximity to the tumultuous moments just before and after emancipation. They provide valuable insight into how ballroom practice in general and the quadrille's form in particular were changing in response to large-scale social transformations. Indeed, some of the changes in musical practice and form suggested by these published pieces may have left traces in the present. If we return to the passage on Egan's third set of creole airs cited above, for example, we see that by 1833 selections from the creole sets were not limited to Jamaica's most prestigious dance circles but could be used in any of various figures. This raises doubts about the idea that the emergence of local choreographic and accompanying musical forms—a crucial step in the process of indigenization—might be tied specifically to the fifth figure.[24] We would argue that the looseness and malleability of performance categories (e.g., "figures") suggested by this passage were the norm for quadrille in many parts of the Anglophone Caribbean, and that one result of this, in many areas, was the transformation and indigenization of all figures, not just the fifth. The profusion and multiplication of varying forms and styles that this flexibility produced over time created much potential for confusion in the later study and analysis of Afro-American folk dances.

## The Reconstitution of European Ballroom Music and Dance in the Anglophone Caribbean: The Question of Cultural Meaning, Past and Present

> "Quadrille dancing seeks the representation of an ideal type of social behaviour." —Daryl Phillip and Gary Smith

In most parts of the Anglophone Caribbean, country dances, quadrille, and related genres derived from European ballroom traditions peaked during the nineteenth century. As we have seen, the numerous variants of quadrille that enjoyed great popularity in Jamaica during the first half of that century had fallen out of favor among the upper strata of colonial society by the 1860s. Although these were replaced by new European-derived varieties—schottisches, polkas, mazurkas, and others—the ballroom fads that took hold one after the other as the century wore on were not to produce robust, widespread, and long-lasting hybrids in the Anglophone territories comparable to those of

Latin America and the Hispanophone Caribbean (Chasteen 2004). At the turn of the century, with independence from colonial rule still many decades away, even the largest Anglophone island, Jamaica, possessed no well-established creolized elite ballroom genres of its own that might be brought into the service of efforts to establish a local "national" identity.

One of the most intriguing things about European ballroom-related genres in the Anglophone Caribbean, then, is the very fact of their survival to the present. It is interesting to note that those that do still exist are found predominantly in rural areas, among people of relatively modest means. In short, throughout the English-speaking Caribbean, the creolized offspring of the European ballroom dances originally introduced by colonial rulers, such as contradance, quadrille, and Lancers, survive primarily as aspects of Afro-Caribbean "folk culture." How did this come to be? Why have these "colonial" expressive forms, originally marked as "European," survived (even if barely, in some cases) to the present in rural Caribbean communities, among these "reconstituted peasantries" (Mintz 1974), despite their virtual disappearance long ago among the more privileged classes? These questions bring us back to the historical processes of adaptation and transformation discussed earlier, suggesting that there was much more to these cultural processes than the written record reveals.

One reason for the continuing existence of such ballroom-related genres among rural people, one might argue, is their continuing local "meaningfulness" within particular social contexts. As suggestive as the available historical documentation is of cultural and musical exchange and creolization during the period of slavery, it tells us very little about the deeper meanings with which transformed versions of European ballroom dances may have been invested by the enslaved in the Caribbean. We can be certain that the transformations in musical structure and performance style hinted at in written records from the time were accompanied by transformations of meaning—in some instances, these reworkings no doubt involved resignification of a fundamental kind—but we lack much in the way of direct evidence. The writers who left such records neglected to search out the deeper meanings these creolized genres had for those who created them and passed them on. And so we can only guess at the actual meanings that might have become attached to musical practices of European origin as these were remade and resignified, hundreds of times over, by Africans and their descendants across the region.[25]

The malleability of the quadrille's formal aspects among both colonizers and colonized raises interesting questions about the room for resignification that lay open to the socially marginalized throughout Jamaican history. One of the most common tropes associated with the historiography of European-derived or -related dances performed by Africans and their descendants in the Americas is the notion that slaves "copied," "imitated," or "mimicked" their masters. In music and dance studies, however, mimesis is undertheorized and its motivations largely unexamined, a circumstance that has tended to reproduce colonial perspectives on the "abilities" of the slaves.[26] In his work on square dancing and quadrille among Indian ("Aboriginal" or "First Nation") people in Manitoba, Byron Dueck (drawing on the ideas of Michael Taussig [1993] and others) moves away from such unexamined assumptions, arguing that mimesis in this part of Canada is "a social response to the cultural alterity encountered in contexts of colonial domination" and a way of "attain[ing] power over the difference" (Dueck 2006: 2). Dueck further proposes that mimesis is not a unidirectional process but "involves coeval or simultaneous processes only possible when both groups engage one another in the shared spaces created by colonialism."

In the Caribbean context, the notion that mimesis, as Dueck suggests, involves "sharing" is important in interpreting not only the interactions and musical exchanges that took place between colonizers and colonized but also those that took place among the enslaved themselves. Among highly heterogeneous slave communities, many new expressive and other cultural forms were built upon general social and behavioral patterns and ideas that were broadly shared (despite Africa's tremendous ethnic diversity) across much of West and Central Africa; these new syncretic forms eventually contributed to the development of new, large-scale African American cultures in the Caribbean and elsewhere (Mintz and Price [1976] 1992: 18–19). Dance was among the broadly shared practices based on common African cultural principles that played an important role in this process. Katrina Hazzard-Gordon (1996: 105), for example, has argued that "though the ceremonial context and the specific uses of movement of each enslaved ethnic group's dances were different, the basic vocabulary of West African movement was strikingly similar across ethnic delineation." Doris Green (1996), in contrast, has provided evidence of the choreographic heterogeneity of traditional African dance, thereby pointing us to some of the differences between groups that may have still been prevalent in the Caribbean of the early nineteenth century. At times, these differences could have posed barriers to interaction between dancers from different ethnic backgrounds, even as, at other times or in other contexts, the broadly shared understandings and common choreographic "vocabulary" mentioned above might have provided a basis for interethnic adaptation and solidarity. This simultaneous heterogeneity and similarity, on different levels, no doubt existed not just in Jamaica but throughout the Caribbean, and it likely presented Africans and their descendants, as they forged their own new plantation communities and cultures, with untold opportunities for richly meaningful acts of mimesis.

Another way in which the idea of mimesis as a relational process is particularly interesting is that it leads us to reconsider what might have been shared between slave and colonizer, and how this, in turn, might have enlarged the possibilities for creative interaction among the enslaved themselves. If generic African "vocabularies" of dance movement were widely shared among slaves of different ethnic backgrounds and could serve as a means of bridging cultural differences, why could colonial ballroom dances based on broadly shared choreographic forms—such as the country dance and quadrille—not be adapted in similar ways? Might not these generic European forms, as they were creolized, also have facilitated—perhaps even eased—sociocultural contact and exchange between ethnically diverse segments of the slave population? Certainly, the present-day choreographic heterogeneity of quadrille dancing throughout the Caribbean supports the notion that originally European ballroom dancing was adapted to a wide variety of social contexts in the slave societies of the Caribbean; and these no doubt included gatherings of ethnically diverse individuals, both African and creole (i.e., locally born), who were actively involved in the formation of new expressive forms along with new identities.

Hazzard-Gordon's research sheds additional light on this question, suggesting that "mimesis" in this case could have entailed a good deal more than mere "imitation" of culturally alien forms. In describing line and circle dances among various West African ethnic groups, she notes that "African religious line dances in the plantation context shared a similar line formation with the numerous secular European reels, in which men and women faced each other in lines."[27] Given this background, the apparent "copying" of Continental figure dancing by enslaved Africans could have—at least for some—provided a curtain of secular (European-identified) respectability behind which to conceal or mask sacred (African-identified) ceremonial practices. The heterogeneity of quadrille's functions and meanings throughout the Anglophone Caribbean would seem to point toward this kind of possibility as well—a question to which we return below.[28]

Given the absence of ethnographically grounded evidence on subaltern versions of European ballroom music and dance forms for most of their history—and even today, it must be noted, we lack high-quality information on such resignified European-derived genres for much of the Anglophone Caribbean—we are left with the temptation to read from the relatively little we know of present-day cultural practices back into the distant past (and vice versa). Such attempts to span wide gulfs in time and space in the absence of written documentation are fraught with difficulties—especially when the temporal and geographic distances are as vast, and the social and cultural variables as complex, as they are in the present case. Nonetheless, from the limited information available to us, we can advance a few general statements about the varieties or kinds of cultural meaning with which these ballroom-related forms and practices have been invested over time.

It is not surprising if these adopted European genres, as some of the early descriptions suggest, came to play a significant role in the development of culturally marked social hierarchies within slave communities, even as these music and dance forms were transformed through creolization. It is clear enough that dances of European origin, such as quadrille, were represented by the Europeans who introduced them as culturally superior—as forms of "civilized" behavior—and that these dances quickly became categorically opposed in colonial ideology to what the Europeans thought of as the "savagery" of contrasting varieties of African-derived or -identified music and dance (Guilbault 1985: 34). Because of this, music and dance, like other aspects of expressive culture, became powerfully coded means of social identification in these colonial plantation societies; and mastering quadrille and other European-identified dances—even in their more creolized forms—was one way of conveying important messages about social position in an increasingly stratified slave society.[29] Such tendencies are visible in the historical descriptions from Jamaica that reveal the fondness of the "brown" middle strata of slave society for these ballroom genres and their corresponding disdain for the drum-based dances (some of them identified with specific African "nations") still prominent among the African-born population (see, for example, Beckwith [1929] 1969: 213). Viewing things from a broader perspective, Yvonne Daniel (2006: 6) writes, "like European performers, African performers who danced the complicated figures were exhibiting their social education and good manners. Freed African performers also used European dance structure to project a differentiated status over enslaved or field Africans. Eventually, however, both house and field, enslaved and free, imitated and thereby promoted European movement, structure, and values within quadrille performance."

Even today, some of quadrille's prominent social characteristics reflect this historical background. For instance, in several parts of the Anglophone Caribbean, quadrille and other ballroom-related genres seem often to be associated with notions of "propriety," "dignity," "refinement," "gracefulness," "nobility," "stateliness," "gentility," "decency," "elegance," "elevation," and other such morally charged concepts that are not easily divorced from this history.[30] As Daniel (2006: 6) learned when carrying out a comparative study of quadrilles in various parts of the Caribbean, "everywhere, the dance form aims for a sense of elegance and propriety, as well as social entertainment and fun." The extent to which this widespread language of social valuation represents a reflection of contemporary color-coded class structures and related ideologies of social inequality still in force today versus a lingering, ideologically insignificant trace of a distant and no longer "living" colonial past (one perhaps recontextualized in egalitarian, or at least less hierarchical, terms) no doubt varies across the region.[31]

But in the postcolonial Anglophone Caribbean, where people of African descent most often constitute large majorities, and where reclamation of the African past has often played an important role in the construction of anticolonial (and sometimes racialized) nationalist identities and ideologies, the idea of promoting European-derived ballroom dances as an aspect of "indigenous" heritage can pose problems. From a "purist" Afrocentric perspective, embracing such European-identified forms (even "Africanized" or creolized versions of them) might be seen as a kind of cultural "betrayal"—a failure to expunge Eurocentric colonial values from postcolonial conceptions of national identity.

When one views things less rigidly, however, much more positive interpretations become possible. Daniel, for instance, on the basis of her comparative work, sees such European-derived ballroom dances, both past and present, in an entirely different light:

> The appropriation of quadrille music by African ancestors must have created a most incredible, if not most uncomfortable, situation for plantation masters, as slaves played European instruments adroitly and danced exquisite quadrille configurations. The music was more Creole than was the dancing, whose structure was primarily European. There was no contradiction for performers, however. For them, their quadrilles were hardly "European." . . . Instead of letting their inhumane treatment dictate the quality of their daily outlooks, actions, and social activities, quadrille performers, past and present, demonstrated liberation of self and mind by expressing socio-spiritual happiness through dancing and music making. They took what would otherwise be an aversion, European dance structure and musical form, and adopted and adapted them; they had fun with and within the dance. In dancing the quadrilles, they subtly and persistently challenged domination, superiority, and power. (2006: 8)

Conflicting interpretations of this complex history and its relationship to the present, as this passage suggests, are not easily resolved.[32] As Stephen Banfield (2007: 144) puts it, "Who was appropriating what? Despite the vitality displayed by a nursery or ballroom tune with inserted syncopation, it is all too easy to romanticize the Jamaican soundscape as cultural cross-fertilization and forget the coercive or co-optive reality of which even musical expression was part."

Did appropriation and performance of European ballroom dances by enslaved Africans in the Caribbean represent an act of resistance and a subversive assertion of humanity (if not actual racial equality)? Or did it, rather, amount to a kind of concession to hegemonic colonial values that actually served to reinforce structures of domination?[33] Both of these interpretations most likely contain some truth, and the degree to which one or the other was true no doubt varied in different times and places. One thing we can be certain of, in any case, is that during the slavery era, as in more recent times, the social significance of these performances and their meanings for performers varied substantially across time and space. After all, despite certain broad commonalities, social and cultural conditions in different parts of the Anglophone Caribbean were never uniform.

To gain some appreciation of how complex this question of cultural signification must have been in the past, one need only consider the range of differing meanings with which these traditions are associated in different areas today. Take, for instance, the island of St. Vincent, which, along with Dominica, represents one of the last places in the insular Caribbean where an ethnically distinct autochthonous population has survived to the present and continues to inhabit a territory of its own. The Vincentian Caribs, concentrated in the northeastern part of the island, are descendants of the original Carib inhabitants but have intermarried to some extent with people of African descent and vary in physical appearance along a continuum from "pure Amerindian" to mixed African-Indian; they no longer speak the Arawakan language of their ancestors, and their present-day culture is in many ways indistinguishable from the creole culture of their Afro-Vincentian neighbors.[34]

Interestingly, the Carib territory is home to what are widely recognized as some of the most vibrant string band traditions in St. Vincent. In this part of the island, the European ballroom-related dances that form the core of the string band repertoire constitute a primary symbol of Carib identity. The genres played here sound much like some of the creolized ballroom musics played elsewhere in the Anglophone Caribbean (with similar instrumentation, including banjo, guitar, *cuatro*, drum, and maracas), and they continue to be associated with a variety of figure dances based on elaborate European-derived choreographies. (For an example, listen to "Quadrille, Third Figure" on this volume's compact disc.) Yet those who have maintained these string band traditions speak of them as profound expressions of indigenous Carib identity and seem to attribute little if any significance to their European or Afro-Creole origins. (This attitude could well change in the near future, however, as the Caribs are increasingly incorporated into expanding networks of surviving indigenous peoples who are joining together to develop new Caribbean concepts of Native American identity spanning the circum-Caribbean region [Forte 2006]; in any case, the question of these dances' origins may become more problematic for the Caribs as various Vincentian and broader Caribbean festival contexts in which they find themselves participating increasingly revolve around the nationalistic performance of "folk culture.")[35] For the time being, the quadrille in particular remains, according to the musicians and dancers who perform it in this part of St. Vincent, one of the "deepest" expressions of Carib identity; indeed, at least one Carib string band leader sees this European ballroom-related tradition, regardless of its origins, as the quintessential embodiment of Caribness.[36] In certain other parts of the island, however, quadrille and other ballroom-related dance musics are performed in a rather different manner—by fife-and-drum ensembles known as "boom drum" bands—and are viewed as local expressions of a broader Vincentian and African-Caribbean identity.[37]

Equally striking is the case of the Jamaican Maroons. The Maroons are descendants of escaped slaves who fought for and won their freedom long before the abolition of slavery in the 1830s. Though generally regarded as the guardians of the most authentically African cultural traditions to have survived in Jamaica, these communities have long taken special pride in the quality of their quadrille dancing (Harris n.d.). In the Windward Maroon community of Moore Town, located in the Blue Mountains, the string band music associated with quadrille dancing and the very different neo-African drum-based music of the religious tradition known as Kromanti Play have been compartmentalized and kept separate; but both are viewed as expressions of "traditional" Maroon identity (Bilby 1985a: 204).[38] Among these Maroons, the European derivation of quadrille, like that of the English family names that have been fused with notions of African "tribal" descent in Moore Town, generally poses no ideological problem (Bilby 2005: 70, 80–81).

In the Cockpit Country on the other side of the island, the Leeward Maroons of Accompong have also long practiced their own versions of old European ballroom dances; in this community, quadrille dancing similarly remains a viable symbol of "traditional" Maroon identity, alongside the more culturally African rites commemorating the Accompong ancestors to which the larger public is invited every January.[39] This was evident, for instance, in the annual Accompong celebration of 2000, during which "traditional" quadrille dancing, performed by Maroon teenagers, formed a prominent part of the program. Backed by prerecorded quadrille music played by a string band, the Accompong dancers executed a series of assiduously choreographed figures on sacred ancestral ground located near the center of the community, next to the monument to the Maroon hero Kojo (Cudjoe).[40]

Perhaps the most remarkable examples of resignification in the Anglophone Caribbean are those in which originally European ballroom dances have become an integral part of African-based religious practices. The best-known illustration of this comes from the island of Montserrat, where an observance known as the Jumbie (or Jombee) Dance—thought to have died out within the last few decades—depended for its spiritual efficacy on the performance of a creolized local version of the quadrille. ("Jumbie" is a word used in most parts of the Anglophone Caribbean to refer to spirits of deceased human beings.) Here, the various figures of the quadrille, much like innumerable varieties of music and dance in West and Central Africa, had become imbued with the power to invoke the spirits of ancestors, who would take possession of dancers at ceremonies held for the management and healing of various spiritual afflictions (Philpott 1973: 161–164; Dobbin 1986).

The majority of the original European colonists of Montserrat were Irish, and strong Irish influence was present in the Jumbie Dance, as in other aspects of Montserratian culture (Messenger 1975). In addition to a fife or another leading melodic instrument known locally as a "pulley" (that is, a concertina, accordion, or melodeon), the ensemble that played this spirit-calling music included two flat frame drums (called *woowoo* and *babala*) that were very similar, if not identical, to the Irish bodhran. There is no doubt that these instruments and the sounds they produced had been resignified in Montserrat in fundamentally African ways. When rubbed with the heel of the hand or a moistened finger, the frame drums could quickly attract jumbies, or spirits of the dead. The melodic instruments, as well as certain songs, could also be used to invoke ancestral spirits and bring on possession. That the music and dance on which these possession ceremonies depended was a kind of hybrid that had been Africanized in important ways yet remained identifiably European in others is evident in such descriptions as the following.

> Four pairs of men and women dance a series of five quadrilles ("sets") played at successively faster tempos. After several hours of dancing, with new partners taking over at the end of each five quadrilles, one or more of the dancers will become possessed, aided by the copious consumption of rum, the wildness of the beat, the heat in the house, and the shouts of the crowd. Turning [i.e., spirit possession] may involve whirling about, apart from the other dancers, or falling to the floor, when the possessed one gasps out a "secret," sometimes in glossolalia. The playing and dancing reveal startling reinterpretations: Western instruments produce Africanesque music, to which dancers perform Irish steps while moving their upper bodies like Africans. (Messenger 1998: 924–925, paraphrasing Philpott 1973: 161–162)

Interestingly enough, the exact same music and dance genres, with the same instrumentation, were also played in a variety of other contexts, such as rum shops and private homes, purely for entertainment; at such times, ancestors were not invoked, and there was no spirit possession. When played in these recreational settings, this "secular" version of quadrille was known simply as "country dance," "drum dance," or "goatskin dance" (Messenger 1998: 924).

Another island with a similar tradition is Tobago (which forms part of the Republic of Trinidad and Tobago but remains culturally quite different from Trinidad). Tobago is known for a distinctive form of music called *tambrin* (from "tambourine"). Tambrin bands feature three or more flat frame drums played with the hands (similar to both the Irish bodhran and the frame drums used in the Jumbie Dance of Montserrat), a leading melody instrument (typically a violin), a triangle, and sometimes other percussion. (Today the traditional fiddle is sometimes replaced by a harmonica.) Although best-known for their performances of a genre known as the "Tobago reel" (said to be of Scottish origin), some of these ensembles have broader repertoires that include other European-derived dances, such as jigs, waltzes, "marching pieces," heel and toe polka, and various figures of the quadrille, as well as entirely local forms, such as bele and calypso.

Much as in Montserrat, these ensembles provide the music for a kind of "jumbie dance" revolving around spiritual healing through possession of ritual specialists by ancestral spirits (Elder 1971; McDaniel 1998c: 959). These ceremonies also feature special "jumbie songs." Folklorist and ethnomusicologist J. D. Elder provides a description of this tradition as it was when he observed it several decades ago: "As the orchestra of drums played the famous 'Tobago Reel' dance songs the spirits 'flew into the heads' (possessed) of the dancers and gave them 'messages' about who had 'put the jumbies on the sick' and what medicines were to be used to cure them. Supporting the drummers with their goat skin tambourines were the fiddlers and female singers chanting the great songs" (Elder 1971: 31). Today, in some parts of Tobago, these orchestras continue to use ballroom-related dance musics, such as reels, quadrilles, and heel and toe polka, to call the spirits of ancestors into the heads of mediums who channel their powers for the benefit of the living, helping them combat illnesses and other spiritually based problems. As in Montserrat, the Tobagonian tambrin bands also sometimes perform some of the exact same genres in a variety of other contexts, such as weddings, in which spirits are not summoned and no possession occurs.[41] (See "Quadrille, Fifth Figure" on this volume's compact disc for an example of a quadrille piece played by a Tobagonian tambrin band.)

These contemporary resignified European-derived dances are of special value to those who wish to gain further insights into the historical processes of creolization that produced the varied assortment of related ballroom genres we see across the Caribbean today. The examples from Montserrat and Tobago are particularly suggestive. Having evolved either during the slavery era or shortly after, both the Jumbie Dance of Montserrat and the tambrin tradition of Tobago represent important windows onto the past. If clearly African-derived spiritual concepts could fuse so thoroughly with originally European ballroom dances on these two islands, there is no reason to believe the same could not have happened elsewhere in the region. The fact that such dances as reels, quadrilles, and polkas, when transplanted to these islands, were invested by Africans and their descendants with meanings that differed radically, and in ways that had profound existential significance, from those originally associated with them in Europe has important implications for our understanding of the cultural processes that contributed to the development of the broader Caribbean "ballroom complex" with which we are concerned here.

Clearly, such examples of cultural appropriation cannot be understood as simple instances of "borrowing" or "imitation"; nor are they easily reconciled with such notions as "deculturation." The fundamental resignification demonstrated by such cases must have seemed deeply subversive to European colonists—if any actually witnessed and understood the meaning of these esoteric practices—for it played havoc with the very definitions, categories, and valuations upon which the racialized social and cultural hierarchies of slave plantation societies were predicated. Not only did it suggest a certain cultural (and existential) autonomy among the enslaved (and their descendants)—a continuing capacity to view the world in their own ways, even as this world became increasingly creolized—but it also successfully and meaningfully merged diverse musical and cultural forms, practices, and ideas that were, according to colonial ideology, separate and incompatible by nature. Indeed, even today, in Caribbean contexts in which hierarchical ideologies and cultural dichotomies from the colonial past linger on, these kinds of deeply meaningful cultural fusions of African-derived ideas and European-derived forms, where they survive, can remain problematic, if not subversive.

It is impossible to say how widespread these spiritualized, African-oriented forms of originally European ballroom dances once were in the Caribbean, though we know they were not limited to Anglophone areas.[42] There is good reason to believe, in any case, that they were much more common in the past than they are today.[43] Given the stigmatization, if not outright outlawing, of expressions of African religiosity across the Anglophone Caribbean during the slavery era and beyond, it is reasonable to surmise that such versions of European dances that had become fused with possession ceremonies would have had to go underground to survive, and many probably died out eventually because of mounting pressures from the hegemonic varieties of Christianity that were opposed to them. Some of these indigenized ballroom dances might actually have existed in virtually indistinguishable dual forms—one associated with "secular" contexts, the other with neo-African religious ceremonies—as was once the case in Montserrat and still is in Tobago. And to judge by what we know of Montserrat—where the Jumbie Dance, following years of persecution by colonial authorities and the established churches (Dobbin 1986), finally disappeared, leaving behind a related "secular" fife-and-drum tradition (featuring quadrille, heel and toe polka, and other such ballroom-derived forms once performed as part of the Jumbie Dance)[44]—it is quite possible that some of the entirely secular versions of ballroom-derived dances now scattered across other parts of the Anglophone Caribbean were once actually associated with such spiritual practices, the memory of which no longer survives. Viewed from this perspective, the "ballroom complex" of the Anglophone Caribbean—as a historical phenomenon, at least—begins to look even less European than cultural nationalists inclined to stress its local distinctiveness might imagine.

Even if these spiritualized versions of the quadrille and related dances constitute the exception to the rule and were never representative, they effectively illustrate a larger point: European ballroom-derived dances were often thoroughly reconstituted in the Caribbean. This process, which we can barely begin to grasp if we rely solely on written accounts from the colonial era, usually involved an infusion of musical characteristics and aesthetic concepts brought from Africa. It also involved resignification of various kinds, some of which, as among the Caribs of St. Vincent and the Maroons of Jamaica, were tied to local notions of ethnic identity but had no apparent spiritual dimension, and others of which, as in Montserrat and Tobago, clearly drew on African-derived religious concepts. Such examples demonstrate not only that these dances became something new and substantially different when they took root in the Caribbean but also that such locally reconstituted forms and practices could vary in the degree to which they reproduced and embodied hegemonic colonial values.

To say that performers of present-day Caribbean versions of European ballroom dances such as the quadrille *always* strive for "elegance" and "propriety," in a "European" or colonial sense, overstates the case. Such a characterization overlooks significant differences between the kinds of performance practices one tends to find in rural areas and those associated with urban locations or otherwise strongly influenced by the attitudes of urban elites. In rural Jamaica, for instance, and in some of the other Anglophone islands, quadrille until recently was often performed in or alongside rum shops—a setting noted for its relaxation of the behavioral strictures associated with "propriety" and "respectability" (Wilson 1973). Anyone who has witnessed these less formal performances can attest that they often display a distinctively African-Caribbean aesthetic—one characterized by a high degree of syncopation, collective improvisation, and overall rhythmic dynamism. This performance style, especially when the music becomes "hot," can hardly be accurately described with such terms as "elegant," "graceful," or "stately" (at least as these are usually construed in Caribbean, not to mention European, contexts).

But such informal performances, relatively free of hegemonic notions of "correctness," are becoming increasingly rare, even in the most remote rural areas. It is not simply a matter of rural, traditional forms of music and dance dying out under pressure from the forces of cultural imperialism associated with expanding mass media, though this has certainly played a role. Just as important are the changes wrought by cultural authorities and planners from urban areas and the local "cultural workers" they have trained. In fact, in most parts of the Anglophone Caribbean, it is difficult nowadays to find performers of these old ballroom-related dances who have not been affected by this kind of cultural intervention from "above." Even the most seemingly remote rural villages seldom remain untouched by state cultural apparatuses.

## Conclusion

As performers are drawn into national and regional competitions and festivals centering on the staged presentation of traditional "folk culture," their performance practices and understandings of their traditions undergo significant modification.[45] Ironically, although these state-sanctioned cultural displays typically aim for authenticity and evince a strong "preservationist" ethic—and, it must be said, in some cases they have probably contributed to the survival of traditions that might otherwise have faded away—they often have the effect of reshaping these traditions in fundamental ways. "Official" forms of folk culture are invariably constructed in part from elite notions of what is interesting, authentic, proper, and correct, and these are not always in line with the understandings and values of the original tradition bearers themselves. And so the modern era has seen resignifications of its own, some of them spurred by this kind of meddling by cultural outsiders with political or other agendas. Greatly complicating the picture, in some areas, is the continuing and growing impact of tourism, which brings its own set of demands for performers who wish to make their traditions "presentable" for foreign audiences of various kinds.

All these factors make it increasingly difficult to ascertain what quadrille and related dances in the Anglophone Caribbean were really like in earlier times, and how much of the discourse of "propriety" and "decency" that tends to surround them in the present is derived from recent interventions versus the historical processes of creolization through which they were born. In fact, this is a question that can only be addressed case by case. And so, until further historical research is done to disentangle these complex factors as they have operated with varying force in different parts of the Anglophone Caribbean over time, all we can say is that there probably has always been, as there still is, great variation in these European ballroom-derived dances and the meanings associated with them.

We must not forget, in any case, that many people in the region—especially those who feel no need or desire to master the "correct" dance steps—are able to enjoy the music of the quadrille and related European-derived forms without the formal choreography and system of values sometimes attached to them. For many, this buoyant "old-time" country music is simply an aspect of "tradition" to be valued and appreciated, often nostalgically, in its own right; and such listeners may give little thought to the kinds of ideological issues raised above. When popular artists refer to quadrille in their recordings—for instance, Bob Marley, who repeatedly intoned the words "ska quadrille" in his 1965 recording of the song "Rude Boy" with the Wailers; or Yellowman, in his 1980s dancehall hit "Skank Quadrille," which pays homage to the same Marley song—it seems usually to have been in this spirit.[46]

Like many other aspects of expressive culture in the Anglophone Caribbean, quadrille and its ballroom-derived relatives reveal the complexity of the creolization processes that produced entirely new and unprecedented fusions in some cases and refurbished yet easily recognizable derivatives in others. Encompassing Africanesque possession rites among supposedly "decultur-ated" subalterns, Europeanesque colonial pageants for the "cultured" few, and innumerable other variations and forms resignified in uniquely local ways, the ballroom complex of this region presents rich opportunities for further study. There is no doubt that we still have much to learn about these reconstituted ballroom traditions.[47] What we already know suggests, in any case, that these culturally ambiguous legacies of European colonialism and African-Caribbean creativity have much more to tell us about both the beauties and the contradictions of cultural life in this part of the world.

## Notes

1. Several writers have discussed examples of enslaved musicians playing and dancing on a colonial model. See, for example, Banfield 2007: 141–145, Hazzard-Gordon 1996, Mintz and Price [1976] 1992: 31, Guilbault 1985: 33, and Floyd and Reisser 1984: 23.
2. We hope this typological sketch of named dances will help the reader avoid terminological confusion. Like musical terms, choreographic terms are often used indiscriminately in writings about European-derived ballroom traditions. In some cases, for example, the term "set" is used to describe a grouped figure dance with or without a caller; in others it is used as a synonym for a suite of dances. It may help here to provide further clarification of the terminology we use in this essay: In longways dance formations, men and women are generally arranged in two lines according to gender and face each other. In square formations, couples are grouped into "sets" of

four people. Round dances are couples dances, while solo dances are danced alone. In some locations, both in the Caribbean and elsewhere, circle dances are sometimes associated with children's games (Post 2004: 93), an association that deserves closer investigation.

3. Giordano 2007: 100. A deeper understanding of European and American social dance conventions can be gleaned from the large selection of nineteenth-century dance manuals available for viewing on the Library of Congress's "An American Ballroom Companion Dance Instruction Manuals Ca. 1490–1920" Web site, available at http://memory.loc.gov/ammem/dihtml/dihome.html.
4. Bilby 1985b: 184. Kenneth Bilby's notion of musical creolization draws on a linguistic model; the related ideas of "acculturation," "transformation," and "blending" have also been addressed by scholars in this connection and dominate much of the literature that surrounds "European"-based music in the Caribbean. See also Szwed and Marks 1988; Floyd 1999: 3; Floyd and Reisser 1984: 22; de Jong 2003; Bilby 1985a, 1985b; and Davis 1994.
5. Floyd's model (1999: 12–13) resonates with similar complexes suggested by Manuel 1994 and León 1964. See also Johnson 2005.
6. The persisting connection between locally rooted, harmonically European popular music and dance genres and quadrille across the Anglophone Caribbean strongly suggests that indigenized European ballroom music nearly everywhere played an important role in the emergence of the creolized forms that would eventually come to be seen as quintessential embodiments of island-specific (and island-wide) identities (and, in the postcolonial era, national identities). Examples of this include Jamaican mento (though it is also found on Providencia and San Andrés, as well as along the Atlantic coast of Central America); St. Vincent washover (which is often characterized as an indigenous Vincentian counterpart to "calypso" [Abrahams 1972: 285]); Antiguan benna; Crucian (USVI) quelbe (Sheehy 1998: 971–972; cf. Joseph Parris Hot Shots n.d.); and Bahamian "rake-'n'-scrape." All of these are, or once were, sometimes performed as figures in local performances of quadrille—usually as one of the final figures (often, though by no means always, the fifth figure). This is largely true of the French Caribbean as well, where, for instance, Martiniquan biguine (*bidjin*) and Haitian *méringue* have a similar relationship with quadrille or other local ballroom-related dances.
7. A description of the quadrille tradition in the Jamaican Maroon community of Moore Town by C.L.G. Harris, the former leader of that community and himself a frequent participant in quadrille dances as a guitarist, gives some idea of the extent to which quadrille performances can vary in rural Jamaica, both in terms of the number of figures and the stylistic categories associated with particular figures: "A set was a series of six separate tunes to which the people danced; these were termed in order 1st figure, 2nd figure and so on to the 6th figure. The 1st to the 4th figures were invariably danced as quadrille but the 5th and 6th were at times danced as *round dance*—a sort of mento in which others usually participated" (Harris n.d.: 114).
8. Both authors have also encountered (and Bilby, recorded) performers in rural Jamaica who state that quadrille, as they know it, has eight figures; others claim as few as five.
9. Guilbault 1998b: 944–945; cf. DeGarmo 1870: 69–70 and Howe 1858: 111. Appended to the *kwadril* may be as many as three closed-couple round dances, includ-

ing a polka, a schottische, and the *lankomèt* (also called a *mazouk*), which is a dance said to have originated in St. Lucia.

10. In some parts of rural Jamaica, certain figures of the quadrille have been given new local names referring to historical events or persons. In the Grants Mountain area of St. Ann parish, for instance, the fourth figure became known as "the Titanic," and the fifth figure as "John Sterling" (Bilby, field notes, July 12, 1975). Whether this practice represents a once common convention or something more limited is unclear; among contemporary musicians, the tradition of naming individual dance figures is followed little, if at all. However, this kind of variation may be one more indication of the flexibility that characterizes quadrille traditions in many parts of the Caribbean.
11. The "shay shay" mentioned here (sometimes written as *sha sha* and pronounced /shíe-she/ or /she-she/ in Jamaican Creole) is a musical form, dance style, and kind of song from the nineteenth and early twentieth centuries that is an antecedent to mento. Despite the frequent occurrence of European forms in Roberts's field notes, Roberts's and Martha Beckwith's publications seem to be concerned primarily with exotic forms—*mento, sha sha*, "catch-me-times"—that were, in fact, figures within these suites. This preoccupation with exotic local forms is also reflected in much subsequent scholarship.
12. Interestingly, a Garifuna-authored source describes the present-day *gunjei* (or *gunjai*) as "a graceful dignified social dance, in which each man dances with each woman in turn" (Cayetano and Cayetano 1997: 129).
13. See also Krehbiel 1914: 116, 120, 121, 123 for a perspective on the Louisiana counjai's relationship to the *koundjo* (or, following Krehbiel, *candio* or *candjo*), a dance with possible African origins, and Abbott and Seroff 2002: 308–312 on the contested origins and possible relationship of "coonjine" or "kunejine" (a term widespread in the southern United States by the late nineteenth century) to Louisiana *coundjaille* and early ragtime and jazz. Little is known about the Haitian *kujai* associated with the ballroom complex; there appear to be few references to it in the literature. George Eaton Simpson (1940), for example, makes no mention of it in his article about the peasant songs of northern Haiti, though he specifically mentions ballroom dances, including the quadrille. Harold Courlander (1960: 136), on the other hand, describes the "koune or coundjaille" as "a dance connected with communal work celebrations," an observation that Gage Averill (1997: 13) echoes in his account of the *koudyay* (thought to be from French *coup de jaille*, meaning "a spontaneous bursting forth"). The *koudyay* described by Averill is a sponsored street celebration "used to reinforce relations of power through patronage and performance." It is impossible at this point to say whether *kujai* is a cognate of either Haitian *koudyay*, Louisiana French Creole *coon jai*, or Garifuna *gunjei*; the available documentation is simply too sparse. See Chapter 6 for further discussion of *koudyay* in Haiti.
14. This practice might actually have started considerably earlier, as in some of the French islands, and simply been ignored by writers of the time. Dena Epstein (1973: 84) cites a source that suggests "Creole Negroes" in Guadeloupe had adopted French dances as early as 1750.
15. Based on his examination of a number of eighteenth- and nineteenth-century Jamaican sources, Richardson Wright (1937: 237) makes the following generalization: "If the mistress of a plantation great house was to give a dance, she called in the negro

musicians of the countryside. They had a quick ear, and could repeat any tune after hearing it once or twice. Some of the bands had a repertoire of twenty or thirty dance tunes for polkas, waltzes, quadrilles, and minuets. Now and then some negro musician could play a sonata without having read a note of it. Of course, none of these slave bandsmen could read a note of music."

16. Kate Van Winkle Keller and Genevieve Shimer (1990: viii–ix) state, "The country dances [in England] went through a gradual evolution. The earliest country dances were dances for sets of two, three, or four couples in round, square, or longways formations, a few of the latter for 'as many as will.' By the mid–eighteenth century most of the set dances had vanished from the ballroom, and only longways for an indefinite number of couples were danced. By 1800, square set cotillions were in the ascendancy, and soon the longways country dances were but a lingering memory." These Continental trends appear to have been reflected fairly closely in the colonies at first, but over time the colonists began to display increasingly divergent local tastes, no doubt partly because of growing participation by slaves and free blacks in ballroom dances.
17. Mrs. Bland's book is a collection of individual sheet music pieces bound together into a single volume, as was the practice at the time. Many of these pieces are marked songs, duets, glees, or "ditties." Others are basic piano-vocal reductions of theater pieces popular in London. Of note is one piece taken from a production set in Barbados and considered the first English antislavery play (*Come Let Us Dance and Sing, the Favorite Finale in Inkle and Yarico* [Longman and Broaderip n.d.]). Although no publication information is printed on some of the pieces, many are products of Bland and Weller. Other represented publishers and printers are Preston, Andrews, Jones, Edmund Lee, Monzani, Longman and Broaderip, and Hime.
18. Richard Blaustein (1995: 192) makes a similar point when discussing relations between "rural, nonelite, nonliterate subcultures" and "urban, elite, literate subcultures" in the context of country dancing (including contradance, quadrille, square dancing, and other such forms) in North America. "While we see concrete evidence of the perpetuation by nonelites of cultural forms once fashionable among cosmopolitan elites," he notes, "we can also observe the continuous adoption and reinterpretation of rural cultural styles by cosmopolitan romantics who have come to identify with 'the folk.'"
19. Cited in Hill 1992: 225. No known copy of this publication exists, but the card catalogue of the National Library of Jamaica has a reference to it that provides some information, including details of the authorship and titles of the selections in the publication. The library record notes that it was simultaneously published in Kingston and London. Their attribution is "182-." Because most of Edelmann's traceable musical activity appears to have happened closer to 1830, it seems safe to assume that Young's publication came first.

    Biographical data on Egan's life comes from Jamaica musicologist Astley Clerk, whose papers are on deposit in the Jamaican National Archives in Spanish Town. For more on the roles of Edelmann and Egan in elite musical life in nineteenth-century Kingston, see Banfield 2007: 141.
20. The titles for these collections were typically *Egan's (Nth) Set of Creole Airs*. Although no copy of Egan's first collection (which, according to Astley Clerk's notebooks may

have been titled *A Selection of Negro Melodies and Creole Waltzes Arranged for Flute or Violin*) is known to exist, the second was issued around 1833, the fourth dates from 1834, and the fifth around 1834–38. (Its title, including the phrase "apprentice tunes," refers to the pre-Emancipation apprenticeship period that began in 1834.)

21. In fact, these works provided the inspiration others needed to publish similarly oriented music. *The Jamaica Despatch and New Courant* reported on September 6, 1834, for example, "We have authority to state that on Saturday next 'The Golden Spring Negro Song,' on the change from Apprenticeship to slavery, and 'The Bath Creole Song' (the words of the latter by J. Daughterty, esq) set for the flute and violin, will be ready for transmission by next week's post."
22. It is interesting to note that dance schools teaching European ballroom genres existed in larger Jamaican towns by the late eighteenth century. Wright (1937: 203) quotes a local newspaper advertisement from 1779 in which a Mr. Godwin "proposes to improve and perfect young Ladies and Gentlemen in Dancing—The Minuet and proper steps to be used in Country Dances, will be taught in a complete manner—Juvenile Gentlemen may attain the Italian Hornpipe, which will conduce to perfection in Country Dances, etc."
23. This publication is also notable because it seems to include at least one title associated with earlier country dance practice. The *finale*, "Love in a Tub," a tune perhaps received from a seventeenth-century theatrical comedy by George Etherege, was choreographed as a longways country dance in an 1816 dance manual called *Treasures of Terpsichore* (Wilson 1816: 70). Whether it was ever danced as such in Jamaica is not known, but given its position in the suite, it could have perhaps been intended as a reprise of earlier longways practice and evidence of choreographic interchangeability within dance suites.
24. Part of the reasoning behind this idea may be based on Jekyll's claim that among the Jamaican peasantry, the fifth figure "sweet them most" (Jekyll [1907] 1966: 217; compare to Szwed and Marks 1988: 30, Carty 1988: 51, and Whylie 2000). Jekyll argues that what distinguishes fifth figures from the others is their pulse (two beat) and comparatively faster speed ([1907] 1966: 220–221). However, Jekyll also notes that musical variation within figures was substantial, which may suggest that local choreographies developed for each figure to suit such variation. In one compelling passage, for example, Jekyll compares the music and choreography of three different fourth figures: "It says much for the expertness of the dancers that they can fit the same steps to tunes of such varying accent as the two last examples present. Here is another which differs again" ([1907] 1966: 235). Interestingly, when the quadrille was performed in Montserrat in the past as part of the "Jumbie Dance" (see below), local performers tended to think of both the fourth and fifth figures in particular as "the hot ones" (Philpott 1973: 162).
25. Peter Manuel's (1994: 271–274) discussion of salsa as a contemporary resignification of originally Cuban forms is helpful in thinking about the kinds of social processes that can produce changes over time in the primary meanings attached to musical genres or forms (including forms that, musicologically speaking, may not have undergone significant restructuring while being resignified). Some of the historical examples of resignification examined here are comparable in certain ways to the case presented by Manuel, while others (such as the "spiritualized" varieties of

quadrille discussed below) represent more radical departures from both the musical structures and social meanings originally associated with the European forms from which they are partly derived.

26. The tendency for musicians in the Caribbean to code switch between sociomusical contexts deserves further analysis in this connection, though it has so far gone largely unrecognized (Bilby [1985b: 203] touches on this in his discussion of "polymusicality"; see also Marks 1974 and Davis 1994). In some ways, it should be noted, this idea of musical heterogeneity parallels the concept of occupational multiplicity outlined by Lambros Comitas (1973) in his study of labor strategies among rural Jamaicans.
27. Hazzard-Gordon 1996: 107. Line dances could also, perhaps, have echoed the choreographic vocabulary of certain kinds of work arrangements.

    Although other authors describe similar dances (e.g., Stewart 1808), Robert Charles Dallas (1790) provides an early description of what a normative New World circle or "ring" dance may have looked like in Jamaica. In this account, we get a sense of slavery's fundamentally coercive nature and some insight into the role gender played in the plantation dynamic: "A ring is formed, in front of which they mean to dance, place themselves—a woman is singled out by a beau-man, who exhibit all their powers of grace and activity—sometimes there are two men dance with one woman [*sic*]; they follow, fan her with their handkerchiefs, court her and leave her alternately, and make you understand, as perfectly as any ballet-dancer in Europe, what they mean. The beau-men had beau-girls, who are the chief dancers, are usually very finely dressed; they are but a small number, in comparison with the others, who keep back and join to sing for them. I was much surprised at the extravagance of some of their dresses, when I was let into the secret by Philanthropos.—'These beau-girls, said he, are the mistresses of the overseers and other white men who think they cannot be too lavish in adorning their persons[;] the beau-men are the favourites of the beau-girls, who secretly furnish them at the expense of their keepers.'—The music of these poor creatures has a wildness that finds its way to the heart—none of their rude instruments could produce any very pleasing effect, without the assistance of their voices; but, so supported, the Banjaw, the Goombay, the Jawbone, inspire mirth and alacrity" (89–90).
28. Certain other supposedly secular expressive forms in the Caribbean have long concealed sacred practice. See Bilby's work on Jankunu (Jonkonnu) in Jamaica (1999; 2007; forthcoming) and Elizabeth McAlister's work on Rara (2002, esp. chap. 3) in Haiti for two examples.
29. Guilbault 2002b: 944; for a similar perspective on ballroom music and dance in Martinique, see Cyrille 2002: 69. Consider also Jamaica, where class position still correlates relatively neatly with the choreographic distinction between camp and ballroom forms of quadrille (Smith 1981: 21–23; Carty 1988: 46–50). Camp, a longways dance, is considered more "African" and is associated with rural Jamaica. In performance, dancers are expected to wear peasant costumes. The ballroom style, a square dance performed in formal dress, is associated with "Europe" and middle and upper classes.
30. See, for instance, Cyrille 2004: 10–11 on quadrille in Dominica; Guilbault 1985: 33–35 on quadrille (*kwadril*) in St. Lucia; and Daniel 2006: 7–8 on a number of dif-

ferent Caribbean locations. (See also Phillip and Smith 1998: 57–61 on the different social valuations attached to African-identified bèlè dancing versus European ballroom-derived jing-ping dances in Dominica.) Similar language is used by the Garifuna (Garinagu) people of Dangriga, Belize, to describe a number of "stylized dances introduced by Europeans" (including quadrille) that are normally performed during the Christmas season; these Garifuna versions of European-derived traditions are maintained by "social etiquette clubs devoted to the proper training of men and women who perform choreographed dances at annual events called 'Grand Ball'" (Greene 2007). See also note 12, on Garifuna *gunjei*.

31. See Shepherd 2005 for a good historical discussion of what the author calls the "ranking game" that produced cultural hierarchies within Jamaican slave society. As she points out, these hierarchies, which reach back into the eighteenth century if not earlier, continue to exert considerable influence in Jamaica today—where "people in the island still adhere to boundary-maintaining mechanisms, elevating English over Jamaican English or Nation Language, uptown residence over downtown residence, Brown over Black and both under White, urban culture over rural living; and among some sectors, wine over white rum, Bach over Buju Banton, the style of Luciano Pavarotti over Jamaica's indigenous Luciano" (2005: 3).
32. A counter-hegemonic interpretation rather different from (and less subtle than) the one suggested by Daniel was common in Jamaica during the 1970s and early 1980s, when the local influence of Rastafarian ideology was particularly strong. This alternate view is encountered, for example, in a British television documentary on Jamaican music from that period, in which the Jamaican Rastafarian narrator Michael Campbell (better known as reggae performer Mikey Dread) states that "under the influence of European music, long before emancipation, the slaves would dress up, dance, and imitate, thereby ridiculing the antics of the slave master. The quadrille, or first figure dancing, is an African mockery of European dances" (*Reggae: Deep Roots Music*, Part One, BBC broadcast, 1982; available on DVD as *Reggae Nashville: Deep Roots Music, Vol. 1: Revival/Ranking Sounds* [Oaks, PA: Screen Edge/MVD Visual, 2006]).
33. For an idea of the complexity of this point, consider the following condescending description of the turn-of-the-century custom called "practice dances," penned by the light-skinned Jamaican journalist and novelist Herbert De Lisser (1910: 107–108): "There is something pathetic about the pride of the West Indian peasant. . . . To marry well, to be buried well, is a wish that is almost universal, and it is shared to the full by the Jamaica peasant. But he does not stop here; he wants to do other things well. If he gives a dance, he wishes it to be a good dance; and as your cook or coachman cannot afford to make a good dance except at long intervals and on the subscription plan, they call the dances they do have by a name which suggests a compromise with pride. They call them 'practice dances.' The theory is that these dances are for learners. But those who attend them are for the most part experts. Yet no one would speak of them as dances pure and simple, for that would be some reflection of one's social life. A dance must be given in a house; dancers must be properly dressed; there must be refreshments. A 'practice dance' may be given in a yard, takes place every week, and you may go to it in your working clothes. You are formally invited of course." Since De Lisser's unsympathetic reading says very little

about the motivations of the participants (to which, in any case, he might not have been privy), it is difficult to interpret the deeper meanings these "practice dances" might have had for practitioners.

34. Though known as "Island Caribs," the ancestors of the present-day Vincentian Caribs did not speak a Cariban language; they spoke, rather, an Arawakan language (a significant proportion of the lexicon of this language, however, was derived from Cariban languages [Granberry and Vescelius 2004: 59–62]).
35. Some idea of what may lie in store for the Vincentian Caribs can be gotten by considering the surviving Carib population of another Caribbean island, Dominica. According to Lennox Honychurch (1997: 289, cited in Phillip and Smith 1998: 125), "the cultural fact is that the Caribs [of Dominica] may have become Creoles, but the social fact is they have chosen to remain Carib." If the Dominican Caribs ever claimed quadrille or other ballroom-related dances as a symbol of their identity, it appears that they no longer do. Phillip and Smith (1998: 125–127) state that "Dominican Caribs themselves have, in recent years, been drawing on contacts with South American Caribs for information and ideas from which they create their dances. . . . The Karifuna [Dominican Caribs] dance to both assert their identity as Caribs and to earn money for local projects back home. Joseph [a Carib leader] points out the fact that their dances are not traditional Carib dances but re-creations taken from the writings of anthropologist and linguist, Douglas Taylor."
36. Interview with Leon Nero, conducted by Kenneth Bilby, Sandy Bay, St. Vincent, June 14, 2004.
37. Kenneth Bilby, field notes, St. Vincent, July 2004; and field recordings of a Vincentian "boom drum" band, Rose Bank, St. Vincent, July 16, 2004.
38. For more on the African-based musical traditions (including Kromanti Play) of Moore Town and other Jamaican Maroon communities, see Bilby 1992 and DjeDje 1998.
39. The dancing of quadrilles, polkas, waltzes, and various "square or set dances" by Maroons in Accompong in the 1940s is briefly described in Leaf 1948: 70–72. Even here in the relatively remote Maroon country—at least according to this visiting North American photographer and travel writer—these dances had retained certain connotations of "nobility." "The dancing was interesting," he notes. "A certain old-world courtesy about these dances had not been lost during the centuries that have passed since these hill people first learned the dances of the European courts" (1948: 72). See also Katherine Dunham's descriptions of quadrille and "set dances" in Accompong during the late 1930s (1946: 22–27).
40. One of the authors, Bilby, observed this performance while attending the annual celebration in Accompong on January 6, 2000. Bilby also observed and occasionally participated (on guitar) in informal performances of quadrille music in both Moore Town and Accompong while carrying out fieldwork in both of these Maroon communities during the late 1970s.
41. Information on the present-day tambrin tradition is from an interview with tambrin bandleader Herbert Smith, conducted by Bilby (Culloden, Tobago, June 24, 2004), as well as field recordings of a tambrin band made in Culloden on the same day.
42. Similar traditions still exist, for instance, in Haiti. There one finds creolized European ballroom dances, such as the *mènwat* (minuet), *kôtrédâs* (contredanse), and *kwadril* (quadrille). Featuring a combination of European instruments (such as violin) and Haitian drums and percussion, these local versions of European ball-

room dances now form an integral part of Vodou ceremonies on some parts of the island (Lowenthal 1978; Yih 1995: 392–443; Honorin 1997: 22–32; McAlister 1997: 40–43). Examples of these Haitian genres may be heard on the compact discs *Fond-des-Nègres, Fond-des-Blancs: Musiques Paysannes d'Haïti* (Paris: Buda Musique 92680-2, 1997) and *Angels in the Mirror: Vodou Music of Haiti* (Roslyn, NY: Ellipsis Arts CD4120, 1997).

43. It is important to note as well that some contemporary ballroom-related traditions in the Anglophone Caribbean that do not involve spirit possession are nonetheless associated with spiritual practices and meanings. According to Miller (2005: 419), for example, Canute Caliste, one of the most important performers of such traditions in Carriacou, claimed to have learned the quadrille from ancestors in dreams; and quadrille dances on this island were traditionally preceded with formal libations, through which the spirits of ancestors were explicitly invited to the performance (though they did not possess the living). It seems likely that in various parts of the Caribbean, spiritual observances of this kind were, like spirit possession, more common in connection with ballroom dances in the past than they are today.
44. This secular fife-and-drum music of Montserrat is associated today with a masquerade dance in which a local version of the quadrille, consisting of five figures, plays an important role (Dewar 1977; Donoghue 2001: 16–17, 38–40). (An example of this kind of Montserratian quadrille music can be heard on this volume's compact disc.)
45. Since 1963, for example, quadrille dance troupes wishing to participate in Jamaica's National Festival for the Arts have been limited to two categories—the informal "camp" and the formal "ballroom" styles—each having its own choreographic standards. Beginning in 1969, any band competing in the festival's mento music competition was required to play a piece of quadrille, whether or not a quadrille was part of its repertory. Since then, such traditional forms as mento and quadrille—where they have not died out completely—have become more standardized, even in more remote rural villages. This may be seen as a testament to how important these festival requirements have become in evaluating traditional "authenticity."

    One of the authors, Daniel Neely, has found that a sense of—if not direct experience with—festival judging standards is widespread throughout Jamaica and that its role in influencing how bands are evaluated even off the concert stage divides contemporary traditional musicians' attitudes about participating in official government sponsored events. Although some point to a sense of patriotic duty to explain the artistic compromises they make in performance, many others remain critical of festival guidelines that they feel do not accurately reflect contemporary practice; rejection of these guidelines is a common justification for nonparticipation (Neely 2008; for other perspectives on staged folklore in Jamaica, see O'Gorman 1987a, 1987b and Thomas 2002).
46. "Rude Boy" can be heard on *Bob Marley and the Wailers, One Love (at Studio One)* (Heartbeat, 1991); "Skank Quadrille" can be heard on *Yellowman, Galong Galong Galong* (Shanachie, 1990). Two particularly interesting examples of musical influence from quadrille in the urban popular arena are Tommy McCook's reggae recordings "Second Fiddle" (Treasure Isle, TIS 211, 1968) and "Third Figure" (Treasure Isle, TIS 222, 1969), their melodies based entirely on quadrille melodies. Other examples of Jamaican popular recordings showing clear musical influence from quadrille or other local European-derived ballroom genres include the rocksteady instru-

mental "Pe Da Pa (Rock and Sock)," by Roland Alphonso and the Soul Brothers (Studio One, SO 2032-B, 1967), and a number of early reggae instrumentals, including "Reggae Jeggae," by Drumbago and the Blenders (Almagamated, FJG 7530, 1968), "Monkey Fiddle," by Tommy McCook (Unity UN 509, 1969), and "Rahtid," by the Dynamites (New Beat, 1969).

47. Two insightful, ethnographically grounded studies that deserve special mention for their attention to some of the complex cultural meanings and historically derived contradictions we have attempted to sketch out here are Guilbault 1985 and Miller 2005, both of which suggest interesting directions for future work along these lines. See also Miller 2008. Two other researchers, Cyrille (see her chapter in this volume) and Daniel, recently completed major comparative projects on quadrille in a number of different Caribbean locations, and their work, as it becomes available, promises to shed much new light on these questions.

## References

Abbott, Lynn, and Doug Seroff. 2002. *Out of sight: The rise of African American popular music, 1889–1895.* Jackson: University Press of Mississippi.

Abrahams, Roger D. 1972. "Christmas and Carnival on Saint Vincent." *Western Folklore* 31 (4): 275–289.

———. 2002. Liner notes to *Nevis and St. Kitts: Tea meetings, Christmas sports, and the moonlight night.* Alan Lomax Collection: Caribbean Voyage. Cambridge, MA: Rounder Records. Rounder 82161-1731-2.

Ahye, Molly. 1978. *Golden heritage: The dance in Trinidad and Tobago.* Trinidad and Tobago: Heritage Cultures.

Allen, William Francis, Charles Pickard Ware, and Lucy McKim Garrison. 1867. *Slave songs of the United States.* New York: A. Simpson.

Averill, Gage. 1997. *A day for the hunter, a day for the prey.* Chicago: University of Chicago Press.

Banfield, Stephen. 2007. "Anglophone musical culture in Jamaica." In *Art and emancipation in Jamaica.* Ed. Tim Barringer, Gillian Forrester, and Barbaro Martinez-Ruiz, 136–149. New Haven, CT: Yale Center for British Art and Yale University Press.

Baxter, Ivy. 1970. *The arts of an island: The development of the culture and of the folk and creative arts in Jamaica, 1492–1962.* Metuchen, NJ: Scarecrow Press.

Beckwith, Martha. [1929] 1969. *Black roadways: A study of Jamaican folk life.* New York: Negro Universities Press.

Bell, Hesketh J. 1893. *Obeah, witchcraft, in the West Indies.* London: Sampson, Low, Marsten.

Benton, Rita. 1964. "Jean Frederick Edelmann, a musical victim of the French Revolution." *Musical Quarterly* 50 (2): 165–187.

Bilby, Kenneth. 1985a. "The Caribbean as a musical region." In *Caribbean contours.* Ed. Sidney Mintz and Sally Price, 181–218. Baltimore: Johns Hopkins University Press.

———. 1985b. "Caribbean crucible." In *Repercussions: A celebration of African American music.* Ed. Geoffrey Haydon and Dennis Marks, 128–151. London: Century Publishing.

———. 1992. Liner notes to *Drums of defiance: Maroon music from the earliest free black communities of Jamaica.* Washington, DC: Smithsonian Folkways. SF 40412.

———. 1999. "Gumbay, Myal, and the great house: New evidence on the religious background of Jonkonnu in Jamaica." *ACIJ Research Review* 4:47–70

———. 2005. *True-born Maroons.* Gainesville: University Press of Florida.

———. 2007. "More than met the eye: African Jamaican festivities in the time of Belisario." In *Art and emancipation in Jamaica.* Ed. Timothy Barringer, Gillian Forrester, and Barbaro Martinez-Ruiz, 120–135. New Haven, CT: Yale Center for British Art and Yale University Press.

———. Forthcoming. "Surviving secularization: Masking the spirit in the Jankunu (Jonkonnu) festivals of the Caribbean and the southern United States." In *Black music scholarship and the bridging of diasporal sacred worlds.* Ed. Samuel Floyd and Shannon Dudley. Berkeley: University of California Press.

Bilby, Kenneth, and Morton Marks. 1999. Liner notes to *Dominica: Creole crossroads.* Alan Lomax Collection: Caribbean Voyage. Cambridge, MA: Rounder Records. Rounder 11661-1724-2.

Blaustein, Richard. 1995. "Old-time fiddling and country dancing in North America: Some reconsiderations." In *Communities in motion: Dance, community, and tradition in America's southeast and beyond.* Ed. Susan Eike Spalding and Jane Harris Woodside, 191–202. Westport, CT: Greenwood Press.

Carpentier, Alejo. 2001. *Music in Cuba.* Ed. Timothy Brennan. Trans. Alan West-Durán. Minneapolis: University of Minnesota Press.

Carty, Hilary. 1988. *Folk dances of Jamaica: An insight.* London: Dance Books.

Cayetano, Sebastian, and Fabian Cayetano. 1997. *Garifuna history, language and culture.* 2nd rev. ed. Belize City, Belize: National Garifuna Council.

Chasteen, John Charles. 2004. *National rhythms, African roots: The deep history of Latin American popular dance.* Albuquerque: University of New Mexico Press.

Comitas, Lambros. 1973. "Occupational multiplicity in rural Jamaica." In *Work and family Life: West Indian perspectives.* Ed. Lambros Comitas and David Lowenthal, 157–173. Garden City, NY: Anchor Press.

Conzemius, Eduard. 1928. "Ethnographical notes on the black Carib (Garif)." *American Anthropologist, New Series* 30 (2): 183–205.

Courlander, Harold. 1960. *The drum and the hoe: Life and lore of the Haitian people.* Berkeley: University of California Press.

Cramer, Louise. 1946. "Songs of West Indian negroes in the canal zone." *California Folklore Quarterly* 5 (3): 243–272.

Cyrille, Dominique. 2002. "Popular music and Martinican-Creole identity." *Black Music Research Journal* 22 (1): 65–83.

———. 2004. "Dance competition, tradition, and change in the commonwealth of Dominica." *Cariso!* [Newsletter of the Alton Augustus Adams Music Research Institute] (Spring): 8–12.

[Dallas, Robert Charles]. 1790. *A short journey in the West Indies, in which are interspersed, curious anecdotes and characters. In two volumes.* London: J. Murray, Fleet Street, and J. Forbes, Covent Garden.

Daniel, Yvonne. 2006. "Come with me and let's talk about Caribbean quadrilles." *Cariso!* [Newsletter of the Alton Augustus Adams Music Research Institute 6:6–12.

Davis, Martha Ellen. 1994. "'Bi-musicality' in the cultural configurations of the Caribbean." *Black Music Research Journal* 1 (2): 145–160.

DeGarmo, William B. 1870. *The prompter: Containing full descriptions of all the quadrilles, figures of the German cotillon, etc.* New York: Raymond and Caulon.

de Jong, Nanette. 2003. "An anatomy of creolization: Curaçao and the Antillean waltz." *Latin American Music Review* 24 (2): 233–251.

De La Beche, Henry T. 1825. *Notes on the present condition of the negroes in Jamaica.* London: Printed for T. Cadell, in the Strand.

De Lisser, Herbert G. 1910. *In Jamaica and Cuba.* Kingston, Jamaica: Gleaner.

Dewar, Ann Marie. 1977. "Music in the Alliouagana (Montserrat) cultural tradition." Bachelor's thesis (typescript in the Montserrat Public Library), University of the West Indies, Cave Hill Campus, Barbados.

DjeDje, Jacqueline Cogdell. 1998. "Remembering Kojo: History, music, and gender in the January sixth celebration of the Jamaican Accompong Maroons." *Black Music Research Journal* 18 (1–2): 67–120.

Dobbin, Jay D. 1986. *The jombee dance of Montserrat.* Columbus: Ohio State University Press.

Donoghue, Eddie. 2001. "Montserrat masquerade: Cultural preservation in the modern world." Manuscript. St. Thomas, U.S. Virgin Islands.

Dueck, Byron. 2006. "Square dancing, mimesis, and Aboriginal public culture." Paper presented at the fifty-first annual meeting of the Society for Ethnomusicology, November 16–19, 2006, in Honolulu, Hawaii.

Dunham, Katherine. 1946. *Journey to Accompong.* New York: Henry Holt.

Edelmann, Jean-Frédéric. 1830. "Letter to the editor." In *The Harmonicon, part II*, 401–402. London: Samuel Leigh.

Elder, J. D. 1971. *Folk song and folk life in Charlotteville.* Port of Spain, Trinidad and Tobago: Universal Printing.

Epstein, Dena. 1973. "African music in British and French America." *Musical Quarterly* 59 (1): 61–91.

Fernandez, Carlos A. 1998. "Costa Rica." In *Garland encyclopedia of world music: Vol. 2: South America, Mexico, Central America, and the Caribbean.* Ed. Dale Olsen and Daniel Sheehy, 680–705. New York: Garland Publishing.

Fiehrer, Thomas. 1991. "From quadrille to stomp: The creole origins of jazz." *Popular Music* 10 (1): 21–38.

Floyd, Samuel, Jr. 1999. "Black music in the circum-Caribbean." *American Music* 17 (1): 1–38.

Floyd, Samuel, Jr., and Marsha J. Reisser. 1984. "The sources and resources of classic ragtime music." *Black Music Research Journal* 4:22–59.

Forte, Maximilian, ed. 2006. *Indigenous resurgence in the contemporary Caribbean: Amerindian survival and revival.* New York: Peter Lang.

Giordano, Ralph G. 2007. *Social dancing in America: A history and reference.* Vol. 1. Westport, CT: Greenwood Press.

Granberry, Julian, and Gary S. Vescelius. 2004. *Languages of the pre-Columbian Antilles.* Tuscaloosa: University of Alabama Press.

Green, Doris. 1996. "Traditional dance in Africa." In *African dance: An artistic, historical and philosophical inquiry.* Ed. Kariamu Welsh Asante, 13–28. Trenton, NJ: Africa World Press.

Greene, Oliver. n.d. "The Garifuna Beluria and the Guadaloupean Léwoz: Comparing the survival of African identity in the new world." LAMECA. Available at http://svr1.cg971.fr/lameca/dossiers/ethnomusicologie/pages/greene_eng_2005.htm.

———. 2007. *Play, Jankunú play: The Garifuna wanaragua ritual of Belize.* DVD. Watertown, MA: Documentary Educational Resources.

Guilbault, Jocelyne. 1985. "A St. Lucian *kwadril* evening." *Latin American Music Review* 6 (1): 31–57.

———. 1993. Musical traditions of St. Lucia, West Indies. Liner notes for *Musical traditions of St. Lucia, West Indies.* Smithsonian/Folkways. SF 40416.

———. 1998a. "Dominica." In *Garland encyclopedia of world music: Vol. 2: South America, Mexico, Central America, and the Caribbean.* Ed. Dale Olsen and Daniel Sheehy, 840–844. New York: Garland Publishing.

———. 1998b. "St. Lucia." In *Garland encyclopedia of world music: Vol. 2: South America, Mexico, Central America, and the Caribbean.* Ed. Dale Olsen and Daniel Sheehy, 942–951. New York: Garland Publishing.

Gushee, Lawrence. 2002. "The nineteenth-century origins of jazz." *Black Music Research Journal* 22 (Suppl. Best of *BMRJ*): 151–174.

Harris, C.L.G. n.d. "The Maroons of Moore Town (a Colonel speaks)." Manuscript.

Hazzard-Gordon, Katrina. 1996. "Dancing under the lash: Sociocultural disruption, continuity, and synthesis." In *African dance: An artistic, historical and philosophical inquiry.* Ed. Kariamu Welsh Asante, 101–130. Trenton, NJ: Africa World Press.

Hill, Errol. 1992. *The Jamaican stage 1655–1900: Profile of a colonial theatre.* Amherst: University of Massachusetts Press.

Honorin, Emmanuelle. 1997. Liner notes to *Fond-des-Nègres, Fond-des-Blancs: Musiques paysannes d'Haïti.* Paris: Buda Musique. Buda 92680-2.

Honychurch, Lennox. 1997. "Carib to Creole: Contact and culture exchange in Dominica." Ph.D. diss., Oxford University.

Howe, Elias. 1858. *Howe's complete ball-room hand book.* Boston: Ditson.

Jekyll, Walter. [1907] 1966. *Jamaica song and story.* New York: Dover Publications.

Johnson, Sara E. 2005. "*Cinquillo* consciousness: The formation of a pan-Caribbean musical aesthetic." In *Music, writing, and cultural unity in the Caribbean.* Ed. Timothy Reiss, 35–58. Trenton, NJ: Africa World Press.

Joseph Parris Hot Shots. n.d. *Quadrille band, vol. 1.* LP. JPHS-01.

Keil, Charles. 1987. "Participatory discrepancies and the power of music." *Cultural Anthropology* 2 (3): 275–283.

Keller, Kate Van Winkle, and Genevieve Shimer. 1990. *The playford ball: 103 early English country dances.* Pennington, NJ: A Cappella Books and the Country Dance and Song Society.

Krehbiel, Henry Edward. 1914. *Afro-American folksong: A study in racial and national music.* New York: Schirmer.

Leaf, Earl. 1948. *Isles of rhythm.* New York: A. S. Barnes.

León, Argeliers. 1964. *Música folklórica cubana.* Havana: Ediciones del Departamento de Música de la Biblioteca Nacional "José Marti."

Lewin, Olive. 1968. "Jamaican folk music." *Caribbean Quarterly* 14:49–56.

———. 2000. *Rock it come over: The folk music of Jamaica.* Kingston, Jamaica: University of West Indies Press.

Long, Edward. 1774. *The history of Jamaica.* Vol. 2. London: T. Lowndes.

Lowenthal, Ira P. 1978. "Ritual performance and religious experience: A service for the gods in southern Haiti." *Journal of Anthropological Research* 34:392–414.

Manuel, Peter. 1994. "Puerto Rican music and cultural identity: Creative appropriation of Cuban sources from danza to salsa." *Ethnomusicology* 38 (2): 249–280.

Marks, Morton. 1974. "Uncovering ritual structures in Afro-American music." In *Religious movements in contemporary America.* Ed. Irving Zaretsky and Mark P. Leone, 60–134. Princeton, NJ: Princeton University Press.

McAlister, Elizabeth. 1997. Liner notes to *Angels in the mirror: Vodou music of Haiti.* Roslyn, NY: Ellipsis Arts. Ellipsis 4120.

———. 2002. *Rara! Vodou, power and performance in Haiti and its diaspora.* Berkeley: University of California Press.

McDaniel, Lorna. 1998a. "Antigua and Barbuda." In *Garland encyclopedia of world music: Vol. 2: South America, Mexico, Central America, and the Caribbean.* Ed. Dale Olsen and Daniel Sheehy, 798–800. New York: Garland Publishing.

———. 1998b. "Grenada (and Carriacou)." In *Garland encyclopedia of world music: Vol. 2: South America, Mexico, Central America, and the Caribbean.* Ed. Dale Olsen and Daniel Sheehy, 864–872. New York: Garland Publishing.

———. 1998c. "Trinidad and Tobago." In *Garland encyclopedia of world music: Vol. 2: South America, Mexico, Central America, and the Caribbean.* Ed. Dale Olsen and Daniel Sheehy, 952–967. New York: Garland Publishing.

McDaniel, Lorna, and Donald R. Hill. 1999. Liner notes to *Carriacou calaloo.* Alan Lomax Collection: Caribbean Voyage. Cambridge, MA: Rounder Records. Rounder 11661-1722-2.

Messenger, John C. 1973. "African retentions in Montserrat." *African Arts* 6 (4): 54–57, 95–96.

———. 1975. "Montserrat: The most distinctively Irish settlement in the New World." *Ethnicity* 2:281–303.

———. 1998. "Montserrat." In *Garland encyclopedia of world music: Vol. 2: South America, Mexico, Central America, and the Caribbean.* Ed. Dale Olsen and Daniel Sheehy, 922–926. New York: Garland Publishing.

Miller, Rebecca. 2000. "The people like melée: The parang festival of Carriacou, Grenada." Ph.D. diss., Brown University.

———. 2005. "Performing ambivalence: The case of quadrille music and dance in Carriacou, Grenada." *Ethnomusicology* 49 (3): 403–440.

———. 2008. *Carriacou string band serenade: Performing identity in the Eastern Caribbean.* Middletown, CT: Wesleyan University Press.

Mintz, Sidney W. 1974. *Caribbean transformations.* Chicago: Aldine.

Mintz, Sidney W., and Richard Price. [1976] 1992. *The birth of African-American culture: An anthropological perspective.* Boston: Beacon Press.

Neely, Daniel T. 2008. "'Mento, Jamaica's original music': Development, tourism and the nationalist frame." Ph.D. diss., New York University.

O'Gorman, Pamela. 1987a. "From field to platform: Jamaican folk music in concert 1." *Jamaica Journal* 20 (1): 45–49.

———. 1987b. "From field to platform: Jamaican folk music in concert 2." *Jamaica Journal* 20 (2): 43–48.

Petley, Christer. 2005. "Slavery, emancipation and the creole world view of Jamaican colonists, 1800–1834." *Slavery and Abolition* 26 (1): 93–114.

Phillip, Daryl. n.d. "Dominica's quadrilles." Division of Culture, Commonwealth of Dominica. Available at http://www.divisionofculture.org/quadrilles.htm. Accessed February 23, 2007.

Phillip, Daryl, and Gary Smith. 1998. *The heritage dances of Dominica.* Canefield, Dominica: Division of Culture.

Philpott, Stuart B. 1973. *West Indian migration: The Montserrat case.* London: Athlone Press.

Pinckney, Warren R. 1992. "Jazz in the U.S. Virgin Islands." *American Music* 10 (4): 441–467.

Post, Jennifer. 2004. *Music in rural New England family and community life, 1870–1940.* Durham: University of New Hampshire Press.

Putnam, Lara. 2002. *The company they kept: Migrants and the politics of gender in Caribbean Costa Rica, 1870–1960.* Chapel Hill: University of North Carolina Press.

Scruggs, T. M. 1999. "'Let's enjoy as Nicaraguans': The use of music in the construction of a Nicaraguan national consciousness." *Ethnomusicology* 43 (2): 297–321.

Sewel, W. E. 1861. "Cast away in Jamaica." *Harper's New Monthly Magazine* 22 (128): 166–182.

Sheehy, Daniel E. 1998. "The Virgin Islands." In *Garland encyclopedia of world music: Vol. 2: South America, Mexico, Central America, and the Caribbean.* Ed. Dale Olsen and Daniel Sheehy, 968–974. New York: Garland Publishing.

Shepherd, Verene A. 2005. "The ranking game in Jamaica during slavery." *Arts Journal* (Guyana) 1 (2): 3–15.

Simpson, George Eaton. 1940. "Peasant songs of northern Haiti." *Journal of Negro History* 25 (2): 203–215.

Smith, Andrea. 1981. "Quadrille in Jamaica." Thesis presented in partial fulfillment of the teacher diploma course, Jamaica School of Dance.

Smith, Ronald. 2002. "Panama." In *Garland encyclopedia of world music: Vol. 2: South America, Mexico, Central America, and the Caribbean.* Ed. Dale Olsen and Daniel Sheehy, 770–785. New York: Garland Publishing.

Steele, Beverley A. 1996. "A folk dance in Grenada." *Bulletin of Eastern Caribbean Affairs* 21 (1): 25–45.

Stewart, John. 1808. *An account of Jamaica, and its inhabitants.* London: Longman, Hurst, Rees and Orme.

———. 1823. *View of the island of Jamaica.* Edinburgh: Oliver and Boyd.

Stolzoff, Norman. 2000. *Wake the town and tell the people: Dancehall culture in Jamaica.* Durham, NC: Duke University Press.

Szwed, John, and Morton Marks. 1988. "The African American transformation of European set dances and dance suites." *Dance Research Journal* 20 (1): 29–36.

Taussig, Michael. 1993. *Mimesis and alterity.* New York: Routledge.

Thomas, Deborah A. 2002. "Democratizing dance: Institutional transformation and hegemonic re-ordering in postcolonial Jamaica." *Cultural Anthropology* 17 (4): 512–550.

Trouillot, Michel-Rolph. 2002. "Culture on the edges: Caribbean creolization in historical context." In *From the margins: Historical anthropology and its futures.* Ed. Brian Keith Axel. Durham, NC: Duke University Press.

University of the Virgin Islands. 2007. "A night of quadrille at the Reichhold Center." Available at http://www.uvi.edu/pub-relations/pressRelease/rel06077.html. Accessed April 3, 2007.

Whylie, Marjorie. 2000. *Mento: The what and the how.* Kingston, Jamaica: Whylie Communications.

Wilson, Peter J. 1973. *Crab antics: The social anthropology of English-speaking negro societies of the Caribbean.* New Haven, CT: Yale University Press.

Wilson, Thomas. 1816. *The treasures of terpsichore or a collection of the most popular English country dances.* 2nd ed. London: Sherwood, Neely and Jones.

Wood, Vivian Nina Michelle. 1998. "The Bahamas." In *Garland encyclopedia of world music: Vol. 2: South America, Mexico, Central America, and the Caribbean.* Ed. Dale Olsen and Daniel Sheehy, 801–812. New York: Garland Publishing.

Wright, Richardson. 1937. *Revels in Jamaica 1682–1838.* New York: Dodd, Mead.

Yih, Yuen-Ming David. 1995. "Music and dance of Haitian Vodou: Diversity and unity in regional repertoires." Ph.D. diss., Wesleyan University.

# Contributors

**Kenneth M. Bilby** is director of research at the Center for Black Music Research, Columbia College, Chicago, and a research associate in the Department of Anthropology at the Smithsonian Institution. He has published numerous articles on Caribbean music, folklore, and culture, and he has produced or compiled fifteen albums (LPs or CDs), several of which feature his own field recordings. His latest book, *True-Born Maroons*, won the 2006 Wesley-Logan Prize of the American Historical Association as an outstanding book on African diaspora history. He is a coauthor of *Caribbean Currents: Caribbean Music from Rumba to Reggae*.

**Dominique O. Cyrille** received her doctorate in musicology from the Université Paris-IV-Sorbonne, Paris, with a dissertation focusing on the traditional dance and music of Martinique, her island of origin. As a Rockefeller Fellow at the Center for Black Music Research for the academic year 2003–4, she carried out extensive fieldwork in St. Lucia, Dominica, and Haiti in order to study the politics of contredanse and quadrille performance. She teaches in the Department of African and African American Studies at Lehman College (City University of New York).

**Edgardo Díaz Díaz** is a specialist in the music of his native Puerto Rico. He has published extensively on the danza, its relation to the Dominican merengue, and other topics. He currently teaches at the City University of New York.

**Michael Largey** is associate professor and chair of the musicology program at Michigan State University. He is the author of *Vodou Nation: Haitian Art Music and Cultural Nationalism* and a coauthor of *Caribbean Currents: Caribbean Music from Rumba to Reggae*.

**Peter Manuel** is professor of music at John Jay College and the Graduate Center of the City University of New York. He has researched and published extensively on musics of various regions, including the Caribbean and South Asia. His books include *East Indian Music in the West Indies: Tân-Singing, Chutney, and the Making of Indo-Caribbean Culture*; *Caribbean Currents: Caribbean Music from Rumba to Reggae* (with Michael Largey and Ken Bilby); *Cassette Culture: Popular Music and Technology in North India*; and *Popular Musics of the Non-Western World: An Introductory Survey.*

**Daniel T. Neely** received his doctorate from New York University with a dissertation on mento, a genre of traditional Jamaican music and a forerunner of reggae music. He has taught ethnomusicology at the New School University and the State University of New York at Stony Brook, and he is currently the director of the New York Music Index and Archive (NYMIA) at the Archive of Contemporary Music. His articles have appeared in the *Beat*, *Esopus*, and *Caribbean Quarterly*. He also plays Irish tenor banjo.

# Contents of the Compact Disc

## CUBA

1. "Cambujá," contradanza, by José Fernández de Coca (ca. 1857). Peter Manuel, guitars and percussion.
2. "¡Ave María Gallo!" contradanza, by José Fernández de Coca (ca. 1857). Peter Manuel, guitars and percussion.
3. "Danza" (Opus 33), by Louis Moreau Gottschalk (1857). Beth Robin, piano.
4. "Luisiana," contradanza, by Manuel Saumell. Beth Robin, piano.
5. "La Tedezco," contradanza, by Manuel Saumell. Beth Robin, piano.
6. "Los ojos de Pepa," contradanza, by Manuel Saumell. Rotterdam Conservatory Orquesta Típica. (Excerpt from *Cuba: Contradanzas & danzones*, Nimbus NI 5502.)
7. "Los tres golpes" ("The Three Blows"), danza, by Ignacio Cervantes. Beth Robin, piano.
8. "Ilusiones perdidas" ("Lost Illusions"), danza, by Ignacio Cervantes. Beth Robin, piano.
9. "El biberón de Benitín" ("Benitín's Nursing Bottle"), danzón. The Orquesta of Enrique Peña, 1918. (From *Hot Music from Cuba 1907–1936*, Harlequin HQ CD 23.)

## PUERTO RICO

10. "Margarita," danza, by Manuel Tavárez. Beth Robin, piano.
11. "Mis amores," danza, by Simón Madera. Angelina Tallaj-García, piano.
12. "Laura y Georgina," danza, by Juan Morel Campos. Beth Robin, piano.
13. "Laura y Georgina," danza, by Juan Morel Campos. The Orquesta de Cocolia (1909).
14. "Impromptu," danza, by Luis Rodriguez Miranda. The Puerto Rico Regimental Band (1909).
15. "El coquí," danza, by José Quintón. Angelina Tallaj-García, piano.

## DOMINICAN REPUBLIC

16. "El sueño" ("The Dream"), danza, by Mariano Arredondo (1864). Angelina Tallaj-García, piano.
17. "Danza criolla," by Julio Alberto Hernández (1933–40). Angelina Tallaj-García, piano.
18. "Para ti," danza, by Julio Alberto Hernández (1941). Angelina Tallaj-García, piano.
19. "Santiago," merengue/danza, by Julio Alberto Hernández (1927). Angelina Tallaj-García, piano.
20. "Celeste aurora," danza, by José de Jesús Ravelo (1924). Angelina Tallaj-García, piano.
21. "Los agrarontes," merengue, by Juan Espínola (1928).

## HAITI

22. "La dangereuse," méringue, by Ludovic Lamothe. Beth Robin, piano.

## CURAÇAO

23. "Erani ta malu," by Jan Gerard Palm. Beth Robin, piano.

## WEST INDIES

24. Quadrille, first and second figures. Chin's Calypso Sextet (Jamaica, 1957). Produced by Ivan Chin. (Courtesy of Ivan Chin.)
25. Quadrille, fourth figure, tambrin band (Tobago). Recorded by Kenneth Bilby in Culloden, Tobago (2004).
26. Quadrille, third figure. Vincentian Carib string band (St. Vincent). Recorded by Kenneth Bilby in Sandy Bay, St. Vincent (2004).
27. Quadrille, third figure. Freedom Mento Band (Jamaica). Recorded by Kenneth Bilby in Glengoffe, Jamaica (2002).
28. Quadrille, fifth figure ("Number Five Dance"). Hybrid Masqueraders Band (Montserrat). Recorded by Kenneth Bilby in St. John, U.S. Virgin Islands (2004).

# Index